The Price System & Resource Allocation

The Price System and Resource Allocation
Fifth Edition

Richard H. Leftwich
Oklahoma State University

Holt, Rinehart and Winston
The Dryden Press
London · Illinois · Sydney · Toronto

A HOLT INTERNATIONAL EDITION
from THE DRYDEN PRESS

ISBN 0 03 910146 0
Printed in Great Britain by
Billing & Sons Ltd., Guildford and London

To Maxine D. Leftwich

Preface

Preface to the Fifth Edition

The fifth edition of *The Price System and Resource Allocation* features several modifications of an evolutionary nature to keep it abreast of contemporary thinking in microeconomics. As in previous editions, the needs of undergraduate students in an intermediate microeconomics course have determined the level of difficulty.

This edition builds on the concept of *welfare* in the sense of *Pareto optimality*. In both the theory of consumer choice and the theory of production the essential conditions for Pareto optimality are established. Then the efficacy of the price system in bringing about these conditions is examined. Toward this end the theory of consumer choice is built on indifference curve analysis with utility analysis presented as a special case of the more general theory. Similarly isoquant-isocost analysis now forms the basis of the theory of production.

Chapter 18 in this edition, like Chapter 17 in the previous editions is essentially a summary chapter. However it has been completely recast to pull together the conditions of Pareto optimality for an economic system along with the conditions of general equilibrium for a price-directed economy. The resulting two sets of conditions are analyzed to determine the circumstances under which they will be identical and the circumstances under which they are divergent.

To provide as much help as possible to students working their way through a comprehensive microeconomics course, the book contains a very large number of illustrations. These appear in the text itself as well as in table and diagram form. For students with a background in calculus the mathematical footnotes should prove helpful. Also this edition contains more applications of microeconomic analysis to economic issues and problems than the previous editions.

Thanks are due to many people for their assistance in preparing this edition. Professor Gerald Lage of Oklahoma State University provided valuable suggestions for the entire book. I wish to acknowledge also the constructive criticisms of Professor Kenneth Gordon of the University of Massachusetts, Professor Elden Reiling of Northern Illinois University, Professor Jack Triplett of Washington University, Professor Roy Ruffin of the University of Iowa and Charles Metcalf of the University of Wisconsin. My graduate assistants, Ms. Shiu-Fang Yu, Mr. William L. Stringer and Mr. Michael D. Brendler were most helpful. Ms. Linda Greer Morales contributed her expertise in the use of the English language at many points throughout the manuscript as she typed it in final form. Especial thanks are due Ms. Jeanne Burns, my secretary, who was invaluable in keeping the whole project under control.

Stillwater, Oklahoma   —R.H.L.
January, 1973

Preface to the First Edition

This book is designed to accomplish a twofold purpose. Primarily it is intended as an undergraduate price theory textbook. In this respect, instructors may find it useful for the price theory section of some basic principles courses, as well as for the usual price theory courses at the junior-senior level. Secondarily, I hope that it will provide a satisfactory review of the principles of price theory and resource allocation for graduate students in economics.

The frame of reference for the book is a stable free enterprise economy. The operation of the price system in guiding and directing resources toward more efficient use can be seen with greater clarity in a stable economy than in one characterized by economic fluctuations. Also a clear understanding of the price theory principles evolving from a stable economy logically precedes the study of price theory principles in a dynamic economy.

Coverage of the book is selective rather than exhaustive. It concentrates on the fundamental principles of price theory. Refinements, ramifications, and highly sophisticated topics are omitted in the belief that these properly belong in advanced courses in price theory. No claim is made for originality. The analysis developed is the property of economists in general. The aim has been for clarity of exposition at a level that upper-division undergraduates can be reasonably expected to attain.

Emphasis is placed on economic efficiency throughout because the concept of economy is in a large measure a concept of efficiency. In this respect more than usual attention is focused on resource pricing, employment, and allocation. Our central problem is that of securing the highest possible level of want satisfaction—both present and future—with available resources and techniques.

With regard to the method of exposition, liberal use is made of graphic analysis. No knowledge of mathematics beyond algebra and plane geometry is required; however, some knowledge of more advanced mathematics will prove helpful. The basic mathematical relations necessary for understanding price theory are introduced as they are needed to progress through the book. The selected readings at the end of each chapter are limited in number. They are selected to provide students with the best classic and contemporary treatments of particular topics.

I owe a debt of gratitude to many who have contributed to the preparation of the manuscript. Especial thanks are due Professor Rudolph W. Trenton of Oklahoma State University and Professor Howard R. Bowen of Williams College, both of whom have read the entire manuscript through its several drafts and have continuously offered encouragement, as well as innumerable helpful suggestions. Thanks are due also to Professor Elliot Zupnick of the College of the City of New York, who reviewed the entire manuscript at a late stage and made many valuable criticisms. Large parts of the manuscript were read by Professors Joseph J. Klos and Eugene L. Swearingen of Oklahoma State University, and I profited materially from their suggestions. I did not always heed the good advice offered; consequently I must take full responsibility for the shortcomings of the book. The typing burden was borne patiently and cheerfully by Mrs. Claudette Voyles with some assistance from Mr. Kenton Ross.

Stillwater, Oklahoma   R.H.L.
April 14, 1955

Contents:

1	Introduction	1
2	The Organization of an Economic System	15
3	The Purely Competitive Market Model	27
4	Basic Applications of the Model	55
5	Consumer Choice and Demand-I	69
6	Individual Consumer Choice and Demand-II	99
7	Market Classifications and the Demand Curve Faced by the Firm	123
8	The Principles of Production	135
9	Costs of Production	163
10	Pricing and Output Under Pure Competition	199
11	Pricing and Output Under Pure Monopoly	229
12	Pricing and Output Under Oligopoly	259
13	Pricing and Output Under Monopolistic Competition	289
14	Pricing and Employment of Resources: Pure Competition	301
15	Pricing and Employment of Resources: Monopoly and Monopsony	321
16	Resource Allocation	343
17	Product Distribution	361
18	Equilibrium and Welfare	381
19	Linear Programming	403

Chapter 1:

Introduction

The era in which we live is marked by pervasive social unrest. Social values and social institutions are being subjected to scrutiny and questioning more intense than any we have seen since the Great Depression. Severe criticism has been leveled at the operation of the capitalist or private enterprise system — some of it pinpoints weaknesses and some of it reveals much ignorance about the nature and performance of such a system.

This book is intended as a contribution to the debate. Its purpose is twofold: (1) to spell out the conditions that must be met in *any* economic system if it is to be efficient; and (2) to show the operation of the price system, with its strengths and weaknesses, in moving the economy toward those conditions. We should recognize at the outset that there are alternative ways of organizing economic activity; this book, however, is concerned predominantly with the price mechanism.

In this introduction we shall survey the nature of economic activity, the methodology of economics, and the relation of price theory to the general body of economic theory. The next two chapters will set the stage for the detailed exposition of price theory that begins in Chapter 4.

Economic Activity

While the boundaries marking off economics from other disciplines or fields of knowledge are hard to draw, general agreement does exist with regard to its main contents. Economics is concerned with man's well-being or welfare. It encompasses the social relationships or social organization involved in allocating scarce resources among alternative human wants and in using those resources toward the end of satisfying wants as fully as possible. The key elements of economic activity are (1) human wants, (2) resources, and (3) techniques of production. These will be discussed in turn.

Human Wants

Economic activity is directed toward the satisfaction of human wants. These provide the driving, motivating force; their fulfillment may be thought of as the end or goal of economic activity. The wants that are important in any economic system may be those of the general public, those of powerful special interest groups, those of government leaders, and others. Different societies are likely to attach different relative weights to whose wants are the most important.

Wants have two characteristics—they are varied, and in the aggregate over time they are insatiable. Insatiability does not necessarily imply that any one individual's desire for a particular commodity is unlimited. The quantity of a good consumed each week that contributes to one's well-being may well be finite. It is commodities in the aggregate for which wants are unlimited, partly because of the wide variety of wants that individuals can conjure up.

Origins of Wants   The insatiability of wants in the aggregate becomes more evident when we consider some of the ways in which wants arise. First of all, wants arise for what the human organism must have in order to continue functioning. The desire for food is the most obvious case in point. In intemperate climates two other desires usually arise from necessity—the desire for shelter and for clothing. One or the other, or both of these, must be fulfilled in some degree if the human organism is to survive the rigors of low temperatures or the extreme heat of the tropics.

Wants arise, too, from the culture in which we live, for every society dictates certain requisites for "the good life"—certain standards of housing and food consumption; patronizing of the arts; and possession and consumption of such items as automobiles, charcoal broilers, television sets, and stereo record players. An individual's status in society is thought to depend to a considerable extent upon his levels of consumption. Consequently, many wants are generated in the process of attempting to improve one's status.

The satisfying of our biological and cultural needs requires a wide variety of goods. Individual tastes vary. Some people like roast beef; some like ham; and some like mutton. Over time the same individual wants to satisfy his hunger with different foods. Tastes in clothing differ, and different social occasions call for different modes of dress. Age differences, climatic differences, social differences, educational differences, and a host of other factors give rise to variety in the goods desired by society in general.

Finally, wants are generated by the activity necessary to satisfy other wants; or want-satisfying activity may be said to create new wants. No better illustration of new wants arising from activity directed toward satisfying an old want can be found than that of a student pursuing a university education. The process of attending a university opens new areas of potential desires that heretofore he had not known existed — intellectual and cultural desires, and many others. The generation of new wants in the process of endeavoring to satisfy old wants plays an important role in the expansibility of human desires.

These sources from which wants arise do not represent an exhaustive classification. But this list illustrates the possibility of the infinite expansion of wants over time and the impossibility of an economy's ever saturating all the wants of all its people.

Want Satisfaction and Levels of Living   The level of want satisfaction achieved in a given economic society is hard to measure. Ordinarily it is expressed in terms of per capita income — sometimes gross and sometimes net, depending on the availability of data. There may be a great dispersion around the average, and the average income figure may be misleading. Nevertheless, per capita income appears to be one of the best measures available of the performance of an economy.

Sometimes people judge the performance of a economy on the basis of whether per capita incomes are at a "satisfactory" level. The implication is that if the level is below "satisfactory" something ought to be done about it — that everyone is entitled to a "satisfactory" level of living. Judgments of these kinds are not very valuable from the point of view of economic analysis.

In the first place the level of living "satisfactory" to a society is entirely relative to the historical time under consideration. A level of living with which most people in the United States would have been quite happy fifty years ago would not be satisfactory today. What is satisfactory today will probably not be satisfactory fifty years from now. As the economy's capacity to produce increases, the concept of what constitutes a "satisfactory" level of living shifts upward. The insatiability of human wants, together with increases over time in productive capacity, leads to an ever-changing concept of what constitutes a "satisfactory" level.

Second, the concept of what constitutes a "satisfactory" level varies among different geographic areas. A level of living high enough to make most Asians content for the present will not be high enough for most Europeans or Americans. People become accustomed to certain living levels and a "satisfactory" one for them becomes just a little higher than what they currently have.

From the standpoint of efficient operation the performance of an economy should not be judged on the basis of whether or not it provides a "satisfactory" level of living. Rather, it should be judged on the basis of whether or not it provides the highest level of living that its resources and techniques will permit at a given time, making due allowance for some part of current production to be set aside to augment future productive capacity. One can ask no more of an economy. It should not provide much less. To the extent that some part of current production is used to augment future productive capacity, the level of living which the economy can provide will grow continuously.

Resources

The level of want satisfaction that an economy can achieve is limited partly by the quantities and qualities of its known resources. Resources are the means available for producing goods that are used to satisfy wants. Hundreds of different kinds of resources exist in the economy. Among these are labor of all kinds, raw materials of all kinds, land, machinery, buildings, semifinished materials, fuel, power, transportation, and the like.

Classification of Resources   Resources can be classified conveniently into two categories: (1) labor or human resources, and (2) capital or nonhuman resources. Labor resources consist of labor power or the capacity for human effort—both of mind and of muscle—used in producing goods. The term *capital* can be misleading, since it is used in several different ways not only by noneconomists but by economists as well. We use the term to include all nonhuman resources that can contribute toward placing goods in the hands of the ultimate consumer. Specific examples are buildings, machinery, land, available mineral resources, raw materials, semifinished materials, business inventories, and any other nonhuman tangible items used in the productive process.[1] We need particularly to guard against confusing capital and money. Money is not capital as the term is used in this book. Money as such produces nothing. It is primarily a medium of exchange—a technique facilitating exchange of goods and services and resources. This technique implies that the values of capital

---

[1] In a basic sense inventories of goods in the hands of ultimate consumers also constitute capital, since it is the satisfaction yielded by goods rather than the goods themselves which consumers desire. Thus, such goods are still means of satisfying ultimate ends or desires of consumers; that is, they have yet to produce the want satisfaction they are supposed to produce. We shall not cut it this fine. Goods in the hands of the ultimate consumer will be called consumer goods rather than capital, and this will avoid some complexities.

items, labor, and consumer goods and services are measured in terms of the monetary unit.

The significance of this classification of resources should not be overestimated. It is more descriptive than analytical. Within each category there are many different kinds of resources, and the differences between two kinds falling within the same classification may be more significant analytically than the differences between two kinds in separate classifications. Consider, for example, a human ditch digger and an accountant. Both fall under the descriptive classification of labor. However, from an analytical point of view, the human ditch digger is more closely related to a mechanical ditch digger, which would fall under the descriptive classification of capital, than he is to the accountant.

Characteristics of Resources   Resources have three important characteristics: (1) most resources are limited in quantity; (2) they are versatile; (3) they can be combined in varying proportions to produce a given commodity. These will be considered in turn.

Most resources are scarce in the sense that they are limited in quantity relative to desires for the products that they can produce. These are called economic resources. Some resources, such as the air used in an internal-combustion engine, are so abundant that they can be had for the taking. These are called free resources, since they command no price. If all resources were free there would be no limitation on the extent to which wants could be satisfied, and no economic problem. Levels of living could soar to infinite heights. Free resources are of no significance for economic analysis and will be disregarded.

We are interested in economic resources. The scarcity of economic resources makes the picking and choosing of which wants are to be satisfied and in what degree necessary. This is the economic problem in a nutshell.

The population of an economy sets an upper limit on the quantities of labor resources available. Various factors—education, custom, general state of health, age distribution—determine the actual proportion of the population that can be considered as the labor force. Over a short period of time the total labor force cannot be expanded very much, but over a longer period it may be variable as population has time to change and as changes occur in the factors determining the actual labor force.

Generally, the total capital equipment of the economy is expanding over time, but this expansion occurs slowly. The amount that an economy can add to its total stock of capital equipment in a year's time without seriously restricting current consumption is a fairly small proportion of its existing capital. Therefore, over a short period of time the quantity of capital available to produce goods is limited.

Any kind of resource can be used in the production of a wide variety of goods. The versatility of resources refers to their capacity to be put to different uses. Common labor can be used in the production of almost every conceivable good. The more highly skilled or specialized a resource becomes, however, the more limited are its uses. There are fewer alternative jobs for skilled machinists than for common laborers. There are still fewer alternative jobs for the brain surgeon, or the ballet dancer, or the big-league baseball player. But even with a high degree of resource specialization supplies of one kind of specialized resource can be developed over time at the expense of supplies of other kinds. Individuals can be trained as physicians rather than as dentists. More bricklayers can be developed at the expense of the quantity of carpenters. More tractors and fewer combines can be produced. The resources of the economy are quite fluid with respect to the forms they can take and the kinds of goods they can produce. The longer the period of time under consideration, the greater their fluidity or versatility.

Possibilities of combining resources in various proportions to produce a given good usually exist. Few, if any, goods require rigid proportions of resources. Generally the possibility exists of substituting some kinds of labor for capital, or for other kinds of labor, and vice-versa. This characteristic of resources is closely related to the characteristic of versatility. Substitution and versatility make it possible for the economy to switch productive capacity from one line of production to another, they make it possible to gear the economy to the changing character of human wants. Resources can be transferred into industries producing goods that are most wanted, and out of industries producing goods that are wanted least.

Techniques of Production   Techniques of production, together with quantities and qualities of resources in existence, limit the level of want satisfaction an economy can achieve. Techniques of production are the know-how and the physical means of transforming resources into want—satisfying form. The nature of techniques available to enterprisers is generally considered to lie largely outside the province of economic theory and in the province of engineering. However, the simultaneous choices of goods to be produced, quantities to be produced, and techniques to be used fall within the scope of economics. Economists usually assume that for the production of any commodity a given range of techniques is available and that for any quantity produced of the commodity the least-cost techniques will be used.

Methodology

In order to make a useful systematic study of economic activity we must learn and apply economic theory to it. But what is economic theory? Like the theory of any other science it consists of sets of principles or causal relationships among the important "facts" or variables that surround economic activity. We shall look first at the construction and functions of sets of economic principles; then we shall turn to the place of price theory within the overall scheme of the discipline.

The Construction of Economic Theory

Any set of principles (a theory) must have a bedrock starting point consisting of propositions or conditions that are taken as given or as being so without further investigation. These we call the *postulates* or the *premises* upon which the theory is erected. In aerodynamics the forces of gravity, the operation of centrifugal force, and air resistance may be among the postulates of a theory involving lift, thrust, and drag. In economics we may build a theory of consumer behavior on the postulate of consumer rationality, defined as the general desire of consumers to secure as much satisfaction as they can in spending their incomes. The first step, then, in the construction of a theory is the specification and definition of its postulates.

The second step is the observation of "facts" concerning the activity about which we want to theorize. For example, if the activity in question is the exchange of groceries between supermarkets and consumers, the activity should be looked into as thoroughly as possible. As facts emerge from continued and repeated observation it will become apparent that some are irrelevant and can be discarded; others will obviously be of significant value. In the grocery exchange case the hair color of consumers is not likely to be important, but the weekly amounts of money that consumers have to spend, the number of supermarkets available to them, and the weekly quantities of groceries available to be purchased will most certainly be important.

The third step—and this one will frequently be taken concurrently with the second—is the application of the rules of logic to the observed facts in an attempt to establish causal relationships among them and in order to eliminate as many irrelevant and insignificant facts as possible. *Deductive* chains of logic may lead us to believe that certain effects follow certain causes in a regular manner. We may reason that consumers with larger incomes are willing to pay higher prices for specific goods. Therefore, an increase in consumer incomes is likely to lead to higher prices. Or, on the other hand, we may reason *inductively*. Repeated observations may indicate that increases in consumer incomes and increases in prices occur simultaneously. So, putting two and two together, we reach the tentative conclusion that higher incomes cause prices to rise. Such tentative statements of cause and effect relationships are called *hypotheses*.

The fourth step in the process of establishing a set of principles is a crucial one. Once hypotheses have been formulated, they must be thoroughly tested to determine the degree to which they are valid; that is, the extent to which they give good results. The tools of statistics are of particular value in this respect. Some hypotheses will not withstand the rigors of repeated testing and, consequently, must be rejected. The testing process may suggest modifications in others; then the modified hypotheses must be tested. Still other hypotheses may be found to hold up most of the time in most of the circumstances to which they are relevant. These we usually refer to as *principles*.

It would be foolish to regard a set of principles as absolute truth. The testing process in economics and in other sciences never ends. At any given point in time we think of principles as the best available statements of causal relations; however, additional data and better testing techniques may enable us to improve on them over time. Economic theory is not a once-and-for-all set of principles. It is viable — evolving and continually growing.

The Functions of Economic Theory

The principal functions of economic theory fall into two categories: (1) to explain the nature of economic activity, and (2) to predict what will happen to the economy. The explanation of the nature of economic activity enables us to understand the economic environment in which we live — how one part relates to others and what causes what. We also want to be able to predict with some degree of accuracy what is likely to happen to the key variables that affect our well-being and to be able to do something about it if we dislike the predicted consequences.

Economists differentiate between *positive economics* and *normative economics* on the basis of whether the users of theory are concerned with causal relations only, or whether they desire some kind of intervention in economic activity intended to alter the course of that activity. Positive economics is supposed to be completely objective, limited to the cause-and-effect relationships of economic activity. It is concerned with the way economic relations *are*. By way of contrast, normative economics is concerned with what *ought* to be. Value judgments must necessarily be made; that is, possible objectives to be achieved must be ranked, and choices made among those objectives. Economic policy making — conscious intervention in economic activity with the intent of altering the course that it will take — is essentially normative in character. But if economic policy making is to be effective in improving economic well-being, it must obviously be rooted in sound positive economic analysis. Policy makers should be cognizant of the full range of consequences of the policies they recommend.

Price Theory and Economic Theory

Price theory (*microeconomic theory*) and the theory of th. economy as a whole (*macroeconomic theory*) provide the basic analytical tool kit of the discipline of economics. The principles of both are used in special subject areas, such as monetary economics, international trade and finance, public finance, manpower economics, agricultural economics, regional economics, and so on. The concentration on microeconomics in this book should in no way be interpreted as minimizing the importance of macroeconomics. Both are essential to a thorough understanding of economic activity.

Price theory (microeconomics) is concerned with the economic activities of such individual economic units as consumers, resource owners, and business firms. It is concerned with the flow of goods and services from business firms to consumers, the composition of the flow, and the evaluation or pricing of the component parts of the flow. It is concerned, too, with the flow of productive resources (or their services) from resource owners to business firms, with their evaluation, and with their allocation among alternative uses. In price theory we usually assume a stable economy—one free from major fluctuations up or down—and reasonably full employment of resources. We shall use these assumptions throughout this book not because fluctuations and unemployment are unimportant but because the structure of price theory can be established in a more unequivocal and simpler way when these assumptions are made.

National income theory (macroeconomics) treats the economic system as a whole rather than treating the individual economic units of which it is composed. The particular goods and services making up the flow from business firms to consumers are not integral parts of the analysis, nor are the individual productive resources or services flowing from resource owners to business firms. The value of the overall flow of goods (net national product) and the value of the overall flow of resources (national income) will receive the focus of attention.

Price index numbers or general price level concepts in macroeconomics replace the individual prices of microeconomics. National income theory concentrates on the causes of change in aggregate money flows, the aggregate flow of goods and services, and the general employment level of resources. Prescription of cures for economic fluctuations and for unemployment of resources follows logically from the determination of their causes. Macroeconomics has much to say about the nature of economic growth and the conditions necessary for the expansion of productive capacity and national income over time.

Price theory and national income theory are closely related and supplement each other extensively. For example, the assumptions that the economy is stable and that reasonably full employment of resources exist are really assumptions regarding the state of the economy viewed from the vantage point of national income theory. A given state of economic affairs defined with respect to national income theory forms the framework within which we shall develop price theory.

Price theory is somewhat abstract. We may as well face this point at the outset. Difficulties will be encountered in this respect, but if we recognize the nature of the difficulties they will seem less formidable. Primarily, we shall find that price theory does not give a description of the real world. It will not tell us why a price differential of two cents per gallon for gasoline exists between Oklahoma City and Cleveland on any given date. However, it should help us to understand the real world. It should show us in general how the price(s) of gasoline is established and the role that gasoline prices play in the overall operation of the economy.

Price theory is abstract because it does not and cannot encompass all the economic data of the real world. To take all the data and factors that influence economic decisions of consumers, resource owners, and business firms into consideration would involve minute descriptions and analyses of every economic unit in existence and that would be an impossible task. Consequently, the function of theory is to single out what appear to be the most relevant data and build an overall conceptual framework of the price system in operation from these. We concentrate on the data and principles that seem to be most important in motivating most economic units. In eliminating less important data and in building up a logical theoretical structure, we lose some contact with reality. But we gain in our understanding of the overall operation of the economy because we reduce the factors to be considered to manageable proportions. We may lose sight of individual trees, but we gain more understanding and a better view of the forest.

The theoretical structure to be established should show the directions in which economic units tend to move and should explain the more important reasons why they tend to move in those directions. It should be a set of logically consistent approximations of how the economy operates. The abstraction and precision of theory is essential to clear thinking and to policy making in the real world, but we should guard against its unqualified application to the real world. We should make theory our tool and not our master.

Welfare

The central theme of this book is economic *welfare*, defined as the economic well-being of those who live and work in the economy. The welfare or well-being of an individual presents no great conceptual difficulties. The simplest case is one in which the individual (or family unit) is thought to be the best judge of what does or does not contribute to his (its) own well-being. The individual's welfare is increased or decreased according to his evaluation of the impact of events that affect him. As outside observers we simply ask how an event affects him and accept his answer at its face value.

The welfare of a group is much more difficult to handle. As a starting point we can say that events that increase the well-being of every individual in the group increase the welfare of the group as a whole. But very often an event that increases the well-being of one person decreases that of another. When such is the case the gain in the welfare of the first must be compared with the loss in the welfare of the second if any conclusions are to be drawn about the welfare of the group as a whole. Comparisons of this sort raise serious problems. How can changes in the well-being of different persons be compared? In some specific cases rough subjective judgments can be made. Taking a Rembrandt away from a connoisseur of art and giving it to a person who does not understand or value art would surely reduce group welfare. In general we have no objective means of measuring and comparing the gain of one person or group of persons with the loss suffered by another individual or group when an event causes both.

We are left with a group welfare concept known as a *Pareto optimum* [2] A Pareto optimum is said to exist when no event can increase the well-being of one person without decreasing the well-being of someone else. Looking at the matter another way, a Pareto optimum does not exist if one or more persons can be made better off without making anyone else worse off. If a Pareto optimum does not exist, a movement toward it—making at least one person better off without making anyone else worse off—increases group welfare.

There is no unique Pareto optimal situation in an economy. Suppose that all production and all exchanges that bestow advantage on anyone without disadvantaging anyone else have taken place. If any redistribution of purchasing power now occurs—for example, the imposition of taxes on the rich and the granting of subsidies to the poor—the conditions of the original Pareto optimum are violated. But a new Pareto optimum, given the new distribution of income, is possible. In fact, there will be a different set of Pareto optimal conditions for every different pattern of purchasing power distribution. If the economy moves from one Pareto optimum to another in this fashion, can we say that the welfare of the group has increased or decreased? There are no objective measures that will provide

[2]Originated by the early twentieth-century Italian economist Vilfredo Pareto.

the answer. We can discuss objectively the conditions that lead to Paretc optimality, given the distribution of income, but if we want to discuss the impact of income redistribution on welfare we must fall back on subjective value judgments to support whatever stand we take.

Summary

Economic activity revolves around three key elements: (1) human wants which are varied and insatiable; (2) resources which are limited, versatile, and capable of being combined in varying proportions to produce a given commodity; (3) techniques for utilizing resources to produce goods and services that satisfy wants. Not only should resources and techniques be used to produce goods that satisfy wants, they should be used also to produce the quantities of those goods that contribute most to aggregate want satisfaction. The goal of economic activity is a level of want satisfaction (level of living) as high as the economy can provide. To achieve this goal the best possible techniques must be used; resources must be fully employed and properly allocated or distributed among the alternative wants of consumers.

The methodology of economics is like that of other sciences. Sets of principles are developed through the formulation and testing of hypotheses. These in turn are outgrowths of logic applied to basic premises and observations of facts.

At the outset, the relationship of price theory to the overall discipline of economics and the relationship of price theory to the real world should be understood. Price theory is an essential part of the economist's tool kit and is used, together with national income theory, in the special subject areas of economics. Rather than explaining in detail the activities of economic units in the real world it establishes general principles concerning activities on the basis of what appear to be the most important economic data. Activities of economic units in the real world approximate or tend toward those of theory. But this loss in the way of detailed contact with the real world means gain in the understanding of the main forces at work.

This book is concerned with welfare in the Pareto optimum sense; that is, it will have much to say about the conditions of economic efficiency for any given income distribution, but it will not have much to say about whether one income distribution is more efficient than another.

Suggested Readings

Friedman, Milton, "The Methodology of Positive Economics," *Essays in Positive Economics* (Chicago Ill.: University of Chicago Press, 1953), pp. 3–43.

Koopmans, Tjalling C., *Three Essays on the State of Economic Science* (New York: McGraw-Hill, Inc., 1957), pp. 129–149.

Lange, Oscar, "The Scope and Method of Economics," *Review of Economic Studies*, vol. XIII (1945–1946), pp. 19–32.

Marshall, Alfred, Principles of Economics, 8th ed. (London: Macmillan & Co., Ltd., 1920), Bk. III, Chap. 2.

Chapter 2:

The Organization of an Economic System[1]

The purpose of this chapter is to give us a brief look at the economy as a whole before we study its details. By developing a preliminary working concept of the economy as a whole, we can fit the details into their proper places as we come to them and can put them into proper perspective. First, we will construct a simple model of a private enterprise economic system. Next, we will discuss the functions of such a system, with special reference to prices as the key mechanism in performing these functions.

A Simplified Model

The widely used "circular flow" diagram of Figure 2-1 furnishes a highly simplified model of an economic system. Economic units are classified into two groups: (1) households and (2) business firms. These interact in two sets of markets: (1) markets for consumer goods and services and (2) resource markets. Households, business firms, consumer goods markets, and resource markets are the component parts of a free enterprise economy. They form the core around which price theory is built.

Households include all individual and family units of the economy and are the consumers of the economy's output of goods and services. With

---

[1]This chapter is based on Frank H. Knight, "Social Economic Organization," reprinted in Harry D. Gideonse and others, eds., *Contemporary Society: Syllabus and Selected Readings*, 4th ed. (Chicago Ill.: University of Chicago Press, 1935), pp. 125–137.

minor exceptions—for example, the indigent—they also own the economy's resources.

Business firms are a more limited group engaged in the buying and hiring of resources and the production and sale of goods and services. They include single proprietorships, partnerships, and corporations at all levels of the productive process. In some cases the same economic unit functions both as a firm and as a household, the family farm being a case in point. We shall assume that its activities as a firm can be clearly separated from its activities as a household and that each activity is classified under the appropriate heading.

The upper half of Figure 2-1 represents the markets for consumer goods and services. Households as consumers and business firms as sellers interact within the markets. Goods and services flow from business firms to consumers; a *reverse* flow of money from consumers to business firms also takes place. Prices of goods and services form the connecting link between the two flows. The value of the flow of goods and services will be equal to the reverse money flow.

The lower half of Figure 2-1 represents the markets for resources. The services of labor and capital in their many forms flow from resource owners (households) to business firms. The reverse flow of money in payment for these resources occurs in such forms as wages, salaries, rents, dividends, interest, and so on, depending on the contractual arrangements under which they are delivered. These are resource prices valuing the services of resources and forming the connecting link between the two flows. In money terms the two flows are equal .

Money circulates continuously from households to business firms and back to households again. The sale of goods and services places money at the disposal of business firms for the purchase of resource services to continue production. The sale or hire of the services of resources places money at the disposal of resource owners for the purchase of goods and services.[2] The money flow takes on four familiar aspects as it makes a complete circuit. It is consumers' cost of living at point 1 in Figure 2-1 as it leaves consumers' hands. It is business receipts for business firms at point 2 . (Aggregate costs of living and aggregate business receipts are the same thing looked at from two different viewpoints.) At point 3 the money flow becomes costs of production; while at point 4 it is consumers' incomes. (Aggregate costs of production and aggregate consumers' incomes are also the same thing considered from two different viewpoints.)

---

[2]In some instances the money flow may be circumvented completely by direct exchange of resource services for goods or for "income in kind" to resource owners. To the extent that this type of transaction occurs, the money flows in each half of the diagram will be less than the value of goods and services and the value of resource services. However, since the bulk of exchange in a free enterprise economy will involve money and prices, we shall leave barter exchanges out of consideration.

Figure 2 – 1　The Circular Flow Model

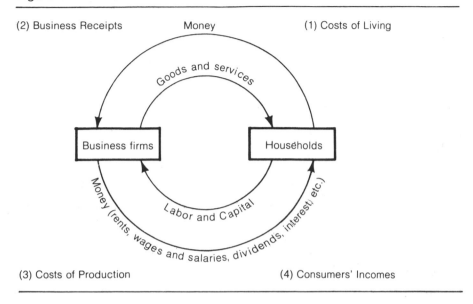

(2) Business Receipts　　　　Money　　　　(1) Costs of Living

Goods and services

Business firms

Households

Money (rents, wages and salaries, dividends, interest, etc.)

Labor and Capital

(3) Costs of Production　　　　　　　　(4) Consumers' Incomes

If the economy is a stationary one—neither expanding nor contracting—the flow of money of the upper half of Figure 2-1 will equal the flow of money of the lower half. The aggregate value of goods and services will equal the aggregate value of resource services. Consumers spend all their incomes; no saving occurs. Likewise, business firms pay out all money received to resource owners and there is no business saving.[3] No net investment occurs. In the production of goods and services capital equipment wears out or depreciates. Some resource services are used to take care of replacement or depreciation, but costs of replacement or depreciation are in reality a part of the cost of producing the goods which caused the depreciation to occur in the first place.

The model can be expanded and made as complex as we want to make it.[4] We can expand it to explain a growing economy, or we can expand it to explain a contracting economy. We can expand it to take government economic activities into account. We can use the model and modifications of it to explain national income analysis. But for our purposes the simple model as presented here will suffice.

---

[3] Profits made by business firms flow into the hands of resource owners in the form of dividends to stockholders or high prices paid to owners of other resources.

[4] For an excellent, somewhat different view of the economy as a whole *see* Milton Gilbert and George Jazi, "National Product and Income Statistics as an Aid in Economic Problems," *Dun's Review*, vol. LII (February 1944), pp. 9–11, 30–38, reprinted in *Readings in the Theory of Income Distribution* (Philadelphia: P. Blakiston's Son & Company, 1946), pp. 44–57.

We shall be concerned with the two sets of markets and the interactions which occur within each of them. In product markets the composition of the flow of goods and services, the prices of each, and outputs of each will be of interest to us. Similarly, in resource markets, the prices, unemployment levels, and allocations of resources will be considered.

The Functions of an Economic System

Every economic system, whether private enterprise or not, must somehow perform five closely related functions. It must determine (1) what is to be produced, (2) how production is to be organized, (3) how the output is to be distributed, (4) how goods are to be rationed over very short-run periods during which their supplies are fixed, and (5) how the productive capacity of the economy is to be maintained and expanded.

Determination of What Is to Be Produced

The determination of what is to be produced in an economy is primarily a problem of determining what wants in the aggregate are most important and in what degree they are to be satisfied. Should the amount of steel currently available be used for the production of automobiles, or tanks, or refrigerators, or for the erection of sports arenas? Or should it be used to provide some of each? Since the resources of the economy are scarce, all wants cannot be fully satisfied. The problem is one of picking and choosing from the unlimited scope of wants those most important to the society as a whole. Essentially, the economy must set up a hierarchy of values for different goods and services that is acceptable to the group and reflects the relative desires of the group for goods and services that the economy can produce.

The value of an item is measured by price in a private enterprise economy, and the valuation process is accomplished by buyers as they spend their incomes. Consumers, for example, are confronted with a wide range of choices with regard to the goods they can buy. The dollar values they place on each of the various goods depend on how urgently consumers as a group desire each good relative to other goods, their willingness and ability to back up desire with dollars, and the supplies of the goods available. The more urgently certain goods are desired, and the more willing consumers are to back up desire with dollars, the higher their prices. The less strong the desire for certain goods, the lower their prices. The greater the available supply of any particular good, the lower its price. Any one unit of the good will be of less importance to the consumer when the supply is great than when the supply is small. The more bread we have available to eat per week, the smaller the value each loaf will be to us. Conversely, the smaller the supply of any particular commodity, the higher consumers will value any one unit of it. Thus, the ways in which consumers spend their incomes establish an array of prices or a price structure in the economy that reflects the comparative values of different goods and services to the consuming public.

Changes in consumer tastes and preferences modify the ways in which consumers spend their incomes. These changes in spending change the structure of prices in turn. Goods which consumers begin to desire more go up in price, while those becoming less desirable to consumers decline in price. The price or value structure of goods and services then changes to reflect changes in consumers' tastes and preferences.

This analysis is positive in nature, telling us how goods are actually valued by means of a system of prices. It does not tell us how goods *ought* to be valued. The latter problem is an ethical one and lies largely outside the scope of price theory. A consumer with a larger income will exert more influence on the value structure than a consumer with a lower income will. Conceivably, biscuits for rich people's dogs may be placed higher in the scale of values than milk for poor people's children, provided there are enough rich people casting their dollar votes in this direction, and there are not enough poor people able to spend dollars for milk. The price system, though working perfectly in this case, may lead to social consequences that are considered undesirable and which we attempt to rectify through the political process. Income redistribution and progressive income taxes are examples of such political processes.

Organization of Production

Concurrent with the determination of what is to be produced, an economic system must determine how resources are to be organized to produce the desired goods in the proper quantities. Organization of production involves (1) drawing resources from industries producing goods that consumers value less and channeling them into the industries producing goods that consumers value more and (2) efficient use of resources by individual firms. These will be considered in turn.

The price system in a free enterprise economy operates to organize production. Firms producing goods and services that consumers want most urgently receive higher prices relative to costs and will be the more profitable. Firms producing goods and services that consumers want less urgently incur losses. The more profitable firms can and do offer higher prices for resources in order to expand. Those incurring losses are unwilling to pay as much for resources. Resource owners, in the interest of increasing their incomes, want to sell their resources to firms offering the higher prices. Therefore, there is a constant channeling of resources away from firms producing goods and services that consumers want least and into the firms producing goods and services that consumers want most. Resources are moving constantly from lower-paying to higher-paying uses, or out of less important into more important uses.

The term *efficiency* in economics differs slightly from the use of the term in physics or mechanics. However, in both contexts it involves the ratio of an output to an input. With regard to mechanical efficiency we know that a steam engine is inefficient because it fails to transform a large part of the heat energy of its fuel into power. Mechanically, an internal-combustion engine is more efficient. However, if fuel for steam engines is cheap and fuel for internal-combustion engines is expensive, cheaper power may be obtained from the steam engine.

This point brings us to the concept of economic efficiency, which is also a ratio of output to input. The economic efficiency of a particular productive process is the ratio of useful product output to useful input of resources. The usefulness of product output, or its value to society, is measured in dollar terms. Similarly, the usefulness or value of resource input is measured in terms of dollars. Thus, the steam engine, which is less efficient mechanically, may be more efficient economically than an internal conbustion-engine provided that it furnishes *cheaper* power for a particular productive process.

The quest for profits provides the incentive for efficient production. The more efficient the firm, given the price of the product, the greater its profits will be. To rephrase the definition of efficiency, it is the value of product output per unit input of resource value. The greater the dollar value of product output per dollar's worth of resource input, the greater economic efficiency is. This statement can also be put the other way around. The less the dollar value of resource input needed per dollar's worth of product output, the greater economic efficiency is. Measurement of economic efficiency requires that values be placed on goods and services. It further requires that values be placed on resources of different types and on the same type of resource in different uses. Resources are valued in the market according to their contributions to the production of goods and services.

Economic efficiency within the firm involves selection of the combinations of resources and the techniques to use in the production process. The choice of techniques to use will depend on relative resource prices and the quantity of product to be produced. The aim of the firm is to produce whatever output it produces as cheaply (efficiently) as it can. Thus, if labor is relatively expensive and capital is relatively cheap, the firm will want to use techniques making use of much capital and little labor. If capital is relatively expensive and labor is relatively cheap, the most efficient techniques are those using little capital and much labor. The techniques to use for most efficient operation will differ with differing levels of output, also. Mass production methods and complicated machines cannot be used efficiently for small outputs; but for large outputs they can be very efficient.

Output Distribution

Distribution of the product output in a private enterprise economy is accomplished by the price system simultaneously with the determination of what is to be produced and the organization of production. Product distribution depends on personal income distribution. Those with larger incomes obtain larger shares of the economy's output than do those with smaller incomes.

The income of an individual depends on two things: (1) the quantities of different resources that he can put into the productive process and (2) the prices that he receives for them. If labor power is the only resource owned by an individual, his monthly income is determined by the number of man-hours he works per month multiplied by the hourly wage rate he receives. If, in addition, he owns and rents out land, the amount of land rented out multiplied by the monthly rental per acre will be his income from land. Income from labor added to income from land is his total monthly income. The example can be expanded to as many different resources as an individual owns.

Income distribution thus depends on the distribution of resource ownership in the economy and whether or not individuals place their resources in employments producing goods that consumers want most; that is, where the highest prices are offered for resources. Low individual incomes result from small quantities of resources owned and/or the placing of resources owned in employments contributing little to consumer satisfaction. High individual incomes result from large quantities of resources owned and/or the placing of resources owned in employments where they contribute much to consumer satisfaction. Thus, income differences may result from improper channeling of certain resources into the productive process by certain individuals, and from differences in resource ownership among individuals.

Income differences that arise from improper channeling of certain resources into the productive process tend to be self-correcting. Suppose a number of individuals are capable of doing the same amount of labor per week in a certain skill category and two groups are employed in the making of two different products. The value of product turned out by a worker in the first group is much higher than the value of product turned out by a worker in the second. Since society values the first group higher than it values that of a worker in the second, the first group of workers will receive greater individual incomes. When workers of the second group perceive the income differential some move to the higher-paying employment. The increased supply of the first commodity lowers consumers' valuation of it, while the decreased supply of the second commodity raises consumers' valuation of it. This in turn lowers the incomes of the first (but now larger) group of workers and raises the incomes of the second (but now smaller) group of workers. When the income differential between workers in the two groups disappears, worker movements from the second to the first group cease. The self-correcting mechanism requires time to work and may, in some cases, be prevented from accomplishing its task by ignorance on the part of the workers of the second group or by institutional barriers that prevent them from moving. In such cases the income differentials become chronic.

A large part of the income differentials arising from differences in resource ownership will not be self-correcting. The major sources of differences in resource ownership are discussed later in Chapter 17. They can be classified under differences in labor power owned and differences in kinds and quantities of capital owned. Differences in labor power owned by different individuals stem from differences in physical and mental inheritance and from differences in opportunities to acquire specific types of training. Differences in kinds and quantities of capital owned come from many sources. These include initial differences in labor resources owned, differences in material inheritance, fortuitous circumstances, fraud, and differences in propensities to accumulate.

In the event society believes that income differences should be smaller, modifications can be imposed on the free-enterprise economy without materially affecting the operation of the price system. Society, through the government, may levy progressive income taxes and make expenditures for welfare purposes. It may subsidize low-income groups in various ways. Redistribution of income will, however, affect the wants to be satisfied by economic activity by changing the effective pattern of social desires for goods and services. Reduction of high incomes makes the individuals who are deprived become less effective in the market place. Augmentation of low incomes makes those who are helped become more effective in the market place. The price system will reorganize production to conform with the new pattern of effective desires for goods and services.

Rationing in the Very Short Run

An economic system must make some provision for rationing commodities over the time period during which the supplies of these cannot be changed. This time period is called the *very short run*. Suppose that wheat were harvested all over the country in the same month each year. From one year to the next the supply of wheat available for consumption would be fixed, assuming there is no carryover from one year to the next. The very short run for wheat in such a case would be one year. The economy must ration the fixed supply in two ways: (1) it must allocate the supply among the different consumers of the economy, (2) it must stretch the given supply over the time period from one harvest to the next.

In a private enterprise economy price will be the device that allocates the fixed supply among different consumers. Shortages will cause the price to increase, decreasing the amount that each consumer is willing to buy. The price will continue to increase until all consumers together are just willing to take the fixed supply. Surpluses will cause price to decrease, increasing the amount consumers are willing to buy until they take the entire supply off the market.

Price will also be the device for rationing the good over time. If the entire supply were to be dumped in consumers' hands immediately after harvest, price would be driven low. At the low price consumption would proceed at a rapid pace. As the next harvest approaches, the disappearance of most of the commodity in the first part of the period leaves very small supplies for the latter part of the period. Consequently, price would be high in the latter part of the very-short-run period.

Speculation plays an important role in smoothing out the consumption of the good over time. Knowing that the price will tend to be low early in the period and high late in the period, speculators will buy up a large part of the supply early in the period, expecting to sell it later at higher prices and thus realize a net gain on their investment in the product. Their purchases will raise the price in the early part of the period above what it would otherwise have been, thus slowing the rate at which the product is consumed at that time. Their sales in the latter part of the period will reduce price below what it would otherwise have been and will provide greater quantities of the product for consumption in the latter part of the period. The actions of speculators modify the price rise that would have taken place over the very-short-run period and bring about a more even flow of the product to consumers over time.

Economic Maintenance and Growth

Every economy in the modern world is expected to maintain and expand its productive capacity. *Maintenance* refers to keeping the productive power of the economic machine intact through provision for depreciation. *Expansion* refers to continuous increase in the kinds and quantities of the economy's resources, together with continuous improvement in techniques of production.

Labor power can be increased through population increases and through the development and improvement of skills by means of training and education. Development and improvement of skills in a private enterprise economy are motivated largely through the price mechanism—the prospects of higher pay for more highly skilled and more productive work. The extent to which skills can be developed and improved is conditioned by training and educational opportunities, together with physical and mental abilities.

Capital accumulation depends on a variety of complex economic motives, and much debate centers about their relative importance. For capital accumulation to occur, some resources must be diverted from the production of current consumer goods and be put to work producing capital goods in excess of the amount needed to offset depreciation.

Improvements in productive techniques make possible the production of greater outputs with given quantities of resources. The motives behind the search for and the discovery of inventions and improvements are not always easy to determine. The inventor may invent because he finds that type of activity interesting. Frequently, improvements in techniques are the by-product of. scholarship intended primarily to advance knowledge. However, a large part of the improvements in productive techniques is a direct result of the quest for profits, as is well-illustrated by the increasing flow of fruitful results coming from the growing research and development departments of large corporations.

The role of the price mechanism and its degree of importance in providing for economic maintenance and growth are not clear. Certainly prices and profit prospects are an important element in determining whether or not maintenance and growth occur. But the area of economic maintenance and growth is virtually an applied subject area in itself. Consequently, we shall be concerned mainly with the first four functions as they are performed in a private enterprise economy.

Summary

Our purpose in this chapter has been to obtain a picture of the economic system as a whole and to gain some appreciation of how the price mechanism guides and directs a private enterprise economy. First of all we set up a simple economic model of a private-enterprise economy. Economic units were classified into two groups: (1) households and (2) business firms. They interact in the markets for consumer goods and services and in resource markets. Households as resource owners sell the services of their resources to business firms. Incomes received are used to buy goods from business firms. Business firms receive income from the sale of goods to consumers. Business incomes in turn are used to buy resources from resource owners.

Second, we listed five basic functions of an economic system and discussed the ways in which a private-enterprise economy performs those functions. A system of prices is the main organizing force. Prices determine what is to be produced. Prices organize production, and they play a major role in the distribution of the product. Prices serve to ration a particular good over its very-short-run period during which the supply of the good is fixed. They are also an element in providing for economic maintenance and growth.

Suggested Readings

Knight, Frank H., "Social Economic Organization," *Contemporary Society: Syllabus and Selected Readings*, Harry D. Gideonse and others, eds., 4th ed. (Chicago, Ill.: University of Chicago Press, 1935), pp. 125–137.
Stigler, George J., *The Theory of Price*, 3rd ed. (New York: Crowell-Collier and Macmillan, Inc., 1966), Chap. 2.

Chapter 3:

The Purely Competitive Market Model

Most people have come in contact with the terms *demand, supply, market,* and *competition* and, not being sophisticated in the use of economic analysis, toss them around in a loose sort of way. Actually these are precise terms to economists and are elements of the purely competitive market model used so extensively in modern microeconomic theory. In building up the model we shall discuss first the concept of pure competition. We shall then turn to the concepts of demand and supply. The analysis of price determination that emerges when the demand and the supply for a particular item are brought together is the essence of the model and will be considered next. Finally, we shall examine the concept of elasticity.

Pure Competition

The term *competition* is used ambiguously both in economic literature and in ordinary conversation. Its common meaning is rivalry. But used along with the word *pure* in economics it carries a different meaning. We shall look first at the conditions necessary for the existence of pure competition and then at its role in economic analysis.

The Necessary Conditions for Pure Competition

Homogeneity of the Product   One requisite for pure competition is that all sellers of a particular kind of product sell homogeneous units of the product, as perceived by the buyers of that product. Buyers think that the units sold by seller *A* are identical to those sold by seller *B* and, as an important consequence, have no reason for preferring the output of any one seller over that of any other seller of the product.

Smallness of Each Buyer or Seller Relative to the Market.   Each buyer and each seller of the product under consideration must be so small in relation to the entire market for the product that they cannot significantly influence the price of whatever it is they are buying or selling. On the selling side the individual seller supplies such a small proportion of the total supply that if he drops out of the market altogether, total supply will not be decreased enough to cause any rise in price. Or, if the individual seller supplies as much as he can produce, total supply will not be increased enough to cause price to fall. As an example let us use the individual seller of most farm products. On the buying side any single buyer takes such a small proportion of the total amount placed on the market that he is unable to influence its price. As consumers we are in this position with respect to most of the items we buy. As individuals we have no impact on the price of bread, meat, milk, safety pins, and so on. The main idea here is that of the insignificance of any one individual buyer or seller of a product.

Absence of Artificial Restraints   Another condition necessary for the existence of pure competition is that no artificial restrictions be placed on the demands for, the supplies of, and the prices of whatever is being exchanged. Prices must be free to move wherever they will in response to changing conditions of demand and supply. There must be no governmental price fixing; nor any institutional fixing; or administering of price by producers' associations, labor unions, or other private agencies. There must be no supply restriction enforced by the government or by organized producer groups. Control of demand through governmental rationing must be nonexistent.

Mobility   An additional requirement of pure competition is that there be mobility of goods and services and of resources in the economy. New firms must be free to enter any desired industry, and resources must be free to move among alternative uses to those where they desire employment. Sellers must be able to dispose of their goods and services wherever the price is highest. Resources must be able to secure employment at their highest paid uses.

"Pure" and "Perfect" Competition

Economists sometimes distinguish between "pure" and "perfect" competition. The distinction is one of degree. The four conditions listed above are usually considered necessary for the existence of pure competition; whereas perfect competition requires that one more condition be met.

The additional requirement is that all economic units possess complete knowledge of the economy. All discrepancies in prices quoted by sellers will be known immediately and buyers will buy at the lowest prices. This forces sellers charging higher prices to lower their prices immediately. If different purchasers offer different prices for whatever they purchase, sellers will know immediately and will sell to the highest bidders. The low bidders must of necessity raise their price offers. In the market for any particular product or resource, a single price will prevail. Examples of perfect competition are very rare, but stock transactions on the New York Stock Exchange may approximate these conditions. The terms of stock transactions are flashed on the Exchange Board as soon as they are concluded. The information is then distributed immediately to interested parties all over the country. Under conditions of perfect competition adjustments of the economy to disturbances in the conditions of demand and supply will be instantaneous. Under conditions of pure competition it will take longer for adjustments to occur because of incomplete knowledge on the part of individual economic units.

Pure Competition in Economic Analysis

Competition in economics is impersonal in its nature. There is no reason for enmity to develop between two wheat farmers over the effect that either one has on the market, since neither has any effect whatsoever. One simply does the best he can with what he has. He is not out to get or defeat the other fellow. By way of contrast, intense rivalry may exist between two automobile agencies or between two filling stations in the same city. One seller's actions influence the market of the other; consequently, in this case pure competition does not exist.

No economist insists that thoroughgoing pure competition characterizes the economy of the United States, nor does anyone claim that it ever has. The question arises, then, as to why we should study the principles of pure competition at all. Three important answers may be given. First, the principles of pure competition furnish a simple and logical starting point for economic analysis. Second, a large measure of competition does exist in the United States today, although perhaps not in pure form. Third, the theory of pure competion provides a "norm" against which the actual performance of the economy can be checked or evaluated.

With regard to the first answer, an analogy can be drawn to the study of mechanics. No one questions the procedure of starting a study of mechanics leaving friction out of consideration. This omission, too, is unrealistic, since friction inevitably occurs in the real world, but the temporary postponement of its consideration allows a clear statement of mechanical principles. Friction is later introduced and taken into account. Competitive economic theory principles occupy about the same role in economic analysis as do frictionless principles in the study of mechanics. Once we understand how the frictionless (competitive) economy works, we can observe the effects of friction (imperfect competition and restraints of various sorts) and take them into account. To study the theory of pure competition does not mean that one must believe that the real world is one of pure competition, nor does it preclude the very legitimate study of imperfect competition. It brings out fundamental cause-and-effect relationships that are also found in imperfect competition. It is simply the logical place to start if one is to understand the principles of imperfect competition and their applications, as well as those of pure competition.

With regard to the second answer, studies indicate that substantial competition does exist in the United States.[1] Enough competition exists and enough economic units buy or sell under conditions approaching pure competition to give us valid answers to a great many economic problems.

Third, in the theory of a market economy pure competition leads to the set of conditions defining maximum economic welfare or well being, given the distribution of income. The actual performance of the economy can then be appraised against its potential "best" performance. Imperfectly competitive or monopolistic forces are important in preventing the attainment of the "best" allocation and use of economic resources. Thus, the purely competitive model frequently is used as the basis for public regulation of imperfectly competitive situations. Presumably it underlies the philosophy and enforcement of the Sherman Anti-trust Act of 1890 as amended, government regulation of public utilities, and many other public policy measures.

Demand

Turning now to the market model we define *demand* for a good as the various quantities of it per unit of time that consumers will take off the market at all possible alternative prices, other things being equal or constant. The quantity that consumers will take will be affected by a number of circumstances, such as (1) the price of the good, (2) consumers' tastes and preferences, (3) the number of consumers under consideration, (4)

---

[1]See F. M. Scherer, *Industrial Market Structure and Economic Performance* (Chicago: Rand McNally and Company, 1971), Chap. 3; and G. Warren Nutter and Henry A. Einhorn, *Enterprise Monopoly in the United States, 1899–1958* (New York: Columbia University Press, 1969).

consumers' incomes, (5) the prices of related goods, (6) the range of goods available to consumers, and (7) consumers' expectations regarding future prices of the product.[2] Additional circumstances could be listed, but these seem to be the most important ones.

Demand Schedules and Demand Curves

The foregoing definition singles out the relationship between possible alternative prices of the good and the quantities of it that consumers will take. The other circumstances are held constant in defining a given state of demand. Usually we think of quantity taken as varying inversely with price. The higher the price of the good, the less consumers will take; and the lower the price of the good, the greater the quantity consumers will take—other things being equal or constant. Some exceptions may occur, in which quantity taken varies directly with price, but these must be few.

Note that the term *demand* is used to refer to an entire demand schedule or demand curve.[3] A demand schedule lists the different quantities of the commodity that consumers will take opposite the various alternative prices of the good. A hypothetical demand schedule is shown in Table 3-1. Product X is the commodity; prices are listed under p_x; and quantities taken are listed under X per unit of time. A demand curve is a demand schedule plotted on an ordinary graph. A demand curve is shown in Figure 3-1. The vertical axis of the graph measures price per unit, and the horizontal axis measures quantity of the good per unit of time. Note that the inverse relationship between price and quantity sold makes the demand curve slope downward to the right.

---

[2] In functional form we can write:

$$x = f(p_x, T, C, I, p_n, R, E)$$

in which:

 x is the quantity of good or service X
 p_x is the price of X
 T represents consumers tastes and preferences
 C is the number of consumers under consideration
 p_n represents the prices of related goods
 R represents the range of goods and services available to consumers
 E represents consumer expectations.

[3] The demand equation for X can be written as:

$$x = f(p_x)$$

where we treat the other variables listed in Footnote 2 as parameters. Or, we can reverse the dependency relationship and write:

$$p_x = g(x)$$

thus expressing the demand equation in the form in which it is usually shown graphically. Although the demand equations and curves are represented in this section as being linear, this need not be the case. Linear demand curves are simply easier to draw and explain than are curvilinear ones.

Table 3-1 Demand Schedule for Product X

Price (p_x)	Quantity (X per U.T.)
$10	1
9	2
8	3
7	4
6	5
5	6
4	7
3	8
2	9
1	10

Figure 3–1   Demand Curve for Product X

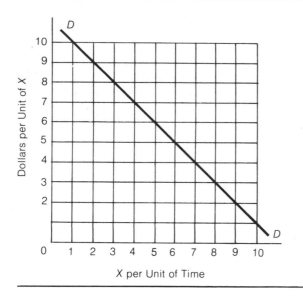

The quantities referred to in Table 3-1 or in Figure 3-1 have no consistent meaning unless they are put in terms of flows per time period. They may be set up on a weekly, monthly, or yearly basis, or whatever time period seems appropriate. It means nothing to say: "At a price of five dollars per unit, six units of product will be taken by consumers." The statement becomes meaningful when we say: "At a price of five dollars per unit, six units of product per week (or month, or whatever the time period happens to be) will be taken by consumers." Hence, we must always remember that we are dealing not merely with quantities but with quantities per unit of

Figure 3–2   Movement along a Demand Curve

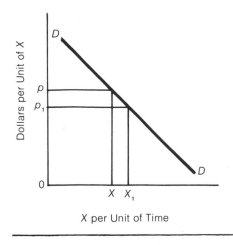

X per Unit of Time

time. They are rates of purchase, such as 500,000 cars per month or 60,000,000 bushels of wheat per month.

The demand curve separates the purchases that consumers are willing to make from those that they are not willing to make. It shows the maximum prices that consumers can be induced to pay for the various quantities indicated on the scale of the horizontal axis; that is, the maximum price at which each of those total quantities can be sold. Or, it can be viewed as showing the maximum quantities that consumers can be induced to take at the price levels indicated on the vertical scale. Any quantity and price shown by a point on or to the left of and below the demand curve is a possible or feasible price-quantity combination to consumers. No point to the right of and above the demand curve is a possible or feasible combination.

A Change in Demand versus a Movement along a Given Demand Curve

A clear distinction must be drawn between a *movement along* a given demand curve and a *change* in demand. A movement along a given demand curve represents a change in quantity taken resulting from a change in price of the good itself when all the other circumstances influencing the quantity taken remain unchanged. In Figure 3-2 a decrease in price from *p* to *p₁* increases the quantity taken from *X* to *X₁*. This is not called a change in demand since it occurs on a single demand curve, and the term *demand* refers to that entire demand curve. In defining demand we assume that the underlying demand circumstances remain constant while we change the price of the commodity and observe what happens to the quantity taken.[4]

When any of the circumstances held constant in defining a given state of demand are changed, the demand curve itself will change. Thus, in Figure 3-3 an increase in consumer incomes will shift the demand curve to the right from DD to D_1D_1. With higher incomes consumers will usually be willing to increase their rate of purchase at each alternative price. A shift in consumer tastes and preferences toward commodity X will have the same results. So, also, will an increase in the number of consumers in the group. An increase in the range of goods available to consumers may cause them to allocate less of their incomes to commodity X, thus shifting the demand curve to the left to position D_2D_2 in Figure 3-3.[5]

The effects on the demand for X of changes in the prices of goods related to X define the nature of the relationships. A related good is a *competitive* or *substitute* good if an increase in its price causes the demand curve for X to shift to the right. The shift results from consumers turning away from the now relatively higher-priced substitute to X.

Suppose, for example, that X is beef and that the price of pork rises. Consumers shift away from pork toward beef, thus increasing the demand for beef. A related good is a *complementary* good if an increase in its price causes a shift to the left in the demand curve for X. The higher price of the related good induces consumers to take less of it. If in taking less of it they have less desire for X, there is an indication of complementarity. In this case suppose that X is milk and that the price of cereal rises enough to curtail cereal consumption. The smaller quantity of cereal consumed reduces the desire for milk — the demand curve for milk shifts to the left.

Supply

The supply of a good is defined as the various quantities of it that sellers will place on the market at all possible alternative prices, other things being equal. It is the relationship between prices and quantities per unit of time that sellers are willing to sell. The same distinction is made between a supply schedule and a supply curve that is made between a demand schedule and a demand curve. A supply curve is a supply

---

If the demand equation were:

$$p_x = a - bx$$

the coordinates of p_x and x would trace out a unique demand curve as long as the parameters a and b remain constant. A change in the value of p_x results in a movement along the curve to the corresponding value of x.

[5]In the equation

$$p_x = a - bx$$

a change in a will shift the position of the curve and a change in b will alter its slope.

Figure 3–3   Changes in Demand

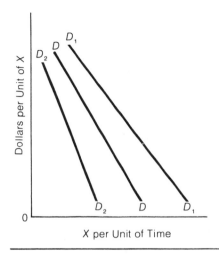

Figure 3–4   Supply Curve for Product X

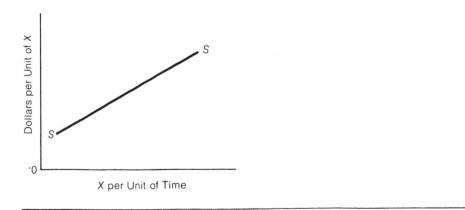

schedule plotted on a graph. Usually the supply curve will be upward sloping to the right, since a higher price will induce sellers to place more of the good on the market and may induce additional sellers to come into the field. A hypothetical supply curve is shown in Figure 3-4.

The "other things" that are held constant in defining a given supply curve are basically (1) the set of prices of the resources used to produce the product and (2) the range of production techniques available.[6]

Like the demand curve, the supply curve is a boundary line between what sellers will and will not do. At any given price sellers would be willing to supply less than the quantity shown by the supply curve at that price, but they cannot be induced to supply more. To be induced to supply any given quantity, sellers must receive at least the price shown by the supply curve at that quantity. They would supply that quantity for a higher price per unit, but they will not supply it for less. Any point on, or above and to the left of, the supply curve represents a possible or feasible quantity supplied at the indicated price. Any point below and to the right of it is not possible or feasible.[7]

Market Price

The demand curve and the supply curve for any given good or service can be placed on a single diagram to show the forces determining its market price. The demand curve indicates what consumers are willing to do, while the supply curve shows what sellers are willing to do. Consumer demand is assumed to be independent of the activities of sellers. Similarly, the supply curve is assumed to be in no way dependent on consumers' activities. Consumers are assumed to operate independently of one another, and so are sellers.

Market Price Determination

Market price determination is illustrated in Figure 3-5. At price level p_1 consumers are willing to take quantity X_1 per unit of time. However, sup-

---

[6]The supply function can be written as:

$$x = s(p_x, p_r, K)$$

in which:

x is the quantity of good or service X

p_x is the price of X

p_r is the set of prices of resources used in producing X

K is the range of production techniques available.

For a short-run supply function we would add M to the list of independent variables, with M representing the number of firms supplying X.

[7]We can express the supply equation as:

$$x = h(p_x),$$

or alternatively, as:

$$p_x = k(x),$$

treating the other independent variables of Footnote 6 as parameters. Again, movements along the supply curve are movements from one set of coordinates to another, with the parameters of the equation remaining constant. A change in supply means a change in the supply equation parameters. Again, linear functions are used because of their simplicity, not because they are more representative of actual supply conditions.

Figure 3-5   Equilibrium Price Determination

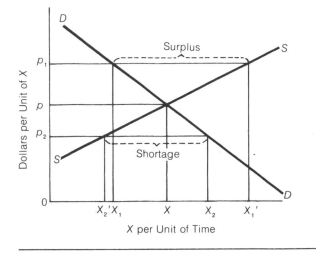

X per Unit of Time

pliers will bring quantity X_1' per unit of time to the market; thus, surpluses of X_1X_1' per unit of time accumulate. Any seller with a surplus believes that if he undercuts other sellers a little he can dispose of his surplus. Thus, an incentive exists for sellers as a group to lower their prices and cut back the quantity supplied. The price will be driven down by the sellers; quantities supplied will decrease; and quantities consumed will increase. Eventually the price will drop to p and consumers will be willing to take exactly the amount that sellers want to place on the market at that price.

Suppose now that sellers initially establish a price of p_2. At this price consumers want quantity X_2 per unit of time, but sellers will place only X_2' per unit of time on the market. This time *shortages* equal to the difference between X_2 and X_2' per time period occur. Faced by shortages consumers bid against each other for the available supply and will continue to do so as long as shortages exist. When the price has been driven up to p by consumers, the shortages will have disappeared and buyers will be taking the quantity that sellers want to sell.

Price p is called *equilibrium price*. Given the conditions of demand and supply for commodity X, it is the price that, if attained, will be maintained. If the price deviates from p, forces are set in motion to bring it back to that level. A price above the equilibrium price brings about surpluses that induce sellers to undercut each other, driving the price back down to the equilibrium level. A price below the equilibrium level results in shortages that cause consumers to bid the price back up to equilibrium. At a price level of p_1 to suppliers so much of the good is placed on the market that the value that consumers place on any one unit of it is less than the supply price. At price p_2 to suppliers the quantity placed on the market is so small that the value of a unit of it to consumers is greater than the supply price. At the equilibrium price p the quantity that suppliers place on the market is such that the supply price and consumers' valuation of a unit of the good are the same.[8]

Changes in Demand and Supply

What happens to the equilibrium price and the quantity exchanged of a good when the demand for it changes? Suppose that *DD* and *SS* in Figure 3-6 represent the demand for and supply of apartment units in a given community. Now suppose that a private college is established in the community and that its enrollment expands rapidly. The greater number of apartment consumers in this group brings about an increase in demand to D_1D_1. At the original price or rental rate p there will be a shortage of *XX'* apartments, and consumers will bid up the price to p_1. The quantity placed on the market and rented out will increase to X_1 as the higher rental rate induces some property owners and builders in the community to construct apartments. After the increase in demand the new equilibrium price and quantity are thus p_1 and x_1, respectively.

The same diagram can be used to illustrate the effects of a decrease in demand on the price and the quantity exchanged of a product. Let D_1D_1 be the initial demand curve for apartments, while *SS* is the supply curve. Now suppose that the state university, located in a city thirty miles away, cuts its tuition rates substantially drawing students away from the private college community. Demand for apartments in the community drops to *DD*, and at the initial equilibrium price p_1 there is a surplus of $X_1'X_1$. Rental rates will decrease and fewer apartments will be rented out, as property owners find it less worthwhile to make available and maintain some of their apartments. The new equilibrium price and quantity will be p and x, respectively.

---

[8]The equilibrium price and quantity are determined mathematically by solving the demand and supply equations simultaneously. If these are, respectively:

$$p_x = g(x).$$

and

$$p_x = k(x)$$

we have two equations, two unknowns, and a determinate solution.
More specifically, representing demand and supply as lines or curves, let the demand and supply equations be

$$p_x = 20 - 3/4\,x \quad \text{(Demand)}$$
$$p_x = 4 + 1/4\,x \quad \text{(Supply).}$$

Solving these simultaneously, we find that $x = 16$ and $p_x = 8$.

Figure 3–6   Effects of a Change in Demand

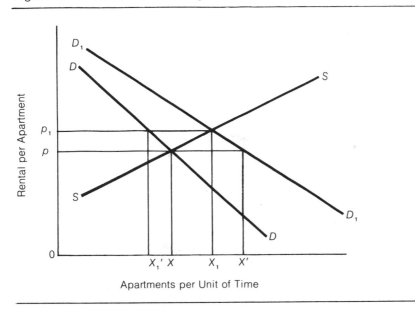

Figure 3–7—Effects of a Change in Supply

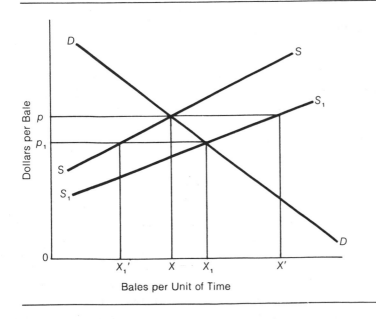

Similarly, changes in supply, given the demand curve for a good, will bring about changes in the equilibrium price and quantity exchanged. In Figure 3–7 let *DD* and *SS* represent the initial demand curve and initial supply curve for bales of cotton. Now suppose that growing conditions become much better than was initially expected, causing supply to increase to S_1S_1. At the initial equilibrium price p there will be a surplus of XX', causing the price to fall to p_1 and the quantity exchanged to increase to X_1. On the other hand, if S_1S_1 were the initial supply curve and a drought reduced the supply of cotton to *SS*, a shortage amounting to $X_1'X_1$ bales per unit of time would occur at the equilibrium price p_1. The price would rise to p, and the quantity exchanged would fall to X.

Elasticity of Demand

The concept of *elasticity of demand* is very useful in economic analysis, as we shall see in the next chapter and throughout the rest of this book. Elasticity of demand is a measure of the responsiveness of the quantity that will be taken to changes in the price of a good or service, given the demand curve for it. If the quantity taken is highly responsive to a small price change, a price increase will cause the total expenditures on the good to decrease; and a price decrease will cause them to rise. If the quantity is not very responsive to price changes, an increase in the price will increase total expenditures on the good, whereas a price decrease will cause them to fall. These points are of such importance that we shall develop them at some length below. But first we shall examine the technical aspects of elasticity measurement.

Measurement of Elasticity

Intuitively the slope of a demand curve appears to be a sufficient measure of the responsiveness of quantity taken to price changes. The slope of a small segment of such a curve can be obtained by observing how much quantity taken changes when the price goes up or down by a certain amount. For example, if a 10¢ decrease in the price of potatoes causes a 100-bushel increase in quantity taken, the slope of that portion of the curve is $-10/100$ or $-1/10$. However, if we redraw the demand curve, measuring the price in dollars instead of cents, the slope of the same segment of the demand curve becomes $(-1/10)/100$, or $-1/1000$. The shift from cents to dollars in measuring the price causes a drastic decrease in the downward slope of the demand curve, even though there has been no real change in the demand curve itself. If we draw the demand curve again, measuring the price in dollars and the quantity taken in pecks, the slope of the same segment of the curve becomes

Figure 3-8 -Measurement of Arc Elasticity

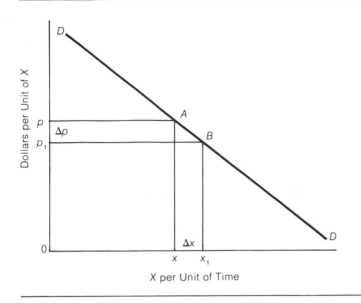

X per Unit of Time

(−1/10)/400, or −1/4000. Obviously, the slope of the demand curve is a very unreliable indicator of how responsive quantity taken is to changes in price.

The comparative slopes of demand curves are also useless as measures of the comparative responsiveness of quantities taken to changes in prices. In comparing the demand curve for wheat with the demand curve for automobiles, suppose we want to know in which case quantity taken is more responsive to a change in price. The comparative slopes of the two demand curves tell us nothing. A one-dollar drop in the price of wheat may increase quantity taken by twenty million bushels per month. A one-dollar decrease in the price of automobiles may increase quantity taken by five automobiles per month. But this situation does not mean that the quantity taken of wheat is more responsive to changes in its price than is the quantity taken of automobiles to changes in the automobile price. A one-dollar change in the price of wheat is a very large relative change. A one-dollar change in the price of automobiles is of little relative consequence. Further, a unit of wheat and a unit of automobile are completely different concepts, and there is no basis for comparing a unit of one with a unit of the other.

The great British economist Alfred Marshall responded to this difficulty by defining elasticity as the percentage change in quantity taken divided by the percentage change in price, *when the price change is small*.[9] In terms of algebra, the definition appears as

$$\epsilon = \frac{\Delta x/x}{\Delta p/p}$$

Consider the movement from *A* to *B* in Figure 3-8. The change in quantity from *x* to x_1 is Δx. The change in price from *p* to p_1 is Δp. The number or coefficient denoting elasticity is obtained by dividing a percentage by a percentage; it is a pure number independent of such units of measurement as bushels, pecks, or dollars. Elasticity will be the same between two given points on a demand curve for wheat, regardless of whether the price is measured in dollars or cents, and regardless of whether the quantity is measured in bushels or pecks. The elasticity computed between two separate points on the demand curve is called *arc elasticity*. The elasticity computed at a single point on the curve for an infinitesimal change in price is called *point elasticity*. We shall discuss the two concepts in turn.

Arc Elasticity

Suppose we want to compute elasticity of demand between *A* and *B* in Figure 3–8, and the coordinates of the two points are as follows:

	p (Cents)	x (bushels)
At point A	100	1,000,000
At point B	90	1,200,000

If we move from point *A* to point *B*, substituting the appropriate numbers in the elasticity formula, we find that:

$$\epsilon = \frac{\frac{200,000}{1,000,000}}{\frac{-10}{100}} = \frac{200,000}{1,000,000} \times \frac{100}{-10} = -2. \qquad [3.1]$$

However, if we move in the opposite direction from point *B* to point *A*, then:

$$\epsilon = \frac{\frac{-200,000}{1,200,000}}{\frac{10}{90}} = \frac{-200,000}{1,200,000} \times \frac{90}{10} = -1.5. \qquad [3.2]$$

[9]Alfred Marshall, *Principles of Economics*, 8th ed. (London: MacMillan & Co., Ltd., 1920), Bk. III, Chap. IV.

The percentage changes in quantity and price are different, depending on the price and quantity from which we start. The difference in the starting points leads us to different values of the elasticity coefficient.

The computations just completed show that arc elasticity between any two points on a demand curve must be an approximation. The farther apart the points between which arc elasticity is calculated, the greater will be the discrepancy between the two coefficients obtained, and the less reliable either will be. If arc elasticity is to be meaningful, it must be computed between points on the demand curve that are close together.

To avoid these discrepancies a modification of the basic elasticity formula can be used. With reference to Figure 3–8, suppose elasticity is calculated as:

$$\epsilon = \frac{\Delta x / x}{\Delta p / p_1}.$$ [3.3]

where p_1 is the lower of the two prices and x is the lower of the two quantities. Using this to compute elasticity between A and B, we find that:

$$\epsilon = \frac{200,000}{1,000,000} \div -\frac{10}{90} = \frac{200,000}{1,000,000} \times -\frac{90}{10} = -1.8.$$ [3.4]

The modified formula provides a very usable average between the two coefficients obtained with the basic formula.[10]

The demand elasticity coefficient shows the approximate percentage change in quantity for a 1 percent change in price and will be negative in sign since the price and the quantity change in opposite directions. However, when economists speak of the magnitude of elasticity they mean the absolute value of the coefficient, ignoring the minus sign. Thus, they say that an elasticity of minus one is greater than an elasticity of minus one-half; and an elasticity of minus two is greater than an elasticity of minus one.

Point Elasticity.   The point elasticity concept is more precise than that of arc elasticity. If the two points between which arc elasticity is measured

---

[10]A slightly more complex arc elasticity formula frequently used is:

$$\epsilon = \frac{x - x_1}{x + x_1} \div \frac{p - p_1}{p + p_1}.$$

Elasticity computed with this formula between points A and B in Figure 3–8 is -1.7. This formula, too, strikes an average between the coefficients arrived at by means of the basic formula when we work first from A to B and then work in reverse from B to A. *See* George J. Stigler, *The Theory of Price*, 3rd ed. (New York: Crowell-Collier and Macmillan, Inc., 1966), pp. 331–333.

Figure 3–9—Measurement of Point Elasticity

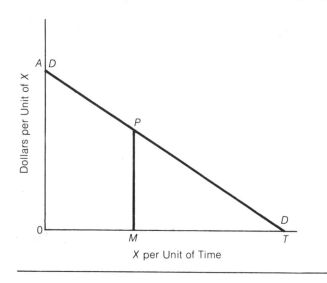

are moved closer and closer together, arc elasticity becomes point elasticity as the distance between the points approaches zero.

Elasticity at a point can be measured by a simple geometric method. Figure 3-9 shows a straight line (linear) demand curve. To measure elasticity at point P we start with the basic formula:

$$\epsilon = \frac{\Delta x/x}{\Delta p/p} = \frac{\Delta x}{x} \times \frac{p}{\Delta p}. \tag{3.5}$$

This can be rearranged to read:[11]

$$\epsilon = \frac{\Delta x}{\Delta p} \times \frac{p}{x}. \tag{3.6}$$

On the demand curve $\Delta p/\Delta x$ is the algebraic expression of the approximate slope of the curve for small price changes from point P. Geometrically, the slope of the demand curve is MP/MT. Therefore, $\Delta p/\Delta x = MP/MT$, or, inverting both fractions, $\Delta x/\Delta p = MT/MP$. Price at point P is MP and quantity at that point is $0M$. Thus, at point P:

---

[11]In terms of calculus:

$$\epsilon = \lim_{\Delta p \to 0} \frac{\Delta x}{\Delta p} \times \frac{p}{x} = \frac{dx}{dp} \times \frac{p}{x}.$$

Figure 3–10   Elasticity Measurements on a Linear Demand Curve

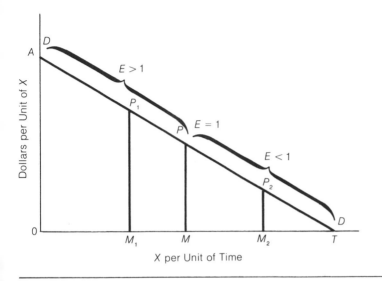

$$\epsilon = \frac{MT}{MP} \times \frac{MP}{OM} = \frac{MT}{OM}.$$

Elasticity coefficients are separated into three classifications with respect to their numerical magnitudes. When elasticity is greater than one, demand is said to be *elastic*. When elasticity equals one, it is said to have *unitary* elasticity. When elasticity is less than one, demand is said to be *inelastic*. These classifications are illustrated on the linear demand curve of Figure 3-10. Assume point P is located so that $OM = MT$. Since elasticity of demand at point P equals MT/OM; elasticity is unitary at that point. Consider any point farther up the demand curve—point P_1, for example. Since M_1T is greater than OM_1, elasticity at point P_1 is greater than one. The farther up the demand curve we move, the greater elasticity becomes, until, as we approach point A, elasticity approaches infinity (∞). Moving down the demand curve to the right from point P, elasticity is less than one and becomes progressively smaller the farther we move. As we approach point T elasticity approaches zero.

This technique for measuring point elasticity can be extended to apply to any point on a nonlinear curve. Suppose elasticity is to be measured at

Figure 3–11   Elasticity Measurement on a Nonlinear Demand Curve

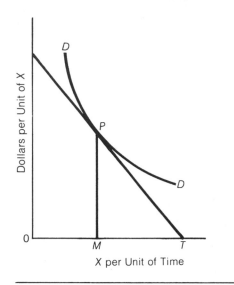

point *P* on the demand curve in Figure 3-11. First, draw a tangent to the demand curve at point *P* and extend it so that it cuts the quantity axis at point *T*. At point *P* the demand curve and the tangent coincide and have the same slopes; therefore, their elasticities must be the same at that point. Measurement of elasticity can proceed as before. Drop a perpendicular from *P* to 0*T* and call its intersection with the quantity axis point *M*. Elasticity of demand at point *P* is equal to *MT/0M*.

Elasticity and Total Money Outlays

One of the most important aspects of demand elasticity is the relationship that exists among price changes, elasticity, and total amount of money spent for the good. The total amount spent can be viewed either as total buyers' outlay (*TO*) or total sellers' receipts (*TR*) for the item. This amount is found by multiplying the quantity sold by the price per unit at which it is sold.

Suppose now that for a certain small price decrease demand is elastic—the percentage increase in quantity sold will exceed the percentage decrease in price. Since the increase in quantity sold is proportionally greater than the decrease in price, such a price decrease will increase sellers' total receipts. Similarly, if demand were inelastic for such a price decrease, the increase in quantity sold would be proportionally less than

Figure 3–12   Elasticity, Price Changes, and TR

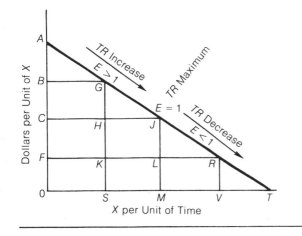

the price decrease, and sellers' total receipts would decline. If elasticity were unitary, the proportional increase in quantity sold would equal the proportional decrease in price, and total receipts would remain unchanged. For price increases the effects on total receipts will be just the opposite.

These results are summarized on the linear demand curve of Figure 3-12 where $OM = MT$. As we move down the demand curve from *A* toward *J* the elasticity of demand is decreasing but exceeds one, and *TR* will be increasing. For example, at price *B* and quantity *S*, *TR* is the area of rectangle 0*BGS;* while at price *C* and quantity *M*, *TR* is the area of rectangle 0*CJM*. By inspection it is apparent that 0*CJM* is larger in area than 0*BGS* As we move down the demand curve from *J* toward *T*, elasticity continues to decrease and is now less than one, and *TR* decreases. At price *F* and quantity *V*, *TR* is the area of rectangle 0*FRV*, and it is evident that this area is smaller than that of 0*CJM*. It follows that at point *J*, where elasticity is unitary, *TR* is maximum.

When a demand curve is a rectangular hyperbola, the elasticity of demand at all points on it is unitary. Such a curve is illustrated in Figure 3-13. Its basic characteristic is that the price multiplied by the quantity taken results in the same total receipts, regardless of what price is charged. For price increases or for price decreases total receipts remain unchanged; that is, $x \times p = x_1 \times p_1 = \ldots = x_n \times p_n$.

A seller contemplating changes in the price of what he sells should be vitally concerned with his product's elasticity of demand for the price

Figure 3 – 13   Unitary Elasticity, Price Changes, and TR

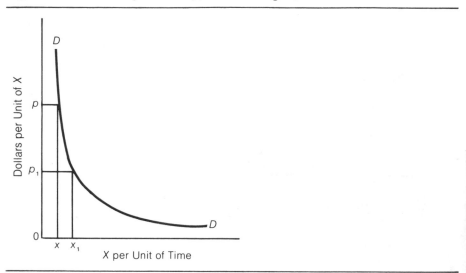

change. If demand were inelastic a price increase would be advisable but a price decrease would not. The former would increase the seller's total receipts, while at the same time it would cut his sales. The latter would increase his sales, but would cut his total receipts.

Factors Influencing Elasticity of Demand

The major factors influencing elasticity remain to be considered. These are (1) the availability of good substitutes for the item under consideration, (2) the number of uses to which it can be put, (3) its price relative to buyers' purchasing power, and (4) whether the price established is toward the upper end of the demand curve or toward the lower end of the curve. These should be thought of as points to look for in trying to determine whether demand will be more or less elastic in the neighborhood of the ruling price.

The availability of substitutes is the most important of the factors listed. If good substitutes are available demand for a given product or resource will tend to be elastic. If the price of whole-wheat bread is decreased while the prices of other kinds remain constant, consumers will shift rapidly from the other kinds to whole wheat. Conversely, increases in the price of whole-wheat bread, while the prices of other kinds remain constant, will cause consumers to shift rapidly away from it to the now relatively lower-priced substitutes.

Figure 3-14 *Dependency of Elasticity on Comparative Percentage Changes*

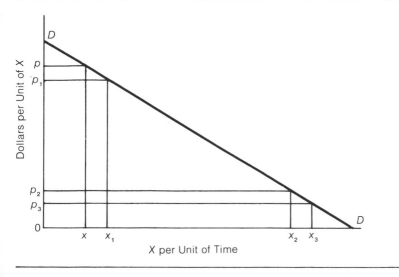

The wider the range of uses for a product or resource, the more elastic demand for it will tend to be. The greater the number of uses, the greater the possibility there is for variation in quantity taken as its price varies. Suppose that aluminum could be used only in the making of airframes for aircraft. Not much possibility would exist for variation in quantity taken as its price varies, and demand for it would likely be inelastic. In reality, aluminum can be put to hundreds of uses requiring a lightweight metal. The possible variation in quantity taken is quite large. Increases in its price subtract from and decreases in its price add to the list of its economically desirable uses. These possibilities tend to make demand for aluminum more elastic.

Demand for goods that take a large amount of the buyers' purchasing power is more likely to be elastic than demand for goods that are relatively unimportant in this respect. Goods such as deep freezers, which require large outlays, make consumers price-conscious and substitute-conscious. An increase in the price of deep freezers will cause shifts toward the use of commercial lockers. Quantity taken, therefore, is likely to vary considerably in response to price changes. For goods such as spices, which take a negligible part of consumers' incomes, changes in price are likely to have little effect on the quantity taken.

If the ruling price is toward the upper end of the demand curve, demand is more likely to be elastic than if it were toward the lower end. This is a purely mathematical determinant of elasticity, and its validity depends on the shape of the curve. It stands on a completely different footing from that of the other three determinants. Figure 3-14 shows a linear demand curve.[12] If the original price is p and changes to p_1, and the original quantity is x and changes to x_1, the percentage change in quantity is large because the original quantity is small compared with the quantity change. The percentage change in price is small because the original price is large compared with the change in price. A large percentage change in quantity divided by a small percentage change in price means that demand is elastic.

If the original price is p_2 and changes to p_3, and the original quantity is x_2 and changes to x_3, the reverse is the case. The percentage change in quantity is small because the original quantity is large. The percentage change in price is large because the original price is small. A small percentage change in quantity divided by a large percentage change in price means that demand is inelastic.

With the possible exception of the first point, concerning availability of substitutes, these are not infallible criteria of elasticity of demand but are expressions of tendencies only. Additionally, they need not all work in the same direction at the same time. One or more may be working against the others, and the magnitude of elasticity will depend on the relative strengths of the opposing forces.

Cross Elasticity of Demand

Cross elasticity of demand is another elasticity concept that is useful in economic analysis. It provides a measure of the extent to which commodities are related to each other. If we consider commodities X and Y, the cross elasticity of X with respect to Y is defined as the percentage change in the quantity of X taken divided by the percentage change in the price of Y. This is expressed mathematically by:[13]

$$\theta_{xy} = \frac{\Delta x/x}{\Delta p_y/p_y}.$$

[3.8]

Goods and services, or resources for that matter, may be related as substitutes or as complements.

When goods are substitutes for each other, the sign of the cross elasticity coefficient between them will be positive. Frankfurters and hamburger

---

[12]The argument of this paragraph does not apply to a demand curve which is a rectangular hyperbola or to one which has greater convexity to the origin than has a rectangular hyperbola. It applies only to those with less convexity.

[13]Or, in terms of calculus:

$$\theta_{xy} = \lim_{\Delta p_y \to 0} \frac{\Delta x}{\Delta p_y} \times \frac{p_y}{x} = \frac{dx}{dp_y} \times \frac{p_y}{x}$$

provide an illustration. An increase in the price of frankfurters will increase hamburger consumption. Changes in the price of frankfurters and in the consumption of hamburger are in the same direction, whether price moves up or down; the cross elasticity is positive.

Goods that are complementary have negative cross elasticity coefficients. Notebook paper and pencils serve as an illustration. An increase in the price of notebook paper cuts paper consumption and, consequently, the consumption of pencils. A decrease in the price of paper will increase its consumption and, also, the consumption of pencils. The change in the price of notebook paper is accompanied by a change in the consumption of pencils in the opposite direction. Therefore, the cross elasticity coefficient will be negative.

Cross elasticity of demand is frequently used in attempts to define the boundaries of an industry; however, its use for this purpose has certain complications. High cross elasticities indicate close relationships or goods in the same industry. Low cross elasticities indicate remote relationships or goods in different industries. A commodity whose cross elasticity is low with respect to all other commodities is sometimes considered to be in an industry by itself. A commodity group with high cross elasticities within the group but with low cross elasticities with respect to other commodities is often said to constitute an industry. Various kinds of men's shoes will have high cross elasticities among each other, but low cross elasticities with regard to other articles of men's clothing. Thus, we have a basis for separating out a men's shoe industry.

One difficulty with cross elasticity as a means of determining industry boundaries is that of establishing how high the coefficients among commodities must be if they are to be considered in the same industry. Cross elasticities among some foods are quite high—those among frozen peas, frozen green beans, frozen asparagus spears, and the like. Others, such as those between frozen vegetable and frozen meat, are likely to be quite low. Is there a frozen food industry? Answers cannot be given unequivocally. Some general economic problems can best be solved by considering all frozen foods in the same industry. More narrow or more specific economic problems will require more narrow industry groupings—a frozen vegetable industry or perhaps even a frozen peas industry. Cross elasticities furnish a guide to, but not a hard and fast determination of, industry boundaries.

Another complication is that of chains of cross relationships. Cross elasticities may be high between passenger cars and station wagons, and between station wagons and pick-up trucks. But passenger cars and pick-up trucks may have low cross elasticities. Are they in separate industries or in the same industry? Again, the nature of the problem we want to attack must be the guide to the proper definition of industry boundaries.

Summary

The nature of pure competition and its role in economic analysis should be clearly understood. Pure competition is essentially the ideal of small-ness of the individual economic unit in relation to the markets in which it operates, the idea of freedom of prices to move in response to changes in demand and supply, and the idea that a considerable degree of mobility for both goods and resources exists in the economy.

The concept of pure competition does not provide an accurate descrip-tion of the real world, but its usefulness is not negated thereby. It supplies the logical starting point for economic analysis. Enough competition does exist so as to give us valid answers to many economic problems. Addi-tionally, competition provides "norms" for evaluation of the actual per-formance of the economy.

Demand shows the quantities per unit of time that consumers will take of a commodity at alternative prices, other things being equal. It can be represented as a demand schedule or a demand curve. We must distin-guish carefully between changes in demand and movements along a giv-en demand curve. Changes in demand result from changes in one or more of the "other things." Movements along a given demand curve assume that the "other things" do not change.

Supply shows the different quantities per unit of time of a commodity that sellers will place on the market at all possible prices, other things being equal, and, together with demand, determines the equilibrium price of the commodity. The equilibrium price of a commodity is that price which if attained will be maintained. Actions of sellers attempting to dis-pose of surpluses will push higher than equilibrium price toward the equi-librium level. Actions of buyers attempting to buy short supplies will drive a lower than equilibrium price toward equilibrium. An increase in demand, given the supply, ordinarily causes an increase in both the price and the quantity exchanged of a good, while a decrease in demand has the oppo-site effect. An increase in supply, given the demand for a good, ordinarily decreases the price and increases the quantity exchanged. A decrease in supply usually increases the price and decreases the quantity ex-changed.

Elasticity of demand measures the responsiveness of quantity taken of a commodity to changes in its price. Elasticity of demand is defined as the percentage change in quantity divided by the percentage change in price when the price change is small. Arc elasticity is an approximate measure of elasticity between two separate points. Point elasticity mea-sures elasticity at one single point on the demand curve. Elasticity of demand is the key element in determining what happens to total business receipts for a commodity when the price of the commodity changes, given demand. When demand is inelastic, increases in price increase total receipts, while decreases in price decrease total receipts. When demand is elastic, the opposite results occur when price is increased or decreased. The degree of demand elasticity for a certain good depends on the availability of substitutes, the number of uses for the good, the importance of the good in consumers' budgets, and the region of the demand curve within which price moves.

The cross elasticity of demand among products is also an important price theory concept. High positive cross elasticities indicate a high degree of substitutability between products and are frequently used to mark off the boundaries of particular industries. High negative cross elasticities indicate a high degree of complementarity between products.

Suggested Readings

Boulding, Kenneth E., *Economic Analysis*, 4th ed., vol. I (New York: Harper & Row, Publishers, Inc., 1966), Chaps. 7 and 8.

Knight, Frank H., *Risk, Uncertainty, and Profit* (Boston: Houghton Mifflin Company, 1921), Chap. 1.

Machlup, Fritz, *The Political Economy of Monopoly* (Baltimore: The Johns Hopkins Press, 1952), pp. 12–23.

Marshall, Alfred, *Principles of Economics*, 8th ed. (London: Macmillan & Co., Ltd., 1920), Bk. III, Chap. IV; and Bk. V, Chaps. I–III.

Stonier, Alfred W., and Hague, Douglas C., *A Textbook of Economic Theory*, 3rd ed. (New York: John Wiley & Sons, Inc., 1964), Chap. I.

Chapter 4:

Basic Applications of the Model

The demand-supply-price model provides some interesting insights into certain kinds of policies pursued both by the government and by private groups. Policies to which the model can be applied most directly consist of price-fixing arrangements and tax policies. Many of these are entered into with the express aim of correcting certain inequities that exist in income distribution. However, using the model as an analytical tool, we find that the results of the arrangements are not always what we expect them to be. We shall look first at policies that fix minimum prices or price floors for specific goods. Then we shall consider maximum pricing or price-ceiling policies. Finally, we shall examine a tax incidence problem.

Minimum-price Policies

Agricultural Price Supports

The outstanding example of minimum-price policies on the part of government is undoubtedly the agricultural price support program developed by the federal government during and since the Great Depression of the 1930s. Prices of farm products sold are thought by proponents of support programs to be too low relative to the prices of products that farmers buy; that is, they are considered to be inequitable or unfair. These relatively low farm prices are thought to be an important factor in causing per capita farm income to be lower than the average United States per capita income. Consequently, price supports have been authorized by Congress and used as a partial answer to the farm-income problem.

The essential price theory features of the program are illustrated in Figure 4-1 with respect to wheat. In an uncontrolled market with the price free to move, the equilibrium price level is p per bushel and the quantity exchanged is X bushels per year. Suppose now that price p is thought to be relatively too low, and a support price is set at p_1. The government supports the price by purchasing the wheat that farmers cannot sell at price p.[1] In Figure 4-1 consumers will buy X_1 bushels per year, leaving a surplus of X_1X_1' for the government to acquire.

A support price will be effective only if it is above the equilibrium level; and if it is effective, surpluses will occur. If it were below p, shortages would induce buyers to bid the price up to the equilibrium level so that the support price would not be effective. Thus, it will be effective only at price levels above p. Yet Congressmen, government officials, farmers, and most of the rest of the general public profess amazement that surpluses accumulate from a price-support program and deduce from the existence of surpluses that something about the program is not being handled properly.

What does the government do in the face of the accumulating surplus? We can predict from what we know about markets that if it can increase the private demand for wheat and/or decrease the supply, the surplus problem will be less intense. The government may find it very difficult to increase the private demand for wheat. At best it may have to rest content with finding uses to which the surplus can be put. It may, for example, subsidize school-lunch programs with free or low-priced wheat from the surplus. Or it may sell wheat overseas at prices below the domestic support price. Neither of these alternatives is problem-free, since the government must make sure that wheat sold abroad does not find its way back into the domestic market and that uses to which it is put domestically do not supplant a part of private demand. Among the measures to decrease supply we find acreage restrictions, holding land out of cultivation through a "soil bank," marketing quotas, and the like.

Interesting questions can be raised as to whether or not agricultural price supports really contribute to greater equity in the economy. Do they reduce income inequalities? Since it is the unit price of the product that is

---

[1] Under the various Agricultural Adjustment Acts the support price is set by means of a storage and loan program. A farmer instead of selling his wheat in the market at price p can obtain a loan on his wheat from the government at price p_1 per bushel, provided he puts the wheat in storage in government-approved facilities. When the loan is due to be repaid, he can either sell his wheat and repay it, or he can turn the wheat over to the government as repayment in full. What would the farmer do if the market price of wheat were above p_1 when repayment is due? What would he do if it were below p_1? In effect, the government is guaranteeing that the price will not fall below p_1. Farmers sell what they can in the market at the price and, in essence, the government buys the surplus.

Figure 4 – 1   Effects of Agricultural Price Supports

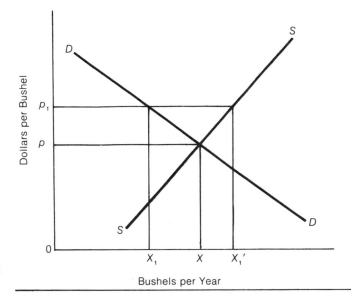

increased, a farmer who raises and sells ten times as much wheat as another will receive ten times the amount of supplemental income that the other receives. The costs of the support program must come from tax revenues. Before the transfer of income from taxpayers to farmers occurs, are the taxpayers richer or poorer than those who are to receive the support payments? What can we say about the overall efficiency of the economy in a situation where farmers are induced either to use resources to produce more than they would have produced at an equilibrium price level or, in the event of supply restrictions, to leave some of the scarce resources of the economy idle?

Minimum Wages

Simple pricing analysis is as applicable to resource markets as it is to markets for goods and services. Labor markets provide excellent examples, since the fixing of minimum prices or wage rates is so widespread and so generally accepted in this country. The fixing of minimum wage rates is done in two ways: (1) by minimum wage legislation and (2) by collective bargaining contracts arrived at through union-management negotiations.

Suppose we concentrate on a market for common unskilled labor, which provides a good example for two reasons: (1) it is purchased competitively in most cases—there are enough users, each taking a small enough proportion of the total supply, so that no one user by itself can influence the wage rate— (2) the legal minimum wage rates set under the Fair Labor Standards Act of 1938, as amended, are effective primarily in unskilled labor markets, especially those in which minority groups and teenagers participate.

What will the effects of a minimum wage rate set above the equilibrium level be? The obvious answer is illustrated in Figure 4-2. At the equilibrium wage rate w workers want to place h man-hours in employment, and this is precisely the quantity that employers are willing to use. A minimum wage rate set below w will have no effect; the equilibrium rate will prevail. But if a minimum wage rate of w_1 is established by either a minimum wage law or a collective agreement of some kind, employers are willing to employ only h_1 man-hours, while the labor force wants to place h_1' in employment. The result will be unemployment amounting to h_1h_1' man-hours per month.

Many find this analytical conclusion unpalatable. Witness, for example, the wide support given the grape pickers of California in their attempts to unionize and obtain higher wage rates from the grape growers. Witness also the almost complete absence of opposition to proposed increases in the federal minimum wage level from $1.60 per hour to $2.00 per hour at a time (1972) when unemployment rates exceeded 6 percent of the labor force. Union leaders are almost unanimous in expressing the opinion that there is no relationship between negotiated wage levels and the rate of unemployment.

What are the effects of the minimum wage on the incomes of workers? In Figure 4-2 the h_1 workers who remain employed at the higher wage rates clearly gain. The h_1h_1' workers who are unemployed just as clearly lose. What about the entire group of the kind of labor under consideration; that is, what happens to the total wage bill? The answer turns on the elasticity of demand. If the labor demand curve is elastic, the total wage bill decreases as the wage rate is increased above the equilibrium level. If demand is inelastic, the total wage bill rises; and if it is of unitary elasticity, the total wage bill will not change.

Supply Restriction

Groups of sellers of a good or of a resource often resort to supply restrictions in order to raise the prices of what they have to sell, with the expectation that the use of this stratagem will increase their incomes. Unions have been accused of limiting their memberships in order to hold wage rates higher than they would otherwise be. In the middle 1930s the Agricultural Adjustment Act was intended to raise the prices of certain farm products by directly curtailing the supplies. The American Medical Association and state medical associations have been said to limit medical

Figure 4 – 2   *Effects of Minimum Wage Rates*

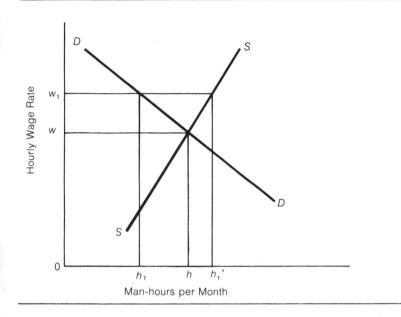

school enrollments for the same purpose. Some university professors are said to require their universities to hire only those with PhD degrees to accomplish the same end.

The mechanics of all these cases are the same. In Figure 4-3 with demand curve *DD* and supply curve *SS* the equilibrium price of whatever is being exchanged is *p* and the quantity bought and sold is *X*. If the supply restriction activities of the sellers of *X* are successful, the supply curve shifts to the left to $S_1 S_1$, raising the price to p_1 and reducing the quantity sold to X_1. Do sellers as individuals gain? Do sellers as a group gain?

Individual sellers who are able to sell as much after the supply restriction as before obviously gain. If some are cut out of the market altogether, they just as obviously lose. If some must now place smaller quantities on the market at higher prices, we cannot say whether they gain or lose without further investigation. Whether sellers as a group gain or lose as a result of the higher price depends again on whether demand is elastic, inelastic, or of unitary elasticity for the price increase.

Maximum-price Policies

Maximum prices, or price controls set by governments, seem to have broad appeal for the general public under at least two sets of circum-

Figure 4–3—Effects of Supply Restriction

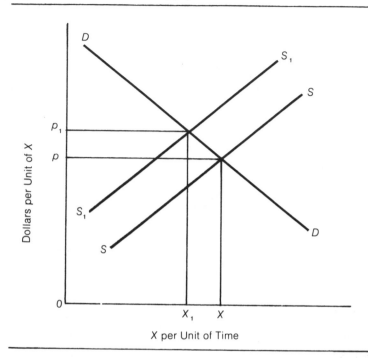

X per Unit of Time

stances. First, when certain items that the public believes are necessities—for example, housing and medical care—seem to be available in quantities thought to be inadequate at prices thought to be too high, there will be sentiment for price controls to keep the items within buying reach of poor people. Second, during the periods of rising price levels that we call inflation, price controls are often thought to be the appropriate remedial measure.

Price Controls for "Necessities"

Housing markets provide a good illustration of the use and effects of price controls for holding down the prices of certain "necessities." Let *DD* and *SS* in Figure 4-4 be the market demand and supply curves for housing units in a ghetto or slum area where prices are not controlled. The equilibrium rent is *p*, and the number of occupied dwelling units is *X*. There is no shortage, since the number of units that consumers want is equal to the number of units that landlords supply at that level of rent.

Now suppose that in the interests of improving the lot of slum dwellers a housing code is enacted that requires substantial repairs and altera-

Figure 4–4– Effects of Rent Controls

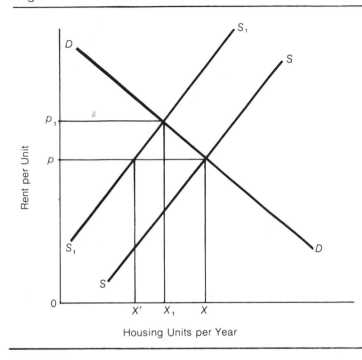

Housing Units per Year

tions to the existing housing units, as well as increased maintenance costs to maintain the code standards. The increased cost of supplying houses is represented graphically by the upward shift in the supply curve to S_1S_1. At the original rent level p there will be a housing shortage amounting to $X'X$. This in turn creates upward pressure on the rent level.

To keep rents within reach of the poor and to prevent landlords from passing on the costs of improvements to tenants suppose that rent controls are put into effect. If they are set at p, what will be the result? The shortage of $X'X$ units will continue to exist, and, because of the restrictions on the level of rent that can be charged, some units that do not comply with the code will stand empty.

Have you ever seen this phenomenon in the slum areas of the nation's large cities and wondered why, if housing is so critical, some apparently sound housing units are unoccupied? At the controlled price it is simply not worth the cost for landlords to put some of the units that they own into condition as required by the codes. They can obtain higher returns by investing their money elsewhere in the economy. Even if there are no price controls, we expect the enactment of housing codes to raise rents and reduce the number of housing units made available.

Price Controls to Stop Inflation

In markets where prices are not controlled, prices serve to ration the available supplies of goods among consumers who want them. Suppose that X in Figure 4-5 is one of many goods produced and sold in the economy. Demand and supply are DD and SS, respectively. The price moves to the equilibrium level p_0, where it rations the available supply among consumers. Each consumer in the economy gets as much as he wants at the equilibrium price level; there is neither a shortage nor a surplus.

If there now occurs a substantial increase in consumer money incomes, what happens in the absence of price controls? Demand for X increases to some such level as D_1D_1, and in the absence of price controls consumers bid the price up toward p_1. As this sequence occurs, and as it becomes more profitable to produce X, producers seek larger quantities of the resources needed to make the product. The same thing is happening in the production of other goods and services; and as producers bid for resources, resource prices rise. If there were some unemployed resources initially available in the economy, unemployed units may be drawn into production, permitting expansion of the outputs of some goods and services. But when unemployment has been eliminated, this source of expansion is no longer possible. Increases in demand when full employment prevails must be reflected in price increases, with no increases on the average in the economy's outputs.

Increases in the prices of resources used in producing any one good or service shift the supply curve for that item to the left. In Figure 4-5 resource price increases move the supply curve of X to S_1S_1. The new equilibrium price is p_2, and the new equilibrium quantity is x_2. Industry X, as we show it, has been able to increase slightly the quantities of the resources it uses and also its product output; but most of the increase in demand is reflected in an increase in the price of the product. The new equilibrium price p_2 induces consumers to ration themselves to the quantity made available at that price.

Effective price controls will change the picture. Consider once more the initial equilibrium situation for X, in which demand and supply are respectively DD and SS. Suppose again that an increase in consumer incomes shifts demand to D_1D_1. This time, however, assume that the price of X is controlled — is not permitted to rise above p_0 — and that resource prices as well are not permitted to rise. The immediate impact is a shortage amounting to x_0x_0'. Consumers want more at the controlled price than suppliers will place on the market; they no longer want to limit their consumption to the quantity available. Since the price cannot operate to ration the available quantities, how is the rationing to be done? By a first-come first-served actuality, with its accompanying queues or waiting in line for the

Figure 4-5- Effects of Price Controls

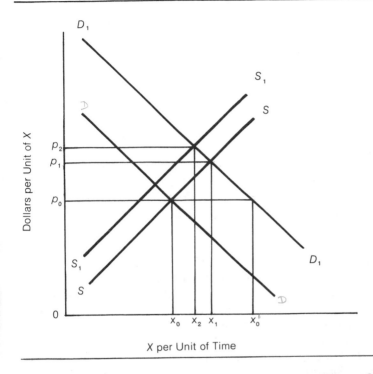

X per Unit of Time

product? By suppliers' whims favoring certain customers? By government imposed rationing schemes? Or by some other method?

Maximum-price policies have an additional impact on the operation of a market system—they make it impossible for relative prices of different products to reflect changes in consumers' relative valuations of different goods and for the price system to reorganize production to accommodate such changes. Figure 4-5 reflects a situation in which an increase in consumer incomes makes product X more valuable to consumers relative to all other available goods than it was before. In the absence of controls some additional quantities of resources flow into the production of X, raising the equilibrium quantity produced from x_0 to x_2. With the price of X controlled at p_0 and with resource prices controlled at whatever their initial levels were, this reallocation will not take place.

As Professor Milton Friedman has aptly put it, placing a set of price controls on a market economy is like locking the rudder on a ship. It does away with the means of steering it along the paths desired by consumers.[2]

---

[2]Milton Friedman, "Why the Freeze Is a Mistake," *Newsweek* (August 30, 1971), p. 23.

Prices cannot perform the function of reflecting the relative values of different goods and services and of organizing production according to consumer desires. Some other mechanism—for example, some kind of government rationing program and some kind of arbitrary allocation of resources among producers—must be substituted for it.

Excise Tax Incidence

A classic application of the model is its use to analyze the incidence of an excise tax placed on a good or service. An excise tax may be a given amount per unit of product, such as a state gasoline tax, or it may be a percentage of the selling price of the product, such as a state sales tax. The former is called a *specific tax;* the latter is termed an *ad valorem* tax. The analysis is essentially the same for either type, but since the specific tax is a little easier to manipulate graphically we shall focus the discussion upon it.

Let cigarettes be the product to be taxed. Suppose that the equilibrium price of cigarettes is p per pack in Figure 4-6 and the quantity exchanged is x packs per week. Now suppose that a tax of t per pack is placed on the product. How much of the tax is passed forward to buyers? How much of it must be paid by sellers? Does the incidence depend on from whom the tax is collected? Many people think so.

Consider first the case in which the tax is collected from cigarette sellers—retail stores. In Figure 4-6 (a) the supply curve SS shows the amounts per pack that sellers as a group must receive to induce them to place on the market the various quantities that comprise the horizontal axis of the diagram. Thus, imposition of the tax t simply shifts the supply curve upward by the amount of the tax. If sellers are to be induced to place x packs per week on the market, they must receive an amount p per pack for themselves; that makes it necessary for them to collect $p + t$ from buyers.

Buyers will not take x packs per week at a price, including tax, of $p + t$ per pack. At this level of expenditure per pack the demand curve shows that they will take x_t' only, leaving a surplus of $x_t'x$ per week on sellers' hands. Undercutting by individual sellers will move the price plus tax down to level $p_1 + t$, at which buyers will take the entire quantity x_1 that sellers will offer at a price, not including the tax, of p_1. The difference between p and $p_1 + t$ shows the amount of the tax that is passed along to buyers. The difference between p_1 and p shows the amount of the tax that must be borne by sellers.

The incidence will be the same if the tax is collected from buyers instead of from sellers. The demand curve and the supply curve, DD and SS,

Figure 4-6   The Incidence of an Excise Tax

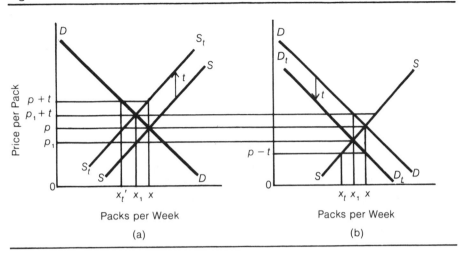

Packs per Week

(a)

Packs per Week

(b)

in Figure 4-6 (b) are identical to those of Figure 4-6 (a). Consider now that *DD* represents the outlays per pack that consumers are willing to pay for each of the various quantities per week, measured along the horizontal axis. The demand curve from the consumers' viewpoint is not affected by the imposition of the tax t, but from the sellers' viewpoint the tax shifts the demand curve downward by the amount of the tax to $D_t D_t$. Consumers will buy x packs per week only if they are required to pay p per pack. After the imposition of the tax only $p - t$ per pack would be left for sellers; consequently sellers' offerings would be reduced to x_t, leaving a shortage of $x_t x$. Bidding for the short supply by buyers will increase the price received by sellers to p_1. Quantity exchanged will be x_1, and buyers will be paying a total of $p_1 + t$ per pack. The incidence of the tax is the same as in the previous case. Buyers now pay $(p_1 + t) - p$ per pack more than they did before the tax. Sellers receive $p - p_1$ less.

The elasticity of demand and the elasticity of supply will affect the relative shares of the tax borne buyers and sellers. Suppose, for example, that given *DD* the elasticity of supply were greater at all prices than we have shown in Figure 4-6. What happens to the incidence of the tax? Or, given *SS*, suppose that the elasticity of demand were greater at all prices. Again, what would be the impact on the incidence of the tax?

Payroll (social security) taxes are really excise taxes of an *ad valorem* type. Does it really matter whether the employer and the employee are each billed for half the tax? Would the incidence of the tax be different if it were all charged against the employer? The employee?

Summary

The market-price model provides useful insights into the effects of certain governmental and private-group economic policy making. It shows that effective agricultural price supports of the storage-and-loan type will result in the accumulation of surpluses of the supported products, and that effective minimum wages will usually cause unemployment. Policies of supply restriction used in order to increase prices may or may not increase the total income of all sellers, although they will certainly increase the incomes of some sellers at the expense of those cut out of market.

Price ceilings are sometimes placed on products in order (1) to protect consumers from high prices of some items thought to be necessities and (2) to control inflation. The model shows that effective price controls used for the first purpose will insure that a shortage comes into being and persists over time, creating a rationing problem. When price controls are used to control inflation prices can neither serve the purpose of rationing the available supplies among consumers nor reflect the relative values that consumers as a group place on different goods and services.

Application of the model to the problem of excise tax incidence shows that there is no difference if the tax is levied on buyers or on sellers. Additionally, the incidence of the tax will vary, depending on the elasticities of demand and supply.

Suggested Readings

Brozen, Yale, "The Effect of Statutory Minimum Wage Increases on Teenage Unemployment," *Journal of Law and Economics*, vol. 12 (April 1969), pp. 109–122.

Knight, Wyllis R., "Agriculture," in Walter Adams, ed., *Structure of American Industry*, 4th ed. (New York: The Macmillan Co., 1971).

Radford, R. A., "The Economic Organization of a P.O.W. Camp," *Economica*, vol. XII (November 1945) pp. 189–201.

Chapter 5:

Consumer Choice and Demand—I

The theory of consumer choice provides a logical starting point for the systematic development of microeconomic principles. In this chapter we focus on indifference curve analysis, the general theory of consumer choice. The utility analysis of Chapter 6, a special case of the general theory, contains much that is of both historical interest and current value.

Indifference curve techniques date from the 1880s; however, they were not developed and integrated into the main body of economic thought until the 1930s. A British economist, Francis Y. Edgeworth, introduced the use of indifference curves in 1881.[1] Edgeworth's techniques, with some modifications, were adopted by an Italian economist, Vilfredo Pareto, in 1906.[2] It remained for two British economists, John R. Hicks and R. G. D. Allen, to popularize and extend the use of indifference curve analysis in the 1930s,[3] and it has since become a standard and necessary part of an economist's analytical equipment.

---

[1]Francis Y. Edgeworth, *Mathematical Psychics* (London: C. K. Paul & Co., 1881).

[2]Vilfredo Pareto, *Manuel d'economie politique* (Paris: V. Giard & E. Briere, 1909). The work was first published in Italian in 1906.

[3]John R. Hicks and R. G. D. Allen, "A Reconsideration of the Theory of Value," *Economica* (February, May 1934), pp. 52–76, 196–219.

The Consumer's Preferences

We begin the study of an individual consumer's behavior by examining his preferences.[4] These are summed up in graphic form as his *indifference map*. We then examine the main characteristics of the *indifference curves* that make up the indifference map.

The Consumer's Indifference Map

In the modern world a consumer has a large number of goods and services among which he can express preferences. In terms of possible combinations of these the variety confronting him approaches infinity. What can we say in an analytical way about the consumer's behavior with respect to this wide range of possibilities?

In order to say much of anything it will be necessary to make certain assumptions about the basic nature of his preferences. We assume, first, that the consumer is able to set up a preference ranking of the combinations confronting him. He can determine which combinations he prefers to others; and he can determine to which combinations he is indifferent. Second, we assume that the preferences of the consumer are consistent or transitive. If he prefers combination *A* to combination *B* and combination *B* to combination *C*, then he must prefer combination *A* to combination *C*. Again, if combination *D* is equivalent to combination *E* and combination *E* is equivalent to combination *F*, then combination *D* is equivalent to combination *F*. Third, we assume that the consumer prefers more of any good or service to less of it; that is, he is not satiated with any specific one.[5]

These assumptions enable us to construct an individual consumer's indifference map conceptually. To simplify matters we shall act as though the world contains only two goods— *X* and *Y*. The consumer is asked to rank the many possible available combinations, showing us those that he prefers over others, as well as those among which he is indifferent.

A set of combinations among which the consumer is indifferent can be expressed as an indifference schedule or an indifference curve. If, for example, he considers all the combinations listed in Table 5-1 as equivalent to one another, these constitute an *indifference schedule*. Plotting these combinations (and all those intermediate to the ones in the schedule) in Figure 5-1 we have *indifference curve* I.

---

[4]The basic consuming unit in an economy is more often a family than a single individual. The term "individual consumer" is used broadly to cover both families and unattached individuals.

[5]Satiation with any one good is not impossible. We have all seen it occur temporarily with food, liquor, and with other items. But, as we shall see, rational economic behavior usually rules out satiation with items that are not abundant enough to be had for the taking.

Table 5-1 An Indifference Schedule

X (Bushels)	Y (Pints)
3	7
4	4
5	2
6	1
7	1/2

Figure 5–1   Indifference Curves

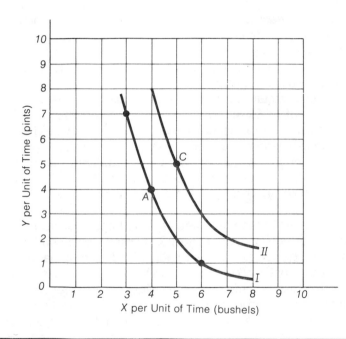

Although Figure 5-1 contains only two indifference curves an infinite number can be drawn. The commodity space enclosed by the X and Y axes contains all possible combinations of the two goods. A combination such as C, containing five bushels of X and five pints of Y, will be preferred to combination A, containing four bushels of X and four pints of Y. (Remember the third assumption.) Other combinations equivalent to C can be located, and these trace out indifference curve II. In this manner we can draw as many indifference curves as we wish. All combinations on higher indifference curves—those farther from the origin—are preferable to those lying on lower indifference curves. The whole set of a consumer's indifference curves constitutes his indifference map.[6]

Indifference Curve Characteristics

A set of indifference curves exhibits three basic characteristics: (1) the individual curves slope downward to the right; (2) they are nonintersecting; and (3) they are convex to the origin of the diagram. These features will be considered in turn.

The downward slope to the right of indifference curves is assured by the assumption that a consumer always prefers more of a good to less of it. If an indifference curve were horizontal this would mean that the consumer is indifferent between two combinations, both of which contain the same amount of Y but one of which contains a greater amount of X than the other. Such a curve could occur only if the consumer were receiving enough X to be saturated with it; that is, additional units of X alone would add nothing to his total satisfaction. Similarly, if an indifference curve were vertical this would mean that the two combinations of X and Y, both with the same amount of X but with one containing more Y than the other, yield equivalent satisfaction to the consumer. Again, such would be the case only if the consumer had reached a saturation point for Y. For the consumer to remain indifferent among combinations when he gives up units of one commodity, the loss must be compensated for with additional units of another commodity. The result, shown graphically, is the downward slope to the right.

Indifference curves will be nonintersecting if the transitivity assumption holds. Referring to Figure 5-2, combination C is preferred to combination A. Combination A is equivalent to combination B. But combination C is also equivalent to combination B. According to the transitivity assumption, C should be *preferred* to B. Thus, the intersection of indifference curves violates the transitivity assumption. To say that indifference curves are nonintersecting is not to say that they are parallel or that they are equidistant from each other. They may run farther apart at some points and closer together at others. The only restriction placed on them here is that they do not intersect.

---

[6]The consumer's preference function or indifference map can be represented by:

$$U = f(x, y)$$

In which U represents levels of preference expressed in ordinal terms only. The equation for one indifference curve is:

$$U_1 = f(x, y)$$

In which U_1 is a constant; that is, a given level of preference. Other values assigned to U define other indifference curves, all of these making up the consumer's indifference map. These assigned values show the order of preference magnitudes, not absolute (measurable) magnitudes.

Figure 5–2 Consequences of Indifference Curve Intersection

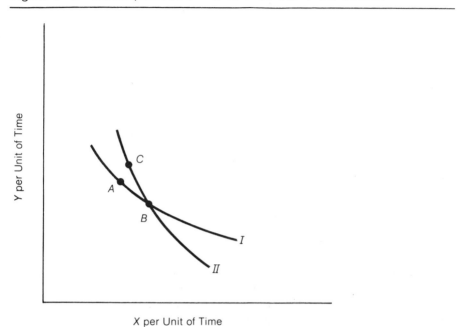

We cannot prove conclusively at this point in our study that indifference curves are convex to the origin, but we can show that it is likely they are. To get at the issue we shall introduce first the *marginal rate of substitution* concept.

The marginal rate of substitution of one product for another, say of X for Y (*MRS*$_{xy}$), is defined as the amount of Y the consumer is just willing to give up to get an additional unit of X—the trade-off betweer. bundles of goods among which he is indifferent. In Figure 5-1 suppose the consumer is initially taking 7 pints of Y and 3 bushels of X. To move to a consumption rate of 4 bushels of X he would be just willing to give up the consumption of 3 pints of Y per unit of time. The marginal rate of substitution for this move is 3. The more Y and the less X the consumer has, the more important a unit of X is to him compared with a unit of Y. Fo. example, a. point A in Figure 5-3 he would be willing to give up a considerable amount of Y to get an additional unit of X. At point B he has a large amount of X and very little Y; hence, a unit of Y would be more important to him as compared with a unit of X than it was at point A, and he would be willing to give up very little of Y to get an additional unit of X. The X axis is marked off in equal quantity units between A and B. At point A the indifference curve shows that the consumer is just willing to give up CD of Y to get an additional unit of X. As the consumer acquires more of X per unit of time and less of Y, the importance of a unit of Y becomes progressively greater as compared with the importance of a unit of X. The amounts of Y he is just willing to give up to get additional units of X become progressively smaller; that is, the marginal rate of substitution of X for Y is decreasing.[7]

If the marginal rate of substitution of X for Y is decreasing, the indifference curve must be convex toward the origin. If it were constant, the amounts of Y the consumer would give up to get additional units of X would be constant instead of decreasing; and the indifference curve would be a straight line sloping downward to the right. If the marginal rate of substitution were increasing, the indifference curve would be concave to the origin.[8]

Complementary and Substitute Relations

If the consumer thinks of goods and services as being related to one another the relationship may be either one of complementarity or one of substitutability. Generally speaking, two goods are complements if an increase (decrease) in the consumption level of one increases (decreases) the relative desirability to the consumer of the other. Goods are substitutes for each other if an increase (decrease) in the consumption level of one decreases (increases) the relative desirability of the other.

These definitions can be made more explicit with the aid of indifference curve concepts. Suppose that the consumer is no longer confined to a two-commodity world, but that he has choices among X, Y, and a host of other goods and services. Let the quantities of the other goods and services be measured in terms of monetary units, while X and Y are measured in bushels and pints as before. The consumer now has the possibility not only of substituting X for Y but also of substituting X for money or Y for money. At any given consumption level for Y there will be some combi-

---

[7]It may be helpful to work out *MRS* arithmetically between different points on indifference curve I of Figure 5-1 before proceeding to the more abstract geometric representation of it in Figure 5-3.

[8]The total differential of the preference function of Footnote 5 is:

$$f_x dx + f_y dy = dU.$$

For a given indifference curve $dU = 0$, so:

$$f_x dx + f_y dy = 0$$

and:

$$-\frac{dy}{dx} = \frac{f_x}{f_y} = MRS_{xy}.$$

In order for the indifference curve to be convex to the origin:

$$\frac{d(MRS_{xy})}{dx} < 0.$$

Figure 5-3- Diminishing Marginal Rate of Substitution

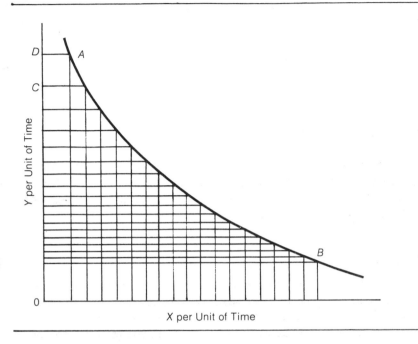

nations of X and money among which he is indifferent, and there will be some combinations of X and money that are preferred to others. In other words, a set of indifference curves for X and money can be established, and at any point on any one indifference curve we can define the MRS_{xm} as the amount of money the consumer is just willing to give up to get an additional unit of X. This, then, is the value that the consumer attaches to a unit of X at that point. Similarly, at any given consumption level for X a set of indifference curves for Y and money can be established; and the MRS_{ym} measures the value that the consumer attaches to a unit of Y at any given point on one of those indifference curves.

Suppose that we know the consumer's consumption levels of X, Y, and other goods measured in monetary units, as well as his sets of indifference curves among them. Then we also know his MRS_{xy}, his MRS_{xm}, and his MRS_{ym}. Now, if he increases his consumption of Y, holding his consumption of X constant, and the MRS_{xm} increases, X is complementary to Y. That is, the increase in the consumption of Y has made a unit of X more valuable to the consumer. On the other hand, if the increase in the consumption of Y decreases the MRS_{xm}, X is a substitute for Y—a unit of X has become less valuable to the consumer.

Examples of complementary and substitute goods abound in the world around us. Tennis rackets and tennis balls, bread and jelly, coffee and doughnuts, automobiles and gasoline are among the many sets of complementary goods. Sets of substitute goods include ham and steak, automobile travel and airplane travel, electric razors and safety razors, and many others.

Constraints on the Consumer

What the consumer is able to do has thus far been left to one side; we have presented a picture of his tastes and preferences only. The constraints on his consumption activitie, are shown by *budget lines*, sometimes called *lines of attainable combinations*.

The Budget Line

The consumer's purchasing power and the prices of what he wants to buy determine his budget line. His purchasing power is usually referred to as his income. The term is not limited to his current earnings but is used broadly to include any supplements to or deletions from whatever his earnings may be. We think of his income, defined in this way, as a weekly, monthly, or yearly average. The prices faced by the consumer are the market prices of the items he purchases.

To show how the budget line is established, we again limit the consumer to a two-good world. Let his income be $100 per week and the prices of X and Y be $2 and $1, respectively. If he were to spend his entire income on X, he could consume 50 units per week—he would be at point A in Figure 5-4. On the other hand, if he were to buy Y and no X he could consume 100 units of Y and would be at point B. If he is at point B and desires to include X in his consumption pattern, he must decrease his consumption of Y to do so. A decrease of 2 units in his consumption of Y releases $2 that can be used to purchase a unit of X. Every one-unit increase in the quantity of X consumed per unit of time requires a two-unit decrease in his consumption of Y, as long as p_y remains at $1 and p_x is $2. Thus, his budget line is a straight line joining points B and A.

The slope of the budget line is determined by the ratio of the price of X to the price of Y. Suppose the consumer's income is I_1, the price of X is p_{x1}, and the price of Y is p_{y1}. If he should spend all of his income on Y, I_1/p_{y1} in Figure 5-5 shows the total number of units of Y that he could purchase. If he were to spend all his income on X, I_1/p_{x1} shows the number of

Figure 5–4   The Budget Line

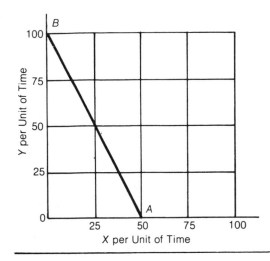

Figure 5–5   Changes in the Budget Line

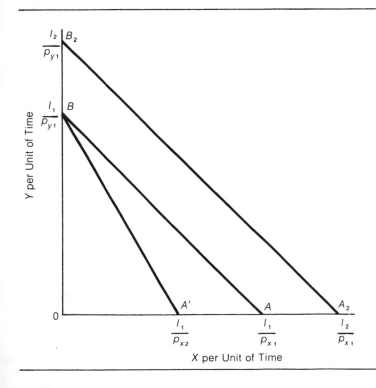

units of X that he could purchase. The budget line BA joins the two extreme points.[9] In more general terms the slope of a budget line is:

$$-\frac{I/p_y}{I/p_x} = -\frac{I}{p_y} \times \frac{p_x}{I} = -\frac{p_x}{p_y}. \qquad [5.1]$$

Note that the consumer can obtain any combination of goods within or on the boundaries of the triangle BOA in Figures 5-4 or 5-5. All of these constitute his set of *feasible* combinations. The budget line BA separates the feasible combinations—what the consumer is able to purchase—from those combinations beyond his financial reach.

Shifts in the Budget Line

Changes in the consumer's income and changes in the prices of the goods and services that he faces will shift his budget line. Suppose that his income is I_1 initially and that the prices of X and Y are p_{x1} and p_{y1}, respectively. His budget line will be BA in Figure 5-5. If the price of X now increases to p_{x2}, while his income and the price of Y remain constant, the budget line will become BA'. There is no change in the amount of Y that his income will purchase if it is all spent on Y; however, the higher price of X reduces the amount of X he could purchase if his money were all spent on X from 0A to 0A'. The new budget line therefore joins B and A'.

Returning to the initial budget line BA, suppose that the consumer's income rises from I_1 to I_2 while the prices of X and Y remain constant. The budget line shifts to the right parallel to itself to B_2A_2. The larger income enables the consumer to purchase greater amounts of X if X alone is purchased, or Y if Y alone is purchased, so that A_2 lies to the right of A and B_2 lies above B. Since the prices of X and Y have not changed, both budget lines have a slope of $-p_{x1}/p_{y1}$ and are therefore parallel.

The Consumer's Preferred Position

The theory of consumer behavior is built on the premise that individual consumers attempt to move toward those combinations of goods and services available to them that are most preferred; that is, that they seek to maximize satisfaction. To show the conditions under which attainment of

---

[9]The budget line equation for the two-commodity example of the text is:
$$xp_x + yp_y = I.$$
Solving for y, we obtain:
$$y = \frac{I}{p_y} - \frac{p_x}{p_y} \times x$$
indicating that the Y-axis intercept is I/p_y and that the slope of the line is $-p_x/p_y$.

Figure 5-6 The Consumer's Preferred Combination

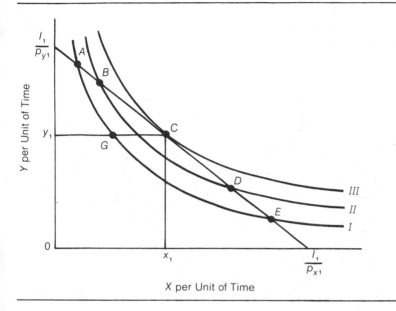

this goal is accomplished, the consumer's preference factors (his indifference map) and the factors restraining him (his budget line) are brought together in Figure 5-6. Any combination such as A, B, C, D, or E on the budget line is available to him. So is any combination such as G lying to the left of or below the budget line. Because of his budget restraint combinations lying to the right of or above the budget line are not available to him.

The most preferred combination must lie on the budget line. If the consumer were to take combination G, there would be a violation of the assumption that he always prefers more of a good to what he currently has. By moving from G to C he obtains more X without sacrificing any Y and consequently gets on a higher indifference curve. This sort of move is always possible for a combination below the budget line. Of the combinations on the budget line the consumer chooses the one that is on the highest indifference curve touched by the budget line. This will be combination C. Combinations A, B, D, and E all lie on lower indifference curves. Combination C is on the highest indifference curve that he can reach and, further, is the only combination available to him on that indifference curve. Thus, the consumer's preferred combination is always that at which his budget line is tangent to an indifference curve. In Figure 5-6 it contains x_1 of X and y_1 of Y.

Tangency of the budget line to an indifference curve means that the rate at which the consumer is *willing* to give up Y to obtain X is equal to the rate at which he would be *required* by the market to give up Y to obtain X; that is, his $MRS_{xy} = p_x/p_y$.[10] The slope of an indifference curve at any point on it is his MRS_{xy} at that point. The slope of a budget line at any point on it is p_x/p_y. At the point of tangency—that is, at C—the slopes of the two curves are necessarily the same.

Consider point A in Figure 5-6. The slope of indifference curve I is greater than the slope of the line of attainable combinations. In other words the amount of Y the consumer *is willing* to give up to get an additional unit of X is greater than the amount of Y he *would have* to give up to get an additional unit of X (that is, $MRS_{xy} > p_x/p_y$). The consumer would give up units of Y for additional units of X because he can move to a preferred position by doing so. The same would be the case at point B. At point D the slope of indifference curve II is less than the slope of the line of attainable combinations, meaning that the amount of Y the consumer is willing to give up to get an additional unit of X is less than the amount he would have to give up (that is, $MRS_{xy} < p_x/p_y$). Therefore, the consumer would not move beyond point C to such a point as D, for such a movement is toward a less-preferred position. He is in equilibrium, or is in his most preferred position at point C, where the marginal rate of substitution of X for Y is equal to the ratio of their respective prices and he is disposing of his entire income.[11]

---

[10]Recognizing that the indifference curves and the budget lines both have negative slopes, we shall disregard the minus signs of the slope measurements and consider the number values only. This practice is conventional and avoids problems arising from mathematical semantics.

[11]To solve the consumer's maximization problem mathematically, let his preference function be:

$$U = f(x, y) \tag{1}$$

The budget restraint is:

$$xp_x + yp_y = I$$

or:

$$xp_x + yp_y - I = 0. \tag{2}$$

To maximize (1) subject to (2) we use the Lagrange multiplier method, forming a new function in which V is a function of x and y such that:

$$V = g(x, y) = f(x, y) + \lambda(xp_x + yp_y - I). \tag{3}$$

For maximization of V:

$$\frac{\delta V}{\delta x} = f_x + \lambda p_x = 0, \text{ or: } f_x = -\lambda p_x \tag{4}$$

$$\frac{\delta V}{\delta y} = f_y + \lambda p_y = 0, \text{ or: } f_y = -\lambda p_y \tag{5}$$

$$\frac{\delta V}{\delta \lambda} = xp_x + yp_y - I = 0, \text{ or: } xp_x + 1p_y = I. \tag{6}$$

Dividing (4) by (5) and letting (6) stand as it is, the conditions for maximum satisfaction become:

$$-\frac{f_x}{f_y} = -\frac{p_x}{p_y} \tag{7}$$

with:

$$xp_x + yp_y = I. \tag{8}$$

The ratio of the partial derivatives f_x and f_y represents the slope of the indifference curve tangent to the budget line.

Suppose in Figure 5-6 that Y is milk and X is honey and that the consumer's budget for the two is fixed. The consumer is initially at point A, and we shall assume that MRS_{xy} at this point is 4—he is just *willing* to give up 4 pints of milk for an additional pound of honey. Let the price of milk p_y be \$1 per pint and the price of honey p_x be \$2 per pound. At these prices the market requires that he give up only 2 pints of milk to increase his consumption of honey by 1 pound. Under this set of conditions the consumer can do what the market requires—he can give up 2 pints of milk for a pound of honey—and, since he still has 2 pints of milk that he would have been willing to give up, clearly be in a preferred position.

Demand Curves and Engel Curves

The analytical devices just developed enable us to get at the forces underlying a consumer's demand curve and his Engel curve for any given good or service. We have met the demand concept before, but it was defined in market terms. For the individual consumer the definition is not much different; his demand curve for an item shows the quantities per unit of time that he will take at various possible prices, other things being equal. The concept of an Engel curve[12] is new but is not difficult. It shows the quantities of an item per unit of time that the consumer will take at *various levels of income*, other things being equal.

The Demand Curve

We shall concentrate first on the demand curve for some product X. The consumer's income, the price of Y, and the consumer's tastes and preferences (his indifference curves) are held constant. We vary the price of X and observe what happens to the quantity of X taken.

Changes in the price of X cause shifts in the consumer's budget line. Let the budget line be AB in Figure 5-7 (a). An increase in the price of X to p_{x2} decreases the total number of units of X he can buy to some quantity I_1/p_{x2} if he spends his entire income on that product, and the new budget line becomes AC. It lies below line AB and has a steeper slope.[13]

Line AC will necessarily be tangent to a lower indifference curve than was line AB, and the new combination of X and Y preferred by the consumer will differ from the original one. Initially, the consumer preferred combination x_1 of X and y_1 of Y. The new preferred combination will be x_2

---

[12]Engel curves are named after Ernst Engel, a German pioneer of the last half of the 1800's in the field of budget studies. *See* George J. Stigler, "The Early History of Empirical Studies of Consumer Behavior," *The Journal of Political Economy*, vol. LXII (April 1954), pp. 98–100.

[13]The slope of AB is p_{x1}/p_{y1}. The slope of AC is p_{x2}/p_{y1}. Since $p_{x2} > p_{x1}$, then $p_{x2}/p_{y1} > p_{x1}/p_{y1}$.

of X and y_2 of Y. Different prices of X cause the budget line to assume different positions, with its focal point always remaining at A. Higher prices of X rotate it clockwise, making it tangent to lower indifference curves. Lower prices of X rotate it counterclockwise, making it tangent to higher indifference curves.

The line joining points of consumer equilibrium at these various prices of X is called the *price consumption curve* and is illustrated in Figure 5-7 (a). Note that in reality it shows no prices. It connects the preferred combinations of X and Y when the consumer's tastes and preferences, his income, and the price of one commodity are held constant and the price of the other commodity is varied.

The necessary information for establishing the consumer's demand schedule and demand curve for X is obtained from Figure 5-7 (a). When the price of X is p_{x1}, the consumer will take quantity x_1 of X. This choice establishes one point on his demand schedule or demand curve. At the higher price p_{x2}, the consumer will take the smaller quantity x_2 of X, establishing a second point on his demand schedule or demand curve for X. These points are plotted as E_1 and E_2 in Figure 5-7 (b). Additional price-quantity points can be found in a similar manner and plotted on a conventional demand diagram in the usual way. The resulting demand schedule or demand curve ordinarily shows that the higher the price of X, the lower the quantity taken, and vice-versa.

Elasticity of Demand and the Price Consumption Curve

If we let the X axis represent units of any good X and the Y axis of an indifference curve diagram represent purchasing power not spent on X,[14] the slope of the price consumption curve indicates whether elasticity of demand for the good is unitary, greater than one, or less than one.

In Figure 5-8 (a) the indifference curves are such that the price consumption curve is parallel to the X axis, or has a slope of zero. As the price of X rises from p_{x1} to p_{x2}, the portion of the consumer's income *not* spent on X remains constant at $0y_1$. Thus, the amount spent on X must remain constant also. If a rise in the price of X causes no change in the consumer's spending on X, then his demand for X must have unitary elasticity for the price increase.

The upward slope of the price consumption curve in Figure 5-8 (b) means that demand for X is inelastic. A rise in the price of X from p_{x1} to

---

[14]A given indifference curve thus shows combinations of purchasing power and X among which the consumer is indifferent. The budget line is drawn in the usual way. The price of purchasing power, or p_{y1}, in dollars is $1 a unit. Hence, l_1/p_{y1} is the consumer's income. Since the slope of the budget line is p_{x1}/p_{y1} and p_{y1} equals $1, that slope is p_{x1}.

Figure 5–7 – The Consumer's Demand Curve for One Good

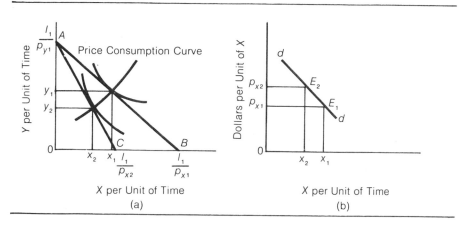

Figure 5–8 – Price Consumption Curves and Elasticity of Demand

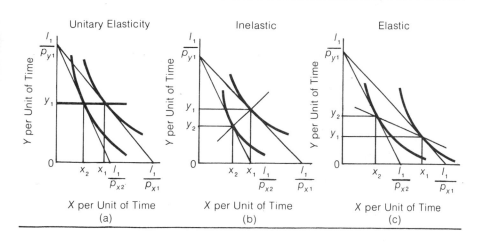

p_{x2} brings about a decrease in the portion of income not spent on X from Oy_1 to Oy_2. In other words, more income is spent on X at the higher price. An increase in expenditures on X as the price of X rises can result only when demand for X is inelastic for the price increases.

Figure 5-8 (c) shows a downward-sloping price consumption curve, meaning that demand for X is elastic. The rise in the price of X increases the portion of income not spent on X from Oy_1 to Oy_2. Therefore, less is spent on X. An increase in the price of X that decreases total expenditure on X results from an elastic demand curve for X between two prices.

Figure 5–9 The Consumer's Engel Curve for One Good

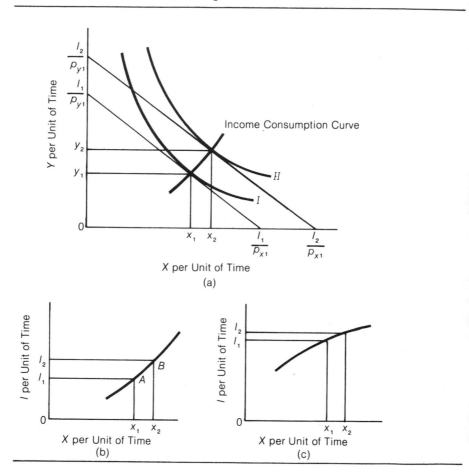

X per Unit of Time
(a)

(b)

(c)

Engel Curves

To obtain the Engel curves for good X or good Y the prices of the goods, along with the consumer's tastes and preferences, are held constant and income is allowed to vary. Given the price of X at p_{x1} and the price of Y at p_{y1}, an increase in income from I_1 to I_2 will shift the budget line to the right parallel to itself as is pictured in Figure 5-9 (a). The consumer could take more units of Y than before at price p_{y1} if he were to spend his entire income on Y. Likewise, if he were to spend his entire income on X at price p_{x1}, he could take more units of X than before. The new budget line must lie to the right and above the old one. Since both have slopes of p_{x1}/p_{y1}, they must be parallel If an increase in income increases the amount of a

Figure 5–10   Engel Curve for an Inferior Good

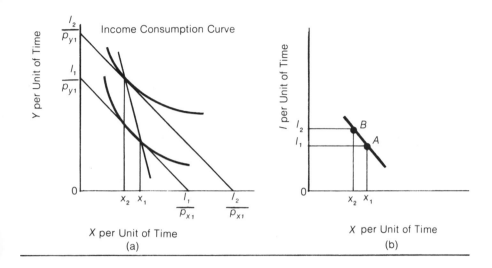

X per Unit of Time
(a)

X per Unit of Time
(b)

good taken, it is said to be a *normal* good. Both X and Y in Figure 5-9 are normal. The line joining all points of consumer equilibrium as income changes is called the *income consumption curve.*

Engel curves for X and Y are plotted from the information provided by the indifference curve diagram of Figure 5-9 (a). Two typical Engel curves are shown in Figure 5-9 (b) and (c), in which income is measured on the vertical axes of the diagrams and quantities per unit of time on the horizontal axes. From Figure 5-9 (a) we note that at an income level of I_1, the consumer will take quantity x_1 of X. This choice is plotted as point A on Figure 5-9 (b). At income level I_2 quantity x_2 will be taken. This choice is plotted as point B. If budget lines corresponding to other levels of income were shown in Figure 5-9 (a), corresponding quantities of X could be determined and plotted against those income levels on Figure 5-9 (b). Assuming that X is a normal good, the higher the income, the greater will be the quantity taken.

Some goods are *inferior* goods rather than normal goods. Their distinguishing characteristic is that as the consumer's income increases, his consumption level of them decreases. Hamburger is a case in point, since at high income levels consumers tend to substitute more expensive meat cuts—prime rib and steak—for it.

A graphic representation of the income consumption curve and the Engel curve for such a good is presented in Figure 5-10. At income level I_1 Figure 5-10 (a) shows that the consumer takes x_1 of X in his most preferred position. This is plotted as point A in Figure 5-10 (b). Similarly, at income level I_2 he takes x_2, and point B on his Engel curve is located. Note that both the income-consumption curve with respect to X and the Engel curve slope upward to the *left*.

Engel curves provide valuable information regarding consumption patterns for different commodities and for different individuals. For certain basic commodities such as food, as the consumer's income increases from very low levels his consumption may increase considerably at first; then, as his income continues to increase, the increases in consumption may become smaller and smaller relative to income increases. A pattern of this type is illustrated in Figure 5-9 (b). For certain other items, such as housing, as the consumer's income increases the quantity purchased per unit of time may increase in greater proportion than income does. Figure 5-9 (c) reflects a situation of this type. It is also quite possible that an item is a normal good at low income levels and becomes an inferior good at high income levels.

Income Elasticity of Demand

The responsiveness to income changes of the quantity per unit of time that a consumer will purchase of an item is measured by his *income elasticity of demand* for that item. The elasticity concept is not a new one at this point, so that we need only spell it out in this particular context. It is defined as:

$$\theta = \frac{\Delta x/x}{\Delta I/I} \qquad \qquad [5.2]$$

that is, the percentage change in quantity divided by the percentage change in the level of income, when the change in the level of income is small.[15] For an arc such as EF in Figure 5-11 (a) the appropriate data can be fed into the elasticity formula to determine the magnitude of elasticity. In Figure 5-11 (b) income elasticity at point A will be MT/OM. The derivation of the point income elasticity measurement is exactly the same as it is for a point price elasticity measurement. At point B would the income elasticity of CC be greater than or less than one? Is there a point on CC at which income elasticity is exactly one? What would an Engle curve with an income elasticity of one at all points look like?

---

[15]In terms of calculus it becomes:

$$\theta = \lim_{\Delta I \to 0} \frac{\Delta x/x}{\Delta I/I} = \frac{dx/x}{dI/I} = \frac{dx}{dI} \times \frac{I}{x}.$$

Figure 5–11   Income Elasticity of Demand

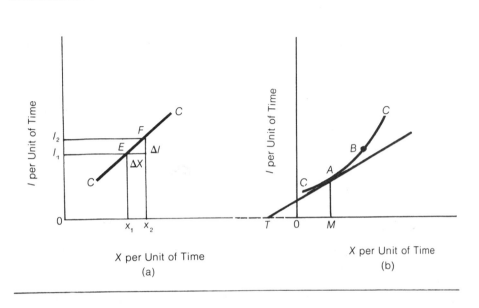

X per Unit of Time
(a)

X per Unit of Time
(b)

Income Effects and Substitution Effects

The inverse relationship usually expressed by a demand curve between the price of an item and the quantity per unit of time that a consumer will take of it is the combined result of a *substitution effect* and an *income effect* of a price change. When the price of an item rises and consumers turn away from it toward now relatively lower-priced substitutes, a decrease in quantity occurs because of the substitution. Additionally, the rise in the price of the item lowers the consumer's real income or purchasing power, causing him to reduce his purchases of all normal goods. To the extent that the reduction in real income affects his consumption of the item under consideration we have an income effect.

The separation of income and substitution effects is illustrated in Figure 5-12. The consumer's income is I_1 and the prices of X and Y are p_{x1} and p_{y1}, respectively. Combination A, containing x_1 of X and y_1 of Y, is the consumer's preferred combination. Suppose the price of X now rises to p_{x2}, rotating the budget line clockwise with I_1/p_{y1} as its focal point until it cuts the X axis at I_1/p_{x2}. Note that because of the increase in the price of X the slope of the new budget line is greater than that of the old one. The slope of the original budget line is p_{x1}/p_{y1}, while that of the new one is

p_{x2}/p_{y1}. Combination B, containing x_2 of X and y_2 of Y is the consumer's preferred combination after the rise in the price of X.

That the consumer's real income has been decreased by the increase in the price of X is illustrated graphically by the fact that combination B lies on a lower indifference curve than combination A does. The movement from combination A to combination B, and the reduction in the quantity of X taken from x_1 to x_2, shows the combined income and substitution effects of the price change.

To isolate the substitution effect and determine its magnitude suppose we increase the consumer's money income enough to compensate him for his loss in purchasing power. The additional purchasing power, or the "compensating increase in income," will move the budget line to the right, parallel to itself; and when just enough has been given the consumer to offset his loss, it will lie tangent to indifference curve II at point C. Combination C is at the same level of preference for the consumer as combination A is; but, because of the now higher price of X, combination A is not available to him. He has been induced to substitute the relatively cheaper Y for the relatively more expensive X in order to avoid a less-preferred position. The income effect of the increase in the price of X has been eliminated by the compensating variation in the consumer's income; hence, the movement from A to C, or the decrease in X taken from x_1 to x', is the substitution effect. It results solely from the change in the price of X relative to the price of Y.

The income effect, apart from the substitution effect, can be determined by taking the compensating variation in income away from the consumer. The budget line shifts to the left, and the highest indifference curve to which it is tangent is indifference curve I. Combination B, y_2 of Y and x_2 of X, is the preferred position. The movement from C to B is the income effect and reduces the quantity of X taken from x' to x_2.

The movement of the consumer from combination A to combination B, with the increase of the price of X from p_{x1} to p_{x2} is thus broken down into two steps, one showing the substitution effect and the other showing the income effect. Usually they operate in the same direction. If X is an inferior good, however, the income effect will work in the opposite direction from the substitution effect. In such a case the increase in the price of X causes a tendency on the part of the consumer to substitute relatively lower-priced goods for X, but at the same time the lower real income of the consumer induces him to increase his consumption of X above what it would otherwise be.

The substitution effect is usually much stronger than the income effect. A consumer who purchases a great many goods will not ordinarily experience a large drop in real income when the price of one of the goods rises.

Figure 5–12 *Income and Substitution Effects*

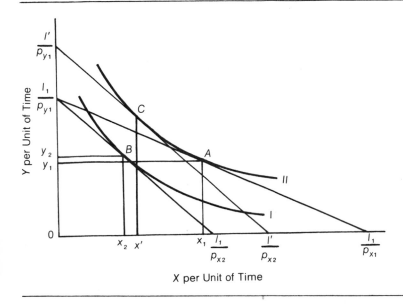

X per Unit of Time

He may experience a large substitution effect, however, when good substitutes are available for the commodity in question.

Exchange and Welfare

The forces giving rise to voluntary exchange of items among individuals and the impact of voluntary exchange on welfare can be readily explained in terms of indifference curve analysis. Suppose we consider two consumers, *A* and *B*, each of whom receives and consumes quantities of two commodities, *X* and *Y*, per unit of time.

Individual *A*'s tastes and preferences for *X* and *Y* are shown on the conventional part of Figure 5-13. The indifference map of *B* is rotated 180° and is superimposed on that of *A* so that the axes of the two diagrams form what is called an Edgeworth box. The diagram for *B* can be placed so that 0*M* represents the entire amount of *Y* received by the two individuals and 0*N* represents the entire amount of *X* received. The indifference curves of *A* are convex to 0, while those of *B* are convex to 0'. Any point on or in the rectangle represents a possible distribution of the goods between the two individuals.

The initial distribution of X and Y can be represented by some such point as F, lying within the rectangle formed by the two sets of axes. Individual A gets Oy_1 of Y per unit of time, and B gets y_1M. The amount of X received per unit of time by A is Ox_1, and that by B is x_1N. Individual A is on indifference curve I_1. Individual B is on indifference curve I'. For A the marginal rate of substitution of X for Y at point F is greater than it is for B. Individual A would be willing to give up more Y to get an additional unit of X than B would require to induce him to part with a unit of X. Thus, the stage is set for exchange.

Whenever the initial distribution of the two commodities is such that an indifference curve of A cuts through an indifference curve of B, either or both parties may gain from exchange. If F is the initial distribution of X and Y, exchanges of Y by individual A to individual B for X could take place in such a way that indifference curve I_1 is followed downward to the right. Individual A would be made no worse off, and individual B would be made progressively better off until the distribution of goods between the two is that represented by point G, at which indifference curve I_1 is tangent to indifference curve I''. No further exchange can occur without making one or both parties worse off then they are at G. Similarly, individual A could exchange Y to individual B for X in such a way that indifference curve I' is followed downward to the right. Such exchanges would leave B no worse off than before but would place A on successively higher indifference curves, or in more preferred positions, until the distribution of goods is that represented by point H, at which indifference curve I' is tangent to indifference curve I_2. Any further exchanges would result in a decrease in well-being for one or both parties.

Again, starting at F, both parties could gain from exchanges that follow a path from F to J, falling somewhere within the area bounded by FG and FH. Both parties would reach higher preference levels until some point J, at which an indifference curve of A is tangent to an indifference curve of B, is reached. Further exchanges would result in one or both parties being made worse off.

Exchanges that alter the distribution of goods from one at which an indifference curve of one consumer intersects an indifference curve of another consumer, toward a distribution within the area bounded by the two indifference curves and within which tangency occurs, lead toward a *Pareto optimum* or an *efficient* distribution of the goods..

In Chapter 1 we defined a Pareto optimum condition as one in which no one can be made better off without making someone else worse off; and it is this condition that occurs at G or J or H or at any other point at which an indifference curve of A is tangent to an indifference curve of B. A line joining all of these tangency points, GJH as extended in Figure 5-13, is called a *contract curve*.

Figure 5–13 The Basis of Exchange

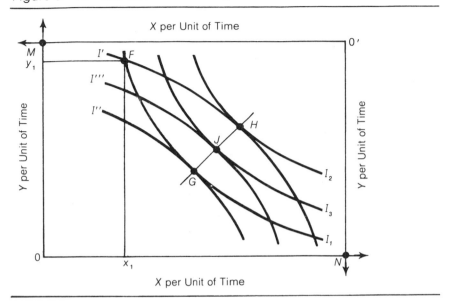

For an efficient distribution of goods between the two parties to exist, or for a Pareto optimum in distribution to exist, the MRS_{xy} for one must be equal to the MRS_{xy} for the other. That is, if the maximum amount of Y that individual A is just willing to give up to get an additional unit of X is equal to the minimum amount of Y that B would accept in exchange for a unit of X, then no gain from such an exchange would occur for either party. These conditions are fulfilled at every point along the contract curve. At each such point an indifference curve of A is tangent to an indifference curve of B; that is, individual A's indifference curve has the same slope as does individual B's, or MRS_{xy} is the same for A as it is for B.

This analysis shows that some redistributions of goods (income) among consumers will increase wefare, but we are left in the dark with respect to others—we cannot say whether or not they make the community better off. Given the initial distribution F, any point on the contract curve from G to H inclusive is a Pareto optimum; and a movement from F to any such point increases the welfare of the community. But there are any number of efficient or Pareto optimum distributions of X and Y between consumers A and B—there is one for every point on the contract curve. If a redistribution from J to H is effected, for example, consumer B is made worse off and consumer A is made better off. Who knows whether the increase in A's welfare is just offset, more than offset, or less than offset by the decrease in the welfare of B?

Some Applications of Indifference Curve Analysis

Indifference curve analysis is useful in analyzing most problems of choices among alternatives. Two common problems—choices between pay in the form of money or in the form of fringe benefits, and choices between work and leisure—provide excellent illustrations of its applications.

Economics of Fringe Benefits

Fringe benefits—such as guarantees of retirement pay, some free medical services, life insurance, the use of company recreational facilities, and many others—have become commonplace as part of the pay package. These are costs to employers, just as wages and salaries are costs, and these benefits constitute a part of what employees earn. The question that we consider here is whether employees would be better or worse off if employers were to pay them the money value (cost) of the fringe benefits as additional wages and salaries, rather than providing these fringe benefits. To keep the choice problem as simple as possible, we assume that there are no tax advantages to employers or employees in paying employees in the form of fringe benefits rather than money.[16]

Suppose initially that an individual's income with no fringe benefits is $0I_1$ dollars, measured along the vertical axis of Figure 5-14 (a). Units of medical service are measured along the horizontal axis, and the amount that the person's total income will purchase at price p_{m1} per unit is $0D$. With the indifference map shown and budget line I_1D, the individual spends I_1C_1 of his income for $0M_1$ units of medical service.

Now, let his employer give the individual a pay increase in the form of free medical service amounting to $0M_1'$ units per month. The fringe benefit obviously increases the welfare of the individual, but the important question is: If the pay increase were given in the form of money rather than in the specific form of a good or service would the individual's welfare be increased by more, less, or by the same amount?

Figure 5-14 (a) illustrates a case in which welfare is increased less by the fringe benefit than it would be by an equivalent amount of money paid to the individual. Free medical services of $0M_1'$ combined with a money income of $0I_1$ shift the budget line to I_1BE. The I_1B segment is determined by the money income $0I_1$—which has not been increased—and the $0M_1'$ (which $= I_1B$) units of medical service that can now be obtained without any decrease in the money income available to the individual to spend as

---

[16]The institutional arrangements that exist in any society obviously affect the choices that are made. But the basic "pure" choice is that between pay in the form of, say, medical services versus pay in the form of money, keeping the choice free of such institutional arrangements as tax laws. Then one can, if he so desires, introduce institutional arrangements and examine the impact of these on the choices made.

Figure 5–14   Fringe Benefits versus Money Income

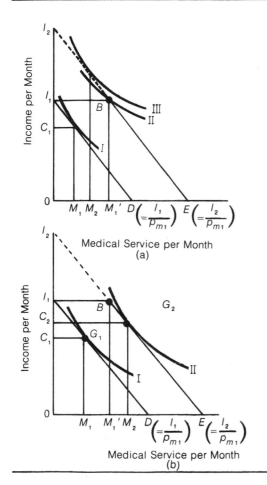

Medical Service per Month
(a)

Medical Service per Month
(b)

he desires. If, however, the individual were to consume more than $0M_1'$ units of medical service per month, he would be required to pay p_{m1} for each unit in excess of $0M_1'$. These circumstances are shown by the BE segment of the budget line. Note that BE is parallel to I_1D since the slope of both curves is equal to p_{m1}. Note also that $DE = 0M_1'$. The new budget line is "kinked" or has a corner in it at B. Indifference curve II is the highest that the individual can reach, so that in this case he consumes the entire amount of free medical services, leaving him $0I_1$ dollars to spend on other goods and service.

If the individual receives a money increase in pay equal in value to, but in lieu of, the fringe benefit medical services, his budget line becomes I_2E.

The increase in money income I_1I_2 is $OM_1' \times p_{m1}$; that is, what the value of the fringe benefit medical services would be in the market. The BE segment of the budget line is the same as it was before, since the individual would, if he were at point B, be spending I_1I_2 dollars for OM_1' of medical services, leaving him with OI_1 dollars to spend as he desires. The segment of I_2E above point B is the significant one. It represents opportunities open to the consumer that were not possible under the fringe benefit arrangement—he can reduce his consumption of medical services below OM_1' units; and for each unit that he so reduces it he will have p_{m1} more dollars to spend on other things. Given the indifference map of 5-14 (a), the individual would indeed reduce his consumption of medical services to OM_2 per month—where indifference curve III is tangent to the I_2E segment of the budget line. This segment was not available to him under the fringe-benefit arrangement. In this case his welfare would be greater if his pay increase were given to him in the form of money rather than in "free" medical services.

If an individual's preferences are such that after a pay increase he wants more medical services per month than the pay increase would buy or provide, his welfare will not be affected by the form of the increase. This situation is illustrated in Figure 5-14 (b). Prior to the pay increase the individual has an income of OI and is in equilibrium at G_1, taking OM_1 units of medical services per month. Now, suppose a pay increase in the form of medical services amounting to OM_1' is given to him, changing his budget line to I_1BE. His new equilibrium position is G_2, and he purchases OM_2 units of medical services per month.

If the pay increase were in the form of money equivalent to the value of the fringe-benefit medical services, his new equilibrium position would also be G_2. The budget line becomes I_2E rather than I_1BE, but since the tangency to an indifference curve occurs in the BE segment common to both budget lines the results are the same either way.

Labor Supply

Indifference curve techniques provide some insights into an individual's choice between leisure and income, or, put the other way around, his choice of the amount of labor time he is willing to supply at different wage rates. Suppose, for example, that the indifference map in Figure 5-15 (a) shows his preference structure for combinations of daily income or leisure. Income is measured on the vertical axis, and leisure is measured on the horizontal axis. Any one indifference curve shows combinations of income and leisure that are equivalent to the individual Higher indifference curves show preferred sets of income-leisure combinations.

A budget line or income line shows the income level that can be obtained by working (giving up leisure) different numbers of hours at a given

Figure 5–15   Work, Leisure, and Labor Supply

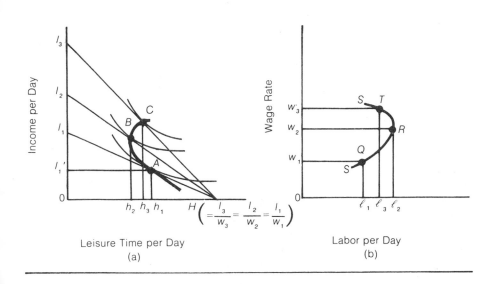

Leisure Time per Day
(a)

Labor per Day
(b)

wage rate. The distance $0H$ represents the maximum number of hours of leisure per day that it would be possible for the individual to trade for work. Some minimum number of hours is required for eating and sleeping. If this number were ten hours per day, then $0H$ would be fourteen hours. At a wage rate of w_1, the individual can earn an income of l_1 $(= 0H \times w_1)$ by working $0H$ hours per day, keeping his tradable leisure at zero. If he works h_1H hours per day his income earned is l_1' $(= h_1H \times w_1)$ and his tradable leisure time is $0h_1$ hours. Note that the slope of the income line is the wage rate w_1.

The individual would be expected to seek out the most preferred combination of income and leisure from all of the combinations that his income line will permit. Given the wage rate w_1, combination A is preferred over all other available to him; this is the highest indifference curve that he can reach. He will work h_1H hours earning an income of l_1' dollars per day. At this point the marginal rate of substitution of leisure for income is equal to the wage rate—the amount of income that he would be willing to sacrifice to obtain an additional hour of leisure is the amount that he would be required to sacrifice in the labor market.

By considering the income lines generated for different wage rates points on the individual's labor supply curve can be determined. At wage rate w_1 the amount of labor supplied will be h_1H ($= 0\ell_1$) per day, and this point is plotted as point Q in Figure 5-15 (b). A higher wage rate w_2 will shift the income line clockwise to I_2H, increasing the amount of labor supplied to h_2H ($= 0\ell_2$). In Figure 5-15 (b) this is plotted as point R. A still higher wage rate w_3 generates income line I_3H and induces the individual to supply h_3H ($= 0\ell_3$) hours of labor per day, giving rise to point T. These and other points located in a similar fashion trace out the labor supply curve SS.

The total impact of a wage rate change on the amount of labor supplied (or leisure demanded) is the combined result of an income effect and a substitution effect. For an increase in the wage rate, such as that from w_1 to w_2, the substitution effect outweighs the income effect; the higher cost of an hour of leisure induces the individual to substitute income for leisure by working more hours per day. The income effect of the wage rate increase would be expected in and of itself to increase the amount of leisure desired and to decrease the amount of work the individual wants to do. The increase in the wage rate from w_2 to w_3 illustrates a situation in which the income effect of a wage increase outweighs the substitution effect. If and when this situation occurs for an individual it makes his labor supply curve bend upward and to the left, as Figure 5-15 (b) illustrates.

Summary

The indifference curve apparatus provides a useful framework for the theory of consumer choice and exchange. A consumer's tastes and preferences are represented by his indifference map. The consumer's opportunity factors—his income and the prices of goods he buys—are represented by his budget line. The point at which his budget line is tangent to an indifference curve represents the combination of goods that the consumer prefers of those available to him.

The consumer's demand curve for one good is obtained by varying the price of the good while holding constant his tastes and preferences, his income, and the prices of other goods. The resulting points of consumer equilibrium trace out the price consumption curve for the commodity. Information for the demand curve can be taken from the indifference curve diagram.

The slope of the price consumption curve for a commodity indicates the elasticity of demand when the commodity under consideration is measured on the X axis and money is measured on the Y axis. A horizontal price consumption curve means that demand has unitary elasticity. When the price consumption curve slopes upward to the right demand is inelastic. When it slopes downward to the right demand is elastic.

Engel curves for commodities are derived by varying the consumer's income, holding his tastes and preferences and the prices of all goods constant. The points of consumer equilibrium form the income consumption curve. The indifference curve diagram furnishes the necessary data for setting up Engel curves.

The change in quantity taken as a result of a price change, as shown by the demand curve for an item, is the combined result of two forces—an income effect and a substitution effect. For normal goods these work in the same direction to produce a decrease in quantity for an increase in price, or an increase in quantity for a decrease in price. For inferior goods the two effects work in opposite directions, but the substitution effect is usually much the stronger of the two.

By means of an Edgeworth box the conditions for an efficient or Pareto optimum distribution of goods among consumers can be established. These are that the MRS_{xy} of one consumer for any two goods, X and Y, must be the same as the MRS_{xy} of any other consumer for the same two goods. Distributions of goods satisfying these conditions form the contract curve. For any distribution of goods not on the contract curve a redistribution can occur that moves to the contract curve and increases community welfare. No conclusions regarding community welfare can be drawn from redistributions that occur along the contract curve.

Among the applications of indifference curve techniques is the analysis of fringe benefits in lieu of money as a part of an employee's total compensation. If an employee voluntarily takes as much or larger quantities of fringe-benefit items than are provided as a part of his compensation, it makes no difference whether that part of his compensation is paid in fringe benefits or in money. Otherwise, he is better off if he is paid entirely in money.

Another application of indifference curve techniques is the analysis of labor-leisure choices of an individual. Higher wage rates raise the price of leisure and induce the individual to substitute income for leisure; that is, to work more. This substitution effect ordinarily has an income effect working against it.

Suggested Readings

Baumol, William J., *Economic Theory and Operations Analysis*, 3rd ed. (Englewood Cliffs, N. J.: Prentice-Hall, Inc., 1972), pp. 207–221.

Boulding, Kenneth E., *Economic Analysis*, 4th ed., vol. 1 (New York: Harper & Row, Publishers, 1966), Chaps. 27–28.

Hicks, John R., *Value and Capital*, 2nd ed. (Oxford, England: The Clarendon Press, 1946), Chaps. 1–2.

Chapter 6:

Individual Consumer Choice and Demand—II

The indifference curve analysis developed in the preceding chapter evolved from an older utility approach to consumer choice, demand, and exchange. The utility approach is a special case of the indifference curve approach. Although the indifference curve approach has become the standard method of treating the theory of choice, references to the utility approach and the extensive use made of it by economists require the student to have a thorough understanding of it.

Utility, or subjective value theory, came on the scene in the 1870s with the almost simultaneous publication of its basic aspects by three economists working independently—William Stanley Jevons of Great Britain, Karl Menger of Austria, and Leon Walras of France. Present-day utility theory owes much to all three theorists.

The Utility Concept

The term *utility* refers to the satisfaction a consumer gets from whatever goods and services he consumes. It is useful analytically to distinguish between total utility concepts and marginal utility concepts under circumstances in which goods are not related to one another and under those in which relatedness occurs.

Nonrelated Goods and Services

Different kinds of items are unrelated, insofar as their consumption is concerned, if the utility or satisfaction obtained by the consumer from one is in no way dependent upon the amount that he consumes of the others. It is unlikely, for example, that the utility obtained from consuming nails has any significant bearing on that obtained from the consumption of gasoline.

Total Utility   The total utility attained from a commodity refers to the entire amounts of satisfaction a consumer receives from consuming it at various rates. The more of an item a consumer consumes per unit of time, the greater will be his total utility or satisfaction from it up to a certain point. At some rate of consumption total utility will reach a maximum. The consumer will not be capable of enjoying any greater satisfaction from it even though more of it is thrust upon him. This state is called his saturation point for that commodity.[1]

A hypothetical total utility curve showing these properties is drawn in Figure 6-1 (a). In plotting the curve we assume that utility can be quantified and that different quantities of utility to the consumer can be added to arrive at a meaningful total.[2]

The saturation point is reached at a consumption level of 6 units of X per unit of time. Up to that level total utility is increasing as consumption increases. Beyond that level, total utility decreases.[3]

Marginal Utility   The marginal utility of a good is defined as the change in total utility resulting from a 1-unit change in consumption per unit of time. In Figure 6-1 (a), if the consumer were consuming 2 units per unit of time and increased his consumption level to 3, his total utility would increase from 18 to 24 units of utility. Marginal utility of the third unit also is equal roughly to the average slope of the total utility curve between points A and B.

The slope of the total utility curve between points A and B shows the increase in utility resulting from a 1-unit increase in consumption and is equal to 6/1 if that segment of the curve is considered to be a straight line. The total utility curve is not necessarily a straight line between A and B,

---

[1]Conceivably, still more units of the good forced upon him can cause his total utility to decrease—if for no other reason than because of storage problems. However, the possibility of decreases in total utility beyond the saturation point is of no importance for our purposes.

[2]Whether utility can be measured cardinally or whether its measurement has ordinal meaning only has been an historical source of controversy in the development of economic thought. The theory presented here does not really require measurability but requires only that the consumer be able to distinguish between greater and lesser amounts of utility. For expositional purposes we shall treat utility as though it were cardinal.

[3]This paragraph assumes that the rate of consumption must be increased by discrete units. Total utility is maximum at 5 as well as at 6 units of X per unit of time. However, there are pedagogical advantages to considering the maximum as occuring at 6 units.

Figure 6–1   Total and Marginal Utility

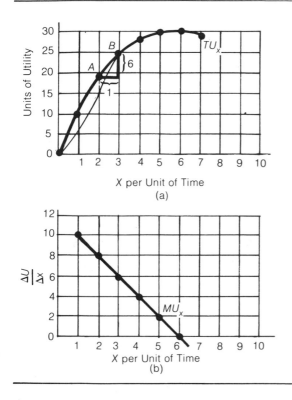

but the error involved in considering it as such is not significant and becomes progressively less the smaller the distance between points. If the distance on the X axis that measures 1 unit of X is infinitesimal, marginal utility at any given level of consumption can be thought of as the slope of the total utility curve at that point.[4]

Marginal utility is reflected by the shape of the total utility curve as the rate of consumption is increased or decreased. In Figure 6-1 (a) marginal utility decreases as consumption per unit of time increases between 0 and 6. This statement can be rephrased by saying that each additional unit of consumption per unit of time adds less and less to total utility, until finally the sixth unit adds nothing at all. Note also that as consumption per unit of

---

[4]In terms of differential calculus, if the total utility curve were:

$$U = f(x) = 12x - x^2$$

then:

$$MU = f'(x) = 12 - 2x.$$

Marginal utility at 2 units of X is 8 units of utility; at 3 units of X it is 6 units of utility.

time increases, the average slope of the total utility curve between any two consecutive consumption levels becomes smaller and smaller until, between 5 and 6 units of X, it becomes 0. The concept of diminishing marginal utility and the concavity of the total utility curve, when viewed from below, are the same thing.

Diminishing marginal utility need not be the case for all levels of consumption between 0 and 6 units of X. The lighter curve in Figure 6-1 (a) could conceivably be the total utility curve between 0 and 3. Suppose, for example, that a single television set in a home with several children causes so much friction over program selection that it adds little to the satisfaction of the family. Two sets — one for the parents and one for the children — may yield more than twice the satisfaction of one. But the successive increases in total utility yielded by three, four, and five sets will surely be successively smaller. Thus, up to some certain consumption level marginal utility may increase as the consumption level increases, and the total utility curve will be convex downward. Beyond that level marginal utility would be decreasing. If a saturation point for a commodity exists for a given consumer, as his consumption level approaches that point marginal utility must be decreasing even though it may have been increasing at lower levels of consumption.

The marginal utility curve can be constructed from the total utility curve of Figure 6-1. In Figure 6-1 (b) the utility axis is stretched out so that the vertical distance measuring one unit is greater than it is in Figure 6-1 (a). The X axis is the same for the two diagrams. Marginal utility at each level of consumption is plotted as a vertical distance above that level of consumption on the X axis. At a consumption level of 6 in Figure 6-1 (a) the average slope of the total utility curve between 5 and 6 is 0. Hence, marginal utility is 0 also; in Figure 6-1 (b) the marginal utility curve intersects the X axis at that consumption level. In Figure 6-1 (b) a line MU_x joining the plotted marginal utilities at each level of consumption is the marginal utility curve for X.

A set of a consumer's marginal utility curves for different commodities, such as that of Figure 6-4 (p. 113), provides a graphic picture of the consumer's tastes and preferences at any given time. For those commodities with which the consumer is easily satiated the marginal utility curves will slope off very rapidly, reaching zero at fairly low levels of consumption. For other commodities with which the consumer is not easily satiated the marginal utility curves will slope off gradually and will reach zero at fairly high levels of consumption.[5] Changes in consumer tastes and preferences

---

[5] as a practical matter no consumer will reach the saturation point for any good that commands a price, except by accident. The reason for this statement will become apparent in the next section of the chapter.

will change the shapes and positions of the marginal utility curves for different commodities.

Related Goods and Services

A great many of the goods and services that an individual consumes are related to each other in some way; that is, the quantity that he takes of one affects the utility that he obtains from others. These may be complementary relationships or they may be substitute relationships. In general, goods that are consumed together, such as bread and butter or tennis rackets and tennis balls, are complementary goods; while those that compete with each other in the consumer's scale of preferences—beef and pork, for example—are substitute goods.

The nature of relatedness is illustrated in the three-dimensional diagram of Figure 6-2 (a). The X and Y axes define a horizontal plane, and total utility is measured as a vertical distance above it. For example, if the individual consumes combination A_1 per week, containing x_1 units of X and y_1 units of Y, his total utility from both will be A_1B_1. Points such as B_1 B_2, B_4, F_1, F_2, and F_5.—showing total utility for different combinations of X and Y—trace out a *total utility surface* lying above the XY plane.

The utility surface pictured in Figure 6-2 (a) shows not only the total utility obtained by the consumer from the consumption of X and Y in various combinations but also how total utility changes as the rate of consumption of one good is changed, given the rate of consumption of the other.

Consider, for example, variations in the consumption of X at each of three different levels of consumption of Y. If no Y is consumed, the total utility of the consumer, as is shown in Figure 6-2 (a), is TU_{x0} for different rates of consumption of X. The same curve is also pictured on the two-dimensional diagram of Figure 6-2 (b). If the amount of Y consumed per week is y_1, total utility is y_1B_0 if no X is taken. Changes in quantity of X with the consumption level of Y held constant at y_1 trace out the total utility curve TU_{x1}. We can visualize the consumer as starting from point B_0 on the utility surface and moving up over the surface directly above the dotted line $y_1A_1A_2A_4$. Again the resulting TU_{x1} curve is plotted in two dimensions in Figure 6-2 (b). The meaning of the third total utility curve for X, Tu_{x2}, is now obvious. If no X is consumed, total utility from y_2 of Y alone is y_2F_0. Holding Y constant at y_2, increasing levels of consumption of X will yield the total utility curve TU_{x2} on the utility surface and in the two-dimensional diagram Figure 6-2 (b). The curves TU_{y0}, TU_{y1}, and TU_{y2} are derived in a similar fashion.[6]

---

[6]If all goods consumed are *independent* of one another the consumer's utility function is of the form:
$$U = f(x) + g(y) + \ldots + n(n).$$
If all goods consumed are *related*, it takes the form:
$$U = f(x, y, \cdots n).$$

Taking the interrelatedness of goods X and Y into account undoubtedly makes utility theory more realistic, but it makes it more complex too. For one thing, there are innumerable possible total utility curves for each product. There is a different total utility curve for X associated with each different quantity of Y that the consumer might consume. Similarly, there is a different total utility curve for Y for each different level of consumption of X. There are also innumerable marginal utility curves for each product. Since the total utility curves for X differ at each different level of consumption of Y, so do the corresponding marginal utility curves for X. For example, in Figure 6-2 (c) MU_{x0}, MU_{x1}, and MU_{x2} are derived from TU_{x0}, TU_{x1}, and TU_{x2}, respectively. Here we see that at a consumption level of x_1 of X the marginal utility of X depends on the amount of Y consumed, as well as on the quantity x_1 of X. If no Y is consumed, it is M_0 or the slope of TU_{x0} at point D_1. If y_1 of Y is consumed, it is M_1 or the slope of TU_{x1} at B_1. If y_2 of Y is consumed, it is M_2 or the slope of TU_{x2} at F_1. Similar reasoning applies to Y. If diminishing marginal utility occurs with any increase in the consumption of either X or Y the utility surface will have the inverted bowl shape exhibited in Figure 6-2 (a); that is, any total utility curve drawn for either X or Y will be convex upward.

Complementary and substitute relations are sometimes defined in terms of what happens to the marginal utility of one good when the quantity consumed of the related goods is changed. If an increase in the consumption of Y causes a decrease in the marginal utility of X, when the quantity consumed of X is not changed, then X is said to be a *substitute* for Y. However, if an increase in the consumption of Y causes an increase in the marginal utility of X, when the quantity of X consumed remains constant, then X is said to be *complementary* to Y.

Indifference Curves

Indifference curve analysis was a logical outgrowth of the utility surface concepts. In Figure 6-3 (a) suppose that a consumer initially consumes good Y only, and that he consumes it at a rate of y_1 per unit of time. His total utility is y_1A_1 or OU_1. Is it not possible that by giving up the consumption of a small amount of Y and by increasing the consumption of S in some amount, he can maintain his level of utility constant? Reducing his consumption of Y and increasing his consumption of X in the manner described, he moves around the indifference surface at a constant distance about the XY plane; and his path traces out the curve A_1B_2. Projected vertically downward on the XY plane the A_1B_2 curve becomes the dashed line y_1x_2. This curve is redrawn with respect only to the XY plane in Figure 6-3 (b).

Figure 6–2 The Utility Surface

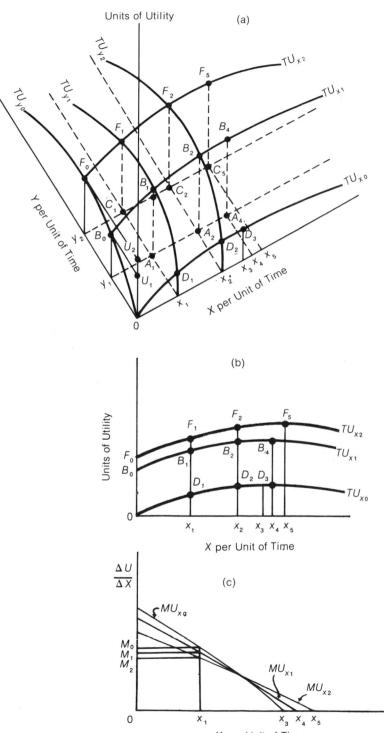

Figure 6-3   Indifference Curves from a Utility Surface

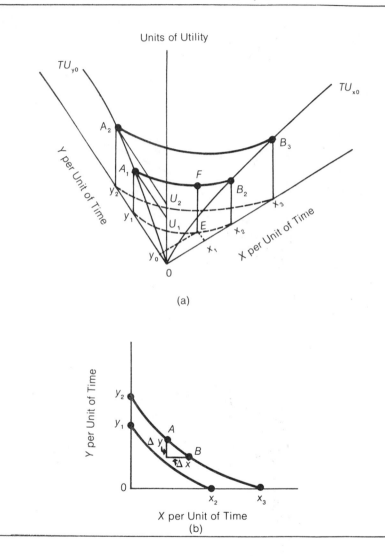

(a)

(b)

The curve y_1x_2 shows all combinations of X and Y that yield levels of utility equal to $0U_1$ or y_1A_1: For example, in Figure 6-3 (a) at point E the consumer is taking y_0 of Y and x_1 of X; this combination yields a total utility of EF (= y_1A_1). Similarly, if he consumes X alone at level x_2, his total utility is x_2B_2 (= y_1A_1). Curve y_1x_2 is in every sense an indifference curve. Since all combinations of X and Y shown by this curve yield the same total utility to the consumer, he is indifferent as to which of them he consumes.

Higher levels of utility are shown by contour lines higher up on the surface, while the lower contour lines show lower levels of utility. Projected on the *XY* plane, the indifference curves corresponding to higher contour lines lie farther from the origin, as does y_2x_3 in Figure 6-3 (b). The projections of lower contour lines lie closer to the origin. These observations are based on the assumption that the utility surface tapers toward a summit as we move up. It is usually thought of as having an inverted bowl shape, although this restrictive shape is not really necessary for the foregoing observations to hold.

The marginal rate of substitution of *X* for *Y* is measured by the ratio of the marginal utility of *X* to the marginal utility of *Y*, or $MRS_{xy} = MU_x/MU_y$. In Figure 6-3 (b) suppose that the consumer is originally consuming combination *A*. If he were to move from combination *A* to combination *B*, he would give up Δ*y* of *Y* and acquire Δ*x* of *X* with *no change* in his total utility level. The loss in utility from giving up *Y* is $\Delta y \times MU_y$. The gain from acquiring *X* is $\Delta x \times MU_x$. Therefore:

$$\Delta y \times MU_y = \Delta x \times MU_x \qquad [6.1]$$

$$\frac{\Delta y}{\Delta x} = \frac{MU_x}{MU_y} = MRS_{xy}. \qquad [6.2]$$

In this discussion we have continued to assume that utility is measurable. For example, in Figure 6-3 (a) the distance $0U_1$ is a definite measurable magnitude, say 8 units of utility, while $0U_2$ is 10 units of utility. Accordingly, in Figure 6-3 (b) we would attach the number 8 to the y_1x_2 indifference curve and 10 to the y_2x_3 curve. However, is it essential that we attach absolute utility *magnitudes* to each indifference curve? Wouldn't it be possible, once we have an indifference map, to attach a utility *ranking* to each curve instead?

If we do so, the 8 and the 10 have no significance as absolute measures. They would show only the order of utility magnitudes; that is, 10 is greater than 8. We could accomplish the same thing by attaching the number 1 to y_1x_2 and the number 2 to y_2x_3.[7]

If the order, but not the absolute measure, of utility magnitudes is all that is required, we can forget about how high the utility surface rises above the *XY* plane. Only its general shape is important. Suppose we think of it as being collapsible from the top down in such a way that contour

---

[7]If the consumer's utility function is represented by:

$$U = f(x, y).$$

Then the equation for one indifference curve is.

$$U_1 = f(x, y)$$

in which U_1 is a constant. Other values assigned to *U* define other indifference curves, all of these making up the consumer's indifference map. It is necessary only that the assigned values show the order of utility magnitudes; it is not necessary that they show absolute (measurable) utility magnitudes.

lines from bottom to top retain their original shapes. If we do so, we are free of the assumption that utility is measurable. The indifference map is the same in all essential respects as those developed earlier in Chapter 5.

Consumer Choice

The utility concepts provide a basis for determining how a consumer will allocate his income among the various goods and services that confront him; but they are somewhat more awkward to use than the more general indifference curve analysis. To keep the discussion as straightforward as possible, we shall employ several simplifying assumptions: (1) we assume that the goods and services contemplated by the consumer are nonrelated; (2) we proceed as though utility were cardinal; (3) we assume that the marginal utility of each item consumed is diminishing.[8] None of these do any violence to the conclusions reached, but they do much to smooth the path toward those conclusions.

Objectives and Constraints

The objective usually postulated for a rational consumer is the maximization of his satisfaction or utility. The consumer's preferences are described by his utility curves for the various goods and services that confront him. His choice problem is to select from these the kinds and amounts that will yield him the greatest possible sum total of utility.

The consumer is constrained by his income (the dollars per unit of time that he has to spend) and the prices of the goods and services available to him. Typically, his income per unit of time is a more or less fixed amount, as are the prices he faces (since he is a pure competitor in the purchase of most things). Faced with these limiting factors, he tackles the problem of choice.

Maximization of Utility

To avoid unnecessary complexity we again limit the consumer to two goods, X and Y, priced at p_x and p_y, respectively. Note that if p_x and p_y are given and constant, we can measure the quantities of these goods in terms of dollar's worths. For example, if a bushel of X costs $2, we can record that physical quantity as two dollar's worths, or a half-bushel as a dollar's worth. Table 6-1 (a) records the consumer's marginal utility sched-

---

[8]Actually, all we need to assume is that the marginal utility of one good decreases relative to the marginal utilities of other goods as consumption of the one is increased in proportion to the consumption of the others. The marginal utility of X could be increasing. However, if the additional consumption of X raises the marginal utilities of other goods that of X has decreased *relative* to those of the other goods.

ules for *X* and *Y*, measuring quantities in dollar's worths and assuming independence between the two goods.[9]

Table 6-1   Marginal Utility Schedules

(a)

Product X		Product Y	
Quantity (Dollar's Worth)	MU_x (Units of Utility)	Quantity (Dollar's Worth)	MU_y (Units of Utility)
1	40	1	30
2	36	2	29
3	32	3	28
4	28	4	27
5	24	5	26
6	20	6	25
7	12	7	24
8	4	8	20

(b)

Product X		Product Y	
Quantity (Bushels)	MU_x (Units of Utility)	Quantity (Pints)	MU_y (Units of Utility)
1	50	1	30
2	44	2	28
3	38	3	26
4	32	4	24
5	26	5	22
6	20	6	20
7	12	7	16
8	4	8	10

If the consumer has an income of $12 per unit of time, what is the allocation of it between *X* and *Y* that will maximize his utility? Suppose he spends only $1 per unit of time. Spent on *Y*, it will yield only 30 units of satisfaction; whereas if it is spent on *X*, it will yield 40. Thus, the dollar will be allocated to *X*. If our consumer increases his expenditure level to $2, where should the second dollar go? Spent on *X*, it will increase his total utility by 36 (the marginal utility of a second dollar's worth of *X*); but spent on *Y*, it adds only 30 units. The second dollar will be spent on *X* and also the third dollar. The situation changes when the expenditure increases from $3 to $4. A fourth dollar spent on *X* will increase the total utility by 28

---

[9]Assuming that the marginal utility schedule of each commodity is independent of the level of consumption of the other commodity, we can go directly and quickly to the conditions necessary for maximization of satisfaction. If *X* and *Y* were substitutes, the more of *X* consumed, the lower the marginal utility of *Y* would be at various consumption levels of *Y*. If they were complements, the more of *X* consumed, the higher the marginal utility of *Y* would be at various consumption levels of *Y*. These possibilities do not change the conditions necessary for maximization of satisfaction but they make numerical exposition of these conditions virtually impossible.

units; but spent on the first dollar's worth of Y, the increase is 30 units. The fourth dollar will go for Y and as expenditure per unit of time is increased dollar by dollar, the fifth should go for Y; the sixth and seventh, one each on X and Y; the eighth, ninth, and tenth on Y; and the eleventh and twelfth, one each on X and Y. The consumer is now taking five dollar's worths of X and seven dollar's worths of Y. The marginal utility per dollar's worth of X is equal to that of a dollar's worth of Y—both are 24 units of utility.

We know that our consumer's utility for the $12 expenditure is maximum, because it was placed dollar by dollar where each dollar made its greatest contribution to his total utility.

Generalizing, we can say that a consumer maximizes his utility by allocating his income among the goods and services (including savings) available to him in such a way that (1) the marginal utility per dollar's worth of any one is equal to the marginal utility per dollar's worth of any other and (2) he is spending all of his income. Savings, which may appear to pose a problem, are simply treated as any other good. A consumer obtains utility from savings; and presumably the marginal utility of savings, like that of other goods and services, diminishes as its quantity is increased.

Now consider another consumer whose marginal utility schedules are those of Table 6-1 (b). The price of X is $2 per bushel and that of Y is $1 per pint. This consumer's income is $15 per unit of time. How should he allocate it between X and Y?

Since the marginal utility schedules are in terms of physical units of X and Y, rather than in terms of dollar's worths, we need a means of converting the information they contain into marginal utilities per dollar's worth. To obtain it consider the fourth bushel of X. If the consumer were taking four bushels of X, the fourth bushel has a marginal utility of 32 units. The fourth bushel (like any other bushel) costs $2. At this consumption level the marginal utility per bushel of X divided by the price of X, or MU_x/p_x, is the marginal utility per dollar's worth of X. Thus, the marginal utility per dollar's worth of X is 16 units at this point. Likewise, the marginal utility per pint of Y at any consumption level divided by the price of Y, or MU_y/p_y, can be read as the marginal utility per dollar's worth of Y at that consumption level. The first condition for maximizing satisfaction becomes:

$$\frac{MU_x}{p_x} = \frac{MU_y}{p_y} = \frac{MU_z}{p_z} = \cdots .$$

[6.3]

The requirement that the consumer be spending all of his income—no more and no less—is expressed as:

$$x \times p_x + y \times p_y + z \times p_z + \cdots = I.$$

[6.4]

His total expenditure on *X* is the price of *X* times the amount of *X* purchased. The same holds for his expenditure on each other good or service, including savings. The total of these must equal his income *I*.

Since the price of *X* is $2 per bushel and the price of *Y* is $1 per pint, we must find some combination of *X* and *Y* at which the marginal utility per bushel of *X* is twice the marginal utility per pint of *Y*. This combination occurs at 6 bushels of *X* and 8 pints of *Y*. However, the total amount spent on *X* would be $12, and the total amount spent on *Y* would be $8. The consumer is exceeding his income. Thus, the second condition for maximization of total utility is not met, although the first one is satisfied. Another possible combination is the one containing 4 bushels of *X* and 7 pints of *Y*. The first condition is met, since 32/$2 = 16/$1. The second condition is met also, since 4 bushels × $2 + 7 pints × $1 = $15. Thus, the consumer should take 4 bushels of *X* and 7 pints of *Y* to maximize his total utility.

We can demonstrate that utility is maximized by transferring a dollar from *X* to *Y*. Giving up a dollar's worth of *X*, or half of the fourth bushel, reduces total utility by 16 units. Spending the dollar for an eighth pint of *Y* increases total utility by 10. There is a net loss of 6 units. A transfer of a dollar in the opposite direction also results in a net loss of utility — 3 units in this case.[10]

The data confronting the consumer may not result in the even solution of this example. Suppose the consumer's income were $14 per unit of time instead of $15. How should he allocate the income? He could give up either a half-bushel of *X* or a pint of *Y*. In either case his total utility would be decreased by 16 units. If his income were $16 instead of $15, he would take half of the fifth bushel of *X*. The increase in total utility would be 13 units. Whereas, if he had taken the eighth pint of *Y*, his total utility would have increased by 10 units only. Thus, the consumer seeking maximum satisfaction should allocate his income among various goods so as to approach as nearly as he can the condition that the marginal utility of a dollar's worth of one good equals the marginal utility of a dollar's worth of any other good purchased.

How would the theory work for a typical family? Suppose the family budget is composed of the following items: food, clothing, housing, automobile, medical care, recreation, and education. Over a short period of time, expenditures in some of the classifications are more or less fixed in

---

[10]The mathematical problem is that of maximizing the consumer's utility function subject to his budget restraint. Using the symbols of the text, his utility function is:

$$U = f(x, y).$$

The budget restraint is:

$$xp_x + yp_y = I$$

or:

$$xp_x + yp_y - I = 0.$$

The maximization problem is identical to that shown in footnote 11, Chapter 5. In that footnote f_x and f_y are MU_x and MU_y, respectively.

amount. The mortgage payments, for example, are a fixed monthly amount. The grocery bill and medical expenditures are sometimes thought to be dictated by necessity rather than choice. The other categories are likely to be more variable, but habit may be influential in determining them in the short run.

Over a longer period of time, however, expenditures on any or all of the budgeted items will be subject to change. The family seeking to get the greatest possible satisfaction from its limited income will reappraise its budget from time to time. The family car begins to rattle a little, and at the same time it appears desirable to add a new bedroom to the house for Junior. It is out of the question to purchase both a new car and a new room, and a choice must be made regarding the direction of expenditure. Still, if either is to be gotten, it will be necessary to cut down on educational expenses for the older daughter, who has been attending a private university. Should she be transferred to the state university where expenses are less? Food and clothing budgeting will also be required in order to make the new car or the new room possible. Likewise, the family will need to economize on recreation, and even on medical expenses. When Junior has a minor illness he will have to get over it without the family calling in the doctor. A whole chain of decisions will be made on the basis of marginal utility principles if maximum satisfaction for the family is to be attained.

The family subjectively estimates the marginal utilities of dollars spent in each of the various directions. Transfer of expenditures from the items where marginal utility per dollar's worth is less toward items where marginal utility per dollar's worth is greater serves to increase total satisfaction.

Demand Curves

The utility approach to consumer choice can be extended to explain the establishment of individual consumer demand curves for goods and services. Again, we limit the consumer to a two-commodity world in which X and Y are independent goods. The consumer's utility curves are given and remain constant throughout the analysis. The marginal utility of each good is assumed to be diminishing.

The Demand Curve for X[11]

To establish the consumer's demand curve for X, suppose that initially the price of X is p_{x1} and the price of Y is p_{y1}. We shall assume that at all times

---

[11]The analysis presented here is essentially that of Walras. See Léon Walras, Abrégé des Eléments d'-économie politique pure (Paris: R. Pichon et R. Durand-Auzias, 1938), pp. 131–133.
The transition from the theory of consumer behavior to demand curves set out in the text differs from the

Figure 6–4   Determination of Quantities Demanded

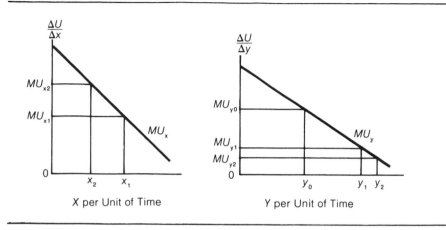

the consumer is operating at the limit of his income restraint. The consumer will maximize satisfaction or be in equilibrium when he is taking that quantity of X and that quantity of Y at which:

$$\frac{MU_{x1}}{p_{x1}} = \frac{MU_{y1}}{p_{y1}}$$ [6.5]

Thus, at price p_{x1} the consumer is taking some definite quantity of X—that quantity which makes the marginal utility of a dollar's worth of X equal to the marginal utility of a dollar's worth of Y. We shall call this quantity x_1.[12]

The consumer's initial position of equilibrium is shown graphically in Figure 6-4. Assuming that p_{x1} is twice p_{y1}, the consumer takes quantity x_1 of X and y_1 of Y. These quantities are such that MU_{x1} is twice MU_{y1}.[13] One point on the consumer's demand schedule or demand curve for X has now been established. At a price of p_{x1} the consumer will take quantity x_1.

The problem is to establish the quantities of X the consumer will take at other prices of X when he is in equilibrium at each of those prices. The price of Y remains constant at p_{y1}. The consumer's marginal utility curves

---

usual Marshallian treatment, which considers the marginal utility of money constant and simply converts the marginal utility curve for a commodity into the demand curve for it. *See* Kenneth E. Boulding, *Economic Analysis*, 4th ed., vol. 1 (New York: Harper & Row, Publisher, 1966), pp. 520–527.

The Marshallian approach ignores the income effects of price changes. The approach used in the text includes income effects as well as substitution effects. This approach in turn makes the utility analysis of the present chapter more nearly parallel to the indifference curve analysis of the last chapter.

[12]He will also be taking some definite quantity y_1 of Y; however, we are primarily concerned with the quantity of X that he takes.

[13]For any given ratio of p_x and p_y, quantities of X and Y taken must be such that $p_x/p_y = MU_x/MU_y$, or $MU_x/p_x \quad MU_y/p_y$.

do not shift; that is, his tastes and preferences remain constant. His income remains constant also.

Suppose that the price of X rises to p_{x2} and that he continues to take the same amount of X that he was taking before. The marginal utility per bushel of X will remain unchanged, but the marginal utility per dollar's worth of X, MU_{x1}/p_{x2}, will be less. If at price p_{x2} the consumer continues taking quantity x_1, he will now be spending more of his income on X than before, leaving less to spend on Y. Since p_{y1} is the fixed price of Y, he will necessarily cut his purchases of Y to some quantity y_0. The decrease in the number of pints of Y consumed causes the marginal utility per pint of Y to go up to MU_{y0} (see Figure 6-4). The marginal utility per dollar's worth of Y is now increased to MU_{y0}/p_{y1}. And:

$$\frac{MU_{x1}}{p_{x2}} < \frac{MU_{y0}}{p_{y1}}. \qquad [6.6]$$

That is, the marginal utility of a dollar's worth of X is less than the marginal utility of a dollar's worth of Y. The consumer is not maximizing satisfaction. Therefore, he will clearly not continue to take quantity x_1 of X after the price has gone up to p_{x2}.

The consumer can increase satisfaction by transferring dollars from X to Y. His loss from taking a dollar away from X is the marginal utility of a dollar's worth of X. His gain from buying an additional dollar's worth of Y is the marginal utility of a dollar's worth of Y, since $MU_{x1}/p_{x2} < MU_{y0}/p_{y1}$, the transfer will yield a net gain in total utility.

The transfer of dollars from X to Y will continue as long as the marginal utility of a dollar's worth of X is less than the marginal utility of a dollar's worth of Y. However, as the consumer gives up units of X, the marginal utility per bushel of X increases, causing the marginal utility per dollar's worth of X to increase, since price remains at p_{x2}. As the consumer buys additional units of Y, the marginal utility per pint of Y declines, as does the marginal utility per dollar's worth of Y. The transfer will stop when the consumer has again equalized the marginal utility per dollar's worth of X with the marginal utility per dollar's worth of Y, and is thus maximizing satisfaction. The quantity of Y taken will have increased from y_0 to some quantity y_2. The quantity of X taken will have decreased from x_1 to x_2. Quantities x_2 and y_2 must be such that:

$$\frac{MU_{x2}}{p_{x2}} = \frac{MU_{y2}}{p_{y1}}. \qquad [6.7]$$

The quantities of X and Y that bring MU_x and MU_y into the proper relationship are shown in Figure 6-4 as x_2 and y_2. We now have another point

Figure 6-5   *Individual Consumer Demand Curve*

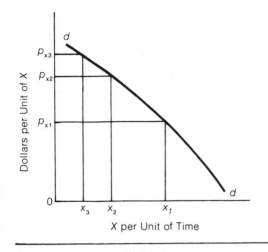

on the consumer's demand curve for X. At price p_{x2} he will achieve equilibrium by taking quantity x_2 of X. The analysis has shown that an increase in the price of X causes a decrease in the quantity taken.

Using $MU_{x2}/p_{x2} = MU_{y2}/p_{yl}$ as a new starting point, we can change the price of X again and repeat this process. In the resulting new equilibrium position the quantity of X taken at the new price is established. Through continued repetition of the process we can determine a series of price-quantity combinations that can be listed as a demand schedule or plotted as a demand curve. Such a curve is shown in Figure 6-5.

Quantities Taken of Other Goods

As a corollary to this analysis it may be instructive to take a closer view of what happens to the quantity of Y taken. When the price of X increases to p_{x2}, is the quantity of Y at the new equilibrium position greater than the original quantity? The answer is, "not necessarily," even though we show it to be greater in Figure 6-4. The crucial factor is the elasticity of demand for X. If demand for X is elastic, the increase in the price of X must decrease total spending on X, leaving more of the consumer's income to spend on Y. In this case, quantity y_2 would indeed be greater than quantity y_1, as we depict it in Figure 6-4. However, if elasticity of demand for X is unitary, total spending on X and total spending on Y will each remain constant and there will be no change in the quantity of Y taken. Should demand for X be inelastic, the price increase in X would increase total spending on X, and decrease total spending on Y; and the new equilibrium quantity of X taken would be smaller than y_1.

Figure 6-6   Construction of a Market Demand Curve

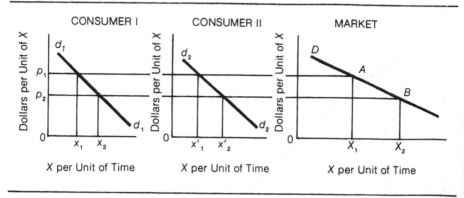

Market Demand Curves

The market demand curve for a commodity is composed of the individual consumer's demand curves for that commodity. We defined the demand curve of an individual consumer in much the same way as we defined a market demand curve. It shows the different quantities that the consumer will take at all possible prices, other things being equal. Thus, by summing the quantities that all consumers in the market will take at each possible price, we arrive at the market demand curve.

The process of summing individual consumer demand curves to obtain the market demand curve is illustrated in Figure 6-6. Suppose there are two consumers, only, who buy commodity X. Their individual demand curves are d_1d_1 and d_2d_2, respectively. At a price of p_1 Consumer I will be willing to take x_1 per unit of time while Consumer II will be willing to take x_1' per unit of time. Together they will be willing to take quantity $X_1(=x_1 + x_1')$ at that price, and A is located as a point on the market demand curve. Likewise, at price p_2 Consumer I will be willing to take x_2 units per unit of time while Consumer II will be willing to take x_2'. Together they will be willing to take $X_2(= x_2 + x_2')$ at that price, and B is located as a point on the market demand curve. Additional points can be located similarly and the market demand curve DD is drawn through them. The market demand curve for a commodity, then, is the horizontal summation of the individual consumer demand curves for the commodity.

Exchange and Welfare

Exchange represents an integral part of economic activity. In modern economies, using the money medium, goods are exchanged for goods;

resources are exchanged for goods; and resources are exchanged for resources. A very common mistake on the part of many people is to think that one of the parties to a voluntary transaction gains while the other loses. In any voluntary exchange of goods among individuals all parties to the exchange expect to increase their satisfaction or welfare. It is the prospect of gain that causes voluntary exchange to occur. This point can be illustrated clearly by means of utility analysis. We shall limit ourselves to two consumers, *A* and *B*, each of whom receives constant quantities per unit of time of two goods, *X* and *Y*. Marginal utility schedules for the two goods for each consumer are shown in Table 6-2.

Table 6-2   The Basis of Exchange

Individual A				Individual B			
Product X		Product Y		Product X		Product Y	
Quantity (Bushels)	MU_x (Units of Utility)	Quantity (Pints)	MU_y (Units of Utility)	Quantity (Bushels)	MU_x (Units of Utility)	Quantity (Pints)	MU_y (Units of Utility)
1	14	1	10	1	20	1	18
2	13	2	9	2	19	2	17
3	12	3	8	3	18	3	16
4	11	4	7	4	17	4	14
5	10	5	6	5	16	5	12
6	9	6	5	6	15	6	10
7	8	7	4	7	14	7	8
8	7	8	3	8	13	8	6
9	6	9	2	9	12	9	4
10	5	10	1	10	10	10	2

Comparative marginal utilities of the goods indicate their comparative worths or values to a consumer. Suppose consumer *A* has 5 bushels of *X* and 6 pints of *Y*. A bushel of *X* at this point contributes 10 units of utility to his total satisfaction. A pint of *Y* contributes 5 units of utility. If he were to lose a bushel of *X*, his loss in satisfaction would be 10 units of utility; or if he were to lose a pint of *Y*, his loss would be 5 units of utility. Thus, a bushel of *X* to him is worth two pints of *Y*. Alternatively, we can say that a pint of *Y* is worth one-half bushel of *X*.

Suppose now that the supplies of goods *X* and *Y* are fixed at 12 bushels of *X* and 12 pints of *Y* per week, and that these are initially distributed between the two consumers so that *A* has 9 bushels of *X* and 3 pints of *Y*, while *B* has 3 bushels of *X* and 9 pints of *Y*. Since for *A* the marginal utility of a bushel of *X* is 6 units of utility and a pint of *Y* is 8 units of utility, a pint of *Y* is worth 1 1/3 bushels of *X* to him. For *B* the marginal utility of a bushel of *X* is 18 units of utility and that of a pint of *Y* is 4 units of utility. Thus, for individual *B* a pint of *Y* is worth only 2/9 of a bushel of *X*.

Under these circumstances both parties will gladly do some exchanging, and exchange will increase community welfare. Individual A will be willing to trade a bushel of X to individual B for a pint of Y; and individual B will be willing to trade a pint of Y for a bushel of X. For individual A the pint of Y gained would be worth 1 1/3 times the bushel of X given up. For individual B the pint of Y given up would be worth only 2/9 of the bushel of X gained. To put it another way, in trading a bushel of X for a pint of Y, individual A would give up 6 units of utility in exchange for 7 units, experiencing a net gain of 1 unit of utility. Individual B would give up 4 units of utility in exchange for 17 units, experiencing a net gain of 13 units of utility. [14]The welfare of both is increased by the exchange, and no one's welfare is decreased.

Once this exchange has been consummated, an additional exchange could result in a further gain for both parties. Individual A, with 8 bushels of X and 4 pints of Y, will no longer be willing to exchange on a bushel-for-a-pint basis, since his loss from such a transaction would be greater than his gain. However, individual B can still gain from trading pints of Y for bushels of X. Since trade is no longer attractive to A on a bushel-for-a-pint basis, B will alter the terms of the trade. If B, who now has 4 bushels of X and 8 pints of Y, were to give up 2 pints of Y for a bushel of X, he would give up 14 units of utility, would gain 16 units, and would still experience a 2-unit net gain in utility. Individual A would find this offer attractive. It would get him 11 units of utility in exchange for 7.

Once the second exchange has occurred, no further gains are available from trade between the two parties; a Pareto optimum has been reached and exchange will cease. Individual A has 7 bushels of X and 6 pints of Y with marginal utilities of 8 and 5 units of utility, respectively. Individual B has 5 bushels of X and 6 pints of Y with marginal utilities of 16 and 10 units of utility, respectively. For A the unit of X is worth 1 3/5 units of Y. Individual B's relative valuations of X and Y are exactly the same; hence, neither can gain from further exchange.

The general principle underlying this discussion is that for exchange to occur, two or more individuals must place different relative valuations on the goods involved. Relative valuations of goods by a single party depend on relative marginal utilities of the goods. Thus, for all consumers to be in equilibrium—that is, for there to be no incentives to exchange—each individual's holdings of goods must be such that the ratio of the marginal utilities of the goods for him is the same as it is for everyone else. In our simple example for A and B to be in equilibrium, MU_x/MU_y for A must equal

---

[14]The one-for-one exchange ratio used here is not the only one at which the initial exchange could occur. Both parties can gain from any exchange ratio at which the amount of X that A is willing to give up to get a pint of Y exceeds the amount of X that B would require to give up a pint of Y.

MU_x/MU_y for B. When these conditions do not hold, it becomes worthwhile for the parties to engage in exchange until they do.

Value in Use and Value in Exchange

The development of a utility theory of choice and exchange enabled economists to explain what the early classical economists of the late eighteenth and early nineteenth centuries called the diamond-water paradox. The paradox was that some goods, like diamonds, have a limited total use value to any one person; yet in markets they have a very high exchange value. Other goods, like water, have a very great total use value to any one person; yet in markets they have a very low exchange value. Early economists were unable to provide a satisfactory explanation of this phenomenon.

Table 6-3   The Diamond-Water Paradox

Water			Diamonds		
Gallons per Year	MU per 100 Gal.	TU	Carats per Year	MU per Carat	TU
100	30	30	1	40	40
200	28	58	2	36	76
300	26	84	3	24	100
400	24	108	4	10	110
500	22	130	5	0	110
600	20	150			
700	18	168			
800	16	184			
900	12	196			
1000	8	204			

The subjective value, or marginal utility, economists of the late nineteenth century used a device like Table 6-3 to provide the answer. Measuring water in 100-gallon units and diamonds in carats, suppose that when consumer A is maximizing satisfaction he consumes 900 gallons of water and 2 carats of diamonds per year. The total utility of water to him is 196 units of utility. But how does he value any of the 100-unit increments of the total supply? The definition of marginal utility informs us that at the 900-gallon consumption level 100 gallons contributes 12 units of utility to his satisfaction level. He would be willing to trade 100 gallons of water for units of any other good that provides a marginal utility of 12 or more units.

Diamonds, on the other hand, provide a total of 76 units of utility at the 2-carat level of consumption. But the marginal utility of a carat of diamonds is 36 units. The consumer would not be willing to trade a carat of diamonds for units of any other good unless the marginal utility of such a good were 36 utility units or more.

The water, which has great use value to him, has a low exchange value because its supply to him is large and its marginal utility to him is low. The diamonds, which have a much lower use value to him, have a high exchange value because their supply to him is small and their marginal utility is high. Exchange value of a good, then, is really determined by the use value to the consumer of the marginal unit; that is, by the marginal utility of a unit of the good.

Summary

The utility approach to the theory of individual consumer choice and demand is a special case of the indifference curve approach. It can be used to explain, among other things, the consumer's allocation of income among the goods that he buys, the consumer's demand curve for any given product, and the exchange of goods among individuals. The conclusions reached depend upon the principle of *relatively* diminishing marginal utility of any one good or service as the consumption of it is increased relative to that of other goods and services.

A consumer seeks to maximize the satisfaction derived from the goods and services obtainable with his given income. Maximization requires that he allocate his income among them in such a way that when he is spending his entire income, the marginal utility per dollar's worth of one is equal to the marginal utility per dollar's worth of every other good or service.

To establish the consumer's demand curve for any one good, we vary its price, holding constant the prices of other goods, the consumer's income, and his tastes and preferences as shown by his utility schedules or curves. At each of the prices the consumer maximizes satisfaction, thus determining the quantity that will be taken at each price. The resulting price-quantity combinations form his demand schedule and can be plotted as his demand curve.

Voluntary exchange of goods among individuals increases the welfare of both parties to the exchange. Incentives for voluntary exchange occur wherever the ratios of the marginal utilities of goods for one consumer differ from the corresponding ratios for another. The condition for simultaneous equilibrium for all consumers is that the ratios of marginal utilities of all goods be the same for all individuals.

Suggested Readings

Boulding, Kenneth E., *Economic Analysis*, 4th ed., vol. 1, (New York: Harper & Row Publishers, 1966), Chap. 24.

Marshall, Alfred, *Principles of Economics*, 8th ed. (London: Macmillan & Co., Ltd., 1920), Bk. III, Chaps. V and VI.

Stigler, George J., "The Development of Utility Theory, I," *The Journal of Political Economy*, vol. LVIII (August 1950), pp. 307–324.

Chapter 7:

Market Classifications and the Demand Curve Faced by the Firm

The discussion of demand in earlier chapters was consumer-oriented, for consumers originate demand. In this chapter we will look at demand from a different viewpoint—that of the individual business firm desiring to produce and sell a product.

No special definition of the firm is necessary at this point. The concept used here is the ordinary one of an individual business concern; it may be a single proprietorship, a partnership, or a corporation. To simplify exposition, we shall assume that a firm produces one product only.

The demand curve faced by a firm for its product shows the amounts that it can sell at different possible prices, other things being equal; and this curve could appropriately be called a sales curve. Its nature depends on the type of market in which the firm sells. Selling markets are usually classified into four different types based on: (1) the importance of individual firms in relation to the entire market in which they sell and (2) whether or not the products sold in a particular market are homogeneous. The market types are (1) pure competition, (2) pure monopoly, (3) oligopoly, and (4) monopolistic competition. Markets of the real world do not always fall neatly into one classification or another, but may be a mixture of two or more. However, it is useful in establishing a frame of reference to analyze the demand curve faced by the firm in each of the four theoretical or pure classifications. Detailed analysis of pricing and output under each will follow in Chapters 10-13.

Pure Competition

The conditions necessary for pure competition to exist in a market were outlined in Chapter 3. In pure competition there are many firms selling identical products with no one firm large enough relative to the entire market to influence the market price. If one firm drops out of the market supply is not decreased enough to cause the price to increase perceptibly. Neither is it feasible for one firm to expand output enough to cause any perceptible decrease in market price. No single seller feels that he affects or is affected by other sellers in the market. No rivalries arise. There will be no reactions of other firms to actions taken by any one firm. Relationships among firms will be impersonal.

The Demand Curve

Under these circumstances the demand curve facing the firm is horizontal at the prevailing market or equilibrium price. At any price above the prevailing market price it can sell nothing. Since all firms of the industry sell identical products, consumers will turn to firms charging the market price if one firm raises its selling price above that level. The proportion of the total market filled by one seller is so small that the firm can dispose of its entire output at the prevailing market price; hence, there is no necessity for lowering the price below that of the other sellers. Any firm attempting to do so will find itself swamped with buyers who promptly bid it back up to the equilibrium level.

A producer of potatoes faces this sort of demand curve. When he hauls his potatoes to market he receives the going market price. On the one hand, if he asks for more than the market price and sticks to his request, he will undoubtedly haul the potatoes home again. On the other hand, no amount of potatoes that he alone can bring to market will drive the price down. He can sell all he desires to sell at the going market price.

Diagrammatically the nature of the demand curve faced by the firm is illustrated by dd on the left-hand side of Figure 7-1. The market demand curve and the market supply curve are DD and SS, respectively. The market price is p; it determines the horizontal infinitely elastic demand curve faced by the firm. The price axes of the two diagrams are identical; however, quantity measurements of the market diagram are compressed considerably as compared with those of the firm diagram. For example, if x_0 measures 10 units of X for the firm, suppose that X_0 measures 10,000 units of X for the total market.

In reality the demand curve faced by the firm is an infinitesimal segment of the market demand curve in the neighborhood of quantity X stretched out over the firm diagram. Any one firm can be thought of as

Figure 7–1 The Demand Curve Facing the Firm – Pure Competition

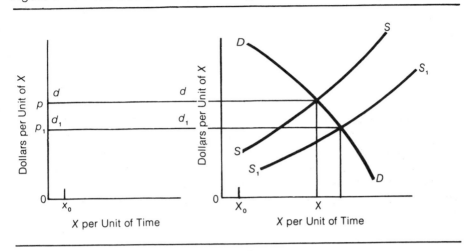

supplying the last small portion of quantity X. Stretching this small segment out over the firm diagram makes the demand curve faced by the firm appear to be horizontal.

Influence of the Firm on Demand, Price, and Output

Any forces that change market demand or market supply will change the market price of the product and, consequently, the demand curve faced by the firm. The firm by itself can do nothing about either the demand curve it faces or the market price. It must accept both as given data. If market supply increases to S_1S_1, the market price decreases to p_1, and the demand curve faced by the firm shifts downward to d_1d_1. Any such change is beyond the control of the individual firm. The firm can only adjust its output, and will gear its output to the prevailing market price.

Pure Monopoly

Pure monopoly is a market situation in which a single firm sells a product for which there are no good substitutes. The firm has the market for the product all to itself. There are no similar products whose price or sales will influence the monopolist's price or sales perceptibly, and vice-versa. Cross-elasticity of demand between the monopolist's product and other products will either be zero or small enough to be neglected by all firms in the economy. The monopolist does not believe that actions of his will evoke retaliation of any kind from firms in other industries. Similarly, he does not consider actions taken by firms in other industries to be of sufficient importance to warrant his taking them into account. The monopolist *is* the industry from the producing point of view. A case in point is the supplier of telephone service to a particular community.

The Demand Curve

The market demand curve for the product is also the demand curve faced by the monopolist. Figure 7-2 shows the market demand curve for the product that is produced and sold by a monopolist. It shows the different quantities that buyers will take off the market at all possible prices. Since the monopolist is the only seller of the product, he can sell at different possible prices in exactly the amounts that buyers will take at those prices.

Influence of the Firm on Demand, Price, and Output

The monopolist is able to exert some influence on the price, output, and the demand for his product. The market demand curve delineates the limits of the monopolist's market. Faced by a given demand curve, he can increase sales if he is willing to lower his price, or he can increase his price if he is willing to restrict his sales volume. Additionally, he may be able to affect the demand curve itself through sales promotion activities of various kinds. He may be able to induce more people to want his product, thus increasing demand; and he may be able to make demand less elastic if he can convince enough people that they cannot afford to be without the product. It follows that if the monopolist is able to increase demand he can increase sales to some extent without lowering the price or, alternatively, he can increase the price to some extent without restricting his sales volume.

Oligopoly

An oligopolistic industry is one in which the number of sellers is small enough for the activities of a single seller to affect other firms and for the activities of other firms to affect him in turn. Changes in the output and the price of one firm will affect the amounts which other sellers can sell and the prices that they can charge. Hence, other firms will react in one way or another to price-output changes on the part of a single firm. Individual sellers are interdependent; not independent as they are under pure competition or pure monopoly.

Figure 7-2   The Demand Curve Facing the Firm—Pure Monopoly

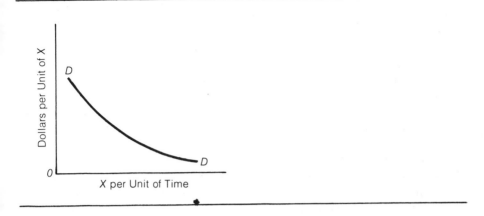

Oligopolistic industries are frequently classified as *differentiated* or *pure*. A differentiated oligopolistic industry is one in which the firms produce and sell *differentiated products*. The products of all firms in the industry are very good substitutes for each other—they have high cross elasticities of demand—but the product of each firm has its own distinguishing characteristics. The differences may be real or fancied. They may consist of differences in quality and design, as is the case in the automobile industry; or they may consist merely of differences in brand names, as is the case in the sale of aspirin tablets.

A pure oligopolistic industry is one in which the firms produce virtually identical products. Purchasers have little cause for preferring the product of one firm to that of another on any basis except price. Examples of industries approaching the pure oligopoly category are the cement, aluminum, and steel industries.

The Demand Curve

There is no typical demand situation facing an oligopolistic firm. The interdependence of sellers in an oligopolistic market makes the determination of the single seller's demand curve difficult. In some situations the demand curve faced by the firm is indeterminate. In others it can be located with some degree of accuracy.

The oligopolistic seller's demand curve will be indeterminate when he cannot predict what the reactions of his rivals will be to price and output changes on his part. The output that the one firm can sell if it changes its price depends on the manner in which other firms react to this price change.

The range of possible reactions is fairly broad. Rivals may just meet the price change; they may change price in the same direction but by less than the change of the original seller; they may exceed the price change; they may improve the quality of their products; they may engage in extensive advertising campaigns; or they may react in other ways. Inability of the individual seller to predict which reactions will occur and in what degree they will occur amounts to inability to determine the demand curve he faces.

When the single seller knows with some accuracy how his rivals will react to price changes on his part, the demand curve he faces becomes correspondingly more determinate. If he can form reliable judgments with regard to the probable effect of rivals' reactions to his own sales, he can take these into account. However, each different reaction by each different rival will result in different quantities that the single seller can market. Consequently, ascertaining the effects of rivals' reactions to the quantities that can be sold at different prices is at best a complex process for the individual firm. A few examples should improve our grasp of the problems involved.

Suppose that there are two producers in a particular industry, and that price changes by either will be just matched by the other. Suppose also that the producers are of approximately equal size and prestige and produce virtually identical products. The market demand curve is *DD* in Figure 7-3. If each firm knows the other will just match his price changes, at any given price each will expect to get approximately half the market. Each will face a fairly determinate demand curve *dd* for his output, and such a demand curve will lie about halfway between *DD* and the price axis.

Suppose now that one producer does not behave in the way just described. With an initial price of *p* suppose that when Firm *A* cuts the price, Firm *B* cuts the price still further. Firm *B* will take some of Firm *A*'s customers away. The demand curve faced by Firm *A* will not then follow *dd* but will follow some path such as the broken line *d'*. Firm *A*, since its rival reacts by cutting price still more, will lose a part of its share of the market when it cuts its price. Firm *A* will not take this situation lying down. It may undercut *B*'s price again, and the situation may develop into a price war — an indeterminate situation.

Suppose that the producers in a given oligopolistic industry form a cartel. Under the cartel arrangement the firms of the industry act as a single unit, each having some voice in the setting of price, output, and other industry policies. When all firms act as a unit the amount that one firm can sell at different possible prices becomes irrelevant. The cartel is concerned with how much the industry as a whole can sell at different possible prices. Thus, the cartel is in much the same position as a pure mo-

Figure 7-3   The Demand Curve Facing the Firm—Oligopoly

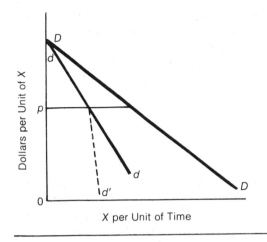

nopolist is, and it is the cartel that faces the market demand curve. The demand curve faced by a single firm fails to be a consideration.

These examples provide a small sample of the possible demand situations faced by an oligopolistic seller. Additional illustrations will be presented in Chapter 12. Our goal at this point is to show that when the demand curve faced by one seller is determinate, the curve's position and its shape will depend on what the reactions of rivals will be to price changes on the part of the single firm.

Influence of the Firm on Demand, Price, and Output

Generally, the oligopolist is able to influence in some degree the demand curve faced by him, his price, and his output. Through sales promotion efforts he may be able to shift the demand curve for what he sells to the right—partly by increasing consumer demand for this type of product, but mostly by inducing consumers to desert his rivals and buy his brand. He may be able to accomplish this through advertising or through design and quality changes, provided such changes give his brand more customer appeal. Rivals will not be sitting idly by in such cases and may retaliate by vigorous campaigns of their own. The firms with the most successful campaigns will be the ones which succeed in increasing demand for their brands.

Whether the firm does or does not face a determinate demand curve, it knows that in general its demand curve slopes downward to the right. To increase sales it must usually lower price—unless the sales increase is made possible by a shift to the right of the demand curve. Higher prices can be obtained at the expense of sales, unless they are obtained through or in conjunction with increases in demand. Generally, the demand curve faced by an individual oligopolist will be fairly elastic because of the existence of good substitutes produced by other firms in the industry. Elasticity of demand, however, as well as the position of the demand curve, will depend on rivals' reactions to the price and output changes of the single seller.

Monopolistic Competition

Monopolistic competition is a market situation in which there are many sellers of a particular product, but the product of each seller is in some way differentiated, in the minds of consumers, from the product of every other seller. As in pure competition there are enough sellers, and each is small enough relative to the entire market so that the activities of one will have no effects on the others. Relationships among firms are impersonal. Product differentiation may take the form of brand names, trademarks, quality differences, or differences in conveniences or services offered to consumers. The products are good substitutes for each other—their cross elasticities are high. Examples of industries approaching monopolistic competition include the women's hosiery industry, various textile products, and service trades in large cities.

The Demand Curve

The shape of the demand curve faced by the firm under monopolistic competition stems from product differentiation. The influence of product differentiation can be seen readily if at first we assume its absence. This assumption leaves us with the case of pure competition and a horizontal demand curve such as dd in Figure 7-4. Now suppose we introduce the concept of product differentiation and observe how dd is affected. When products are differentiated, consumers become more or less attached to particular brand names. At any given price for commodity X some consumers will be on the margin of switching to other brands, while others are attached to X at that price with varying degrees of tightness.

Suppose that for the monopolistic competitor quantity x will be taken at price p. If the firm raises the price, those consumers on the verge of switching to other brands will make the switch, since the other brands are now relatively lower in price. The higher the firm raises its price, the more customers it will lose to relatively lower-priced brands. Since other brands will usually be very good substitutes for that of the firm under considera-

Figure 7–4 The Demand Curve Facing the Firm—Monopolistic Competition

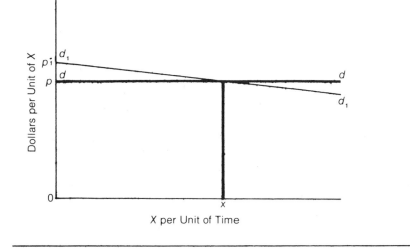

tion, the rise in price necessary for the firm to lose all its customers (pp_1) will not be large. For price increases above p the demand curve faced by the firm will be the lighter line in the diagram. Similarly, if the firm lowers the price below p, it will pick up marginal customers of other sellers, since its price is now relatively lower as compared with other firms' prices. It will not have to lower price much to pick up all the additional customers it can handle. Thus, for decreases in price below p, the lighter line in the diagram shows the demand curve faced by the one firm. The entire demand curve faced by the monopolistic competitor is one such as d_1d_1.

It may be thought that price reductions by one firm that attract customers away from the other firms in the industry will evoke some kind of retaliatory action on the part of the other firms, as in the case of oligopoly. Such is not the case, however, because there are many firms in a monopolistically competitive industry. The firm that reduces its price will attract so few customers from each of the others that the other firms will not notice or feel the loss. Nevertheless, for the one firm the total increase in customers will be substantial.

Likewise, it may seem that the price increases by one firm that drive customers away would increase demand for the products of the other firms. But the customers shifting to other firms will be widely scattered among those firms. Not enough will go to any other single firm to cause any perceptible increase in demand for its product, even though the loss of customers to the price-raising firm is substantial.

Influence of the Firm on Demand, Price, and Output

The individual firm in a monopolistically competitive industry may be able to influence demand for its own product to some perceptible degree through advertising. But the existence of many good substitutes will preclude much success in this direction.

The firm is subjected to highly competitive forces, yet it is to a small extent a sort of monopolist since it has some discretion in setting price and output. However, if the firm raises price very much it loses all its customers; and it does not have to lower price very far to secure all the customers it can handle. Within that limited price range the firm has price-setting discretion. Outside that price range it is subject to competitive forces. The demand curve faced by a firm under monopolistic competition will be highly elastic throughout its relevant range. The cause is not hard to find. The products of all firms in the industry, even though differentiated, are very good substitutes for each other.

Summary

Analysis of the demand situation facing the individual business firm is organized around four market classifications. The conditions of demand facing the individual firm differ from classification to classification, these differences stemming from two sources: (1) the importance of the individual firm in the market in which it sells and (2) product differentiation or product homogeneity.

Pure competition stands at one extreme of the classification and pure monopoly stands at the other. Purely competitive firms sell homogeneous products, and each is so small relative to the entire market that by itself it cannot influence market price. Hence, the demand curve faced by the firm is horizontal at the equilibrium market price. A monopolist is a single seller of a product not closely related to any other product. He faces the market demand curve for his product.

Oligopoly and monopolistic competition fill the gap between these two extremes. Monopolistic competition differs from pure competition in one respect only—products of different sellers are differentiated. This fact gives the monopolistic competitor a small amount of control over his price; however, each firm is so small relative to the entire market that by itself it cannot affect other firms in the industry. It faces a downward-sloping, highly elastic demand curve.

With regard to the number of firms in the industry, oligopoly lies between the extremes of pure competition and monopolistic competition on the one hand and pure monopoly on the other. Its primary characteristic is that there are few enough firms in the industry for the activities of one firm to have repercussions on the price and sales of the other firms. Hence, rivalries develop under oligopoly. The demand curve faced by a single seller depends on what the reactions of rivals will be to market activities on the part of the one firm. If the reactions of rivals cannot be predicted, the demand curve faced by the firm cannot be determined.

Suggested Readings

Fellner, William, *Modern Economic Analysis* (New York: McGraw-Hill, Inc., 1960), Chap. 17.
Machlup, Fritz, "Monopoly and Competition: A Classification of Market Positions," *American Economic Review*, vol. XXVII (September 1937), pp. 445–451.

Chapter 8:

The Principles of Production

In order to understand costs, supply curves, resource pricing and employment, resource allocation, and the distribution of the economy's product output, one must first understand the principles of production. Production theory, like the theory of consumer behavior, is basically a theory of choice among alternatives. The key economic unit is the individual firm rather than the individual consumer. Whereas the individual consumer attempts to maximize satisfaction by the way in which he spends his income on consumer goods, the individual firm attempts to maximize the product output it can obtain with any given cost outlay by the way in which it secures and combines resource inputs. A fundamental difference between the two theories is that the purchasing power of the consumer is more or less fixed, while the possible outlays of the firm are variable. This difference will not be of much concern in the present chapter, but will be important later on.

In this chapter the concept of a firm's production function is first explained, and then the law of diminishing returns is considered. Finally, resource product curves and the efficiencies of various resource combinations are analyzed.

The Production Function

The Concept

The term *production function* refers to the physical relationships between a firm's inputs of resources and its output of goods or services per unit of time, leaving prices aside. It can be expressed in general mathematical terms as:

$$x = f(a, b, c). \tag{8.1}$$

The firm's output is represented by x, and its inputs are represented by a, b, and c. The equation can be expanded readily to include as many different resources as are used in the production of any given commodity. It furnishes a convenient way of relating product output to resource inputs.

Firms can usually vary the proportions in which resources are combined in production processes; and this flexibility brings about several possible types of relations among inputs, inputs and outputs, and among outputs. Where inputs can be substituted for one another in the production of a product, there will be a number of alternative sets of input quantities that will produce a given level of product output, and the firm makes choices among these. By increasing or decreasing the quantities of all resource inputs used, the firm can increase or decrease its output level. It can also increase or decrease output within limits by increasing or decreasing the quantity used of one or more resource inputs, holding the quantities of other resource inputs constant. And, given the bundle of resources available to it, a firm that produces more than one product can increase its output level of one product by reducing its output level of another, transferring the resources thus released to the production of the first.

The input-input, input-output, and output-output relationships that characterize a firm's production function depend on the techniques of production used. Of the range of techniques available, we assume the firm will use those that are most efficient; that is, the ones that will provide the greatest value of output for a given value of input. Generally speaking, an improvement in techniques will increase the output that can be produced from given quantities of resources.

The Production Surface

In many ways a firm's production function is analogous to the preference function or the utility function of an individual consumer, although one must be careful not to confuse the two. A firm uses resource inputs to generate product or service outputs. Usually these quantities have cardinal properties—the product output can be measured, added, and, in most cases, seen. An individual consumer purchases and uses products and services to generate a much more nebulous kind of output—satisfaction or utility.

Suppose, then, that a firm uses two resource inputs, A and B, to obtain outputs of product X. In the three-dimensional diagram of Figure 8-1 (a), the coordinates in the horizontal AB plane show input combinations. Product output associated with each input combination is measured vertically

Figure 8 – 1   A Production Surface and an Isoquant

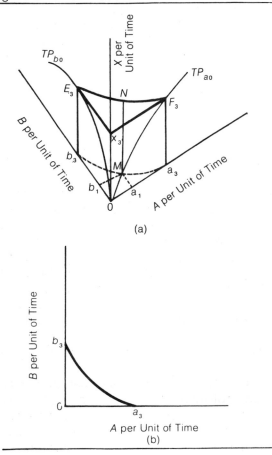

(a)

(b)

above the plane. If no resource A is used, total product curve TP_{b0} is generated by varying the quantity of resource B used. An output of $b_3E_3 (= Ox_3)$ is produced with b_3 of B alone. Similarly, if no resource B is used, TP_{a0} is generated by varying the quantity of resource A used. With a_3 of A the output level is $a_3F_3 (= Ox_3)$. A combination of b_1 of B and a_1 of A yields an output level of MN. The whole range of input combinations generates an inverted bowl-shaped production surface, showing the output associated with every possible input combination.

Isoquants   Contour lines can be drawn around the production surface of Figure 8-1 (a) at each possible level of output. All points on a given contour line are equidistant from the AB plane; that is, any one contour line represents a constant or given level of production. These contour lines can be projected downward onto the *AB* plane, forming a set of *isoquants*, or product indifference curves. Any one isoquant, say b_3a_3 in Figure 8-1, shows the different combinations of *A* and *B* with which the firm can obtain a product output of x_3. If the production surface has an inverted bowl-shape, higher contour lines, when projected to the *AB* plane, become isoquants lying farther from the origin of the diagram. A complete set of isoquants for the firm is called its isoquant map.[1]

Isoquant Characteristics   The general characteristics of isoquants are the same as those of indifference curves. First, they slope downward to the right for those combinations of resources that firms will want to use. Second, they do not intersect. Third, they are convex to the origin of the diagram.

Isoquants slope downward to the right for the resources that can be substituted for one another in the production process. For example, usually there are possibilities of substitutions between capital resources and labor resources used. If less of one is used, more of the other must be used to compensate for the decrease in the first, if the level of output is to remain constant. Exceptions will occur where resources cannot be substituted for one another in production processes.[2] There are no substitutes for raw milk as an input in the production of the pasteurized product. In other cases, in the short run, fixed proportions of a resource may be required.

An intersection of isoquants has no logical economic explanation. An intersection point would mean that a single combination of resources produces two different maximum outputs, thereby implying that an increase in the level of output can be accomplished with no increase in the amount of any resource used. To the right of the intersection point the implication is that by decreasing the quantities of all resources used, product output can be increased. Thus, isoquant intersections are economic nonsense.

Convexity to the origin reflects the fact that while different resources may be substitutes for each other, they are not ordinarily perfect substitutes. Consider labor and capital used in digging a ditch of a certain length, width, and depth. Within limits they can be substituted for each other. But the more labor and the less capital used to dig the ditch, the more difficult it becomes to substitute additional labor for capital. Addi-

---

[1]From the production function:

$$x = f(a, b)$$

a given isoquant is defined by assigning a value to *x*. For example:

$$x_6 = f(a, b).$$

The isoquant map is described by a family of isoquants obtained by assigning different values to *x*.

[2]*See* Sidney Weintraub, *Intermediate Price Theory* (Philadelphia: Chilton Company, Book Division, 1964) pp. 34, 40–42, for a discussion of the exceptions.

Figure 8–2   *Effects on Total Product of Quantity Changes in One Resource*

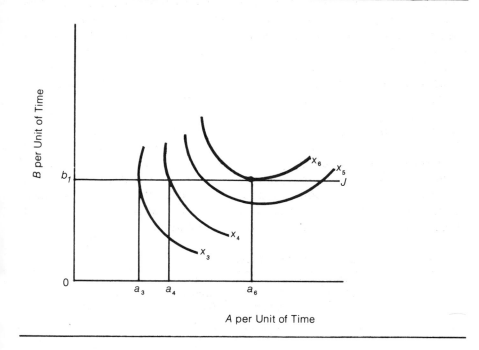

tional units of labor will just compensate for smaller and smaller amounts of capital given up. The same reasoning applies to other resources.

The more of resource A and the less of resource B the firm uses to produce a constant amount of product X, the more difficult it becomes to substitute additional units of A for B; that is, additional units of A will just compensate for smaller and smaller amounts of B given up. This principle is called the principle of *diminishing marginal rate of technical substitution of A for B ($MRTS_{ab}$)*. The $MRTS_{ab}$ is measured at any point on an isoquant by the slope of the isoquant at that point. It is the amount of B lost which will be just compensated for by an additional unit of A at that point.

Product Curves

Product schedules and product curves for either resource A or resource B can be derived from the firm's system of isoquants. With reference to Figure 8-2, suppose the firm considers the employment of alternative quantities of A per unit of time with a fixed amount b_1 of B. A movement to the right along the line b_1J reflects the use of larger quantities of A. Each isoquant intersected by line b_1J shows the product output for each quantity of A. Thus, when a_4 of A is used with b_1 of B, total product will be x_4. The greater the amount of A used, the greater will be the total product until the firm is using a_6 of the resource. With greater quantities of A, line $b_1 J$ intersects lower and lower isoquants, showing that total product decreases. Thus, the firm would never use more than a_6 of A with b_1 of B, even if A were free. The total product curve for larger and larger quantities of A used with the fixed amount of B increases, reaches a maximum at a_6 of A, and then decreases. This curve is shown in Figure 8-3.

The average product and marginal physical product schedules or curves of a resource are derived from its total product schedule or curve. Suppose that a firm conducts a series of experiments to determine the total product output it can get from various quantities of labor per unit of time used with one unit of capital. The results are listed in column (3) of Table 8-1 as the *total product* of labor. As the amount of labor is increased up to 7 units, output increases. At 7 and 8 units of labor the maximum total product that a unit of capital will produce is obtained.

Table 8-1   Product Schedules for Labor

(1) Capital	(2) Labor	(3) Total Product (Labor)	(4) Average Product (Labor)	(5) Marginal Physical Product (Labor)	
1	1	3	3	3	⎫
1	2	7	3½	4	⎬ Stage I
1	3	12	4	5	⎭
1	4	16	4	4	⎫
1	5	19	3⁴/₅	3	⎬ Stage II
1	6	21	3½	2	⎭
1	7	22	3¹/₇	1	
1	8	22	2¾	0	⎫
1	9	21	2⅓	−1	⎬ Stage III
1	10	15	1½	−6	⎭

The *average product* of labor, computed from columns (2) and (3), is the total product of labor at each level of employment divided by that quantity of labor. Note that in column (4) average product rises as the quantity of labor is increased, reaches a maximum at 3 and 4 units of labor per unit of capital, and then decreases as the employment of labor is increased further.

The change in total product per unit change in the quantity of labor employed, holding the quantity of capital constant, is called the *marginal physical product* of labor. In Table 8-1 an increase in the employment of labor from 0 to 1 unit increases total product from 0 to 3; thus the marginal

Figure 8–3   Total Product Curve for One Resource

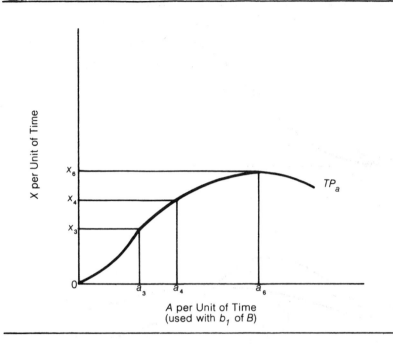

physical product of labor at the 1-unit level of employment is 3 units of product. Two units of labor employed rather than 1 increase total product to 7; and the marginal physical product of labor at the 2-unit level of employment is 4 units of product. The rest of column (5) is computed in similar fashion.

The total, average, and marginal product concepts are shown graphically in Figure 8-4. The vertical axis of Figure 8-4 (a) measures product produced per unit of capital (Product/Capital); and the horizontal axis measures labor used per unit of capital (Labor/Capital). The total product curve (TP_ℓ) is in all essential respects like that of Figure 8-3.[3] When ℓ_1 units of labor are used on the unit of capital, total product reaches a maximum. In the illustration adding still more units of labor per unit of capital causes total product to decrease.

---

[3]The total product curve of Figure 8-4 begins at the origin of the diagram, but it is not necessary that it do so. For some resources not absolutely essential in the production of the product, it may begin above the orign – cottonseed meal fed to cows to increase milk production is a case in point. In other cases no product may be obtained until severl units of the variable resource are applied to the fixed complex of other resources. For example, one man in a steel mill will produce nothing. Two men can do no better. A certain minimum complement of labor is necessary before any production can be obtained. In this case the total product curve of labor begins to the right of the origin.

Figure 8–4   Product Curves for Labor

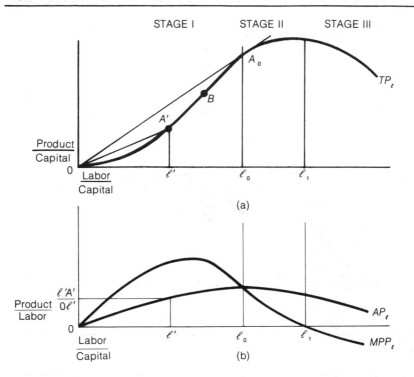

The average product curve for labor (AP_ℓ) drawn in Figure 8-4 (b) is derived from the total product curve (TP_ℓ) of Figure 8-4 (a). The vertical axis of Figure 8-4 (b) measures product per unit of labor (Product/Labor). The horizontal axis is the same as that of Figure 8-4 (a). Since average product is total product divided by the number of units of labor used, average product in Figure 8-4 (a) at ℓ' units of labor is $\ell'A'/0\ell'$, which measures the slope of the line $0A'$. This ratio is plotted in Figure 8-4 (b). As the quantity of labor is increased from zero to ℓ_0, the slopes of the corresponding $0A$ lines increase; that is, the average product of labor increases. At ℓ_0 units of labor the slope of line $0A_0$ is greater than that of any other $0A$ line drawn from the origin to the total product curve. Thus, the average product of labor is maximum at this point. Beyond ℓ_0 units of labor the average product decreases, but it remains positive as long as total product is positive. The slopes of the $0A$ lines corresponding to the various quantities of labor in Figure 8-4 (a) are plotted as the AP_ℓ curve in Figure 8-4 (b).

The slope of the total product curve at any given quantity of labor measures the marginal physical product of labor at that point. Both the slope of TP_ℓ and the marginal physical product of labor (MPP_ℓ) are defined as the change in total product per unit change in the quantity of labor used. Marginal physical product reaches a maximum at point *B*, where the total product curve turns from concave upward to concave downward. At quantity ℓ_1 of labor the total product is maximum; hence, marginal physical product is zero. Beyond ℓ_1, additional units of labor cause the total product to decrease, meaning that the marginal physical product is negative.[4] The slopes of TP_ℓ at the various quantities of labor in Figure 8-4 (a) are plotted as MPP_ℓ in Figure 8-4 (b).

An additional guide to the proper location of the marginal physical product curve is its relation to the average product curve. When average product is increasing, marginal physical product is greater than average product. When average product is maximum, marginal physical product equals average product. When average product is decreasing, marginal physical product is less than average product.[5] These relationships are verified by columns (4) and (5) of Table 8-1.

---

[4]Mathematically, if the total product of labor is represented by:

$$TP_\ell = x = f(\ell),$$

then the average product of labor is:

$$AP_\ell = \frac{x}{\ell} = \frac{f(\ell)}{\ell}$$

and the marginal physical product of labor is:

$$MPP_\ell = \frac{dx}{d\ell} = f'(\ell).$$

[5]To illustrate these relationships, consider a succession of men entering a room, each taller than the one who preceded him. As each man enters, the average height of the men in the room increases; however, except for the first man, average height will be less than that of the man currently entering. The height of each man as he enters is marginal height and is analogous to marginal physical product. Average height is analogous to average product. Thus, for average product (height) to be increasing, marginal physical product (height) must exceed the average.

Now suppose that additional men enter, each successively shorter than the one preceding him and all shorter than was average height before they entered. Average height will decrease, but will not be as low as marginal height. Where average height is maximum, the height of the last man who entered must have been equal to average height, since he caused neither an increase nor a decrease in average height.

Mathematically, if AP_ℓ is increasing, then:

$$\frac{d(AP_\ell)}{d\ell} = \frac{d\left(\frac{f(\ell)}{\ell}\right)}{d\ell} > 0,$$

so:

$$\frac{\ell \cdot f'(\ell) - f(\ell)}{\ell^2} > 0$$

$$f'(\ell) - \frac{f(\ell)}{\ell} > 0$$

and:

$$f'(\ell) > \frac{f(\ell)}{\ell};$$

that is, $MPP_\ell > AP_\ell$. Similarly, it can be shown that if AP_ℓ is constant, $MPP_\ell = AP_\ell$; and if AP is decreasing, $MPP_\ell < AP_\ell$.

The Law of Diminishing Returns

The product schedules of Table 8-1 and the product curves of Figure 8-4 illustrate the celebrated *law of diminishing returns*, which describes the direction and the rate of change that the firm's output takes when the input of only one resource is varied. It states that *if the input of one resource is increased by equal increments per unit of time while the inputs of other resources are held constant, total product output will increase; but beyond some point the resulting output increases will become smaller and smaller.*[6] If the increases in the variable resource are carried far enough, total product will reach a maximum and may then decrease. The law is consistent with observations that there are limits to the output that can be obtained by increasing the quantity of a single resource applied to constant quantities of other resources.

Diminishing returns may or may not occur for the first few one-unit increases in the variable resource used with the fixed quantities of other resources. It is possible for diminishing returns or diminishing increases in total product to occur for all such increments. This is frequently the case with the application of fertilizer to given complexes of seed, land, labor, and machinery.

But a stage of increasing returns may also characterize the initial increases in the variable resource before diminishing returns begin. An example of this situation is the amount of labor used to operate a factory of a given size. Smaller quantities of labor than that for which the factory is designed tend to operate inefficiently because of the multiplicity of jobs to be performed by each individual and because of time lost in changing from one job to another. Equal increments in labor used bring about successively greater increments in total product up to some point. In Table 8-1 through three units of labor, and in Figure 8-4 through ℓ_0 units of labor, we show increasing returns.[7] Beyond these points, increases in the quantity of labor used lead to diminishing returns.

Product Curves and Efficiency

The three product curves just described provide a means for determining how efficient various resource combinations will be in the process of production. At the outset we shall assume that the production function is *linearly homogeneous*, or that *constant returns to scale* prevail — changes of

---

[6]*The different quantities* of the variable resource refers to *alternative* quantities used with constant amounts of other resources, not to a chronological application of additional units.

[7]Whether or not we assume that diminishing returns occur at the outset is not important. Usually, for expository purposes we assume first increasing and then decreasing returns as the quantity of the variable resource is increased.

a given proportion in the quantities of all resources used will change product output in the same proportion. Both capital and labor are ·completely divisible with respect to quantities used; and techniques of production are such that the same techniques will be used for any given ratio of labor to capital, regardless of the absolute amount of resources used. To put this another way, we shall assume that the same techniques would be used if 2 units of labor work 1 unit of capital as are used if 1 unit of labor works 1/2 unit of capital or if 4 units of labor work 2 units of capital. A situation of this kind is called *constant returns to scale*—proportional changes in the quantities of all resources used change product output in the same proportion.[8]

Our major concern is with the *ratio* of the "variable" resource to the "fixed" resource. In arriving at the product curves we are not really limited to one unit of capital or whatever quantity the "fixed" resource happens to be. We can think of the firm as using any amount of capital it wishes to use; but in establishing the product curves, we convert our observations into terms of product obtainable from 1 unit of the "fixed" resource. For example, if 10 units of labor working 2 units of capital produce 38 units of product per unit of time, for purposes of establishing the product curves we would convert the data to an equivalent of 1 unit of capital—that is, 5 units of labor working 1 unit of capital produce an output of 19 units of product per unit of time. An increase in the quantity of capital used, with the quantity of labor being held constant, is equivalent to a decrease in the quantity of labor, with the quantity of capital being held constant.

The Three Stages for Labor

The product schedules of Table 8-1 and the product curves of Figure 8-4 can be divided into three stages. In each of the three stages the average product curve and the total product curve of labor provide information with regard to how efficiently the resources are used for various labor-capital ratios. As the ratio of labor to capital is increased—that is, as more and more labor per unit of capital is used—the average product curve provides information regarding the amount of product obtained per unit of labor for the various ratios. The total product curve provides information regarding the amount of product obtained per unit of capital.

Stage I is characterized by increases in the average·product of labor as more labor per unit of capital is used. These increases mean that the efficiency of labor—the product per worker—increases. The total product obtained per unit of capital as larger quantities of labor are applied to it

---

[8]In mathematical terms, the production function is said to be homogeneous of degree one, meaning that if:
$$x = f(a, b)$$
then:
$$\lambda x = f(\lambda a, \lambda b).$$

also increases in Stage I. The increases in total product show us that the efficiency of capital also increases in Stage I. Thus, increases in the quantity of labor applied to a unit of capital in Stage I increase the efficiency with which both labor and capital are utilized.

Stage II is characterized by decreasing average product and decreasing marginal physical product of labor. But the marginal physical product is positive since total product continues to increase. In Stage II, as larger quantities of labor per unit of capital are used, the efficiency of labor—product per worker—decreases. However, the efficiency of capital—product per unit of capital—continues to increase.

In Stage III the application of larger quantities of labor to a unit of capital decreases the average product of labor still more. Additionally, the marginal physical product of labor is negative and total product is decreasing. The efficiency of labor and the efficiency of capital both decrease when the firm pushes into Stage III combinations.

In looking over the three stages we note two things: The combination of labor and capital that leads to maximum efficiency of labor lies at the boundary line between Stages I and II; the combination of labor and capital leading to maximum efficiency of capital is the one at the boundary line between Stages II and III.

The Three Stages for Capital

Suppose we rework Table 8-1 and Figure 8-4 in such a way that we determine the product schedules and product curves for various quantities of capital applied to one unit of labor. This reworking enables us to show that Stage I for labor is Stage III for capital, that Stage III for labor is Stage I for capital, and that Stage II for labor is also Stage II for capital. We continue to assume that constant returns to scale prevail.

To facilitate comparison of the product curves of labor with those of capital it will be convenient to set up the product schedules of Table 8-2 and the product curves of Figure 8-5 in an unorthodox way. Table 8-2, showing the effects of increasing the ratio of capital to labor, should be read from bottom to top. Figure 8-5 read in the conventional way (from left to right) shows the effects of increasing the ratio of labor to capital; but read from right to left it shows the effects of increasing the ratio of capital to labor.

The Product Schedules   The results of this reworking of Table 8-1 are shown in Table 8-2. Starting at the bottom of Table 8-1, 10 units of labor are used per unit of capital. In a ratio sense this combination means the same thing as using 1/10 of a unit of capital per unit of labor. These numbers are shown in columns (1) and (2) in the last row of Table 8-2. Similarly, in terms of ratios, 9 units of labor per unit of capital are the same as 1/9

Table 8-2   Product Schedules for Capital

(1) Capital	(2) Labor	(3) Total Product (Capital)	(4) Marginal Physical Product (Capital)	(5) Average Product (Capital)	
1	1	3	$(-)1$	3	
$1/2$	1	$3^1/2$	$(-)3$	7	Stage III
$1/3$	1	4	0	12	
$1/4$	1	4	4	16	
$1/5$	1	$3^4/5$	9	19	Stage II
$1/6$	1	$3^1/2$	15	21	
$1/7$	1	$3^1/7$	22	22	
$1/8$	1	$2^3/4$	30	22	
$1/9$	1	$2^1/3$	75	21	Stage I
$1/10$	1	$1^1/2$	15	15	

of a unit of capital per unit of labor; and so on up through the table until we reach the top, where 1 unit of capital is used with 1 unit of labor. The ratios of capital and labor are the same throughout Tables 8-1 and 8-2.

The total product schedule for various amounts of capital applied to one unit of labor is determined from column (3) of Table 8-1. Ten units of labor applied to 1 unit of capital produce 15 units of product. Obviously, then, 1/10 of a unit of capital applied to 1 unit of labor should produce a total product of 15/10 or 1 1/2 units of product. This result is listed in the last row of column 3 in Table 8-2. Since 9 units of labor applied to 1 unit of capital produce 21 units of product, 1/9 of a unit of capital applied to 1 unit of labor will produce a total produce to 2 1/3. Total product of the larger quantities of capital used with 1 unit of labor is computed in a similar way to complete column (3).

The marginal physical product schedule for capital should show the increments in total product per full unit increment in capital at the various ratios of capital to labor used. The first 1/10 of a unit of capital used increases total product from 0 to 1 1/2 units. Therefore, at this ratio of capital to labor the marginal physical product of a unit of capital is 1 1/2 ÷ 1/10 = 3/2 × 10 = 15 units of product. This quantity is listed in column (4) in the last row of Table 8-2.

An increase in capital from 1/10 of a unit to 1/9 of a unit increases total product from 1 1/2 to 2 1/3. The product increment is 7/3 − 3/2 = 14/6 − 9/6 = 5/6 of a unit of product. The capital increment is 1/9 − 1/10 = 10/90 − 9/90 = 1/90 of a unit of capital. Marginal physical product of a unit of capital at this point is 5/6 ÷ 1/90 = 5/6 × 90 = 75 units of product. Column (4) is calculated by similar computations on up through columns (1) and (3) of Table 8-2.

Column (5) of Table 8-2, read from bottom to top, presents average product per unit of capital for the various capital-to-labor ratios. The average product of capital for each ratio is obtained by dividing the total product of capital by the quantity of capital used. Since 1/10 of a unit of capital produces 1 1/2 units of product, average product of capital equals 1 1/2 ÷ 1/10 = 15 at this point. Similarly, 2 1/3 units of product divided by 1/9 of a unit of capital equals an average product of capital at this point of 21 units. The other figures of column (5) are determined by similar computations.

When Table 8-1 is compared with Table 8-2, two columns of Table 8-1 turn out to be identical with two columns in Table 8-2. First, the total product schedule of labor applied to 1 unit of capital [see Table 8-1, column (3)] has become the average product schedule of land applied to 1 unit of labor [see Table 8-2, column (5)]. Second, the average product schedule of labor applied to 1 unit of capital [see Table 8-1, column (4)] has become the total product schedule of capital applied to 1 unit of labor [see Table 8-2, column (3)]. A little reflection will reveal that these relationships are as expected. The total product of more and more labor applied to one unit of capital is the average product of capital (or the product per unit of capital) as the ratio of labor to capital is increased. Likewise, the average product of labor (product per unit of labor) is necessarily the total product of various quantities of capital applied to one unit of labor.

A further observation can be made. Stages I, II, and III are marked off approximately for labor in Table 8-1.[9] Stages I, II, and III for capital are marked off approximately in Table 8-2. That which is Stage I for labor in Table 8-1 has become Stage III for capital in Table 8-2. That which is Stage III for labor in Table 8-1 has become Stage I for capital in Table 8-2. Stage II for labor is also Stage II for capital in both tables.

The Product Curves   In Figure 8-5 product curves for capital per unit of labor, as well as those of labor per unit of capital, are shown. The product curves for both labor applied to a unit of capital and capital applied to a unit of labor are drawn in the diagram. Reading the horizontal axes from left to right, the ratio of labor to capital is increasing, giving rise to the three familiar product curves for labor [TP_ℓ in Figure 8-5 (a); AP_ℓ and MPP_ℓ in Figure 8-5 (b)]. Reading the horizontal axes from right to left, the ratio of capital to labor is increasing. The total product curve of labor when the ratio of labor to capital is increased becomes the average product curve for capital when the ratio of capital to labor is increased. The average product curve for labor when the ratio of labor to capital is increased becomes the total product curve for capital when the ratio of

---

[9]The boundary lines between stages must be approximations when product schedules are set up in table form. Only on continuous graphs can the exact boundaries between the stages be established.

Figure 8–5   Product Curves for Capital

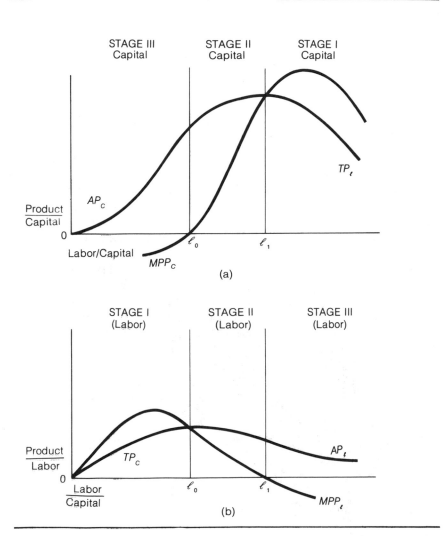

capital to labor is increased. Note that the marginal physical product curve for capital, reading from right to left in Figure 8-5 (a), lies above the average product curve for capital when average product is increasing, cuts the average product curve at its maximum point, and lies below the average product curve when that curve is decreasing. Note also that the marginal physical product curve for capital reaches zero at the ratio of capital to labor at which the total product of capital is maximum. The marginal physical product of capital is negative where increases in the quantity of capital per unit of labor lead to decreases in the total product of capital. The three stages for both capital and labor are shown in Figure 8-5.

Stage II Combinations

Stage II, which is common for both capital and labor, contains all the relevant ratios of labor to capital for the firm. The three stages—their relationships and their characteristics—are summed up in Table 8-3. In Stage I for labor, labor is used too sparsely on the capital; and increases in the ratio of labor to capital will increase its average product. Further, in Stage I for labor (Stage III for capital)* the marginal physical product of capital is negative. Too little labor per unit of capital means precisely the same thing as too much capital per unit of labor. The firm should increase the ratio of labor to capital used (or decrease the ratio of capital to labor used) at least to the point at which the average product of labor will no longer increase and the marginal physical product of capital will no longer be negative. Such an increase will place the firm in Stage II.

In Stage III for labor or Stage I for capital the marginal physical product of labor is negative, meaning that too much labor is used per unit of capital or that too little capital is used per unit of labor. The ratio of labor to capital should be decreased at least to the point at which the marginal physical product of labor is no longer negative; and this increase in the ratio of capital to labor will increase the average product of capital. Now only Stage II ratios remain with us.

Table 8-3   Symmetry of the Three Stages for Labor and Capital

Labor Productivity When the Ratio of Labor to Capital Is Increased		Capital Productivity When the Ratio of Capital to Labor Is Increased	
Stage I	Increasing AP_ℓ	Negative MPP_c	Stage III
Stage II	Decreasing AP_ℓ and MPP_ℓ, but MPP_ℓ is positive	Decreasing AP_c and MPP_c, but MPP_c is positive	Stage II
Stage III	Negative MPP_ℓ	Increasing AP_c	Stage I

The main points emerging from the foregoing discussion are worth emphasizing. The combination of labor and capital that yields maximum efficiency of labor lies at the boundary between Stage I and Stage II for labor (Stage II and Stage III for capital). The one that yields maximum efficiency for capital lies at the boundary between Stage I and Stage II for capital (Stage II and Stage III for labor).

The introduction of resource costs into the picture puts the economic issues facing the firm into proper perspective. Suppose that capital is so plentiful that it costs nothing at all, while labor is scarce enough to command some price. Because whatever cost outlay the firm makes will go for labor, the firm will achieve its greatest economic efficiency (lowest cost per unit of product) at the ratio of labor to capital that maximizes product per unit of labor.This ratio occurs at the boundary between Stages I and II for labor. The output per unit expenditure will increase through Stage I and decrease through Stages II and III.

Suppose labor can be had for the asking and capital is a scarce resource that commands a price. In this case the entire cost outlay goes for capital; and economic efficiency is greatest when the ratio of labor to capital is such that product per unit of capital is maximum. Stage I is again ruled out of consideration, since product per unit of capital (and per unit expenditure) increases as the ratio of capital to labor is increased throughout that stage. At the boundary between Stages I and II for capital (between Stages III and II for labor), product per unit of capital and product per unit of expenditure are maximum.

Suppose now that both labor and capital are economic resources; that is, both are scarce enough to command a price. Increases in the ratio of labor to capital in Stage I for labor increase both the product per unit of labor and the product per unit of capital. These increases also increase the product obtained per unit of expenditure on both; hence, the firm will move at least to the boundary between Stages I and II. If the firm moves into Stage II, increasing the ratio of labor to capital, the product per unit expenditure on labor decreases, while that per unit expenditure on capital increases. Which is more important, the increasing efficiency of capital or the decreasing efficiency of labor? We shall return to the question in a moment. If the firm moves into Stage III for labor the product per unit expenditure on capital and on labor both decrease; hence, when both resources have costs the firm should not go beyond the boundary line between Stages II and III for labor.

Labor to capital ratios of Stage I and Stage III for either resource are ruled out of the firm's consideration under all circumstances. The firm will not operate in Stage I for either resource when capital is free and when labor has costs, or when labor is free and capital has costs, or when both resources command prices. The same reasoning applies to Stage III. Stage II is left as the possible range of relevant ratios of labor to capital.

Which of the ratios of labor to capital falling within Stage II will the firm use? The answer depends on the comparative costs or prices per unit of capital and labor. We have already observed that if capital is free and labor must be paid, the firm will use the ratio at which Stage II for labor begins. If capital must be paid and labor is free, the firm will use the ratio at which Stage II for labor ends. From these points we can deduce that the less the price of capital relative to the price of labor, the closer the ratio should be to the beginning of labor's Stage II. The less the price of labor relative to the price of capital, the closer the ratios should be to the end of labor's Stage II. Thus, for any resource that a firm employs we can say that the firm should use some ratio of that resource to other resources that falls within Stage II for that resource.

A Generalized Stage II

Isoquant diagrams enable us to establish a generalized Stage II—not restricted to a linearly homogeneous production function. Consider the isoquant map in Figure 8-6. From it we can read off the set of resource combinations that will produce any given level of output. In addition, we can locate the total product curves for resource A—a different one for each different level of resource B with which alternative quantities of A are used. We can also locate the total product curves for resource B—one for each different quantity of A with which alternative quantities of B are used.

On any given isoquant the marginal rate of technical substitution of A for B is measured by the ratio of the marginal physical product of A to the marginal physical product of B. In Figure 8-6 suppose that combination M of A and B is used to produce x_6 of X. In moving from combination M to combination Q, holding the output level constant at x_6, the firm gives up MN of resource B for NQ of resource A. The reduction in output from giving up MN of B is $MN \times MPP_b$. The increase in output from NQ of A is $NQ \times MPP_a$. Since the reduction in output from giving up B must equal the increase in output from the additional A, then:

$$MN \times MPP_b = NQ \times MPP_a \qquad [8.2]$$

or:

$$\frac{MN}{NQ} = \frac{MPP_a}{MPP_b}$$

Since:

$$MRTS_{ab} = \frac{MN}{NQ}$$

then:

$$MRTS_{ab} = \frac{MPP_a}{MPP_b}$$

Figure 8-6   Stage II on an Isoquant Diagram

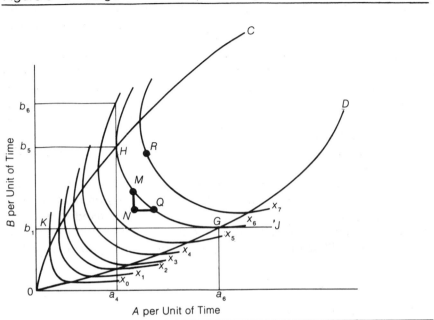

If the $MRTS_{ab}$ is 2, then MPP_a is twice as large as MPP_b, meaning that one additional unit of A will compensate for the loss of 2 units of B.[10]

The line OD joining the points at which isoquants become horizontal is called a *ridge line*. Consider point G on isoquant x_6. Since the slope of the isoquant, or $MRTS_{ab}$, is zero it is apparent that MPP_a is also zero at this point. For a movement to the right along line b_1d the total product of A will decline; and MPP_a is negative for such a movement. This situation means that the firm would be moving into Stage III for resource A. The same thing

---

[10]The marginal rate of technical substitution of A for B on any given isoquant is found by differentiating the isoquant equation as follows:

$$x = f(a, b)$$

and:

$$f_a \, da + f_b \, db = dx = 0.$$

So:

$$-\frac{db}{da} = \frac{f_a}{f_b} = MRTS_{ab}.$$

The partial derivatives f_a and f_b are, respectively, MPP_a and MPP_b. If an isoquant is to be convex to the origin then:

$$\frac{d\left(\frac{f_a}{f_b}\right)}{da} < 0.$$

can be said at every point along OD; consequently any combination of A and B to the right of OD is in a generalized Stage III for resource A. The upward slopes of those portions of the isoquants lying to the right of OD reflect the negative MPP_a in Stage III for A.

Line OC joining the points at which isoquants become vertical is also a ridge line. At point H an increase in resource B along line a_4H as extended will decrease the total product of B; that is, MPP_b is negative for the increase. The same thing can be said for any increase in B from a point on OC. Consequently, any combination of A and B that lies above OC is in Stage III for resource B.

The combinations comprising the area between ridge lines OD and OC thus constitute a generalized Stage II for both resources. These are the combinations that are relevant for the production decisions of the firm. We need not restrict our thinking to a linearly homogeneous production function or to a production function in which one resource is fixed in quantity. A change in the quantity of either resource from a combination such as R in the generalized Stage II area will result in diminishing returns for that resource.

The Least-cost Combination

Which of the Stage II combinations should a firm use in the production of its product? We assume that the firm's objective is to produce as efficiently as possible. To attain this goal means that whatever the level of output the firm chooses, the resource combination should be the one that keeps its cost outlay for that output as low as possible. This point can be put another way — whatever cost outlay the firm makes, it should use the resource combination that will produce the greatest amount of product for that cost outlay.

The problem facing a firm is essentially the same as that facing a consumer. Isoquants show the outputs the firm gets from "consuming" various combinations of resources. These are analogous to indifference curves, which show the "outputs" of satisfaction a consumer gets from consuming various combinations of goods and services. To complete the analogy we need the firm's counterpart of the consumer's budget line.

This counterpart is called an *isocost* or "equal-cost" curve. Let the firm's total cost outlay on resources A and B be T dollars, while the resource prices are p_a and p_b, respectively. In Figure 8-7 the amount of B that the firm can get if it buys no A is $\dfrac{T}{p_b}$. The amount of A that the firm can get if it buys no B is $\dfrac{T}{p_a}$. A line joining these two points shows all combinations of the

Figure 8–7　Cost Minimization

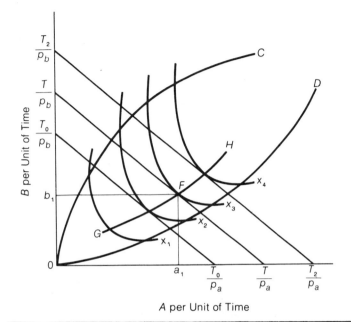

A per Unit of Time

two that cost outlay *T* will purchase. This line is called an isocost curve.[11] Its slope is:

$$\frac{T/p_b}{T/p_a} = \frac{T}{p_b} \times \frac{p_a}{T} = \frac{p_a}{p_b}.$$ [8.3]

The maximum output obtainable with a given cost outlay is that of the highest isoquant touched by the isocost curve. In Figure 8-7, given the firm's production function, resource prices of p_a and p_b, and a cost outlay of *T*, the maximum amount of *X* that can be obtained is x_3. This is produced with a_1 of *A* and b_1 of *B*. Any other combination that will produce x_3 lies above the isocost curve generated by cost outlay *T;* and as long as p_a and p_b remain constant, other combinations could be obtained only by increasing the cost outlay.

Changes in the firm's cost outlay, given the prices of resources *A* and *B*, will shift the isocost curve parallel to itself. If the cost outlay were a

---

[11]The set of isocost curves confronting a firm using two resources, *A* and *B*, can be represented by the equation:

$$ap_a + bp_b = T$$

smaller amount T_0, the isocost curve would shift to the left. Thus, in Figure 8-7 T_0 would be the least possible cost of producing output x_2. If the cost outlay were a greater amount, T_2, the isocost curve would shift to the right, and T_2 would be the least possible cost of producing output x_4. The line GH joining all points of equilibrium (least-cost resource combinations) for each possible cost outlay is called the *expansion path* of the firm.

The condition that must be met if the firm is to minimize costs for a given level of output is that the $MRTS_{ab} = p_a/p_b$. In Figure 8-7 the slope of the isoquant x_3 equals the slope of the isocost tangent to it at point F. Cost outlay T is thus the least possible cost of producing output x_3. The slope of the isocost at the point of tangency is p_a/p_b. The slope of the isoquant at the point is MPP_a/MPP_b. Therefore, at F the least-cost resource combination for producing x_3 is $MPP_a/MPP_b = p_a/p_b$. Rearranging the equation, we can write $MPP_a/p_a = MPP_b/p_b$. Thus, to secure a given output at the least possible cost the marginal physical product of a dollar's worth of one resource must be equal to the marginal physical product of a dollar's worth of every other resource used.[12]

Multiple Products

When two resources, A and B, are used to produce two products, X and Y, some distributions of the resources between the two uses will be more efficient than others. In the discussion that follows it makes no difference

---

[12]To minimize costs:

$$T = ap_a + bp_b \qquad [1]$$

for a given level of output:

$$x_1 = f(a, b) \qquad [2]$$

differentiate (2), obtaining:

$$\frac{db}{da} = -\frac{f_a}{f_b}. \qquad [3]$$

Then take the first partial derivative of T with respect to a, obtaining:

$$\frac{\delta T}{\delta a} = p_a + p_b \frac{db}{da}. \qquad [4]$$

Substituting (3) in (4) and setting the derivative equal to zero, we have:

$$\frac{\delta T}{\delta a} = p_a - p_b \frac{f_a}{f_b} = 0 \qquad [5]$$

and the necessary minimum-cost condition becomes:

$$\frac{p_a}{p_b} = \frac{f_a}{f_b}. \qquad [6]$$

that is:

$$MRTS_{ab} = \frac{p_a}{p_b}, \text{ or } \frac{MPP_a}{p_a} = \frac{MPP_b}{p_b}.$$

The sufficient condition for minimum cost is that at the point of tangency of the isoquant curve and the isocost line, the isoquant curve be convex to the origin, or:

$$\frac{d^2b}{da^2} > 0. \qquad [7]$$

Figure 8–8   Efficient Resource Distributions

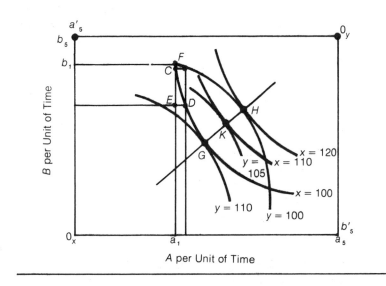

A per Unit of Time

whether the products are produced by the same or by different firms. We assume that the supplies of resources *A* and *B* are fixed amounts per unit of time; that is, the resource supply curves are perfectly inelastic.

The Edgeworth box in Figure 8-8 provides a convenient method for determining which distributions are most efficient. Let the quantity of resource *A* be $0_x a_5$ or $0_y a'_5$, and the quantity of resource *B* be $0_x b_5$ or $0_y b'_5$. Isoquants showing production levels of *X* are convex to the 0_x origin; and those showing production levels of *Y* are convex to the 0_y origin. Suppose the initial distribution of the two resources is shown by point *F* with $0_x a_1$ of *A* and $0_x b_1$ of *B* used in the production of *X*; and with $a_1 a_5$ of *A* and $b_1 b_5$ of *B* used in the production of *Y*.

Are these the best combinations of available resources for the production of *X* and *Y*? The output levels are 100 units of each. The slope of the $x = 100$ isoquant at point *F*, or $\dfrac{MPP_a}{MPP_b}$, in the production of *X* is greater than the slope of the $y = 100$ isoquant, or $\dfrac{MPP_a}{MPP_b}$, in the production of *Y*. This information means that if a unit of *A* is transferred from the production of *Y* to the production of *X*, with the output of *X* held constant at 100 units, the quantity of *B* released from the production of *X* is more than enough to compensate in the production of *Y* for the release of the unit of *A*. Suppose, for example that ED in Figure 8-8 represents the unit of A transferred from the production of Y to the production of X. If the production of X is held at the 100-unit level, EF units of B are released from the production of X. But to hold the output of Y constant at the 100-unit level, only CF units of B are needed to compensate for the unit of A transferred out. Thus we have a surplus of EC units of B if production of X and Y is held at the original levels.

The released units of B can be used to increase one or both of the product outputs. If the output of X is held at 100 units and the surplus B is turned to the production of Y, this usage constitutes a movement downward to the right around isoquant $x = 100$ and to a Y isoquant above the 100-unit level. Transfers of A from the production of Y to the production of X and of B from the production of X to the production of Y, carried from point F to point G, increase the output of Y to 110 units *without* decreasing the amount of X produced. If the released units of B were used to increase the output of X, holding Y constant at 100 units, a movement from F to H could take place, increasing the production of X to 120 units. The released B can be used to increase the production of both X and Y, moving from point F to some point K between G and H, where an X isoquant is tangent to a Y isoquant. As we have located it, point K represents output levels of 110 units of X and 105 units of Y. Clearly, in all of these cases the efficiency with which resources are used is increased.

Any one of the points—G, H, or K—is Pareto optimal. Resource redistributions from F to any one of these points increase the output of at least one of the products without decreasing the output of the other. But once the resource distribution becomes G, H, or K no further transfers of *any kind* can be made without decreasing the the output of at least one of the goods. A Pareto optimal distribution of resources is said to be an *efficient* distribution.

The condition that must be met for an efficient resource distribution is that $MPP_{ax}/MPP_{bx} = MPP_{ay}/MPP_{by}$; that is, the point locating the efficient distribution in the Edgeworth box must be a point of tangency between an isoquant of one product and an isoquant of the other. In Figure 8-8 the contract curve GKH extended is the locus of all such points. Any point on it, once reached, is Pareto optimal. We must be careful not to make more of this analysis than is there. All we have learned is that any distribution of resources, like F, that is not on the contract curve is inefficient. The output of one or both products can be increased by a redistribution of the resources between the two uses to a distribution that lies on a segment of the contract curve like GH—within the arcs of the isoquants that pass through F. The analysis tells us nothing about how much X and how much Y society wants produced. More information is needed to handle this problem.

Figure 8-9   Transformation Curve for Two Products

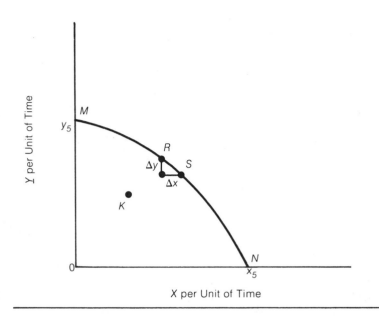

Transformation Curves

The information provided by the contract curve of Figure 8-8 is frequently displayed in the form of a *transformation curve* for the two products, showing the combinations of them that can be produced efficiently given the resource supplies and techniques of production available for producing them. In Figure 8-8, if all the resources available in the economy are used to produce Y, the total output of the product is shown by the Y isoquant that passes through 0_x. If this amount of Y is y_5, we can plot the combination as point M in Figure 8-9. Product X can be produced only if some of product Y is given up, with resources being transferred from the production of Y to the production of X. In Figure 8-8 the process of giving up successively more Y to produce successively more X is represented by a movement along the contract curve from 0_x toward 0_y. Each pair of tangent isoquants provides the X and Y output combinations that are plotted as the transformation curve in Figure 8-9. The larger the output of X, the smaller the amount of Y that can be produced; thus, the transformation curve must slope downward to the right. If all of the available resources are used to produce X, the total output is x_5 units per unit of time, as is shown by point N in Figure 8-9.

The approximate slope $\Delta y / \Delta x$ of the transformation curve between two points close together, such as R and S, measures the *marginal rate of transformation* of X and Y, or MRT_{xy}.[13] This is defined as the amount of Y that must be given up to produce an additional unit of X. The MRT_{xy} is shown as increasing in Figure 8-9, meaning that the less Y and the more X the economy chooses to produce, the more Y it must give up in order to produce an additional unit of X. The primary explanation of this relationship is that some of the economy's resources tend to be more specialized to the production of X, while others are much more useful in producing Y. When all of the economy's resources are used in producing Y, not much Y must be sacrificed to produce a unit of X, since those resources more specialized to the production of X are the ones that are transferred. However, the larger the output of X becomes, and the smaller the output of Y becomes, the more necessary it is to transfer those resources more specialized to the production of Y to production of the additional X. Consequently, larger and larger amounts of Y must be given up for one-unit increases in the output of X.

The transformation model provides an excellent summary of the production choices available to a society. If some of its resources are unemployed, the combination of goods will be one such as K lying below the transformation curve. The output of one or both products can be increased without decreasing the output of any other good. An inefficient distribution of resources brings about the same result. The combinations on the curve show the production possibilities or alternatives when resources are fully employed and are distributed or allocated efficiently. They are Pareto optimal production possibilities.

Summary

The principles of production lay the foundation for the analyses of costs, supplies, resource pricing and employment, resource allocation, and product distribution. These topics will be considered in later chapters.

The term production function is applied to the physical relationship between resource inputs and product output of a firm. Product output is determined partly by the quantities of resource inputs and partly by the techniques of production used by the firm. The production function can be summed up graphically as a production surface and displayed in two dimensions as an isoquant map.

---

[13]In terms of calculus, MRT_{xy} at any given point on the transformation curve is the slope of the curve at that point; that is dy/dx.

Holding the quantities of all other resources constant, the quantity of any one resource can be varied and the effects on product output can be observed. As the quantity of the variable resource is increased, the law of diminishing returns will become effective. We distinguished among total product, marginal physical product, and average product of the variable resource. The product schedules or product curves of the variable resource were divided into three stages. Stage I is characterized by increasing average product. In Stage II average and marginal physical product of the variable resource are decreasing, but its marginal physical product is still positive. In Stage III the marginal physical product of the variable resource is negative. We deduced that only those ratios of the variable resource to other resources lying within Stage II may be economically efficient for the firm to use.

The precise combination of variable resources that the firm should use depends on the marginal rate of technical substitution among those resources and on their respective prices. To maximize product with a given cost outlay, or to minimize cost for a given amount of product, resources should be combined in ratios such that the $MRTS_{ab} = p_a/p_b$; that is, so that the marginal physical product per dollar's worth of one equals the marginal physical product per dollar's worth of each other resource used.

An Edgeworth box is useful in showing the distributions of resources among products that are efficient in a Pareto optimal sense. The resulting contract curve provides the necessary information for establishing a transformation curve showing the optimal production possibilities for the economy.

Suggested Readings

Cassels, John M., "On the Law of Variable Proportions," *Explorations in Economics* (New York: McGraw-Hill, Inc., 1936), pp. 223–236. Reprinted in *Readings in the Theory of Income Distribution* (Philadelphia: P. Blakiston's Sons & Company, 1946), pp. 103–118.

Heady, Earl O., *Economics of Agricultural Production and Resource Use* (Englewood Cliffs, N.J.: Prentice-Hall, Inc., 1952), Chap. 2.

Knight, Frank H., *Risk, Uncertainty, and Profit* (Boston: Houghton Mifflin Company, 1921), pp. 94–104.

Tangri, O. P., "Omissions in the Treatment of the Law of Variable Proportions," *American Economic Review*, vol. LVI (June 1966), pp. 484–493.

Weintraub, Sidney, *Intermediate Price Theory* (Philadelphia: Chilton Company, Book Division, 1964), Chap. 3.

Chapter 9:

Costs of Production

Supplies of particular commodities are determined by costs of production; therefore, to understand supplies we must understand costs. Cost analysis is rooted in the principles of production. We shall start this discussion with the meaning of costs and follow through with a discussion of the short-run and long-run cost curves of the individual firm.

The Concept of Costs

The concept of costs of production as used in economic analysis differs somewhat from common usage of the term. The economic concept is more precise and consistent. Common usage ordinarily conveys some idea of the money involved in turning out a product; and it is not always clear which categories of expenditure are included and which excluded. To build up the concept as it is used in economics we shall consider first the alternative cost principle and then the implicit and explicit aspects of costs.

The Alternative Cost Principle

The basic idea of the alternative cost principal is contained in the transformation curve described in the last chapter. Under conditions of full employment, and when resources are efficiently allocated among goods and services, an increase in the output of any one product requires the sacrifice of some amounts of alternative products. If a certain kind of labor is used in making both washing machines and refrigerators, an increase in the output of refrigerators entails a reduction in the quantity of washing machines available, since labor must be withdrawn from that use. If steel is used in making automobiles and football stadiums, an increase in football stadiums leaves less steel available for making automobiles, reducing the number of automobiles that are manufactured. Thus, the production of any product requires the sacrifice of some value of alternative products.

Economists define the costs of production of a particular product as the value of the foregone alternative products that resources used in its production could have produced. This principle is called the *alternative cost principle*, or the *opportunity cost principle*. The costs of resources to a firm are their values in their best alternative uses. The firm, in order to secure the services of resources, must pay for them amounts equal to what they can earn in those alternative uses. In the earlier example of labor, the cost of the labor in the manufacture of washing machines is the value of refrigerators that the labor could have produced. Unless the manufacturer of washing machines pays that amount for the labor, it will go into or remain in refrigerator production. The steel example is similar. Automobile manufacturers must pay enough for steel to attract or hold the desired amounts away from alternative employments of steel — and this value is its cost to the automobile firm from the economist's point of view.

Explicit and Implicit Costs

Explicit costs of production are the outlays made by a firm that we usually think of as its expenses. They consist of explicit payments for resources bought outright or hired by the firm. The firm's payroll, payments for raw and semifinished materials, payments of overhead costs of various kinds, and payments into sinking funds and depreciation accounts are examples of explicit costs. They are the costs that accountants list as the firm's expenses.

Implicit costs of production are the costs of self-owned, self-employed resources, frequently overlooked in computing the expenses of the firm. The salary of a single proprietor who sets aside no salary for himself but who takes the firm's "profits" as payment for his services is an excellent example. A still more common implicit cost is the return to the owners of a firm on their investment in plant, equipment, and inventories.

The consideration of the firm owner's salary as a cost can be easily explained. In accordance with the alternative cost principle, the cost of the single proprietor's services in producing his product is the value of the foregone alternative product that would have been produced had he worked for someone else in a similar capacity. We consider as a part of the firm's costs, then, a salary for the proprietor equal to the value of his services in his best alternative employment. This cost is an implicit cost, which does not take the form of an "expense" outlay.

The consideration of a return on investment as a cost of production is more tricky. Return on investment usually is thought of as coming from the firm's profits rather than as being a cost of production. In the simplest case, consider a single proprietor who has invested in (purchased) the land, building, and equipment for his business establishment. A return on his investment equal to what he could have earned had he invested the same amount elsewhere in the economy is an implicit cost of production. Had he invested elsewhere his investment would have purchased resources to produce other goods. What those resources could earn in those alternative uses would determine the return on investment that he could have earned had he invested there.

The same principle on a larger scale applies to a corporation. Stockholders are the real owners of the corporation's land, plant, equipment, and inventories[1] — they have invested money in resources used by the corporation. Dividends equal to what stockholders could earn had they invested elsewhere in the economy are implicit costs of production from the point of view of the economist. The costs of resources obtained by the firm with stockholders' investments are, according to the alternative cost principle, the value of the alternative products foregone by holding the investment where it is. To hold the investment where it is, the corporation must pay a return to stockholders equal to what they could earn if they should invest elsewhere in the economy.

Costs, Resource Prices, and Efficiency

Costs of production incurred by the firm consist of both explicit and implicit obligations to resource owners. These obligations are just large enough to obtain and hold resources in the employment of the firm. Usually the firm's "expenses" include the explicit obligations only. Thus, costs of production as viewed by the economist differ somewhat from (and will usually be larger than) the firm's accounting "expenses."

Our discussion of costs will be oversimplified to some extent. We will be concerned with a firm's costs of production at various alternative product outputs. Costs at each output depend on (1) the amount the firm must pay for resources — that is, resource prices — and (2) the techniques available for combining resources to produce the output. We shall eliminate

---

[1]Additionally, the corporation may have borrowed money by selling bonds to increase the amounts of its plant and equipment. Thus, bondholders, too, have invested money in the corporation. Interest payments on the bonds — the return on the bondholders' investments — are explicit payments and are recorded as costs by the corporation as well as by the economist.

the problem of resource pricing by assuming that the firm is a pure competitor in the purchase of resources. The single firm takes such a small proportion of the total amount of any given resource in existence that by itself it cannot influence the resource price. The firm can get all it wants of any one resource at a constant price per unit. Thus, differences in costs at different output levels result from differences in the efficiency of the techniques that the firm can use at each of those outputs. The effects on costs of possible changes in resource prices as a result of output changes on the part of a firm can be taken into consideration later on, after resource pricing has been discussed.

The Short-run and Long-run Viewpoints

In analyzing a firm's costs of production a distinction is made between the short-run and long-run viewpoints. These are essentially planning rather than calendar time concepts; they refer to the time horizon over which the firm's planning stretches. We shall examine them in turn.

The Short Run

The *short run* is a planning period so short that the firm is unable to consider varying the quantities of some resources used. It is possible to think of a period so short that no resource can be varied in quantity. Then, as the planning period is lengthened, it becomes possible to vary the quantity of one. A progressive lengthening of the period permits more and more resources to become variable in quantity until ultimately they all fall into the variable category. Any period between that in which no resources can be varied in quantity and that in which all resources but one are variable can legitimately be called the short run. However, to facilitate exposition we ordinarily use a more restricting definition.

The possibilities of varying the quantities of different resources depend on their nature and the terms of hire or purchase. Some, such as land and buildings, may be leased by the firm for given time periods; or, if they are owned outright, it may take some time to acquire additional quantities or to dispose of a part of the quantities already owned. The quantity of top management is not ordinarily readily variable. Heavy machinery especially designed for the firm's use cannot be quickly increased or decreased in quantity. Typically, the period required for variation in the quantities of such resources as power, labor, transportation, raw materials, and semifinished materials will be shorter than that required for variation in the quantities of land, buildings, heavy machinery, and top management.

The usual interpretation of the short-run concept used here is a planning period so short that the firm does not have time to vary the quantities of such resources as land, buildings, heavy machinery, and top management. These are the firm's short-run *fixed resources*. Our concept of the short run does allow variation in the quantities of such resources as labor, raw materials, and the like. These are the firm's *variable resources*.[2]

The calendar time length of the short run will vary from industry to industry. For some industries the short run may be very short indeed. Such will be the case where the quantities of fixed resources used by a firm in the industry are typically small or can be added to or subtracted from in a short space of time. Various textile industries and many service industries are cases in point. For other industries the short run may be several years. It takes time to add to the productive capacity of an automobile firm or a basic steel firm.

The quantities of fixed resources used determine the size of the firm's plant.[3] The size of plant sets the upper limit to the amount of output per unit of time that the firm is capable of producing. The firm can vary its output up to that limit, however, by increasing or decreasing the quantities of variable resources used in the fixed size of plant.

The fixed resources or the plant may be compared with a meat grinder. The variable resources will be analogous to unground meat. In this case the output of ground meat per unit of time can be varied by varying the input of unground meat. There will be some upper limit beyond which the output cannot be increased, regardless of how much unground meat is on hand to push through it.

The capital and labor example of the preceding chapter can also be viewed in a short-run context. We can think of the fixed amount of capital as the fixed size of plant, and the variable quantities of labor as the variable resources used with it.

The Long Run

The *long run* presents no definitional difficulties. It is a planning period long enough for the firm to be able to vary the quantities per unit of time of all resources used. Thus, all resources are variable. No problem of classifying resources as fixed or variable exists. The firm can vary its size of plant as it desires, from very small to large or vice-versa. Infinitesimal variations in size are usually possible.

---

[2]The dividing line between fixed and variable resources is not always clearcut. In particular cases some of the resources listed here as "variable" may require more time for alterations in quantity taken than some listed as "fixed." For example, contractual arrangements for the purchase of power or labor may be such that quantities of these cannot readily be varied. Yet it may be possible for the firm to lease out, sublease, or sell some part of its "fixed" resources on short notice.

[3]The term *plant* is used here in a broad context to cover the whole scope of the firm's operations. A firm may operate several establishments at different locations; we shall view these all together as the firm's "plant."

Short-run Cost Curves

Classification of resources in the short run as fixed and variable enables us to classify their costs as fixed costs and variable costs. *Fixed costs* are the costs of fixed resources. *Variable costs* are those of variable resources. The distinction between fixed and variable costs will be basic for the discussions of total costs, average costs, and marginal costs that follow.

Total Cost Curves

In the short run the total costs of a firm depend partly on the output level produced. The component parts of total costs are total fixed costs and total variable costs. We shall look at these in turn.

Total Fixed Costs   *Total fixed costs* are the entire set of obligations per unit of time incurred by the firm for fixed resources. Since the firm does not have time to vary quantities of fixed resources used per unit of time, total fixed cost will remain at a constant level regardless of the output produced per unit of time. Suppose, for example, that the firm occupies a certain amount of land. If it owns the land outright the cost must be amortized over the expected life of the firm. The amortization costs are a fixed amount per unit of time and are independent of the firm's output. The same principle applies to buildings and heavy machinery. Top management salaries are also fixed—usually by contract—for the short run and are independent of the firm's output.

A hypothetical total fixed cost schedule is presented in Table 9-1; the corresponding total fixed cost curve is plotted in Figure 9-1. Note that the total fixed cost curve is independent of the output level, is parallel to the quantity axis, and lies above it by the amount of the total fixed costs.

Total Variable Costs   *Total variable costs* are the obligations incurred for variable resources. They depend on the output level and must necessarily rise as the firm's output increases. Larger outputs require larger quantities of variable resources and, hence, larger cost obligations. For example, the larger the output of an oil refinery, the larger the quantity of crude oil inputs it must purchase; hence, the larger will be the crude oil costs. Table 9-1 lists a hypothetical total variable cost schedule. *TVC* in Figure 9-1 is the corresponding total variable cost curve. These costs show a characteristic usually typical of a firm's total variable costs. Up to a certain output level their rates of increase decrease as the firm's output of product and input of variable resources increase. Beyond that output level the rate of increase in total variable cost increases. The successive increases in total variable cost are smaller and smaller up to 7 units of output in Table

Table 9-1   Total Cost Schedules for a Firm

Quantity of X	Total Fixed Cost	Total Variable Cost	Total Cost
1	$100	$ 40	$140
2	100	70	170
3	100	85	185
4	100	96	196
5	100	104	204
6	100	110	210
7	100	115	215
8	100	120	220
9	100	126	226
10	100	134	234
11	100	145	245
12	100	160	260
13	100	180	280
14	100	206	306
15	100	239	339
16	100	280	380
17	100	330	430
18	100	390	490
19	100	461	561
20	100	544	644

Figure 9-1   Total Cost Curves of a Firm

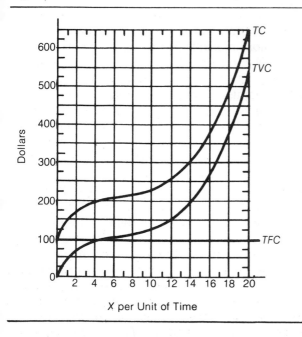

9-1 and Figure 9-1. Beyond 8 units of output the successive increases become larger and larger.

The changes in total variable cost shown in Table 9-1 and the shape of the total variable cost curve of Figure 9-1 reflect increasing and diminishing returns to variable resources as larger and larger quantities of them are used with the firm's fixed resources of its given size of plant. Consider the simple case in which a firm uses only one variable resource, resource A. A conventional total product curve for A is drawn on the right-hand side of Figure 9-2, showing increasing returns to A for quantities up to a_3 and diminishing returns for larger quantities. The point of inflection on the TP_a curve is at F.

The TP_a curve is easily converted into the total variable cost curve of the firm once the price of the variable resource A is known. Let the price of A be p_{a1}, so that for any given input of A, total variable cost is that quantity of A multiplied by its price. Measure total variable cost (dollars' worth of A) on a horizontal axis stretching to the left of the origin. Total variable cost when a_1 of A is used is $a_1 \times p_1$, and the corresponding output of product is x_1. On the left-hand diagram these coordinates locate point D' on the firm's total variable cost curve. Points E', F', and G' are located in a similar manner, and all such points together trace out the firm's total variable cost curve.

The TVC curve in the left-hand diagram is a mirror image of the TP_a curve in the right-hand diagram. If, for example, p_{a1} is $1 and we let the distance on the horizontal axis that measures one unit of A to the right of the origin be equal to the distance that measures $1's worth of A to the left of the origin, the reflection is exact. The point of inflection F' on TVC is the precise counterpart of F on TP_a. Both curves are concave upward from the origin to their respective inflection points and are concave downward beyond the inflection points, because of increasing returns on A for quantities up to a_3 and decreasing returns for still greater quantities. If we rotate the left-hand side of the diagram 90° clockwise, letting the product axis become the horizontal axis, the TVC curve takes on the same shape as that of Figure 9-1. It is concave downward out to the inflection point and concave upward beyond that point.

In the usual case a firm uses several variable resources rather than only one, but the principles at work are the same as those of the single resource example. With a given size of plant we can think in terms of increasing the complex of variable resources used. As we start from a very small complex, increasing returns to the variable resources may occur—equal increments in outlays on the entire complex may result in larger and larger increments in output—and the TVC curve consequently will be convex downward. But as larger and larger outlays are made, diminishing returns to the complex come into play—equal increments in TVC result in smaller and smaller increments in output—and the TVC curve becomes

Figure 9-2   Relation between the
TVC Curve and the Total Product Curve of Variable Resources

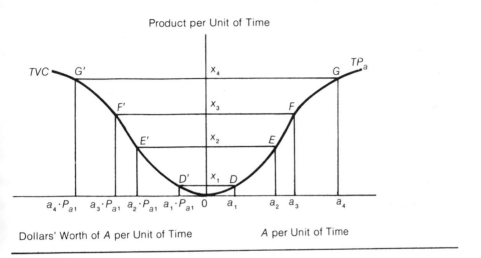

Product per Unit of Time

Dollars' Worth of *A* per Unit of Time   *A* per Unit of Time

concave upward. At some output level the fixed size of plant will have reached its absolute maximum capacity to produce. Now the total variable cost curve turns straight up. Increased obligations incurred for still larger quantities of variable resources will lead to no increases in output at all.

Total Costs   Total costs of the firm for various output levels are the summation of total fixed costs and total variable costs for those output levels. The total cost column of Table 9-1 is obtained by adding total fixed cost and total variable cost at each level of output. Likewise, the total cost curve of Figure 9-1 is obtained by summing the *TFC* curve and the *TVC* curve vertically. The *TC* curve and the *TVC* curve must necessarily have the same shape, since each increase in output per unit of time increases total cost and total variable cost by the same amount. The output increase does not affect total fixed cost. The *TC* curve lies above the *TVC* curve by an amount equal to *TFC* at all output levels.[4]

[4]The short-run total cost function can be represented mathematically as:

$$C = k + f(x)$$

in which:

$$TC = C$$
$$TFC = k$$
$$TVC = f(x).$$

Per Unit Cost Curves

Per unit cost curves are used extensively in price and output analysis — more so than the total cost curves are. Per unit cost curves show the same kind of information as total cost curves, but in a different form. The per unit cost curves are the average fixed cost curve, the average variable cost curve, the average cost curve, and the marginal cost curve.

Average Fixed Costs   Average fixed costs or fixed costs per unit of product at various levels of output are obtained by dividing total fixed cost by those outputs. Thus, the average fixed cost column of Table 9-2 is computed by dividing the total fixed cost column of Table 9-1 by the different quantities of *X*. The average fixed cost schedule is plotted in Figure 9-3 as the *AFC* curve.

Table 9-2   Per Unit Cost Schedules of a Firm

Quantity of X	Average Fixed Cost	Average Variable Cost	Average Cost	Marginal Cost
1	$100.00	$40.00	$140.00	—
2	50.00	35.00	85.00	30
3	33.33	28.33	61.66	15
4	25.00	24.00	49.00	11
5	20.00	20.80	40.80	8
6	16.67	18.33	35.00	6
7	14.29	16.43	30 72	5
8	12.50	15.00	27.50	5
9	11.11	14.00	25.11	6
10	10.00	13.40	23.40	8
11	9.09	13.18	22.27	11
12	8.33	13.33	21.66	15
13	7.69	13.85	21.54	20
14	7.14	14.72	21.86	26
15	6.67	15.93	22.60	33
16	6.25	17.50	23.75	41
17	5.88	19.41	25.29	50
18	5.55	21.67	27.22	60
19	5.26	24.27	29.53	71
20	5.00	27.20	32.20	83

The greater the output of the firm, the smaller average fixed cost will be. Since total fixed cost remains the same regardless of output, fixed costs are spread over more units of output; and each unit of output bears a smaller share. Therefore, the average fixed cost curve is downward-sloping to the right throughout its entire length. As output per unit of time increases, it approaches but never reaches the quantity axis. Thus, it becomes apparent that firms with large fixed costs — the railroads, for example, with their tremendous fixed charges on roadbeds and rolling stock —

Figure 9-3   Per-Unit Cost Curves of a Firm

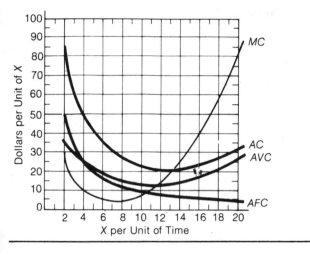

can substantially reduce their fixed costs per unit by producing larger outputs.

Average Variable Costs   Variable costs per unit of output are computed in the same way as fixed costs per unit of output. The *average variable cost* column of Table 9-2 is obtained by dividing total variable cost in Table 9-1 at various outputs by those outputs. Plotted graphically, the average variable cost column of Table 9-2 becomes the *AVC* curve of Figure 9-3.

The average variable cost curve usually will have a U shape. Its U shape can be explained in terms of the principles of production. Suppose, for example, that a factory is designed to employ approximately one hundred workers. The size of plant is fixed, and labor is the only variable resource. The amount of product produced if only one man is employed will be extremely small, but if an additional man is employed the two can split up the jobs to be performed and can more than double the single man's output. In other words, the average product of labor increases with the employment of the additional man. If a doubling of labor (variable) costs will more than double output, labor costs per unit of output (average variable costs) will decrease. Thus, throughout Stage I for labor, the average product per worker increases, and average variable costs decrease. When enough men are employed to go into Stage II, average product of labor decreases, or, what amounts to the same thing, average variable costs increase. The average variable cost curve in this case is a sort of monetized mirror reflection of the average product curve for labor.

The same general principles apply when a complex of several variable resources is used by the firm. At small input levels of the complex, product per unit of cost outlay or "average product" of the complex will be increasing, meaning that average variable costs will be decreasing. As input levels are increased, "average product" reaches a maximum, and then decreases. Average variable costs correspondingly reach a minimum and then increase.

When a complex of variable resources is used by the firm, combinations or ratios of the variable resources to each other must be considered also. Suppose the firm for which the cost curves of Figure 9-3 are drawn uses three variable resources — A, B, and C — with its given size of plant. Resource prices are p_a, p_b, and p_c, respectively. If the firm's output is to be six units of product, and if its average variable cost is to be as low as possible ($18.33) for that output, the variable resources must be combined in such proportions that:

$$\frac{MPP_a}{p_a} = \frac{MPP_b}{p_b} = \frac{MPP_c}{p_c}.$$

If they are not so combined, average variable cost for that output will exceed $18.33. Similarly, each point on the average variable cost curve can be attained only if the firm combines variable resources in the proper proportions for each and every output at which those points are located. Failure to do so will result in higher costs.

Average Costs   *Average costs* or the overall costs per unit of output can be obtained in either of two ways. If total costs at various outputs in Table 9-1 are divided by the respective outputs, the result is the average cost column of Table 9-2. Alternatively, in Table 9-2, average fixed costs and average variable costs added together at each of the output levels produce the average cost column. Graphically, the AC curve in Figure 9-3 represents the average cost column of Table 9-2 plotted against outputs. The AC curve is also the vertical summation of the AFC curve and the AVC curve.

The average cost curve, too, is usually thought to be a ∪-shaped curve. Its ∪ shape depends on the efficiency with which both fixed and variable resources are used. Given the size of plant, the greater the output of the firm, the greater the efficiency of the fixed resources as a group; that is, the smaller average fixed cost becomes. In Figure 9-3 variable resources are used more and more efficiently until output reaches 11 units. Up to this level average cost must be decreasing, because the efficiency of both fixed and variable resources is increasing. Between 11 and 13 units of output average fixed costs decrease, but average variable costs increase as variable resources become less efficient. However, the decreases in average fixed cost more than offset the increases in average variable cost, so that average cost continues to decrease. Beyond 13 units of output per unit of time decreases in the efficiency of variable resources more than offset increases in the efficiency of fixed resources and average cost rises. We should note an obvious fact in passing: The minimum point on the average variable cost curve lies at a lower output level than does the minimum point on the average cost curve.[5]

Marginal Cost *Marginal cost* is defined as the change in total costs resulting from a one-unit change in output. It can be defined just as accurately as the change in total variable costs resulting from a one-unit change in output, since a change in output changes total variable costs and total costs by exactly the same amounts. Marginal cost depends in no way on fixed costs. The marginal cost column of Table 9-2 can be computed from either the total variable cost column or the total cost column of Table 9-1. It is plotted graphically as *MC* in Figure 9-3.

Figure 9-4 shows the relationship between a marginal cost curve and the total cost curve from which it is derived. Consider output x on the total cost diagram of Figure 9-4 (a). Total costs at that output are T. Now let us increase output by one unit to x_1. Total costs increase to T_1. Marginal cost of the x_1 unit is $T_1 - T$. The marginal cost of a unit of output at any level of output can be found in the same way. The marginal cost values plotted against outputs in Figure 9-4 (b) form the marginal cost curve. At any given output on the marginal cost diagram marginal cost at that output is measured by the distance from the base line up to the marginal cost curve. Thus, at output x_1 marginal cost of the x_1 unit is M dollars. This represents the same number of dollars as does $T_1 - T$ on the total cost diagram.

The marginal cost curve usually is ∪-shaped, and its shape comes from that of the *TC* curve. Up to the x_2 level of output the *TC* curve is concave downward; or, what amounts to the same thing, each one-unit increase in output per unit of time up to that point will increase total costs

---

[5]The average cost function is derived from Footnote 4 by dividing the total cost function by output and is:

$$\frac{C}{x} = \frac{k}{x} + \frac{f(x)}{x}$$

in which:

$$AC = \frac{C}{x}$$

$$AFC = \frac{k}{x}$$

$$AVC = \frac{f(x)}{x}$$

Figure 9–4   The Relationship between MC and TC

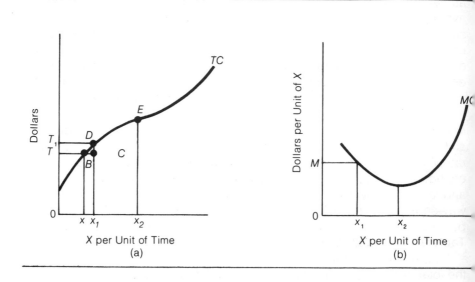

by a smaller amount than did the preceding one. Hence, marginal cost is decreasing as output is increased to that level. Point E on the TC curve is the point of inflection. At output level x_2, at which the point of inflection occurs, marginal cost takes on its minimum value. At outputs greater than x_2 the total cost curve is concave upward, meaning that each one-unit increase in output per unit of time increases total costs by more than the preceding one did. Therefore, marginal cost will be increasing for outputs beyond that level.

Marginal cost at any given output can be thought of geometrically as the slope of the total cost curve at that output. The approximate slope of the total cost curve of Figure 9-4 (a) between B and D is CD/BC. BC is equal to one unit of output, and CD is equal to $T' - T$, or marginal cost of the x_1 unit. The slope of the total cost curve between B and D is thus equal to marginal cost of the x_1 unit. For the typical firm one unit of output is measured by an infinitesimal distance along the quantity axis. The large size of the unit of output (x to x_1) in Figure 9-4 (a) is for purposes of illustration only. If one unit of output is measured by an infinitesimal distance along the quantity axis, marginal cost at any given output is numerically equal to the slope of the total cost curve at that output. The slope of the TC curve of Figure 9-4 (a) is decreasing between zero and output x_2 (although TC is rising) and is increasing beyond x_2. Thus, marginal cost first decreases and then increases as output increases.

Figure 9–5   The Relationship between MC and AC

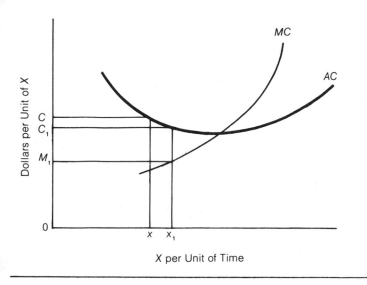

Relationship of MC *to* AC *and to* AVC

The marginal cost curve bears a unique relationship to the average cost curve derived from the same total cost curve. When *AC* is decreasing as output increases, *MC* is less than *AC*. When *AC* is increasing as output increases, *MC* is greater than *AC*. It follows that at the output at which *AC* is minimum, *MC* is equal to *AC*. These relationships are shown in Figure 9-5.

For example, suppose the firm's output is *x*. Its average cost is $0C$. We know that average cost at any output equals the total cost of that output divided by the output; therefore, $0C = TC/x$ at output *x*. Suppose now that the output is increased by one unit to x_1 and that the addition to total costs is $0M_1$, which is the marginal cost of the x_1 unit. Suppose further, as we have shown in Figure 9-5, that marginal cost of the x_1 unit is less than the average cost $0C$ of *x* units. Since the additional unit of output per unit of time adds a lesser amount to total costs than was the average cost of *x* units, the average cost of x_1 units must be less than the average cost of *x* units. However, the average cost of x_1 units will not be pulled down as low as the marginal cost of the x_1 unit. Thus $0C_1 < 0C$, but $0C_1 < 0M_1$; or, when average costs are decreasing, marginal cost is necessarily less than average cost. Similarly, when an additional unit of output adds an amount to total costs equal to the old average cost, the new average cost will equal the old and will also be equal to marginal cost of the additional unit of output. Also, when an additional unit of output adds a greater amount to total costs than was the original average cost, the new average cost will be greater than the original but will be less than the marginal cost of the additional unit. These relationships can be verified by reference to Table 9-2 and Figure 9-3.

The relationships between marginal cost and average variable cost will be identical with the relationships between marginal cost and average cost, and for the same reasons. When average variable cost is decreasing, marginal cost will be less than average variable cost. When average variable cost is minimum, marginal cost and average variable cost will be equal. When average variable cost is increasing, marginal cost will be greater than average variable cost. These relationships can also be verified by Table 9-2 and Figure 9-3.

The complete set of short-run per unit cost curves is pictured in Figure 9-3. The marginal cost curve cuts the average variable cost curve and the average cost curve at their respective minimum points. An increase in fixed costs would shift the average cost curve upward and to the right in such a way that the marginal cost curve would still intersect it at its minimum point. No change in the marginal cost curve would be involved, since marginal cost is independent of fixed cost.[6]

As we have presented them, the variations in the component parts of short-run costs as the firm varies output do not depend on changes in the price paid per unit for each of the various resources used by the firm. We assumed at the outset that the firm can get all it wants of any resource at a constant price per unit; that is, it buys them under conditions of pure competition. The shapes of the short-run curves as they are presented

---

[6]Starting from the total cost function:

$$C = k + f(x)$$

the marginal cost function becomes:

$$\frac{dC}{dx} = f'(x)$$

and is thus seen to depend in no way on k. Further, if average cost is decreasing, then:

$$\frac{d\left(\frac{C}{x}\right)}{dx} = \frac{x\frac{dC}{dx} - C}{x^2} < 0,$$

or:

$$\frac{dC}{dx} - \frac{C}{x} < 0;$$

which means that MC is less than AC. Similarly, it can be shown that MC is greater than AC if:

$$\frac{d\left(\frac{C}{x}\right)}{dx} > 0$$

and MC equals AC if:

$$\frac{d\left(\frac{C}{x}\right)}{dx} = 0.$$

here are solely reflections of the efficiency with which resources can be used at the alternative output levels obtainable with a given plant size.

Still, in the real world we observe such things as quantity discounts on resources purchased in large amounts by the firm. This situation represents a departure from pure competition in the buying of resources, or a departure from the assumptions on which our cost curves are based. Should quantity discounts occur, the total variable cost curve and the total cost curve will increase less as output is increased than they would otherwise. Correspondingly, quantity discounts would cause the average variable cost curve and the average cost curve to show greater decreases, then smaller increases, than they would otherwise show as output is increased. Further modifications of short-run cost analysis will be developed in Chapters 14 and 15.

The Optimum Rate of Output

The output at which short-run average cost is lowest is the output at which a given size of plant is most efficient. Here the value of the inputs of resources per unit output of product is least. This output is called the optimum rate of output. The term *optimum* as we use it means "most efficient." Whatever the size of plant built by the firm, the output of minimum average cost is the optimum rate of output for that plant. As we shall see later the optimum rate of output for a given plant size is not necessarily the output at which the firm makes the greatest profits. Profits depend on revenue as well as costs.

Long-run Cost Curves

In the long-run planning period any size of plant is a possibility for the firm. All resources are variable. The firm can change the quantities used per unit of time, of land, buildings, machinery, management, and all other resources. There will be no average fixed cost curve. We need to concern ourselves with the long-run average cost curve, the long-run total cost curve, and the long-run marginal cost curve.

It will be helpful to think of the long run as a set of alternative short-run situations into any one of which the firm can move. At any given time we can adopt the short-run viewpoint, considering the alternative output levels that can be produced with the size of plant in existence at that time. Yet, from the point of view of a long-run planning period, the firm has opportunities to change the short-run picture. The long run may be compared with the action sequence of a motion picture. If we stop the film and look at a single picture we have a short-run concept.

Figure 9–6 The Long-run Average Cost Curve, Three Alternative Plant Sizes

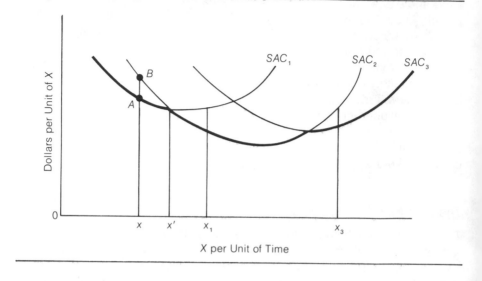

X per Unit of Time

Long-Run Average Cost

Suppose that it is technologically possible for the firm to build only three alternative sizes of plant. These are represented by SAC_1, SAC_2, and SAC_3 in Figure 9-6. Each *SAC* curve is the short-run average cost curve for a given plant size. In the long run the firm can build any one of these, or it can shift from one to another.

Which one should the firm build? The answer depends on, and will vary with, the long-run output per unit of time to be produced. Whatever the output is to be, the firm will want to produce at an average cost as low as possible for that output.

Suppose the output level is to be *x*. The firm should construct the plant represented by SAC_1, which will produce output *x* at a smaller cost per unit (*xA*) than either of the other two will. Costs would be *xB* per unit if SAC_2 were used. For output *x'* the firm would be indifferent between SAC_1 and SAC_2; but for output x_1, it would prefer to use SAC_2. For output x_3 the firm would construct and use the plant represented by SAC_3. We are now in a position to define the *long-run average cost curve*. It shows the least possible cost per unit of producing various outputs when the firm can plan to build any desired size of plant. In Figure 9-6 the heavy portions of the *SAC* curves form the long-run average cost curve. The light portions of the *SAC* curves are irrelevant. The firm would never operate at the light portions in the long run, because it could reduce costs by changing plant size.

Figure 9-7 The Long-run Average Cost Curve, Infinite Alternative Plant Sizes

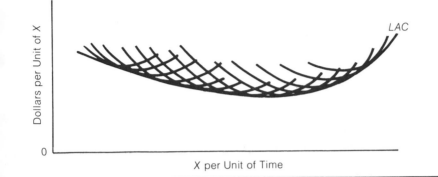

The possible plant sizes that a firm can build as a long-run undertaking usually are unlimited in number. For every conceivable size there will be another infinitesimally larger or infinitesimally smaller. A series of *SAC* curves such as those of Figure 9-7 results, and even here any number of additional *SAC* curves can be drawn between any two of those in the diagram. The outer portions of the *SAC* curves form a heavy line, the long-run average cost curve. Since the long-run average cost curve is made up of very small segments of the various *SAC* curves, it can be considered as a curve just tangent to all possible *SAC* curves representing the plant sizes that the firm conceivably could build. Mathematically it is an envelope curve to the *SAC* curves.

Every point on the long-run average cost curve requires that the firm be using a least-cost combination of resources. For a given output long-run total cost and long-run average cost are least when *all* resources used are combined in proportions such that the marginal physical product per dollar's worth of one equals the marginal physical product per dollar's worth of every other resource used. This statement means that a dollar spent on management must add the same amount to total product as a dollar spent on raw materials. A dollar spent on labor and a dollar spent on machinery must both yield the same addition to total product, and so on for all resources. Should these conditions not be fulfilled — if a dollar spent on management adds less to total product than a dollar spent on machines — then some shifts in expenditures from management to machines will increase total product without increasing total costs; or, looking at the matter another way, the shifts will provide a decrease in total cost or a decrease in average cost, holding total product constant. Thus, the cost levels shown by the long-run average cost curve for various outputs can be attained by the firm only if the least-cost resource combination is used for each output.

Economies of Size

The long-run average cost curve is usually thought to be a U-shaped curve. Such will be the case if firms become successively more efficient up to some particular size or range of sizes, and if they then become successively less efficient as the range of plant sizes from very small to very large is considered. Increasing efficiency associated with larger and larger plant sizes is reflected by *SAC* curves lying successively at lower levels and farther to the right. Examples are provided by SAC_1, SAC_2, and SAC_3 in Figure 9-8. Decreasing efficiency associated with still larger plant sizes would be shown by *SAC* curves lying successively at higher levels and farther to the right. The resulting *LAC* curve would thus have a general U shape.

The forces causing the *LAC* curve to decrease for larger outputs and sizes of plant are called economies of size. Two important economies of size are (1) increasing possibilities of division and specialization of labor and (2) increasing possibilities of using advanced technological developments and/or larger machines. These economies will be discussed in turn.

Division and Specialization of Labor   The advantages of division and specialization of labor have long been known to both economists and the general public.[7] A small plant employing few men cannot specialize the men on particular operations as readily as can a larger plant employing a larger work force. In the small plant the typical worker performs several different operations in the process of producing the commodity. He may not be particularly proficient at some of them. In addition, he may lose time in changing from one set of tools to another in performing different operations.

In a larger plant greater specialization may be possible, with the worker performing that process at which he is most adept. Specialization on a particular process eliminates the time lost in changing from one set of tools to another. Also, the worker performing a single type of operation develops shortcuts and speed in performing it. The efficiency of the worker is likely to be higher and cost per unit of output correspondingly lower where division and specialization of labor are possible. A word of warning may be necessary though. In some cases it may be possible to carry specialization to the point at which the monotony of the task begins to counteract increases in the efficiency of the individual's performance.

Technological Factors   The possibility of lowering costs per unit of output by technological methods increases as the plant size is increased. In

---

[7]*See* Adam Smith, *The Wealth of Nations*, Edwin Cannan, ed. (New York: Modern Library, Inc., 1937), Bk. I, Chaps. I-III.

Figure 9-8   *Economies and Diseconomies of Size*

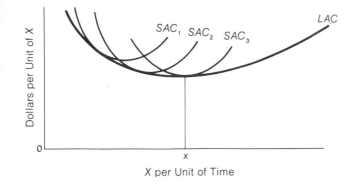

the first place the cheapest way of producing a small output will usually not be one which also employs the most advanced technological methods. Consider, for example, the production of automobile hoods. If the output were to be two or three hoods per week, then certainly large automatic presses would not be used. The cheapest way to produce the hoods probably would be to hammer them out by hand. The cost per unit would still be comparatively high. There would be no cheap way of producing the small output or of operating the small plant for the production of a small output.

For larger outputs and plant sizes mass-production technological methods can be used to effect reductions in per unit costs. In this example, if output were to be several thousand units per week, then a larger plant with automatic presses could be installed, and costs per unit would become substantially lower than was possible with the small plant.

In the second place technological considerations are usually such that in order to double the capacity of a machine to produce a doubling of material, construction, and operating costs of the machine is not necessary. For example, it is cheaper to build and operate a 600-horsepower diesel motor than it is to build and operate two 300-horsepower diesel motors. The 600-horsepower motor has no more working parts than a single 300-horsepower motor. Additionally, the 600-horsepower motor does not require twice the amount of materials used in building a single 300-horsepower motor. The same type of example can be made for almost any machine. Technological possibilities represent a very important explanation of the increasing efficiency of larger and larger plant sizes, up to some limit.

Diseconomies of Size

The question now arises as to why, once the plant is large enough to take advantage of all economies of size, still larger plant sizes are likely to result in less efficiency. It would appear, offhand, that the firm would be able at least to maintain the economies of size. The answer usually given to the question is that there are limitations to the efficiency of management in controlling and coordinating a single firm. These limitations are called diseconomies of size.

As the size of the plant is increased, management, like the lower echelons of labor, may become more efficient through division of tasks and specialization in particular functions; but the argument commonly made is that beyond some certain size the difficulties of coordinating and controlling the firm multiply rapidly. The contacts of top management with the day-to-day operations of the business become more and more remote, causing operating efficiency in production departments to decrease. Decision-making responsibility must be delegated, and coordination must be established among the decision-making subordinates. The paper work, travel expenses, telephone bills, and additional employees necessary for coordination pile up. Occasionally, plans of separate decision-making subordinates fail to mesh and costly slowdowns occur. To the extent that increasing difficulties of coordination and control reduce the efficiency per dollar outlay on management as the size of the plant is increased, per unit costs of production will increase.

The discussion so far may be interpreted to mean that as the size of plant is increased, economies of size cause the long-run average cost curve to decrease, and then, when all economies of size are realized, diseconomies of size straightway begin. Such is not necessarily the case. Once the plant is large enough to take advantage of all economies of size, there may be a range of larger plant sizes where diseconomies are not yet evident. In this case the long-run average cost curve will have a long horizontal series of minimum points rather than the single minimum point of the conventional long-run average cost curve. When the plant has become sufficiently large for diseconomies of size to become apparent, the long-run average cost curve turns upward to the right. Another possibility is that some diseconomies begin to occur in a plant too small to realize all economies of size. If the economies of size for larger plants more than offset the diseconomies, the long-run average cost curve slopes downward to the right. Where diseconomies of size more than offset economies of size, the long-run average cost curve slopes upward to the right.

The Optimum Size of Plant

The term *optimum size of plant* is applied to the most efficient of all the sizes of plant that the firm can build. The optimum size of plant is the one

Figure 9-9   The Optimum Size of Plant

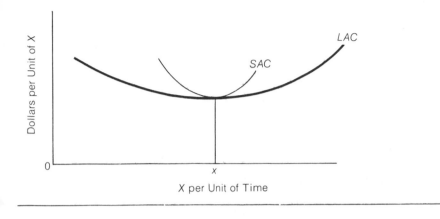

for which the short-run average cost curve forms the minimum point of the long-run average cost curve. It can also be thought of as that size of plant with a short-run average cost curve tangent to the long-run average cost curve at the minimum points of both. The short-run average cost curve of the optimum size of plant in Figure 9-9 is *SAC*.

Firms will not invariably construct plants of optimum size and operate them at optimum rates of output. As we shall see, they will do so under conditions of pure competition in the long run; however, under pure monopoly, oligopoly, and monopolistic competition they are not likely to do so. The size of plant that will operate at the lowest cost per unit for given outputs will vary with the output to be produced. For example, in Figure 9-9 plant *SAC* will produce output x more cheaply than will a plant of any other size; and output x can be produced at a lower cost per unit than can any other output. But for outputs greater or less than x per unit costs will necessarily be higher. Plant sizes other than the optimum will produce such outputs at lower costs per unit than will the one of optimum size.

How can we determine the size of plant to be constructed for a specific output? Consider Figure 9-10. Suppose the firm is producing output x_1 with plant SAC_1. Plant SAC_1 is being operated at less than its optimum rate of output. Now the output level is to be increased to x_2. The increase can be accomplished in either of two ways: (1) by increasing the output rate with plant SAC_1 or (2) by changing to a larger plant size. Which method should the firm use? Either method will allow the firm to reduce costs per unit. Method 1 will cause SAC_1 to be used at its optimum rate of output. Costs are lower than c_1. However, if the firm should use Method 2 economies of size from the larger plant will allow even greater per-unit cost reductions for output x_2 than will Method 1. Costs per unit will be c_2

Figure 9-10   Appropriate Plant Size for a Given Output

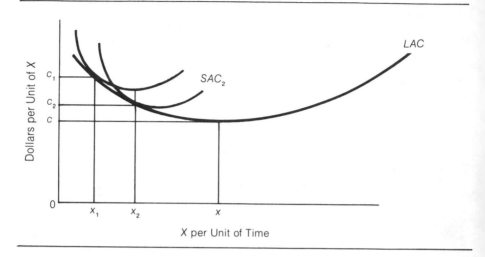

with plant SAC_2, and this is the lowest cost at which that output can be produced. For outputs between 0 and x the firm will achieve lowest per-unit costs for any given output by using a less than optimum size of plant at less than the optimum rate of output. Similarly, for any given output greater than x lowest cost per unit will be achieved if the firm uses a greater than optimum size of plant at a greater than optimum rate of output. The applicable general principle is this: To minimize cost for any given output the firm should use the plant size for which the short-run average cost curve is tangent to the long-run average cost curve at that output.

Long-run Total Cost and Long-run Marginal Cost

No discussion of a firm's long-run costs would be complete without reference to its long-run total cost curve (LTC). Although the LTC curve provides no information beyond that supplied by the LAC and LMC curves, it does present an alternative view of long-run costs that from time to time proves useful.

The LTC curve can be built up easily enough from the firm's LAC curve. Suppose that the LAC curve of the firm is that of Figure 9-10. At output levels x_1, x_2, and x, long-run total costs will be $x_1 \times c_1$, $x_2 \times c_2$, and $x \times c$, respectively. Long-run total costs can be computed from other output levels in the same way. We would expect that the resulting LTC curve would look like that of Figure 9-11 (b) starting at the origin of the diagram and moving upward to the right in much the same fashion as a total variable

Figure 9 – 11   From Isoquants to the LTC Curve

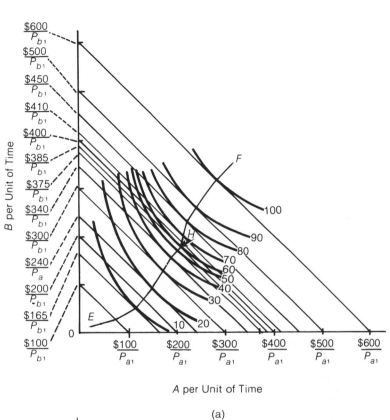

(a)

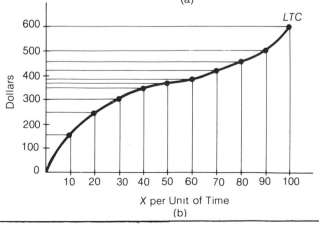

(b)

cost curve. The *LTC* curve as we have drawn it reflects first decreasing long-run average costs and then increasing long-run average costs.

The *LTC* curve can also be constructed using isoquant-isocost analysis. The production function represented by the isoquant map in Figure 9-11 (a) generates a typical long-run cost curve for a firm. The number on each isoquant indicates the level of output that the isoquant represents. The prices of resources A and B are constant at p_{a1} and p_{b1}, respectively, and determine the slope $(-p_{a1}/p_{b1})$ of the family of isocost curves. Alternative possible total cost outlays are shown as the numerators of the various fractions $(TC0/p_b$ and $TC0/p_a)$ along both the B and the A axes. Note that the isocosts showing $100 increments in total cost outlay are spaced equally from one another.

The isoquants are spaced to reflect first economies of size and then diseconomies of size as the firm's plant size is increased. To put this point another way, the spacing reflects increasing efficiency and then decreasing efficiency in the use of resources as the plant size is increased. As we move along the expansion path, equal increments in the firm's output require decreasing increments in total cost outlay until point H is reached. Beyond point H increasing increments in cost outlay are required to bring about equal increments in output. The resulting total cost curve is that of Figure 9-11 (b).

The long-run marginal cost curve shows the change in long-run total cost per unit change in the firm's output when the firm has ample time to accomplish the output change by making the appropriate adjustments in the quantities of all resources used, including those which constitute its plant. Or we can think of the *LMC* curve as measuring the slopes of the *LTC* curve at various output levels.

From the *LTC* curve of Figure 9-12 we can deduce that *LMC* would be less than *LAC* where *LAC* is decreasing—that is, from 0 to output x—and would be greater than *LAC* for output levels beyond x where *LAC* is increasing. At output x, *LMC* and *LAC* are equal. These relationships are shown in Figure 9-13 by the *LAC* and *LMC* curves. The *LMC* curve bears the same relationship to its *LAC* curve that any given *SMC* curve bears to its *SAC* curve.

Relationships between LMC *and* SMC

When the firm has constructed the proper size of plant for producing a given output, short-run marginal cost will equal long-run marginal cost at that output. Suppose, for example, that the given output is x_2 in Figure 9-13. The firm would use the plant represented by SAC_2, which is tangent to the *LAC* curve at that output. The corresponding total cost curves would be STC_2 and *LTC* in Figure 9-12. We can verify that STC_2 would lie above

Figure 9–12 The Relationship between Short-run and Long-run Total Costs

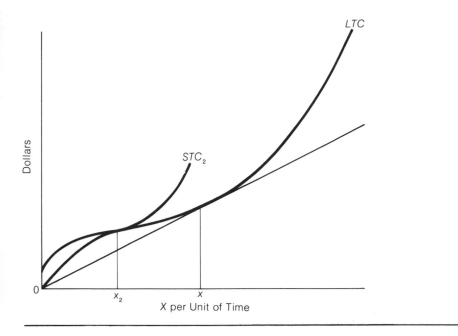

Figure 9–13 Relationship between SMC and LMC for a Given SAC and LAC

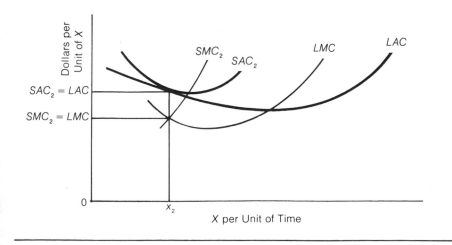

LTC at output levels below x_2 because SAC_2 is greater than LAC at those output levels. At output x_2, STC_2 would be equal to LTC, because SAC_2 and LAC are equal. At outputs greater than x_2, STC_2 would again exceed LTC because SAC_2 for those outputs again lies above LAC. At output x_2, where SAC_2 is tangent to LAC, STC_2 must also be tangent to LTC. At outputs in the neighborhood of, but below x_2, the STC_2 curve must have a smaller slope than the LTC curve. At output levels greater than x_2, the STC_2 curve must have a greater slope than the LTC curve. At x_2, where STC_2 is tangent to LTC, both curves have the same slope.

Because the slope of the STC_2 curve is short-run marginal cost for that size of plant, and because the slope of LTC is long-run marginal cost, it follows that $SMC_2 < LMC$ at outputs just smaller than x_2; $SMC_2 > LMC$ at outputs just larger than x_2; and SMC_2 equals LMC at output x_2. These relationships are shown in Figure 9-13.

Summary

Costs of production are the obligations incurred by the firm for resources used in the production of its product. The cost of any given resource is determined by its value in its best alternative use. This principle is called the alternative cost doctrine. Costs of production differ from the usual concept of the firm's "expenses," which usually coincide with explicit resource costs. In determining costs of production implicit resource costs also must be included. The analysis of costs presented in the chapter assumes that the firm by itself cannot influence the price of any resource that it buys.

In the short run, resources used by the firm are classified as fixed and variable. The obligations incurred for them are fixed costs and variable costs. Total fixed costs and total variable costs for different outputs are the component parts of total costs. From the three total cost curves we derived the corresponding per unit cost curves—average fixed cost, average variable cost, and average cost. The short-run average cost curve shows the least per unit cost of producing different outputs with a given plant size and is a ∪-shaped curve. In addition, we derive the marginal cost curve. The output at which short-run average cost is least is called the optimum rate of output for a given size of plant.

All resources can be varied in quantity by the firm in the long run; consequently, all costs are variable. The long-run average cost curve shows the least per-unit cost of producing various outputs when the firm is free to change its plant to any desired size. It is the envelope curve to the short-run average cost curves of all possible sizes of plant, and it is usually ∪-shaped. The factors causing its ∪ shape are called economies of size and diseconomies of size. The long-run marginal cost curve shows the change in total costs resulting from a one-unit change in output when the firm is free to vary the quantities used of all resources. The size of plant which is the most efficient of all is called the optimum size of plant.

For whatever output the firm produces in the long run, if the least per unit cost is to be obtained for that output the plant size must be such that its short-run average cost curve is tangent to the long-run average cost curve at that output. For such a plant size short-run marginal cost will equal long-run marginal cost at the output of tangency.

Suggested Readings

Stigler, George J., *The Theory of Price*, 3rd ed. (New York: Crowell-Collier and Macmillan, Inc., 1966), Chaps. 6 and 9.

Viner, Jacob, "Cost Curves and Supply Curves," *Zeitschrift für Nationalökonomie*, vol. III (1931), pp. 23–46; reprinted in American Economic Association, *Readings in Price Theory*, George J. Stigler and Kenneth E. Boulding, eds. (Homewood, Ill.: Richard D. Irwin, Inc., 1952), pp. 198–232.

Appendix to Chapter 9
The Geometry of Short-run Per-unit Cost Curves

The relationships between total cost curves and per-unit cost curves can be shown geometrically. Using the three total cost curves as a starting point, we shall derive from them the corresponding per unit cost curves. Then we shall show geometrically the relationship between the average cost curve and the marginal cost curve.

The Average Fixed Cost Curve

The average fixed cost curve of Figure 9-14 (b) is derived from the total fixed cost curve of Figure 9-14 (a). The quantity scales of the two diagrams are the same. The vertical axis of Figure 9-14 (a) measures total fixed costs, whereas that of Figure 9-14 (b) measures fixed cost per unit.

Consider output x in Figure 9-14 (a). At that output total fixed cost is measured by xA. Now consider the straight line $0A$. The slope of $0A$ is $xA/0x$, which is numerically equal to average fixed cost $0R$ in Figure 9-14 (b). Likewise, at output x_1 average fixed cost $0R_1$ in Figure 9-14 (b) equals the slope of $0A_1$ or $x_1A_1/0x_1$.

At successively larger outputs the slopes of the corresponding $0A$ lines become smaller and smaller, showing that average fixed cost decreases as output increases; however, it can never reach zero. The numerical slopes of the $0A$ lines plotted against the respective outputs for which they are drawn comprise the average fixed cost curve of Figure 9-14 (b).

Geometrically, the AFC curve is a rectangular hyperbola. It approaches but never reaches both the dollar axis and the quantity axis. It is convex to the origin of the diagram. The distinguishing feature of a rectangular hyperbola is that at any point on the curve, such as L, the values represented on each axis when multiplied together produce the same mathematical product as the multiplication of the corresponding values at any other point on the curve, such as M. In other words, $0x \times 0R = 0x_1 \times 0R_1$. Such must necessarily be the case for the average fixed cost curve. Because total fixed costs are constant, and because average fixed cost at any output times that output equals total fixed cost, the mathematical product of any

Figure 9 – 14   The Geometry of TFC and AFC

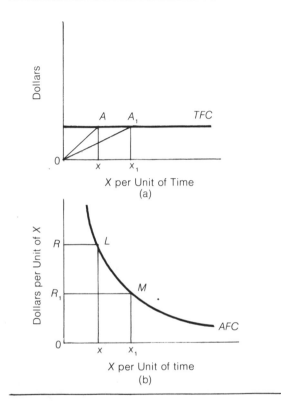

X per Unit of Time
(a)

X per Unit of time
(b)

output times its corresponding average fixed cost must equal the mathematical product of any other output times its corresponding average fixed cost.

The Average Variable Cost Curve

The average variable cost curve in Figure 9-15 (b) is derived from the total variable cost curve in Figure 9-15 (a). The process of derivation is similar to that used in obtaining the *AFC* curve. At output x, *TVC* equals xB; hence, *AVC* at output x equals $xB/0x$, equals the slope of line $0B$. At x_1, *AVC* equals $x_1B_1/0x1$, equals the slope of $0B_1$. At x_3, *AVC* equals $x_3B_3/0x_3$, equals the slope of $0B_3$. At x_4, *AVC* equals $x_4B_4/0x_4$, equals the slope of $0B_4$. The numerical slopes of the $0B$ lines plotted against their respective outputs trace out the *AVC* curve of Figure 9-15 (b).

Figure 9–15   The Geometry of TVC and AVC

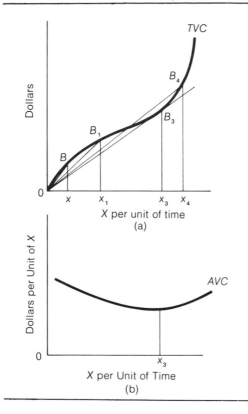

The geometric derivation of the *AVC* curve makes it clear that the curve takes it shape from the *TVC* curve. Between 0 output and output x_3, the *0B* line for each successively larger output must have a smaller slope than the one for the preceding output. Hence, between 0 and x_3, the *AVC* curve must be decreasing. At output x_3, line $0B_3$ is just tangent to the *TVC* curve and thus has a smaller slope than any other *0B* line can possibly have. At x_3, *AVC* is as low as it can get. At outputs greater than x_3, the *0B* lines will increase in slope, meaning that *AVC* is increasing. The *AVC* curve must have a v shape if we have correctly established the shape of the *TVC* curve.

The Average Cost Curve

The average cost curve in Figure 9-16 (b) is derived from the total cost curve in the same way that the *AVC* curve is derived from the *TVC* curve.

Figure 9–16   The Geometry of TC and AC

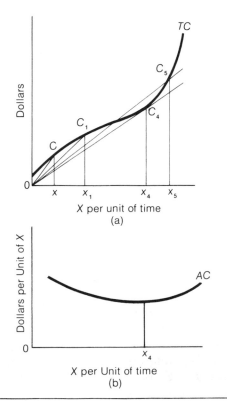

X per unit of time
(a)

X per Unit of time
(b)

At output x, TC equals xC, so AC equals $xC/0x$, equals the slope of line $0C$. At output x_1, AC equals $x_1C_1/0x_1$, equals the slope of $0C_1$. At output x_4, AC equals $x_4C_4/0x_4$, equals the slope of $0C_4$. At output x_5, AC equals $x_5C_5/0x_5$, equals the slope of $0C_5$. The slopes of the $0C$ lines plotted against the corresponding outputs locate the AC curve in Figure 9-16 (b).

If the shape of the TC curve is correct, the AC curve must be a $\vee$ - shaped curve. The $0C$ lines decrease in slope as output increases up to output x_4. At output x_4, $0C_4$ is tangent to the TC curve and, consequently, is the one of least slope. Here AC is minimum. At greater outputs, the slopes of the $0C$ lines are increasing; that is, AC is increasing.

The Relationship of AC and MC

The relationship between AC and MC can be shown geometrically with the aid of the TC curve of Figure 9-17. Consider output x_1. Average cost at

Figure 9–17   The Geometry of AC and MC

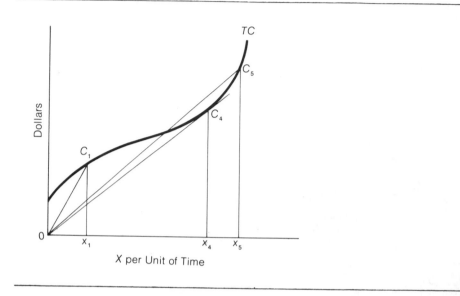

x_1 is equal to the slope of line $0C_1$. Marginal cost at output x_1 is equal to the slope of the *TC* curve at that output. The line $0C_1$ has a greater slope than does the *TC* curve at output x_1; hence, average cost at x_1 is greater than marginal cost at the same output. This will be the case for any output up to x_4. At output x_4, the slope of the line $0C_4$ is equal to the slope of the total cost curve at that output, meaning that average cost and marginal cost are equal at that output. As we have seen already, average cost is minimum at output x_4. At output x_5, the slope of line $0C_5$ is less than the slope of the *TC* curve, meaning that marginal cost is greater than average cost at that output. This relationship will hold at any output above x_4; that is, at outputs for which average cost is increasing. Thus, when average cost is decreasing, marginal cost is less than average cost. When average cost is minimum, marginal cost equals average cost. When average cost is increasing, marginal cost is greater than average cost.

Chapter 10:

Pricing and Output under Pure Competition

Demand, production, and cost analyses are brought together in this chapter to examine the pricing and output mechanism under market conditions of pure competition. The model to be developed presents a pure or frictionless view of how production is organized in a private enterprise economy. Ways in which monopoly elements modify the operation and the results of the system are taken into account in the following three chapters.

Pure competition was defined in Chapter 3. Its prime characteristics are: (1) product homogeneity among the sellers of an industry; (2) many buyers and sellers of the product—that is, enough of each so that no one is large enough relative to the entire market to influence product price—(3) an absence of artificial restraints on demand, supply, and product price; and (4) mobility of goods and resources.

The Very Short Run

The *very short-run* period, or market period, refers to situations in which supplies of products are already in existence. For example, demand for a product may be seasonal, with production scheduled ahead of the season in which the product is to be sold. The clothing industries are cases in point. Spring, summer, fall, and winter production are based on estimated seasonal demands and occur well in advance of the season of sales. Other examples are fresh fruit and vegetable retail markets. Retailers purchase stocks of perishable goods. Once the stocks are on hand they must be disposed of before they spoil. Still another example is that of a product produced seasonally for a demand that continues the year around. Production of wheat and other farm crops is typical of this type of situation. Two basic problems must be solved by the economy in the very short run: (1) how are existing supplies of goods to be allocated or rationed among the many consumers who want them, and (2) how are given supplies to be rationed over their entire very short-run periods?

Rationing among Consumers

Price is the mechanism for rationing or allocating a fixed supply among consumers who want it. Suppose the period during which the supply is fixed is one day, and that the demand curve of Figure 10-1 shows the different quantities per day that consumers will take from the market at different possible prices. The supply curve is vertical, since the supply for the day is fixed. Price p will clear the market. Everyone who wants the commodity at that price will receive it in the desired amounts. At a price below p a shortage will develop, and consumers will drive the price up. At a price above p a surplus will exist, and individual sellers will lower their prices to get surpluses off their hands. At price p consumers voluntarily ration themselves to the fixed supply.

Rationing over Time

Prices also serve to ration a fixed supply over time, but the rationing process is more complex. Suppose that the very short-run period is one year. Suppose, however, that the demand curve of Figure 10-2 is based on a four-month period only. To simplify matters, suppose further that the demand curves for each of the three four-month periods of the year are alike. Assume that sellers correctly anticipate the market for each four-month period and sell or hold their supplies accordingly.

Since the diagram applies to a four-month period only the supply curve for the first four-month period will not be vertical. Sellers have the option of selling during any of the three four-month periods. The higher the price offered during the first period, the greater the quantity of the good they would be expected to place on the market during that period. Thus, the supply curve for the first four-month period will be upward-sloping to the right as in $S_1 S_1$. The market price will be p_1, and the quantity sold will be x_1.

The supply curve for the second four-month period would be expected to lie above $S_1 S_1$, except at low prices, and to be less elastic. It would lie above $S_1 S_1$ because sellers, to be induced to hold quantities over, would require sufficiently higher prices for different quantities to cover storage

Figure 10–1   Very Short Run Rationing among Consumers

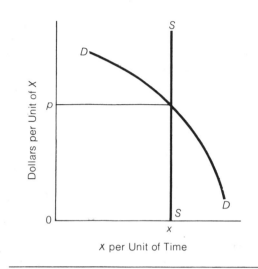

Figure 10–2   Very Short Run Rationing over Time

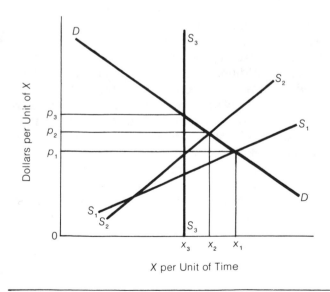

costs and a normal rate of return on investment in the goods carried over.
At extremely low prices, however, the second four-month period may lie to

the right of S_1S_1. The possibility of low prices in the second period would be more serious to sellers than would a similar possibility in the first period, since the opportunities for disposing of supplies held over are reduced. Consequently, sellers may be induced to place more on the market than they would be willing to at those same prices in the first period. The smaller elasticity at various prices is also a result of the narrowing of opportunities for disposing of the supplies held over. The periods during which supply can be disposed of now have been reduced to two. The supply curve for the second period would look something like S_2S_2. The price would be p_2, and the quantity sold would be x_2.

The third four-month period will be identical with the case shown in Figure 10-1. The remaining supply must be disposed of in the third period; consequently, the supply curve will be S_3S_3 in Figure 10-2. Note that S_3S_3 lies above S_2S_2 except at low prices, and that it is less elastic than S_2S_2. In fact, S_3S_3 is completely inelastic. The price will be p_3, and the quantity sold will be x_3.

The successively higher prices for the four-month periods will occur as shown only if sellers correctly anticipate demand and the amounts that should be held over. If sellers misjudge the future market and hold large quantities over to the second and third periods, the prices during those periods may fall below that of the first period. If sellers' anticipations are correct, the price for each successive period should be sufficiently higher than that of preceding periods to pay storage costs, a normal rate of return on investment in held-over supplies, and conpensation for the risks involved in holding supplies over to succeeding periods.

Thus, price is the rationer of fixed supplies over time. Sellers, or speculators, as the case may be, in holding supplies off the market during the early part of the overall very short-run period cause the price to be higher during that time than it would otherwise have been. By their speculative activity they smooth out both the prices and quantities sold over the entire period. In the absence of any speculative activity relatively large quantities would be placed on the market early in the period, holding the price down. Small quantities available in the latter part of the period would cause the price to be high. The speculative activity described above, while it does not eliminate the upward price trend over time, does much to narrow the differential between the early and late parts of the period. Activity of this type occurs regularly in the markets for those storable farm products lying outside the price-support program.

A Corollary

A corollary to this discussion is that once a good is on the market in fixed quantity, costs of production play no part in the determination of its price. The price will be determined solely by the fixed supply, together with demand for the product.[1] It is futile for holders of such a product to try to recoup production costs. A purely competitive seller who cannot consume the product himself will prefer to dispose of his holdings at any price above zero rather than keep it indefinitely. Old bread and overripe bananas are cases in point. Costs of production enter the picture only when there is some possibility of varying the supply produced over the time period under consideration. Such a possibility exists in both the short and the long run, which we have yet to consider.

The Short Run

The short run is a time period in which the firm can vary its output but does not have time to change its size of plant. The number of firms in the industry is fixed, because new firms do not have time to enter and existing firms do not have time to leave. Any changes in industry output must come from the fixed plant capacity of existing firms. Since each firm is too small, relative to the market in which it sells, to be able to affect the market price of the product, the problem facing the firm is that of determining what output to produce and sell. For the market as a whole the market price and market output must be determined.

The Firm

As a starting point we use the premise that a firm's objective is to maximize its profits or to minimize its losses if it cannot make profits. This premise can be modified to include such objectives as sales maximization with a minimum-profit constraint, concern for the environment, enhancement of community cultural activities, and the like. But usually we expect a firm to make those choices that will enable it to make more profits rather than less, and such choices lead toward profit maximization. *Profits* are defined as the difference between the firm's total receipts (*TR*) and its total costs (*TC*).

Profit Maximization: Total Curves. Profit maximization involves a comparison of total costs with total receipts at various possible output levels and choice of the output at which total receipts exceed total costs by the greatest amount. Total receipts, or total revenue at different outputs, are plotted against short-run total costs at various levels of output in Figure 10-3. The total cost curve is the short-run total cost curve of the preceding chapter. The total receipts curve needs further elaboration.

---

[1]Note that in the example of Figure 10-2 market supply is fixed at an absolute quantity for the third period only.

Since the firm can sell either large or small outputs at the same price per unit, its total receipts curve will be a linear upward-sloping curve starting at zero. If sales of the firm are zero, so are total receipts. If sales are one unit of output per unit of time, the firm's total receipts are equal to the price of the product. At two units of output and sales, total receipts will be twice the price of the product. Each one-unit addition to the firm's sales per unit of time will increase total receipts by a constant amount—the price per unit of product—hence, the total receipts curve is upward-sloping and linear.[2]

Profits of the firm are maximum at output x, where the vertical spread between TR and TC is greatest. The amount is measured by the vertical distance AB. At output x the slopes of the two curves are equal. At outputs just smaller than x the slope of TR exceeds that of TC; hence, the two curves spread farther and farther apart as output increases. At outputs just greater than x the slope of TC exceeds that of TR hence, the two curves come closer and closer together as output increases.

The amount by which the firm's total receipts change when its sales are changed by one unit is called *marginal revenue*. Under conditions of pure competition, since the product price is fixed in the firm's view, the change in total receipts brought about by a one-unit change in sales is necessarily equal to the product price. Marginal revenue and the product price for the purely competitive seller are the same thing. In Figure 10-3 an increase in sales from x_0 to $(x_0 + 1)$ increases TR by an amount equal to p. Thus, marginal revenue and product price are equal to the slope of the TR curve.[3]

The necessary conditions for profit maximization can be restated in terms of marginal revenue and marginal cost. Since marginal cost is equal to the slope of the TC curve and marginal revenue is equal to the slope of the TR curve, profits are maximized at the output at which marginal cost equals marginal revenue.[4] At outputs smaller than x we can see that marginal revenue is greater than marginal cost. Therefore, larger out-

---

[2]The total receipts curve can be written as:

$$R = f(x) = xp.$$

[3]The relationship between marginal revenue and total revenue is the same as that between marginal utility and total utility, between marginal physical product and total product of a resource, and between marginal cost and total cost.
Since:

$$R = f(x) = xp,$$

in which p is a constant, then:

$$MR = \frac{dR}{dx} = f'(x) = p.$$

[4]This statement must be used with caution. Consider output x' in Figure 10-3. At output x' *losses* are maximized rather than profits, but marginal cost equals marginal revenue. This matter will be clarified in the discussion of per-unit curves that follows.

Figure 10-3   Short-run Profit Maximization: Total Curves

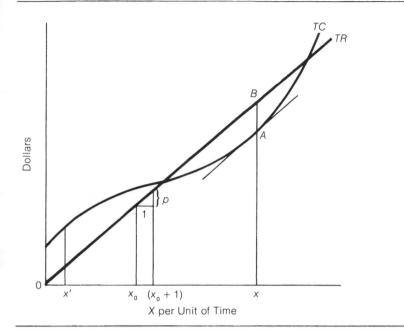

puts up to x will add more to the firm's total receipts than to the firm's total costs and, consequently, will make net additions to profits. Beyond output x marginal cost is greater than marginal revenue. Thus, larger outputs beyond x add more to total costs than to total receipts and cause profits to decrease.[5]

Profit Maximization: Per-unit Curves.   Analysis of the firm's profit-maximizing output is usually put in terms of per-unit cost and revenue curves. The basic analysis is the same as above, but the diagrammatic treatment

---

[5]Denoting profits by π and letting the total cost function be $C = g(x)$, then:

$$\pi = R - C = f(x) - g(x).$$

The necessary conditions for profit maximization are:

$$\frac{d\pi}{dx} = f'(x) - g'(x) = 0,$$

or:

$$f'(x) = g'(x);$$

that is:

$$MR = MC.$$

The sufficient conditions are:

$$\frac{d^2\pi}{dx^2} < 0.$$

is in a different form. The firm's short-run average cost curve and short-run marginal cost curve are shown in Figure 10-4, as is the demand curve faced by the firm. Since marginal revenue is equal to the price per unit, the marginal revenue curve coincides with the demand curve faced by the firm. Both are equal, at all possible output levels of the firm, to the market price of the product.

Profits are maximum at the output level at which marginal cost equals marginal revenue; that is, at x, where SMC equals MR.[6] At any output less than x, say x_0, marginal revenue x_0B exceeds marginal cost x_0A. Larger outputs up to x will increase total receipts more than they increase total costs; hence, profits will increase up to that point. Beyond output x, SMC is greater than MR, and movement to those larger outputs will increase total costs more than they increase total receipts, causing profits to decrease. Therefore, x is the output of maximum profits. Total profits of the firm appear in Figure 10-4 as the area of the rectangle *cpmn*. Profit per unit is the price p minus average cost c at output x. Total profit is equal to profit per unit multiplied by sales; that is, total profit equals $cp \times x$. Note that at output x profit per unit is not maximized, nor is there any reason why it should be. The concern of the firm is with total profits, not with profit per unit.

Loss Minimization. If it should happen that the market price of the product is less than short-run average costs at all possible output levels, the firm will incur losses instead of making profits. Since the short run is defined as a time period so short that the firm cannot change its size of plant, liquidation of the plant in the short run is not possible. The choices open to the firm are: (1) whether to produce at a loss or (2) whether to discontinue production. Fixed costs will be incurred even if the second alternative is chosen.

The firm's decision rests on whether or not the price of the product covers average variable costs (or whether total receipts cover total variable costs). Suppose the market price of the product is p_0 in Figure 10-5. If the firm produces x_0, at which SMC equals MR_0, total receipts equal $p_0 \times x_0$. Total variable costs also equal $p_0 \times x_0$; hence, total receipts just cover total variable costs. Total costs are equal to total variable costs plus total fixed costs; therefore, if variable costs are just covered, the firm's loss with be equal to total fixed costs. It makes no difference whether the firm produces or not. In either case losses equal total fixed costs.

If the market price is less than minimum average variable costs the firm will minimize losses by discontinuing production. The loss will equal total fixed costs when the firm produces nothing. If the firm should produce at a

---

[6]MC equals MR at output x', but this is an output of maximum loss. For profit maximization MC must equal MR and *additionally* the MC curve must intersect the MR curve from below.

Figure 10-4   Short-run Profit Maximization: Per-unit Curves

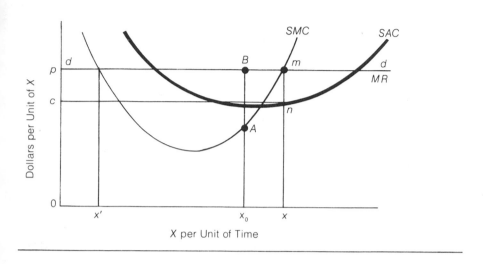

Figure 10-5   Short-run Loss Minimization

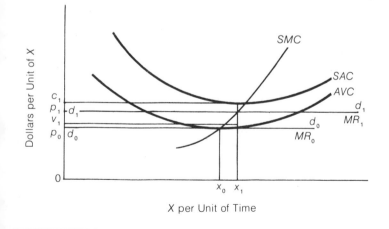

price less than p_0, average variable costs would be greater than price and total variable costs would be greater than total receipts. Losses would equal total fixed costs plus that part of total variable costs not covered by total receipts.

At a price greater than minimum average variable costs, but less than minimum *SAC*, it pays the firm to produce. At such a price as p_1 an output of x_1 results in losses that are less in amount than total fixed costs. Total receipts are $p_1 \times x_1$. Total variable costs are $v_1 \times x_1$. Total receipts exceed total variable costs by an amount equal to $v_1 p_1 \times x_1$. The excess of total receipts over total variable costs can be applied against total fixed costs, thus reducing losses to an amount less than total fixed costs. Loss in this case equals $p_1 c_1 \times x_1$.

Suppose, for example, that the firm under consideration is a wheat farmer who owns his farm and his machinery. The farm is mortgaged and the machinery is not yet paid for. Mortgage and machinery payments constitute his fixed costs and must be met whether or not he produces wheat. Outlays for seed, gasoline, fertilizer, and his own labor represent his variable costs. If he produces nothing there are no outlays on variable resources.

Under what circumstances should he produce nothing at all and hire his labor out to someone else? If expected receipts from the wheat crop are not sufficient to cover the costs of seed, gasoline, fertilizer, and his own labor, he should not produce. If he produces under these circumstances his losses will equal mortgage and machinery payments plus that part of his variable costs not covered by his receipts. If he does not produce, his losses will equal mortgage and machinery payments only. Thus, he should not produce.

Under what circumstances will it be to his advantage to produce even though incurring losses? If expected receipts will more than cover the variable costs the excess can be applied to the mortgage and machinery payments and production should be undertaken. Under these circumstances a decision not to produce means the loss will be the full amount of the fixed costs. If he produces, his loss will be less than his total fixed costs.

At output level x_1 when the market price is p_1 equality between *SMC* and *MR* shows that losses are minimum. At a lower output *MR* is greater than *SMC* and increases in output will add more to total receipts than to total costs, thus reducing losses. Beyond x_1, *SMC* is greater than *MR*, meaning that increases in output add more to total costs than to total receipts. The increases in output will increase the losses. Hence, losses are minimum at the output where *SMC* equals *MR*.

To summarize, the firm maximizes profits or minimizes losses by producing the output at which *SMC* equals *MR*, or the price. There is one exception. If the market price is less than the firm's average variable costs, losses will be minimized by stopping production altogether, leaving losses equal to total fixed costs.

Short-run Supply Curve of the Firm. That part of the firm's *SMC* curve that lies above the *AVC* curve is the firm's *short-run supply curve* for the product. The *SMC* curve shows the different quantities that the firm will place on the market at different possible prices. At each possible price the firm will produce the amount at which *SMC* equals *p* (and *MR*) to maximize profits or minimize losses. Supply drops to zero at any price below *AVC*.

The Market

The market or industry price has been taken as given so far, but we now have the tools necessary to see how it is determined. Market price emerges from interactions between demanders of a good on the one hand and suppliers of the good on the other. We discussed the forces underlying a market demand curve in previous chapters, but we have yet to establish the market supply curve. The short-run market supply curve for a commodity is a short step beyond the individual firm supply curve. After we establish it, we shall consider short-run equilibrium for an entire market.

Short-run Supply Curve of the Market As a first approximation we can think of the *market short-run supply curve* as the horizontal summation of the short-run supply curves of all firms in the market. This supply curve shows the quantities of the commodity that all firms together will place on the market at various possible prices. Such a market short-run supply curve is valid if resource supplies to the group of firms in the market are perfectly elastic; that is, if changes in resource inputs and product output by all firms simultaneously have no effect on resource prices. We shall return to this point shortly.

Short-run Equilibrium. Diagrammatically, Figure 10-6 shows determination of market price, market output, and the output of one representative firm of the industry. The output axis of the market diagram is considerably compressed as compared with that of the firm diagram. The price axes of the two diagrams are identical. The market demand curve for the product is shown as *DD* in the market diagram. The *SAC* and *SMC* curves of the representative firm are drawn in the firm diagram. The horizontal summation of all individual firm supply curves establishes the market short-run supply curve *SS*. The short-run equilibrium market price will be *p*. The demand curve and the marginal revenue curve faced by the firm will be horizontal at that level. To maximize profits the representative firm, and each firm in the market, will produce the output at which *SMC* = *MR* = *p*. The firm output is *x*. The combined outputs of all firms is the market output

Figure 10-6   Short-run Equilibrium: Firm and Industry

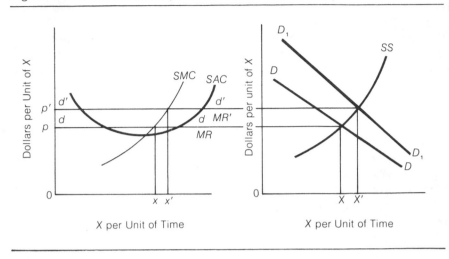

X per Unit of Time   X per Unit of Time

X. The market as a whole and each individual firm in the market are in short-run equilibrium.

An increase in market demand for the product to D_1D_1 will increase the short-run equilibrium price and output. The increase in demand will cause a shortage of the good at the old price p. The price will be driven up by consumers to p'. The demand curve and marginal revenue curve faced by the firm shift up to the level of the new market price. To maximize profits each firm will increase its output up to the level at which its SMC equals its new marginal revenue and the new market price. The new output level for the representative firm will be x', and the new market output will be X'.

Supply Curve Modifications   When an expansion or contraction of resource inputs by all firms acting simultaneously cause resource prices to change, the market short-run supply curve is no longer the horizontal summation of individual firm supply curves. Even though one firm cannot affect resource prices through expansion or contraction of the quantities it buys, all firms acting at the same time may be able to do so. If the expansion of the market output and resource inputs increases resource prices, individual firm cost curves will shift upward. If expansion decreases resource prices, firm cost curves will shift downward. The possibility exists, too, that some resource prices will increase and some will decrease. The effect may be to change the shape of the cost curves slightly and to cause some shift up or down, depending on whether resource price increases or resource price decreases are predominant.

The net effect of resource price increases when expansion occurs will be to make the market short-run supply curve less elastic. In Figure 10-6 the increase in demand increases price and marginal revenue, inducing firms to expand output. But suppose the output expansion causes resource prices to increase, shifting *SAC* and *SMC* upward. The upward shift in *SMC* is also a shift to the left, meaning that the new *SMC* curve will equal marginal revenue or price at a smaller output than would be the case had the *SMC* curve not shifted. Similarly, resource price decreases resulting from expansion of the market output will cause the market supply curve to be more elastic than the market supply curve shown in Figure 10-6. The market short-run supply curve in this case is obtained by summing individual firm profit-maximizing outputs at each possible level of the market price.

The Long Run

The possibilities of output variation in a purely competitive industry are much greater in the long run than in the short run. In the long run output can be varied through increases or decreases in the utilization of existing plant capacity—as is the case in the short run. But more important, in the long run firms have time to increase or decrease their plant sizes, and there is ample time and opportunity for new firms to enter or for existing firms to leave the industry. The two latter possibilities greatly increase the elasticity of the long-run market supply curve as compared with the short-run market supply curve. Long-run adjustments in the size of plant by individual firms will occur simultaneously with the entrance or exist of firms to and from the industry, but they can be more easily understood if they are considered first by themselves.

The Firm

Size of Plant Adjustments The firm's determination of the size of plant to use can be put into proper focus by assuming that entry into the industry is blocked in some way. Suppose the firm is faced with a certain market price, say *p* in Figure 10-7. Its long-run average cost curve and long-run marginal cost curve are *LAC* and *LMC*, respectively. To maximize long-run profits the firm should produce output *x* at which long-run marginal cost equals marginal revenue. The plant size that enables the firm to produce output *x* at the least possible cost per unit is *SAC*, and for that size of plant short-run marginal cost also is equal to marginal revenue. Profits of the firm are *cp* × *x*.

Digression on Profits   A note on profits is in order before proceeding further, since the concept of profit is ambiguous enough to require explicit definition. *Economic profits* are a pure surplus or an excess of total receipts over *all* costs of production incurred by the firm. Included as costs are obligations incurred for all resources used equal to what those resources could earn employed in their next best alternative use; that is, the opportunity or alternative costs of all resources used. These costs include returns to the owners of capital used equivalent to what they could get had they invested in capital elsewhere in the economy. They include implicit returns to labor owned by the operator of the business. Thus, profits are so much "gravy" for the firm.

The contrast between the concept of economic profits as defined and the accountant's concept of a corporation's net income or "profits" should help make this definition clear. Corporation income taxes will be ignored. A corporation's "profits" are determined by the accountant as follows:

Gross income
− Expenses (including interest payments on bonds,
                          amortization expenses, depreciation expenses, and so on)
= Net income or "profits"

However, from the point of view of economics, certain costs have been left out of consideration. Obligations incurred to the owners of the corporation's capital (its stockholders) are as much costs of production as are those incurred for labor or for raw materials. The corporation is usually thought to make payments to capital owners in the form of dividends from the corporation's "profits," but from the point of view of economic theory such a conception is incorrect. To arrive at economic profits dividend payments equal to what investors could earn had they invested elsewhere in the economy should be subtracted from the corporation's net income as follows:

Net income or "profits"
− Average dividends
= Economic profits

What happens to profits made by an individual firm? They accrue primarily to the owners of the firm in the form of higher returns to investors in the business or in the form of increases in the value of the owners' holdings. The former means higher-than-average dividends to stockholders in the case of the corporation, or a higher income in the case of a single proprietor or partner than he could have earned had he invested and/or worked elsewhere. The latter means that some of the economic profits are

Figure 10-7 Plant Size Adjustment in the Long Run

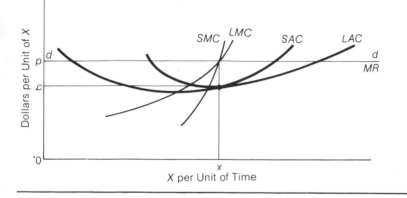

plowed back into the firm to expand or improve it. This action increases the value of the owners' holdings. Profits may be used sometimes to pay other resource owners returns that are more than the opportunity costs of their resources.

The Firm and the Market

Long-run Equilibrium   *Long-run equilibrium* for a firm means that it has either no incentive or no opportunity to change what it is doing. If profit maximization is its objective, the firm of Figure 10-7 is in long-run equilibrium. Its $LMC = MR = p$, so that there is no incentive to change the size of its plant. Its $SMC = MR = p$, so that there is no incentive to move from an output level of x per unit of time.

Long-run equilibrium for the industry implies more than that the firms in the industry are in long-run equilibrium. In addition, there must be no incentive for new firms to enter the industry or for existing firms to leave. In other words, there must be no lure of economic profits to induce the entry of new firms, nor can there be the pain of losses to induce present firms to leave.

If entry into the industry is open—and in pure competition it is not blocked—profits like those made by the firm of Figure 10-7 will attract new firms. The industry promises a rate of return to investors greater than that they can earn on the average elsewhere in the economy. The entry of new firms increases the supply of product X and causes the price to move downward from its original level p. Each individual firm in the industry, faced with a downward-shifting demand curve and marginal revenue curve, will cut its output level below x and will reduce its scale of plant below SAC. In the interests of maximizing profits outputs will be cut to levels at which the long-run marginal cost curve cuts the successively lower marginal revenue curves.

Economic profits can be made by firms in the industry until enough firms have entered to drive the price down to p_1, as is shown in Figure 10-8. At that point individual firms will have cut their plant size back to the optimum as is shown by SAC_1; and they will operate at the optimum rate of output. Economic profits have been eliminated by the entry of new firms, and there is no incentive for more firms to enter. No losses are being incurred, and thus there is no incentive for firms to leave the industry. The firms in the industry are doing satisfactorily; they are earning returns for all resources equal to what those resources could earn in alternative employments.[7]

The industry is in long-run equilibrium when all firms of the industry are in the position shown in Figure 10-8. For every firm $LAC = SAC = p$ at the output being produced, and at no other output can lower average costs be obtained. Also, for each firm there is no incentive to increase or decrease scale of plant or output since $LMC = SMC = MR$.

For a long-run industry equilibrium to exist, individual firms must also be in a long-run equilibrium. The converse of this assertion will not hold. An individual firm could be in long-run equilibrium while making profits—as in Figure 10-7, for example. But in this case the industry would not be in equilibrium. The existence of long-run industry equilibrium requires long-run individual firm equilibrium at a no-profit, no-loss level of operation.

Similarly, long-run industry and individual firm equilibrium requires that short-run equilibrium exist at the same time. But short-run individual firm and industry equilibrium can exist even though there is long-run individual firm and/or industry disequilibrium. Long-run equilibrium of an

---

[7]In the discussion of the long run we shall assume that for all firms, both in the industry and potentially in it, the minimum points of the LAC curves lie at the same level. This condition is a necessary one for defining the long-run equilibrium position of an industry.

In reality long-run equilibrium is never likely to be achieved in any industry. It is a will-o'-the-wisp that industries forever chase but never catch. Before an industry can reach equilibrium, conditions defining the equilibrium position change. Demand for the product changes, or costs of production change as a result of resource price changes, or techniques of production alter. Thus, the chase goes on toward a new equilibrium position. The long-run (and other) equilibrium concepts are important, however, because they show us the motivation for and the direction of the chase. Additionally, they show us how the chase works toward (in most cases) solution of the economic problem.

The argument usually made regarding equality of minimum long-run average costs of firms in the industry rests on the alternative cost doctrine. Initial inequalities in such costs may result from superior management of particular firms; from favorable locations of certain firms with respect to power, markets, and sources of raw and semifinished materials; or from other similar causes. According to the alternative cost doctrine these differentials will not persist. The superior manager who can make profits for his firm could do the same for other firms in the industry and, perhaps, in others outside the industry. His prospective value to other firms becomes his cost to the firm in which he works; thus, the cost of his services to the one firm increases to the point at which he can make pure profits for none. The same argument applies to a favorable location. The cost of the favorable location becomes its value to other firms which could use it to advantage. Its value to other firms is the capitalized value of the returns it could earn for them. Hence, the profits it can earn for any one firm disappear as its cost is correctly determined.

Figure 10-8 Long-run Equilibrium

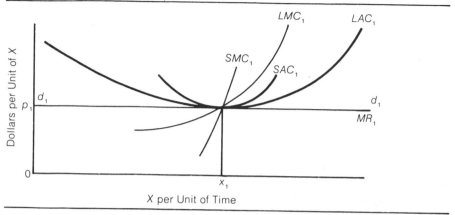

industry is a more general concept than is either long-run equilibrium for a firm or short-run equilibrium for both a firm and an industry.

Although this analysis serves to introduce the concept of long-run equilibrium in a purely competitive industry, it is by no means a complete analysis of the long-run adjustments within the industry that occur as a result of some disturbing force. Usually cost changes as well as price changes will take place as new firms, attracted by profits, enter the industry. The nature of the cost adjustments, if any, will depend on whether the industry is one of increasing costs, constant costs, or decreasing costs. Each of these will be analyzed in turn below.

Increasing Costs   Consider first an industry of *increasing costs*. The nature of increasing costs will become evident as we move through the analysis. Suppose that the industry is initially in long-run equilibrium. Then suppose that the disturbing force is an increase in demand for product X. We shall trace through the short-run and long-run effects of the increase in demand. Then the long-run market supply curve for the product will be established.

Long-run equilibrium diagrams for the industry and for a representative firm of the industry are shown in Figure 10-9. The market demand curve is *DD*, and the market short-run supply curve is *SS*. The firm's long-run average cost curve and short-run average cost curve are *LAC* and *SAC*, respectively. The firm's short-run marginal cost curve for scale of plant *SAC* is *SMC*. The long-run marginal cost curve is omitted. It is not essential for the analysis and unduly complicates the diagram.

Since the industry and the firm are in long-run equilibrium, they are necessarily in short-run equilibrium, too. Therefore, we can think of the market demand curve and the market short-run supply curve as establishing the industry price p. The demand curve and the marginal revenue curve faced by the firm are horizontal and are equal to price p at all levels of output for the firm. The firm produces the output at which SMC (and LMC) equals marginal revenue or price. Individual firm output is x. Industry output X is the summation of individual firm outputs at price p. There are just enough firms in the industry to make the price equal to minimum short-run and long-run average costs for the firm at output x. The firm is using the optimum size of plant at the optimum rate of output. There are no economic profits or losses being incurred.

Now suppose we consider the short-run effects of an increase in demand to D_1D_1. The market price will rise to p'. The firm, in order to maximize profits, will increase output to x', the output at which SMC equals the new marginal revenue. Industry output will increase to X'. The firm will be making profits equal to output x', multiplied by the difference between price p' and short-run average costs at output x'. The short-run effects of the increase in demand are: (1) an increase in price and (2) some increase in output as existing plant capacity is worked with greater intensity.

Turning now to the long-run effects, the existence of profits will bring new firms into the industry. As new firms enter, increasing the industry's productive capacity, the market short-run supply curve will shift to the right. The more firms that enter, the farther to the right the curve will move. The increase in supply will cause price to move downward from the short-run high of p'. As the price goes down, individual firms will cut output back from the short-run high of x'.

In an increasing cost industry the entry of new firms causes the whole set of cost curves for existing firms to shift upward. Such a shift will occur in an industry that uses significant proportions of the total supplies available of the resources necessary for making its product. Suppose, for example, that one such resource is a special steel alloy. The entry of new firms in the industry increases the demand for such resources, thus increasing their prices. As resource prices rise, the set of cost curves shifts upward accordingly.

Any given set of cost curves presupposes that the firm can get all it wants of any one resource at a constant price per unit. No single firm causes the prices of resources to change, since it does not take a large enough amount of any resource to be able to affect its price. It is the greater demand for resources brought about by the entry of new firms into the industry and, perhaps, by the simultaneous expansion of output by existing firms that causes resource prices to rise. The forces causing resource prices to rise lie completely outside the control of the individual firm, and are said to be *external* to the firm. The increases in resource

Figure 10-9   Effects of Changes in Demand: Increasing Costs

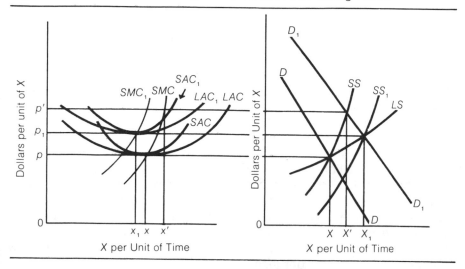

prices and the consequent upward shifts of the cost curves are thus the result of *external diseconomies* of increasing production in the industry.

A two-way squeeze is put on profits by the entry of new firms as the price falls and costs rise. New firms enter until the price decreases enough and costs rise enough for the price to be equal again to minimum long-run average costs for individual firms. All profit is squeezed out. In Figure 10-9 the new price is p_1, and the new cost curves are LAC_1, SAC_1, and SMC_1. The entry of new firms stops and the industry is once more in long-run equilibrium. The new long-run market price of p_1 lies between the original long-run price of p and the short-run high of p'. The new firm output is x_1 at which SMC_1 is equal to the new long-run marginal revenue and price. Industry output will have increased to X_1, since the increased capacity of the industry has moved the short-run supply curve to SS_1 [8]

Some question may arise with regard to the new long-run output of the firm. Will it be equal to, greater than, or less than the old long-run output of x? The answer depends upon the way in which the cost curves shift upward. Whether the cost curves shift straight up, a little to the left, or a little to the

---

[8]To keep an already complex exposition as simple as possible, a long-run development of a transitory nature has been ignored in the argument of the text. The short-run high price, resulting from the increase in demand for the product, not only attracts profit-seeking new firms into the industry but also creates an incentive for existing firms to increase their plant sizes beyond the optimum. This situation will be the case since for the individual firm maximum long-run profits are obtained at the output at which long-run marginal cost equals marginal revenue and price (see Figure 10-7). Then, as the entrance of new firms lowers price, the output at which long-run marginal cost equals price becomes smaller. The firm is induced to reduce its plant size. When enough firms have entered to eliminate profits, the firm once more will be building the optimum size of plant.

right depends on the comparative price increases of different classes of resources. If all resource prices increase proportionally, the same combinations of resources will be the least-cost combinations. The cost curves will shift straight up, and the new long-run firm output will be equal to the old. Suppose, however, that short-run fixed resources go up relatively more in price than do those which are considered variable in the short run. The firm will want to economize on the now relatively more expensive fixed resources. The proportions of the relatively more expensive fixed resources to the relatively cheaper variable ones will be decreased to secure least-cost combinations. The optimum size of plant will tend to be slightly smaller in the new long-run equilibrium position than it was in the old. Hence, the new long-run equilibrium firm output will tend to be smaller than the old, as is shown in Figure 10-9. If short-run fixed resources increase proportionally less in price than do short-run variable resources, least-cost combinations favor larger sizes of plant. The firm will want to economize on the now relatively more expensive resources and use larger proportions of those which constitute the plant. The new optimum size of plant and the new output will tend to be larger than the old.

The long-run industry supply curve is LS in Figure 10-9. It joins all points of long-run equilibrium for the industry. Alternatively, the industry long-run supply curve can be thought of as the horizontal summation of the minimum points of all individual firm LAC curves as the entry of new firms shifts their cost curves upward. The industry long-run supply curve shows the industry outputs that will be forthcoming at different possible prices when there is ample time for size of plant adjustments as well as for the entry and exit of firms.

Constant Costs   The pattern of analysis for an industry of constant costs is basically the same as that for an industry of increasing costs. Starting from the position of long-run equilibrium shown in Figure 10-10, suppose that an increase in demand occurs. The short-run effects are the same as before. The price will increase to p'; the firm's output will increase to x'; and the market output will increase to X'. Economic profits will be made by the individual firms of the industry.

New firms will be attracted into the industry in the long run. As before, the short-run market supply curve will shift to the right as new firms enter, causing the price to decrease.

In a *constant cost* industry the entry of new firms does not increase market demands for resources sufficiently to cause their prices to increase. Of the total supplies of resources necessary for the production of X, this industry takes a small enough part so that no influence is exerted on their prices by the new firms coming in. If the entry of new firms has no effect on resource prices, the cost curves of existing firms will remain as

Figure 10 – 10   Effects of Changes in Demand: Constant Costs

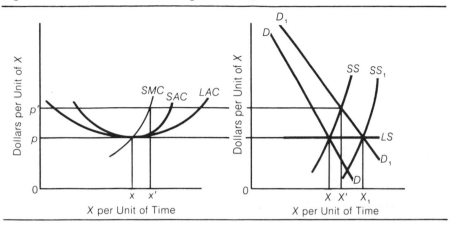

they were before. Profits will be made until enough firms have entered to bring the price back down to *p*. Price and minimum long-run average costs will be equal, and long-run equilibrium will be re-established. The new short-run supply curve will be SS_1. Individual firm output will be that at which *SMC* equals marginal revenue and price *p*. The entry of new firms will have increased industry output substantially to X_1. The long-run supply curve will be *LS* and will be horizontal at the level of minimum long-run average costs.

Decreasing Costs   Decreasing cost cases are probably rather rare. Analytically, they parallel increasing and constant cost cases. As before, we start with an industry and its firms in long-run equilibrium and then assume demand increases. The short-run effects are the same as before. In Figure 10-11 the market price will increase to *p'*; firm output goes up to *x'*; and the industry output increases to *X'*. Pure profits equal to *x'* times the difference between *p'* and *SAC* at output *x'* will be made by the representative firm.

New firms will be attracted into the industry in the long run because of the pure profits available. The industry short-run supply curve moves to the right as new firms add to the industry's productive capacity. Price goes down as new firms enter.

In a *decreasing cost industry* the entry of new firms must cause resource prices to fall. The decrease in resource prices as new firms enter causes the cost curves to shift downward. Both the price of *X* and costs of prodution are decreasing. Eventually the declining product price overtakes the declining cost curves and profit is squeezed out. The new long-run equilibrium price is p_1 and is less than the original price of *p*. Individual

Figure 10–11   Effects of Changes in Demand: Decreasing Costs

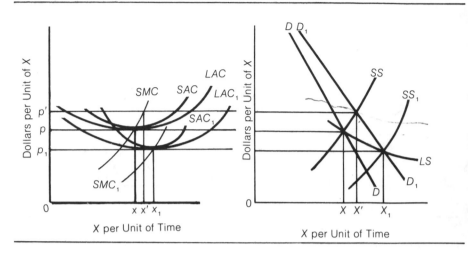

firm output is x_1, at which both short-run and long-run marginal costs equal marginal revenue or price. The new industry output is X_1. The long-run supply curve *LS* will be downward-sloping to the right.

What are the circumstances that could conceivably give rise to decreasing costs? Suppose the industry in question is a young one growing up in a new territory.[9] Transportation facilities and the organization of markets, both for resources and the final product, may not be well-developed. An increase in the number of firms in the industry and, consequently, in the size of the industry may make feasible the development of improved transportation and marketing facilities that will substantially reduce the costs of individual firms. For example, industrial growth of an area may stimulate development and improvement of railway, highway, and air transportation service into and out of the area. However, good explanations of decreasing costs are rather hard to find; whatever the explanations given for particular cases, they usually stem basically from improvements in the quality of resources furnished or from greater efficiencies developed in the resource-furnishing industries.

Decreasing costs, or *external economies* of increasing production, as discussed above, should not be confused with the *internal economies of size* possible for a single firm with a smaller than optimum size of plant. The individual firm has no influence over external economies. These result solely from expansion of the industry or from forces outside the control of

---

[9]In this case the chances of its being one of pure competition are small.

the firm. Internal economies of size are under the control of the firm. The firm can secure them by enlarging its plant.

Probably, increasing cost industries are the most prevalent of the three cases analyzed. Decreasing costs are most unlikely to occur. Industries of constant cost and of decreasing cost are likely to become industries of increasing cost as they become older and more well-established. Granting the possibility of decreasing costs, once the decreasing costs or external economies of increasing production have been taken advantage of, the industry must surely become one of constant or increasing costs.

The disturbing force triggering these chains of adjustments was assumed to be an increase in demand for the product. It could just as well have been a decrease in demand, in which case losses would occur for individual firms and exit from the industry would have occurred until long-run equilibrium was again established. Or, in lieu of changes in demand, we could have assumed that major technological developments caused disequilibrium to occur, and these would induce new firms to enter the industry until long-run equilibrium was re-established.

The Welfare Effects of Pure Competition

In a private enterprise economic system what effects on welfare would be expected if the market structure in which producers and sellers operate were purely competitive? A complete assessment of the expected effects must wait until we have examined resource pricing and employment in detail; however, some tentative statements can be made at this point.

The welfare effects of purely competitive forces can be brought out by summarizing how the purely competitive mechanism operates. Suppose that initially disequilibrium exists—there is a random array of prices, outputs, and distribution of productive capacity (resources). There are two "givens" throughout the discussion: (1) pure competition exists in all markets and (2) the distribution of purchasing power does not change. We will focus attention on two goods, food (F) and clothing (C).

The Very Short Run

In the very short run consumers, confronted with the initial prices of goods and services, attempt to allocate their incomes so as to maximize satisfaction. Since supplies are initially fixed, prices move to the levels that will just clear the markets. All exchanges that are mutually beneficial occur as prices move toward their equilibrium levels; and, since such exchanges benefit the exchanging parties without decreasing the welfare of anyone external to the exchanges, community welfare increases. Community welfare with fixed supplies is maximum when for each consumer:

$$\frac{MU_f}{p_f} = \frac{MU_c}{p_c}$$

or:

$$\frac{MU_f}{MU_c} = \frac{p_f}{p_c}$$

or:

$$MRS_{fc} = \frac{p_f}{p_c}$$

The Short Run

If the plant capacity in food and clothing production is fixed and outputs of both products are not at short-run profit-maximizing levels, will the consequent adjustments increase welfare? Suppose that firms producing food are operating at outputs such that $SMC_f < p_f$, and that clothing firms are producing outputs at which $SMC_c > P_c$. The production of clothing will be reduced and the production of food will be increased. Community welfare will be increased in the process. Consumers value variable resources used in producing F more than they value them used in producing other goods. This differential valuation is the meaning of $SMC_f < p_f$. The price p_f is the value that consumers place on any one unit of F at the current supply level. At current production levels of F the short-run marginal cost of F is the value of the products that the resources used in producing the last one-unit increment in F can turn out in their best alternative uses. Consequently, consumer welfare can be increased by transfers of resources from those other uses into the production of F; that is, from uses in which those resources produce a smaller value of product into the use where their output is of greater value. Similarly, $SMC_c > p_c$ means that consumers value resources used in producing C less than they value them used in producing other goods. Consumer welfare can be increased by resource transfers from C into the production of other goods.

The purely competitive market mechanism induces producers to accomplish the output changes that consumers desire. To maximize profits or to minimize losses in the short run producers of F want to increase their outputs to levels at which $SMC_f = p_f$. Producers of C desire to contract their outputs to levels at which $SMC_c = p_c$. Producers in industry F offer slightly higher prices for the necessary variable resources. In industry C output contraction decreases demand for variable resources used in that industry, which in turn depresses the prices offered for those variable resources. To the extent that F and C use the same kinds of variable resources, voluntary reallocation by resource owners, from the lower-paying to the higher-paying uses sufficient to equalize their remuneration in the two uses, will occur. If the two industries use different kinds of variable resources, a general reallocation of variable resources may occur throughout the economy. Reallocation may occur from industry C to other industries which can use the kinds of variable resources used in producing C. In turn, reallocation of the kinds of resources used in industry F from other industries to industry F may occur. The overall short-run resource reallocation which occurs will be limited, however, by the existing plant capacity in the two industries. Short-run equilibrium exists in the two industries when $SMC_f = p_f$ and $SMC_c = p_c$.

The Long Run

Although the short-run reorganization of production increases the welfare of consumers, it stops short of maximizing it because of fixed plant capacity in each industry. In the long run there is ample time for productive capacity to move; that is, for firms to enter and to exit whenever incentives to do so occur.

Suppose that in short-run equilibrium firms in industry F show profits while those in C incur losses. The profits in F and the losses in C mean that consumers value investment in plant and equipment more in industry F and less in industry C than they value it in other uses; their welfare will be increased by transfers of investment out of C, where they value it less, and into F, where they value it more. The incentives motivating producers bring about this result.

The short-run losses in C bring about rates of return on investment in that industry below what investment elsewhere in the economy will earn. Consequently, disinvestment in C will occur—through failure to take care of depreciation on plant and equipment and through the eventual liquidation of some existing firms. As firms leave industry C the supply of C decreases, causing its price to rise. The decreased demands for resources in industry C lower their prices, decreasing costs of production for individual firms. The exit of firms will cease when the decreasing supply has increased the price and lowered costs enough so that losses are no longer being incurred. A smaller number of firms in C will be producing with optimum-sized plants and optimum rates of output, but in total they will produce a smaller combined output at a higher price than in the short run.

At the same time short-run profits in industry F will be attracting resources (productive capacity) into that industry. The profits indicate a higher return on investment than investors can earn elsewhere in the economy. This is a lucrative field in which to invest. New firms are established in the industry. Increasing demands for resources raise resource prices and the cost curves both of entering firms and firms already in the industry. The entry of new firms increases industry supply, driving the price down. New firms enter until the increasing supply lowers the price of F to the level of the higher average costs. Entry stops when profits no longer appear to be obtainable to entering firms. Firms are forced to use optimum plant sizes and operate them at optimum rates of output to avoid losses. More firms are in the industry; their combined outputs are greater; and the product price is lower than it was in the short run.

The reallocation of resources may be direct or indirect. If the plant capacity of firms in industry C can be easily converted to the production of product F, firms in industry C may simply switch over to producing the more profitable F. Or, if the production processes of the two industries are unrelated, reallocations will be of the indirect nature described above, with firms folding in industry C and new firms emerging in industry F. In either case profits and losses, and differential prices for resources in the two industries, bring about the desirable reallocation of resources or productive capacity.

With the re-establishment of long-run equilibrium the two industries again achieve the greatest possible economic efficiency. Individual firms in each industry operate optimum plant sizes at optimum rates of output. Consumers receive units of each product at prices equal to the minimum obtainable average cost per unit. Some of the economy's resources or productive capacity has been switched from the production of one commodity to another in response to changes in consumer tastes and preferences.

Equilibrium and Welfare

The achievement of long-run equilibrium conditions in purely competitive markets appears to lead to maximum consumer welfare. As we examine the other market structures we shall find that they fall short of reaching the summit—one of our tasks is to assess the extent to which they fall short. The purely competitive model provides an excellent bench mark for this purpose, and thus several conditions or characteristics of pure competition and long-run purely competitive equilibrium that have important welfare implications are worth noting.

First, pure competition leads to that organization of productive capacity at which *prices of products are equal to their per-unit costs — marginal and average.* There are no profits or losses. Productive capacity (resources) is so allocated that it is valued equally by consumers in all its alternative uses, and no reallocation can increase welfare.

Second, *each firm operates at peak efficiency,* producing its product output at the least possible cost per unit. In long-run equilibrium the firm is induced to operate an optimum size plant at the optimum rate of output in order to avoid losses. It takes advantage of all possible economies of size as well as using the most efficient resource combination for the output level it produces.

Third, *resources are not diverted into sales promotion efforts.* No necessity exists for individual firms to engage in aggressive activities to promote sales when they sell in purely competitive markets. One firm alone cannot influence product price, and the products produced by all firms in the industry are homogeneous. Since the individual firm can sell all it wishes to sell at the going market price, sales promotion to increase its volume is unnecessary. The homogeneity of the product produced by all sellers largely precludes sales promotional activities on the part of one to raise his price. Buyers have so many alternative sources of supply that price increases on the part of one seller cause his sales to drop to zero.

Summary

This chapter draws together the analysis of demand and the analysis of costs to show how the price system organizes production under the special conditions of pure competition. Pricing and output are discussed from the time viewpoints of the very short run, the short run, and the long run.

Supplies of goods are fixed in amount in the very short run. Price serves to ration existing supplies among consumers. Additionally, price rations the fixed supply over the duration of the period of the very short run.

Individual firm outputs can be varied within the limits of their fixed sizes of plant in the short run. In order to maximize profits individual firms produce the outputs at which their short-run marginal costs equal marginal revenue or product price. Industry price of a product is determined by the interactions of all consumers and all producers of the product. Individual firms may make profits or incur losses in the short run.

In the long run additional firms will enter industries that make profits, and some existing firms will leave industries in which losses occur. Thus, productive capacity expands in the former industries and contracts in the latter. Expansion of productive capacity lowers market price of the product and decreases individual firm profits. Contraction of productive capacity increases market price and reduces losses. Long-run equilibrium exists in each industry when the number of firms in the industry is just sufficient for profits not to be made nor losses incurred. When an industry is in long-run equilibrium, product price equals average cost of production. Each firm must be operating an optimum scale of plant at the optimum rate of output if losses are to be avoided.

Industries may be characterized as increasing cost, constant cost, or decreasing cost industries. Increasing costs occur when the entrance of new firms into an industry increases the prices of resources used to produce the product. The resulting higher costs are called external diseconomies. In constant cost industries the entrance of new firms does not increase demand for resources enough to raise their prices. Consequently, no changes in the costs of existing firms occur. Decreasing costs, which must be rare in the real world, occur when the entrance of new firms causes resource prices and costs of production to fall. These are termed external economies.

Pure competition has certain welfare effects or implications that are important. In the first place consumers get products at prices equal to their per unit costs of production. Second, pure competition, where pure competition can exist, results in the greatest economic efficiency. Third, there is little motivation for sales promotion efforts on the part of individual firms.

Suggested Readings

Boulding, Kenneth E., *Economic Analysis*, 4th ed., vol. 1, (New York: Harper & Row Publishers, 1966), Chaps. 18 and 19.

Marshall, Alfred, *Principles of Economics*, 8th ed. (London: Macmillan & Co., Ltd., 1920), Bk. V, Chaps. IV and V.

Viner, Jacob, "Cost Curves and Supply Curves," *Zeitschrift für Nationalökonomie*, vol. III (1931), pp. 23–46.

Chapter 11:

Pricing and Output under Pure Monopoly

The nature of pure monopoly was explained in Chapter 7; however, it may be good to recount its essential characteristics. Pure monopoly is a market situation in which there is a single seller of a product for which there are no good substitutes. The product sold by the monopolist must be clearly different from other products sold in the economy. Changes in the prices and outputs of other goods must leave the monopolist unaffected. Conversely, changes in the monopolist's price and output must leave the other producers of the economy unaffected.

Pure monopoly in the real world is rare. Local public-utility industries approximate it. Other industries that approach this type of market structure include the manufacturing of locomotives, telephone equipment, and shoe machinery, as well as the production of magnesium and nickel.[1] But monopoly is not total unless substitutes are nonexistent. In the public utility field gas and electricity are to some extent substitutes. Aluminum also has substitutes, as do the metal alloys produced with the aid of molybdenum and magnesium.

Whether or not monopoly exists in pure form, the principles of pure monopoly provide an indispensable tool for analyzing problems of pricing, output, resource allocation, and welfare. In the first place monopoly tools of analysis are the most fruitful ones to apply to industries approach-

---

[1]F.M. Sherer, *Industrial Market Structure and Economic Performance* (Chicago: Rand McNally & Co., 1970), p. 59.

ing pure monopoly or which act in many instances in a monopolistic fashion. Second, monopoly tools of analysis and modifications of them are invaluable in the study of oligopoly and monopolistic competition. We shall discuss first some of the basic concepts of monopoly analysis. A discussion of short-run and long-run pricing and output will follow. Next we shall analyze the effects of monopoly on welfare. Control of monopoly pricing will then be considered. Finally, we shall turn our attention to price discrimination.

Costs and Revenues under Monopoly

Costs of Production

For the analysis of pure monopoly the cost concepts used are those that were built up in Chapter 9 and used in the case of pure competition. Pure monopoly differs from pure competition with respect to product sales, not with respect to costs of production. We shall assume that the monopolistic seller of a product is a purely competitive buyer of resources and has no effect on resource prices.[2] He can get as much of any resource as he desires without affecting its price per unit.

Revenues

The difference between the purely competitive firm and the monopolist lies on the selling side. Since the pure competitor can sell all he wants at the going market price, his marginal revenue and price are equal. The monopolist faces the market demand curve for his product; hence, the more he sells per unit of time, the lower must be his price. There are important implications here for the monopolist's marginal revenue in relation to price.

Marginal revenue at different levels of sales per unit of time for the monopolist will be less than the price per unit at those sales levels. Consider Table 11-1. A typical demand schedule faced by a monopolist is shown by columns 1 and 2. Total revenue at different levels of sales is listed in column 3, and at any given level of sales equals the price multiplied by the quantity sold. The marginal revenue column shows the changes in total receipts resulting from one-unit changes in the sales level. With the exception of the first unit, marginal revenue is less than the price at each level of sales. Suppose the firm's current level of sales in 3 units of X.

---

[2]Modifications of cost curves to take account of a single firm's influence on resource prices are deferred to Chapter 15. If used here the modifications would make no essential difference in the development of the chapter.

Table 11-1   Demand, Total Revenue and Marginal Revenue Schedules

(1) Price	(2) Quantity per Unit Time	(3) Total Revenue	(4) Marginal Revenue
$10	1	$10	$10
9	2	18	8
8	3	24	6
7	4	28	4
6	5	30	2
5	6	30	0
4	7	28	(−)2
3	8	24	(−)4
2	9	18	(−)6
1	10	10	(−)8

Price per unit is $8 and total receipts are $24. Now suppose the firm desires to increase sales per unit of time to 4 units of X. It must reduce the price per unit to $7 in order to expand sales. The fourth unit sells for $7. However, the firm takes a $1 loss per unit on its previous sales volume of 3 units. The total loss of $3 must be deducted from the selling price of the fourth unit in order to compute the net increase in total receipts resulting from the one-unit increase in sales. Thus, marginal revenue at a sales volume of 4 units is seen to be $7 − $3 = $4 (the difference between $28 and $24).

When the demand schedule and marginal revenue schedule of Table 11-1 are plotted on the same diagram, the marginal revenue curve lies below the demand curve. In fact, the marginal revenue curve bears the same relationship to the demand curve as does any marginal curve to its corresponding average curve. The demand curve is the firm's average revenue curve. When any average curve—average product, average cost, or average revenue—decreases as the firm's output increases, the corresponding marginal curve lies below it.[3]

A useful proposition in economic analysis states that at any given level of sales by the firm, marginal revenue equals product price minus the ratio of price to elasticity of demand at that sales level; that is,

---

[3]If the demand curve is of the form:

$$p = a - bx,$$

then:

$$TR = xp = xa - bx^2$$

and:

$$MR = \frac{d\,(TR)}{dx} = a - 2bx.$$

A geometric method of finding the marginal revenue curve for a given demand curve is developed in Appendix I of this chapter.

$MR = p - p/\epsilon$.[4] The proposition ties together the relationships among the firm's marginal revenue, total revenue, price, and elasticity of demand. Consider the demand curve faced by a purely competitive firm as is shown in Figure 11-1 (a). Elasticity of demand at all outputs approaches infinity (∞). Because $MR = p - p/\epsilon$ and because $\epsilon \to \infty$, p/ϵ approaches zero and MR approaches p; that is, for all practical purposes $MR = p$ at all outputs. Now consider a monopolist faced by the straight-line demand curve of Figure 11-1 (b). At output M, halfway between zero and T, $\epsilon = 1$. At smaller outputs $\epsilon > 1$ and at larger outputs $\epsilon < 1$.[5]

We noted in Chapter 3 that an increase in sales when $\epsilon > 1$ causes TR to increase. This means that when $\epsilon > 1$, MR must be positive. The equation $MR = p - p/\epsilon$ states the same thing. If $\epsilon > 1$, then p/ϵ must be less than p and MR must be positive. The greater ϵ is, the smaller p/ϵ will be, and the smaller will be the difference between p and MR. At the output where $\epsilon = 1$, TR is maximum and MR should be zero. The formula supports this point. If $MR = p - p/\epsilon$ and $\epsilon = 1$, then $MR = p - p = 0$.

In Chapter 3 we also learned that increases in sales when $\epsilon < 1$ causes TR to decrease. MR must be negative in this case. If $MR = p - p/\epsilon$ and $\epsilon < 1$, then $p/\epsilon > p$ and MR is negative. The formula is consistent with our earlier observations regarding the relationships between elasticity and total revenue when sales are increased.

The Short Run

Profit Maximization: Total Curves

Profit maximization under conditions of pure monopoly is subject to the same basic rules as those applying to the firm under pure competition. When plotted, the total receipts schedule of Table 11-1 becomes a total

---

[4] If $TR = xp$, then:

$$MR = \frac{d(TR)}{dx} = p + x\frac{dp}{dx} \tag{1}$$

$$= p + \frac{p}{\frac{dx}{dp} \times \frac{p}{x}}. \tag{2}$$

Since:

$$\epsilon = -\frac{dx}{dp} \times \frac{p}{x}, \tag{3}$$

then, substituting in (2), we find:

$$MR = p - \frac{p}{\epsilon}. \tag{4}$$

This proposition is proved geometrically in Appendix II of this chapter.

[5] See pp. 43–48.

Figure 11 – 1   Implications of Demand Elasticity for Marginal Revenue

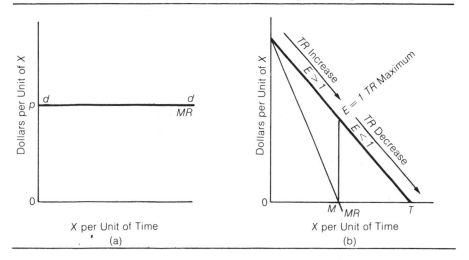

Figure 11 – 2   Short-run Profit Maximization: Total Curves

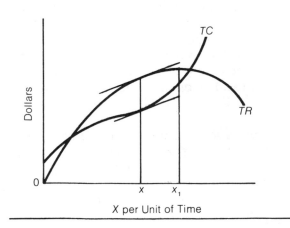

receipts curve like that of Figure 11-2. Note the difference between the monopolist's *TR* curve and that of a purely competitive firm. The difference results from the fact that to sell greater outputs the monopolist must charge lower prices. Therefore, at some output such as x_1 he will have reached maximum total receipts. Still larger sales will cause total receipts to decrease rather than increase. The monopolist will maximize profits at output *x*, where the difference between *TR* and *TC* is greatest. The output at which the difference between the *TR* and *TC* curves is greatest is that at which their slopes are equal (tangents to the curves at this output are parallel). Since the slope of the *TC* curve is marginal cost and the slope of the *TR* curve is marginal revenue, profits are maximum at the output at which marginal revenue equals marginal cost.[6]

Profit Maximization: Per-unit Curves

Diagrammatic representation of short-run profit maximization by a monopolist in terms of per unit costs and receipts is presented in Figure 11-3. Profits are maximum at output *x*, at which *SMC* equals *MR*. The price per unit that the monopolist can get for that output is *p*. Average cost is *c* and profits are equal to *cp* multiplied by *x*. At smaller outputs *MR* is greater than *SMC;* thus, larger outputs up to *x* add more to total receipts than to total costs and increase profits. At larger outputs *MR* is less than *SMC;* hence, increases beyond *x* add more to total costs than to total receipts and cause profits to decrease.[7]

Two Common Misconceptions

There is a common misconception that a monopolist necessarily makes profits. Whether or not profits are made depends on the relationship between the market demand curve faced by the monopolist and his conditions of cost. The monopolist may incur losses in the short run and, like the purely competitive firm, continue to produce if the price more than covers average variable costs. In Figure 11-4 the monopolist's costs are so high and his market is so small that at no output will the price cover average costs. His losses are minimum, provided price is greater than average variable costs, at output *x*, at which *SMC* equals *MR*. Losses are equal to *pc* × *x*.

Another common misconception is that the demand curve faced by a monopolist is inelastic. Most demand curves, with the exception of those faced by firms under conditions of pure competition, range from highly elastic toward their upper ends to highly inelastic toward their lower ends[8] and cannot be said to be either elastic or inelastic. They are usually both, depending on the sector of the demand curve under consideration. The output that maximizes a monopolist's profits will always be within the

---

[6]The mathematics of profit maximization for a monopolist are the same as for a purely competitive firm (*see* pp. 203–205).

[7]The intersection of *MR* and *SMC* tells us nothing other than that profits are maximum or losses are minimum at that output. The price is shown by the demand curve at that output and not by the *MR* curve. Profits are determined by the price and *average cost*, not by the price and *marginal cost*.

[8]The situation could conceivably be reversed, but such an occurrence would be unusual. A demand curve that is inelastic toward the upper end and elastic toward the lower end would necessarily be one with a greater degree of curvature than that of a rectangular hyperbola.

Figure 11–3 Short-run Profit Maximization: Per-unit Curves

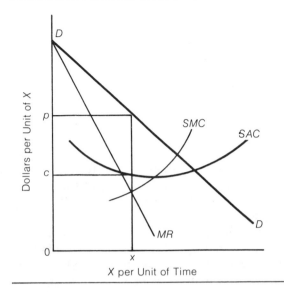

Figure 11–4 Short-run Loss Minimization: Per-unit Curves

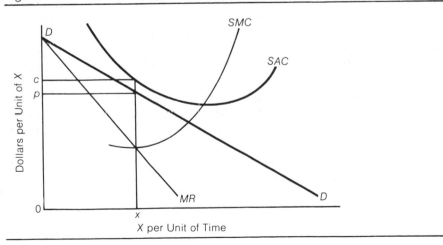

elastic sector of his demand curve if he has any costs of production. Marginal cost is always positive; therefore, at the output at which marginal cost equals marginal revenue, marginal revenue must also be positive. If marginal revenue is positive, then the elasticity of demand must be greater than one.

The Long Run

Entry into the Industry

Whereas entry of new firms into an industry of pure competition is easy in the long run, entry into a monopolistic industry is blocked. The monopolist must be able to forestall the entry of new firms when profits are being made or he does not remain a monopolist. Entry into the industry will change the market situation in which the firm operates.

The monopolist may block entry into his field in several ways. He may control the sources of raw materials necessary for the production of his product. The Aluminum Company of America, for example, prior to World War II was reputed to own or control over 90 percent of the available supplies of bauxite, the basic raw material used in the making of aluminum.[9] Or he may hold certain patents that prevent other firms from duplicating his products. In the manufacture of shoe machinery a single company has held patents simultaneously on virtually all equipment used in the manufacture of shoes. Instead of selling machinery outright to shoe manufacturers, the company leased it to them and collected royalties. The shoe manufacturer who obtained any equipment from another source would then find himself unable to obtain key equipment from the company.[10] The market of a monopolist may be so limited relative to the size of his optimum scale of plant that even though one firm makes profits, the entry of another would drive prices so low that both would incur losses. Thus entry is blocked. Still other methods of blocking entry occur. In the public utility field exclusive franchises granted by the governmental unit concerned will do the job. These are some of the more important monopolizing devices.[11]

The requirement that entry be completely blocked if pure monopoly is to remain pure monopoly helps explain why it is rare. Except in cases where the government blocks entry it is extremely difficult for a monopolist to suppress the rise of substitutes when profits can be made in his field. Patents similar to those of the monopolist can be secured, although putting them to use in producing substitute products may be difficult in some cases. Some patents may become obsolete as new ideas and processes supersede those of the past. Where sole ownership of raw materials is the monopolizing device used, substitute raw materials frequently can be developed to make a product that is a reasonably good substitute for the original.

---

[9]Clair Wilcox, *Competition and Monopoly in American Industry*, Temporary National Economic Committee Monograph No. 21 (Washington, D.C.: Government Printing Office, 1940), pp. 69–72.

[10]*Ibid.*, pp. 72–73.

[11]A more complete list of devices for restricting entry into particular industries is given on pp. 278ff.

Figure 11–5 Long-run Profit Maximization: Less than Optimum Plant Size

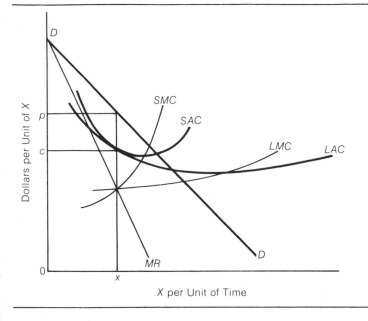

Size of Plant Adjustments

Since entry into the industry is blocked, the monopolist adjusts his long-run output by means of size of plant adjustments. Three possibilities exist. First, the relationship between the monopolist's market and his long-run average costs may be such that he will build a plant of less than optimum size. Second, the relationship may be such that he will build an optimum size of plant. Third, the monopolist may, under certain circumstances, be induced to build a larger than optimum size of plant.

Less than Optimum Size of Plant   Suppose the monopolist's market is so limited that his marginal revenue curve cuts his long-run average cost curve to the left of its minimum point. Figure 11-5 illustrates this situation. Long-run profits are maximum at the output at which *LMC* equals *MR*. The output is *x* and the price is *p*. The monopolist should build the size of plant that will produce output *x* at the least possible average cost, so that the short-run average cost curve *SAC* should be tangent to the *LAC* at output *x*. If *SAC* is tangent to *LAC* at output *x*, *SMC* is necessarily equal to *LMC* at that output.[12] Also, because output *x* is the output at which *LMC* equals *MR*, *SMC* is equal to *MR* at the same output. Thus, a monopolistic firm in long-run equilibrium is necessarily in short-run equilibrium too.

[12]*See* Chap. 9, pp. 188–190.

Profits are equal to $cp \times x$. Any change in the size of plant or in the rate of output of *SAC* will decrease profits.

In this case the monopolist will build a less than optimum size of plant and operate it at a less than optimum rate of output. His market is not large enough for him to expand the plant sufficiently to take advantage of all economies of size. The size of plant that he uses will have some excess capacity. If he were to make it smaller than *SAC*, so that no excess capacity occurs, he would at the same time lose some of the economies of size that *SAC* offers. The loss would more than offset any "gains" from fuller utilization of a smaller plant size.

Local power companies in small- and medium-sized towns often operate plants of smaller than optimum size at less than their optimum rates of output. The relatively small local market for electricity limits the generating plant to a size too small to use the most efficient generating equipment and techniques. Yet the well-planned plant will have some excess capacity — both to take advantage of economies of size and to meet peak output requirements.

Optimum Size of Plant   Suppose the monopolist's market and his cost curves are such that his marginal revenue curve hits the minimum point of his *LAC* curve as in Figure 11-6. The long-run profit-maximizing output is x, at which $LMC = MR$; this will necessarily be the output at which *LAC* is minimum. The monopolist, to produce x at the least possible cost per unit for that output, should build plant *SAC*, the optimum size of plant. In this case $SMC = LMC = MR = SAC = LAC$ at output x. The firm is in both short-run and long-run equilibrium. The price is p; the average cost is c; and profits are equal to $cp \times x$. Under the assumed conditions the firm operates an optimum size of plant at the optimum rate of output.

Greater than Optimum Size of Plant   Suppose the monopolist's market is large enough for his marginal revenue curve to cut his *LAC* curve to the right of its minimum point. This situation is diagrammed in Figure 11-7. The long-run profit-maximizing output is x. The proper plant to build is *SAC*, which is tangent to *LAC* at output x. At output x, $LMC = SMC = MR$; hence, the monopolist is in short-run equilibrium as well as long-run equilibrium.

Under the assumed conditions the monopolist builds a larger than optimum size of plant and operates it at more than the optimum rate of output that maximizes profits. His plant is so large that diseconomies of size occur. It pays him to use a plant a little smaller than the one that would produce output x at its most efficient rate of output. By operating *SAC* at more than its most efficient rate of output he can obtain a lower per-unit cost than would be possible with a larger plant. The diseconomies of size of a still larger plant are of a greater cost magnitude than is the operation of *SAC* beyond its optimum rate of output.

Figure 11–6   *Long-run Profit Maximization: Optimum Size of Plant*

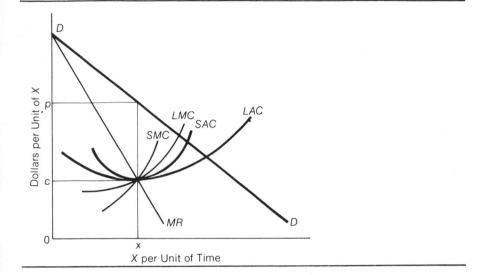

Figure 11–7 *Long-run Profit Maximization:Greater than Optimum Plant Size*

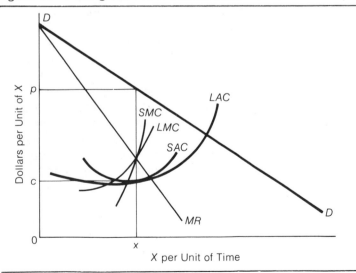

Price Discrimination

In some cases a monopolist may find it possible and profitable to separate and keep separate two or more markets for his product. Under such
conditions he will charge a different price for his product in each of the

markets. Two conditions are necessary for such *price discrimination* to occur. First, he must be able to keep the markets apart. Otherwise, his product will be purchased in the market with the lower price and resold in the market with the higher price, thus ironing out the price differential the monopolist attempts to establish. Second, for price discrimination to be profitable, the elasticities of demand at each price level must differ among the markets. The reason they must differ will become evident as the analysis progresses.

Distribution of Sales

Consider first the way in which a discriminating monopolist would distribute his sales between two (or more) markets. For any given volume of sales, ignoring costs for the moment, he would sell in the market in which an additional unit of sales per unit of time adds most to his total receipts. This amounts to saying that he would distribute his sales among the markets in such a way that marginal revenue in each market is equal to marginal revenue in the other market(s). In this way he will obtain the greatest total receipts from a given volume of sales.

Diagrammatically, suppose the monopolist can sell in the two separate markets of Figure 11-8. The demand curves are D_1D_1 and D_2D_2, respectively. For convenience the quantity axis of Market II is reversed, with units of X measured from right to left instead of from the usual left to right. If the volume of sales is less than x_0, he should sell the entire amount in Market I, since the additions to his total receipts from sales in that market will exceed any addition to his total receipts made from selling in Market II. If his total volume of sales equals x_1 plus x_2, he should sell x_1 in Market I and x_2 in Market II so that marginal revenue in Market I equals marginal revenue in Market II. The level of marginal revenue will be r in each market. To show that this distribution brings in the greatest possible total receipts, suppose that the sales volume in one market is cut by one unit, and in the other market it is increased by one unit. Cutting sales by one unit in either market reduces his total receipts from that market by an amount equal to r. Increasing sales by one unit in the other market will add less to total receipts than r, since marginal revenue from an additional unit of sales per unit of time in that market will be less than r. With the proper distribution of sales, the price in Market I will be p_1 and the price in Market II will be p_2.

The reasons why elasticity of demand at each possible price must differ between the two markets now becomes clear. Since $MR = p - p/\epsilon$, if elasticities were the same in the two markets at equal prices the corresponding marginal revenues would also be the same. The distribution of sales that makes marginal revenue in Market I equal to marginal revenue

Figure 11-8　Distribution of Sales among Markets: Price Discrimination

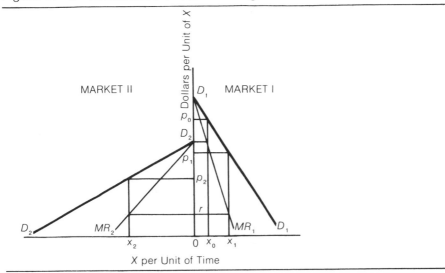

in Market II would make the price in Market I equal to the price in Market II. If such were the case there would be neither point nor profit in separating the markets.

Profit Maximization

The monopolist's cost curves, together with the marginal revenue curve for his total sales volume, are needed to solve his profit-maximizing problem. Let his average cost curve and his marginal cost curve be those of Figure 11-9. They are appropriate for his entire output regardless of how it is distributed. The marginal revenue curve for the entire sales volume when sales are properly distributed is ΣMR in Figure 11-9. The demand curve and the marginal revenue curve for Market II have been drawn in the usual way. Then MR_1 and MR_2 are summed horizontally to obtain ΣMR.

The profit-maximizing problem is now reduced to a simple monopoly problem. The total output of the monopolist should be x, at which $MC = \Sigma MR$. The distribution of sales and the prices charged should be x_1, sold at price p_1 in Market I; and x_2, sold at price p_2 in Market II. Marginal revenue in Market I equals marginal revenue in Market II equals r with this distribution of sales. If total output and sales were less than x, marginal revenue in one market or the other (or both) would be greater than r, and marginal cost would be less than r. Increases in production up to x would therefore add more to total receipts than to total costs and would increase profits. If total output and sales were expanded beyond x, marginal cost would exceed *r* and marginal revenue in one market or the other (or both) would be less than *r*. Such increases in production would add more to total costs than to total receipts and would decrease profits. With output *x* properly distributed between the two markets, profits in Market I will equal $cp_1 \times x_1$; and profits in Market II will equal $cp_2 \times x_2$. Total profits will be $cp_1 \times x_1$ plus $cp_2 \times x_2$.

Examples of Price Discrimination

Price discrimination is frequently encountered in public utility industries. Electric power companies usually separate commercial from domestic users of electricity. Having a separate meter for each user enables the company to keep the markets apart. Elasticity of commercial users' demand for electricity is higher than that of domestic users; consequently, a lower rate is charged commercial users. This discrimination stems from the greater possibilities of commercial users adapting substitutes for the power company's product. Large commercial users may find it possible not only to find substitute sources of power but to generate their own electric power. Although domestic users may, and sometimes do, generate their own electric power, generating plants for their power needs are so small that costs per unit tend to be prohibitive.

Another example of price discrimination occurs in the field of foreign trade in the classic case of "dumping." Goods are sold abroad for a lower price than the domestic or home price. The markets are separated by transportation costs and tariff barriers. Elasticity of the demand curve facing the seller in the foreign market is usually higher than that in the domestic market. Although the seller may be a monopolist in the domestic market he may find himself confronted abroad with competitors from other countries. Substitutes for his product on the world market increase the elasticity of the foreign demand curve he faces.

The Welfare Effects of Pure Monopoly

What impact does the introduction of pure monopoly into the purely competitive world of the last chapter have on consumer welfare? The effects appear most striking when we assume that some markets are characterized by pure competition while others are characterized by pure monopoly. As in the purely competitive case, a complete statement of the effects must wait until resource pricing and employment have been discussed.

Short-run Output Restriction

If all industries were initially purely competitive and were in long-run equilibrium, monopolization of one or more of them would reduce consumer

Figure 11-9   *Profit Maximization: Price Discrimination*

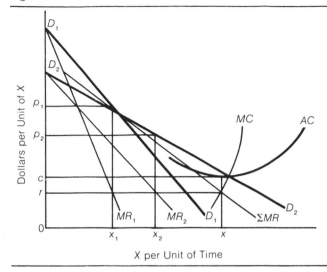

Figure 11-10   *Monopolistic Output Restriction*

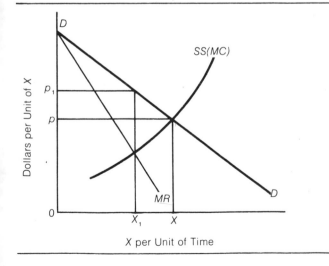

welfare. Suppose, for example that *X* in Figure 11-10 represents one industry in a purely competitive economy. The market demand curve is *DD* and the market short-run supply curve (the sum of the individual firm marginal cost curves) is *SS*. The market price is *p* and the industry output level is *X*. Although the average cost curves are not drawn in on the figure to illustrate the point, suppose that the industry is in long-run equilibrium and that a Pareto optimum exists throughout the economy.

What would be the short-run impact of monopolization of industry X? If the productive capacity of the industry were brought under the control of a single firm, demand would look different to the monopolist than it did to the individual firms making up the industry when it was purely competitive. The purely competitive firms each saw a horizontal demand curve at the market price p. Each firm saw a marginal revenue curve that coincided with that demand curve and produced an output level at which short-run marginal cost was equal to marginal revenue or price p. The monopolist sees the market demand curve sloping downward to the right and a marginal revenue curve that lies below the demand curve like MR in Figure 11-10. Assuming that the monopolist takes over intact the physical facilities of the industry and that no diseconomies of size are thereby engendered, SS (the industry supply curve or marginal cost curve under pure competition) is also the marginal cost curve of the monopolist. To maximize profits the monopolist would reduce the industry's output level to X_1 and raise the price to p_1. The reduction in the output of X would release some of the resources used in the industry, and these would be used to increase the outputs of other goods, reducing their prices in the process.

As resources are transferred out of X into other uses, welfare is reduced. The marginal cost of X at any output level is the value in other uses that consumers attach to the resources used to produce a unit of X. The price of X at that output level is the value they attach to the same resource bundle used to produce X. We note, in Figure 11-10, that as the output level of X is reduced from X toward X_1 the marginal cost of X falls below its price, indicating that resources are being transferred from uses where their values to consumers are greater to uses where their values to consumers are less. This change must necessarily reduce the level of well-being of at least some members of the society.

Long-run Output Restriction

Welfare will also be held below the optimum level in the long-run by the monopolization of an industry. Profits can persist in the long run because entry into the industry is blocked. Where long-run profits occur, the product price exceeds average costs, indicating that productive capacity in the industry is too small relative to productive capacity elsewhere in the economy. Consumers value those resources making up plant capacity more when they are used in the profit-making industry than when they are used elsewhere—therefore welfare is less than it could be.

A major problem posed by monopoly in a private enterprise economy, then, is that it prevents the price mechanism from organizing production in a Pareto optimal way. The monopolized industries are induced to produce with existing productive capacity output levels that are too small—marginal costs are less than the respective product prices—and the monopolies prevent productive capacity itself from expanding where consumers desire expansion; that is, where profits are made. The use of too few resources in the monopolized industries necessarily means the use of too large quantities in competitive industries, if full employment of resources exists.

Inefficiency of the Firm

In addition to the welfare impact of output restriction the monopolistic firm ordinarily will not use resources at their peak potential efficiency. The purely competitive firm in long-run equilibrium uses the optimum size of plant at the optimum rate of output. The size of plant and the output that maximize the monopolist's long-run profits are not necessarily optimal.[13] However, if monopoly is to be compared with pure competition on this point, the comparison is legitimate only for industries in which pure competition can exist. In an industry with a limited market relative to the optimum rate of output of the optimum size plant, monopoly may result in lower costs or greater efficiency than would occur if there were many firms, each with a considerably less than optimum size plant. In such a case even though monopoly may result in greater efficiency than any other type of market organization, resources still are not used at peak potential efficiency.

Sales Promotion Activities

It may be to the advantage of the monopolist to engage in some sales promotion activities, whereas under pure competition there is little point in activities of this kind. The monopolist may use sales promotion to enlarge his market; that is, to shift his demand curve to the right. Also, if he can convince the public that consumption of his product is highly desirable or even indispensable, elasticity of demand at various prices may be decreased. Additionally, such activities may be used to shield him from potential competition and to protect his monopoly position. His objective in this case will be to get his firm name so closely tied to his product that potential competitors will find it futile to attempt to enter the market. At this point it is difficult to assess the impact of sales promotion activities on welfare. We will be in a better position to analyze these effects when we have completed the chapter on oligopoly.

---

[13]*See* p. 225.

Regulation of Monopoly

The tools of monopoly analysis so far discussed provide some indications of how monopoly might be regulated to offset at least in part the adverse effects of monopoly on welfare. Two possible governmental regulatory devices are: (1) direct regulation of monopoly price and (2) regulation through taxation.

Price Regulation

Authority is frequently invested in state regulatory commissions to govern the rates or prices charged by public utilities, such as gas and electric power companies. The economic problem involved is determination of the rate that will induce the monopolist to furnish the greatest amount of product consistent with his costs and with consumer demand.[14]

The profit-maximizing output of a monopolist in the absence of price regulation is shown in Figure 11-11.[15] The monopolist maximizes profits at output level x, where marginal cost equals marginal revenue. The price will be p and profits are $cp \times x$. Since entry into the industry is blocked, the profits may exist over time.

By establishing a maximum price below p the regulatory commission can induce the monopolist to increase output. Suppose a maximum price of p_1 is established—at the level at which the marginal cost curve cuts the demand curve. The demand curve faced by the monopolist becomes $p_1 AD$. Between output levels of zero and x_1 sales will be made at p_1 per unit. The monopolist cannot charge more, but the public will take his entire output within those limits at that price. For output levels greater than x_1 the monopolist must lower the price below p_1 to clear the market; hence, the market demand curve applies.

The change in the demand curve faced by the firm alters the marginal revenue curve as well. From zero to x_1 the new demand curve is infinitely elastic—it is the same as the demand curve faced by a firm under pure competition—and marginal revenue equals p_1. Beyond output x_1 the market demand curve and the original marginal revenue curve are relevant. After the maximum price is established, the marginal revenue curve of the monopolist is $p_1 ABC$.

The monopolist's profit-maximizing position must be re-examined in view of the altered demand and marginal revenue situation. With the establishment of the maximum price x is no longer the profit-maximizing

---

[14]Economic aspects of the problem frequently are subordinated to political aspects, but we shall omit the latter.

[15]The analysis can be presented in either long-run or short-run terms. A short-run explanation has the virtue of being less complex.

Figure 11–11 *Regulation of Monopoly by Price Control*

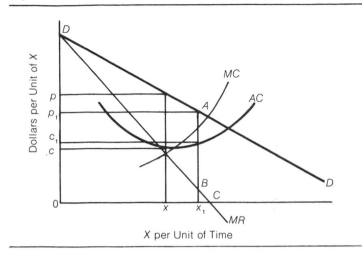

output. Profits will be maximized at the level of output at which the marginal cost curve cuts the new marginal revenue curve. At x marginal revenue exceeds marginal cost; consequently, increases in output up to x_1 increase profits. At outputs beyond x_1 marginal cost would exceed marginal revenue—which drops off sharply, or is said to be "discontinuous" at x_1—causing profits to decrease. The new profit-maximizing output is x_1 a larger output than before. Even though profits of $c_1p_1 \times x_1$ occur, welfare has been increased.

Taxation

Taxes levied on monopolists are often thought to be appropriate regulatory devices to prevent them from reaping the full benefits of their monopolistic positions. We shall consider two types: (1) a specific tax or a fixed tax per unit on the monopolist's output[16] and (2) a lump-sum tax levied without regard to output.[17]

---

[16]The general effects would be the same if an *ad valorem* tax, a fixed percentage of the product price, were levied.

[17]The general effects would be the same if the tax were a fixed percentage of the monopolist's profits.

Figure 11 – 12   Regulation of Monopoly by a Specific Tax

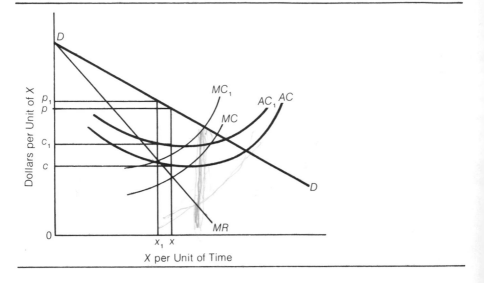

A Specific Tax   Suppose a specific tax is levied on the monopolist of Figure 11-12. His original average cost and marginal cost curves are *AC* and *MC*, respectively. His original price and output are *p* and *x*. The tax is a variable cost and shifts the average and marginal costs upward by the amount of the tax. Faced with the new cost curves, AC_1 and MC_1, the monopolist cuts his output to x_1 and raises price to p_1 in order to maximize profits.

The monopolist is able to pass a part of the specific tax to the consumer through a higher price and a smaller output. At the same time the monopolist's profits will be smaller after the tax than before. Before-tax profits were $cp \times x$. After-tax profits are $c_1p_1 \times x_1$. To make certain that after-tax profits are smaller than before-tax profits, think for a moment of the firm's total revenue and total cost curves. Total receipts of the monopolist at various outputs are unchanged by the tax, but total costs at all outputs will be greater. Profits at all possible outputs will be smaller than before and maximum profits after the tax necessarily will be smaller than they were before. If all the monopolist's profits were taxed away through specific taxes, prices still higher and outputs still smaller than those shown in Figure 11-12 would result. It appears that a specific tax on the monopolist's product would reduce welfare rather than increase it.[18]

---

[18]Consider, however, the possible effects of specific taxes levied on the outputs of pure competitors in the economy, which would induce them to reduce their output levels, releasing resources to the monopolized industries and inducing the latter to expand their outputs.

Figure 11 – 13   Regulation of Monopoly by a Lump-sum Tax

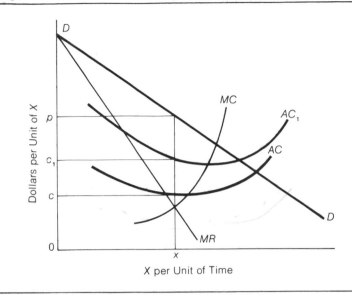

A Lump-sum Tax   Suppose a lump-sum tax is imposed on the monopolist of Figure 11-13 — for example, a license fee imposed by a city on its
only swimming pool. The original average and marginal cost curves are
AC and MC. The original price and output are p and x. Since the lump-
sum tax is independent of output, it is a fixed cost to the monopolist. It
shifts the average cost curve to AC_1, but it has no effect on the marginal
cost curve. Consequently, the profit-maximizing price and output remain
at p and x; but profits fall from $cp \times x$ to $c_1p \times x$.

The lump-sum tax must be borne by the monopolist alone. He is unable
to pass any part of it on to the consumer through higher prices and
smaller outputs. Attempts to do so will decrease his profits even more. All
of the monopolist's profits may be taxed away in this manner with no effect
whatsoever on output and price. The lump-sum tax by itself has no impact
on welfare.

Summary

Pure monopoly is rare in the real world; however, the theory of pure monopoly is applicable to those industries in which it is approximated
and to firms that act as though they were monopolists. Additionally, it furnishes necessary tools of analysis for the study of oligopoly and monopolistic competition.

The differences between the theory of pure monopoly and the theory of pure competition rest on the demand and revenue situations faced by the firm and on the conditions of entry into industries in which profits are made. Marginal revenue is less than price for the monopolist. His marginal revenue curve lies below the demand curve that he faces. Entry into monopolistic industries is blocked.

The monopolist maximizes short-run profits or minimizes short-run losses by producing the output and charging the price at which marginal revenue equals short-run marginal cost. Monopolists may incur losses and, if so, continue to produce if price exceeds average variable cost. The monopolist operates within the elastic sector of his demand curve.

In the long run the monopolist maximizes profits at the output at which long-run marginal cost equals marginal revenue. The size of plant to be used will be the one with its short-run average cost curve tangent to the long-run average cost curve at the profit-maximizing output. Short-run marginal cost will equal long-run marginal cost and marginal revenue at that output.

A monopolist finds it profitable to practice price discrimination when he can keep markets for his product separate and when elasticity of demand for each market is different at each possible price. The price-discriminating monopolist produces an output and distributes it among his markets in such a way that marginal revenue in each market equals marginal revenue in every other market and is also equal to his marginal cost.

Monopoly has important implications for welfare in a private-enterprise economy. Where it exists along with competitive industries, it leads to output restriction and prices that are higher than marginal costs. The possibility of long-run profits under monopoly exists because of blocked entry into monopolized industries. Where profits occur, consumers are willing to pay more for a product than is necessary to hold the resources making that product in the industry concerned. Blocked entry limits transfer of resources into and expansion of output of a monopolized profit-making industry, and thus reduces welfare. A monopolistic firm is not likely to operate optimum size plants at optimum rates of output. Some sales promotion efforts may be made to enlarge the monopolist's market, to decrease elasticity of demand for his product, and to discourage potential competition.

The theory of monopoly throws some light on effective means of monopoly regulation. A maximum price set below the monopoly price will benefit consumers through both the lower price and an increased product output. A specific tax levied on the monopolist's product will be shifted partly to consumers through output restriction and higher prices. A lump-sum tax must be borne entirely out of the monopolist's profits.

Suggested Readings

Dewey, Donald, *Monopoly in Economics and Law* (Chicago: Rand McNally & Company, 1959).

Harrod, R.F., "Doctrines of Imperfect Competition," *Quarterly Journal of Economics*, vol. XLVIII (May 1934), pp. 442–470.

Marshall, Alfred, *Principles of Economics*, 8th ed. (London: Macmillan & Co., Ltd., 1920), Bk. V, Chap. XIV.

Robinson, Joan, *The Economics of Imperfect Competition* (London: Macmillan & Co., Ltd., 1933), Chaps. 2, 3, 15, 16.

Appendix I to Chapter 11
Derivation of the Marginal Revenue Curve

The marginal revenue curve can be derived geometrically from a given demand curve. A straight-line demand curve will be used to develop the method which will then be modified to cover the case of a nonlinear demand curve.

Straight-Line Curves

Consider first what a marginal revenue curve is. In Figure 11-14 the quantity units are purposely large. Suppose a single unit of sales adds an amount OK to the firm's total receipts. Both total receipts and marginal revenue are equal to Area I, or $OK \times 1$. When sales are increased to two units of X per unit of time, suppose total receipts increase by an amount OL. Marginal revenue of a unit now equals Area II, or $OL \times 1$. Area II does not overlap Area I but lies entirely to the right of it. The dotted line from the top of Area II to point L is a reference line only, to assist in reading marginal revenue from the dollar axis. Total revenue from the two units equals marginal revenue when sales are one unit, plus marginal revenue when sales are increased to two units; in other words total revenue equals Area I plus Area II. Marginal revenue when sales are increased to three units per unit of time equals OM, or, what amounts to the same thing, equals Area III. Total revenue is now equal to Area I plus Area II plus Area III. The stairstep curve from K to N is the marginal revenue curve for the firm through three units of sales.

For a typical firm a single unit of output is measured by an infinitesimal distance along the X axis. If the distance measuring a single unit of output is infinitesimal, the marginal revenue curve no longer looks like the discontinuous or stairstep curve of Figure 11-14 but looks as smooth as the MR curve in Figure 11-15. The point to be made from Figure 11-14 is that any given level of sales total receipts are equal to the area under the marginal revenue curve up to that quantity. In Figure 11-14 total receipts from three units of sales equal the sum of Areas I, II, and III as we have said. The same is true in Figure 11-15 where total receipts when sales are OM are equal to Area $OASM$.

Figure 11–14 Marginal and Total Revenue

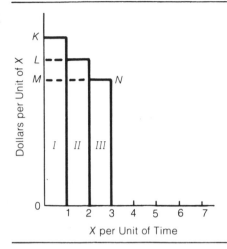

Figure 11–15
Derivation of the Marginal Revenue Curve from the Demand Curve

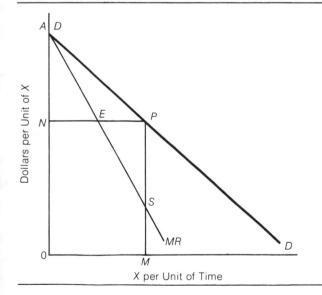

Assume that the demand curve faced by a monopolist is the straight line *DD* of Figure 11-15, and that we want to determine marginal revenue at sales level 0*M*. Ignore the *MR* curve of the diagram temporarily. Price at quantity 0*M* will be *MP* or 0*N*. Suppose now that *MR* is drawn in Figure 11-15 as a tentative marginal revenue curve. It should start from the vertical axis at a common point with the demand curve.[19] Reference to Table 11-1 shows that the marginal revenue curve for a straight-line demand curve also will be a straight line spreading away from the demand curve as the sales level increases.

What conditions must be fulfilled if marginal revenue is to be correctly measured at sales level OM? If MR were the marginal revenue curve, area $OASM$ would equal total receipts. Also, area $ONPM$ (that is, price times quantity) equals total receipts. Hence, area $ONPM$ must equal area $OASM$. Area $ONESM$ is common to both the larger areas, and if subtracted from each, the area of triangle ANE must be equal to the area of triangle EPS. Angle NEA equals angle SEP because the opposite angles formed by two intersecting straight lines are equal. Since triangles ANE and EPS are right triangles, with an additional angle of one equal to the corresponding angle of the other, they are also similar triangles. If MR is correctly drawn, triangles ANE and EPS are equal in area as well as similar, and thus will be congruent. If they are congruent, SP must equal NA since the corresponding sides of congruent triangles are equal. Therefore, to correctly locate marginal revenue at sales level OM, we must measure the distance NA and set point S below point P such that SP equals NA. Marginal revenue at OM will be MS.

Use of the geometric method for deriving marginal revenue from a given demand curve is much simpler than the proof. Suppose we locate the marginal revenue curve for demand curve DD in Figure 11-16. Select several points such as P, P_1, and P_2 at random on the demand curve. The corresponding levels of sales are OM, OM_1, and OM_2. Corresponding prices will be ON, ON_1, and ON_2. Now drop below P by an amount equal to NA and call the newly located point S. Marginal revenue at sales level OM is MS. Drop below P_1 by an amount equal to N_1A. Call this point S_1. Marginal revenue at OM_1 equals M_1S_1. Repeat the process at P_2, so that S_2P_2 equals N_2A. A line joining the S points is the marginal revenue curve.

Nonlinear Curves

The procedure with a slight modification can be used to locate the marginal revenue curve for a nonlinear demand curve. Suppose the demand curve is DD in Figure 11-17. The demand curve and the marginal revenue curve start from a common point on the vertical axis, and we should locate marginal revenue at several different sales quantities, say OM, OM_1, and OM_2. The corresponding points on the demand curve are P, P_1, and P_2. The

---

[19]Actually, it coincides with the demand curve at a sales level of one unit. However, if the distance measuring a unit of sales on the quantity axis is infinitesimal, we can assume that both curves start from a common point on the vertical axis.

Figure 11–16   Location of the MR *Curve for a Linear Demand Curve*

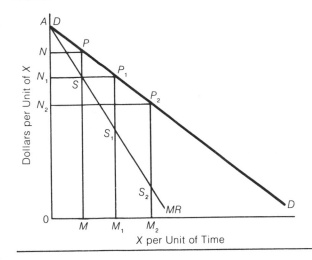

Figure 11–17   Location of the MR *Curve for a Nonlinear Demand Curve*

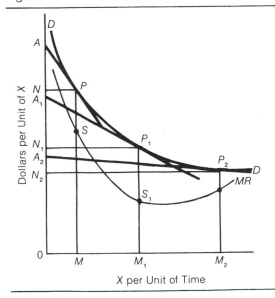

corresponding prices are ON, ON_1, and ON_2. Now draw a tangent to the demand curve at point P so that the tangent cuts the vertical axis. Call this point A. If the tangent were the demand curve, we could easily find marginal revenue for it at sales level OM. We would drop below P by an amount equal to *NA* and set point *S* so that *SP* equals *NA*. Actually the tangent and demand curve *DD* are the same curve and have the same slope at the point of tangency. Therefore, *MS* will be marginal revenue for *DD* at sales level *0M*, as well as being marginal revenue for the tangent when the tangent is thought of as being the demand curve. Marginal revenue at sales $0M_1$ can be found by drawing a tangent to *DD* at P_1. The tangent intersects the vertical axis at A_1. Drop below P_1 by an amount equal to N_1A_1 and marginal revenue at $0M_1$ is M_1S_1. Repeat the procedure at P_2, so that S_2P_2 equals N_2A_2. Marginal revenue at $0M_2$ is M_2S_2. A line joining the *S* points is the marginal revenue curve for *DD*. Note that when the demand curve is not a straight line the *A* points on the vertical axis shift as different levels of sales are considered.[20]

---

[20]A common mistake in locating the marginal revenue curve for a given demand curve is that of merely drawing the marginal revenue curve so that it bisects the distance between the demand curve and the vertical axis. This procedure will locate the marginal revenue curve accurately for a linear demand curve only. If the demand curve has any curvature to it—that is, if it is convex or concave when viewed from below—such a procedure is not valid. If the demand curve is convex from below, the marginal revenue curve will lie to the left of a line bisecting the distance between the vertical axis and the demand curve. If the demand curve is concave from below, the marginal revenue curve will lie to the right of such a line.

Even in the case of a linear demand curve the procedure described here is correct in a mathematical sense only. It is not sound logically from the point of view of economics. For example, in Figure 11-15 point *E* lies on the marginal revenue curve for demand curve *DD*. Sales level *0M* (or *NP*) and price *0N* (or *MP*) are used in locating point *E*. However, there is no economic reason why sales level *0M* or price *0N* (or *MP*) should have any connection at all with marginal revenue at one half of sales level *0M*. The connection is purely a mathematical one stemming from the fact that *DD* is a straight line. With regard to sales level *0M* and price *0N*, the only marginal revenue value which could be derived from them logically is marginal revenue at that sales level and that price.

Appendix II to Chapter 11
Price, Marginal Revenue, and Elasticity of Demand

The proposition that marginal revenue equals price minus the ratio of price to elasticity of demand at that price is proved geometrically with the aid of Figure 11-18. Suppose the sales level is $0M$. The demand curve is either DD or D_1D_1 — which are tangent at that level of sales. At sales level $0M$ the elasticity of both curves is the same, and the corresponding marginal revenues will also be the same. For convenience, draw the marginal revenue curve corresponding to D_1D_1. Elasticity of demand at $0M$ equals $MT/0M$. However, $MT/0M$ is equal to PT/AP, since a line (PM) parallel to one side of a triangle ($A0$) cuts the other two sides into proportional segments. Likewise, $PT/AP = 0N/NA$. Because $0N = MP$ and $NA = SP$, $0N/NA = MP/SP$. Elasticity of demand at $0M$ is equal to $MT/0M = PT/AP = 0N/NA = MP/SP$, or $\epsilon = MP/SP$. Dividing through by ϵ and multiplying through by SP, $SP = MP/\epsilon$. From the diagram it can be seen that $MS = MP - SP$. Because $SP = MP/\epsilon$, then $MS = MP - MP/\epsilon$, or:

$$\text{marginal revenue} = \text{price} - \text{price/elasticity.}$$

Figure 11–18   Price, Elasticity of Demand, and Marginal Revenue

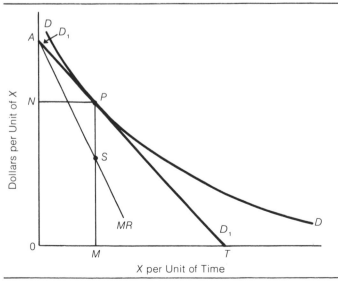

Chapter 12:

Pricing and Output under Oligopoly

Market situations in which there are few enough sellers of a particular product for the activities of one to be of importance to the others are called oligopoly situations as we have said. A single seller occupies a position of sufficient importance in the product market for changes in his market activities to have repercussions on the others in that market. Other sellers react to the market activities of the one, and their reactions in turn have repercussions on him. The individual seller is aware of this inter-dependence and in changing his price, output, sales promotional activity, or quality of product he must take the reactions of others into account.

The analysis of pricing and output under oligopoly lacks the neatness and precision of the theories of pure competition and of monopoly. The imprecision is partly because of what we shall call oligopolistic uncertain-ty — in many cases an oligopolist cannot be sure what his rivals' reactions will be to various kinds of activities on his part — and partly because oligopoly covers such a wide range of cases, each with its own unique characteristics. There is not now, nor is there likely to be in the foreseeable future, a general theory of oligopoly. Consequently, in this chapter we shall try to get some feel for the problems and principles involved in analysis of oligopolistic industries. Several selected models will be developed with this objective in mind.

First, we shall briefly discuss costs, demand, and product differentia-tion as they are to be used in the analysis. Next, we consider collusion versus independent action by oligopolists. Then we turn to short-run pric-ing and output, long-run pricing and output, and nonprice competition. Finally, we examine the effects of oligopolistic market structures on the operation of the economy.

Costs, Demand, and Product Differentiation

Costs of Production

We continue to assume in this chapter that the oligopolistic firm buys its resources competitively. Its cost curves are like those of the purely competitive firm and the pure monopolist.

Demand

Differences in the conditions of demand as seen by the individual firm constitute the main feature setting oligopoly apart from the other types of market structure. Since what one firm is able to do in the market is conditioned by the ways in which other firms react to the market activities of the one, the extent of this oligopolistic uncertainty is highly variable from case to case In some situations the firm is quite knowledgeable as to the reactions it can expect from other firms and so it can determine the demand curve it faces with some confidence. In other situations the firm does not possess this knowledge, and the position and shape of the demand curve it faces are highly conjectural. Interdependence of demand among the firms of an industry and oligopolistic uncertainty give rise to a whole host of problems and strategies on the part of firms that we do not find in the other market classifications.

Pure and Differentiated Oligopoly

The distinction between differentiated oligopoly and pure oligopoly will not play a prominent role in our analysis. As a practical matter, sellers in most oligopolistic industries sell differentiated products.[1] Nevertheless, some of the fundamental principles of differentiated oligopoly, as well as of pure oligopoly, are seen most clearly when we assume that pure oligopoly exists. For example, instead of a single market price for a product produced under differentiated oligopoly, a cluster of prices may occur. Automatic toasters may range in price from $19.95 to $29.95. The various price levels reflect consumers' views regarding the respective qualities of the different sellers' wares and the availability of different makes. Analysis may be simplified and basic pricing principles not distorted seriously if we assume that pure oligopoly exists, thus reducing the cluster of prices

---

[1]Industries approaching pure oligopoly include cement, basic steel, and most of the other basic metal-producing industries. Even here there are elements of differentiation among the products sold in a particular industry. Locational factors, service, and personal friendships may differentiate the products of the various sellers in an industry.

to a single market price for the product.[2] Wherever necessary, we shall specify whether conditions of differentiated or pure oligopoly are assumed.

Collusion versus Independent Action

Oligopolistic market structures invite collusion among the firms in an industry, but at the same time collusive arrangements are difficult to maintain. There are at least three major incentives leading oligopolistic firms toward collusion. In the first place they can increase their profits if they can decrease the amount of competition among themselves and act monopolistically. In the second place collusion can decrease oligopolistic uncertainty. If the firms act in concert they reduce the likelihood of any one firm's taking actions detrimental to the interests of the others. In the third place collusion among the firms already in an industry will facilitate blocking newcomers from that industry. However, once a collusive arrangement is in existence, any single firm has a strong profit incentive to break away from the group and act independently. These forces will be examined in some detail throughout the chapter.

A classification of oligopolistic markets according to the degree of collusion that occurs will facilitate discussion of representative oligopolistic models. We shall distinguish among cases of perfect collusion, imperfect collusion, and cases characterized by independent action on the part of individual firms.[3]

Perfect Collusion

Cases of perfect collusion consist primarily of cartel arrangements. A cartel is a formal organization of the producers within a given industry. Its purpose is to transfer certain management decisions and functions of individual firms to a central association in order to improve the profit positions of individual firms. Overt formal cartel organizations are generally illegal in the United States, but they have existed extensively in countries outside the United States and on an international basis.[4] Even in the United States voluntary tacit organizations and collusion may give certain industries most of the characteristics of a cartel.

---

[2]One such distortion is that product differentiation may affect control of the individual seller over price. Attachment of consumers to the products of single sellers will reduce the changes in quantities sold for price adjustments upward or downward within a certain price range; that is, it will make the demand curve faced by the individual seller less elastic within that price range.

[3]*See* Fritz Machlup, *The Economics of Sellers' Competition* (Baltimore: The Johns Hopkins Press, 1952), pp. 363–365.

[4]*See* George W. Stocking and Myron W. Watkins, *Cartels in Action* (New York: The Twentieth Century Fund, Inc., 1946).

The extent of the functions transferred to the central association varies in different cartel situations. We shall consider two representative cartel types.[5] The first, selected to illustrate almost complete cartel control over member firms, will be called *the centralized cartel*. The second illustrates cases in which fewer functions are transferred to the central association. It will be designated as *the market-sharing cartel*.

In the centralized cartel the decision making with regard to pricing, output, sales, and distribution of profits is accomplished by the central association, which markets the product, determines prices, determines the amount that each firm is to produce, and divides profits among member firms. Member firms are represented in the central association, and cartel policies presumably result from exchanges of ideas, negotiation, and compromise. However, a firm's power to influence cartel policies is not necessarily proportional to its representation in the central association. Its economic power in the industry may significantly influence cartel policies.

The market-sharing cartel is a somewhat looser form of organization. The firms forming the cartel agree on market shares with or without an understanding regarding prices. Member firms do their own marketing but are careful to observe the cartel agreement.

Imperfect Collusion

Imperfectly collusive cases are made up mostly of tacit informal arrangements under which the firms of an industry seek to establish prices and outputs and yet escape prosecution under the United States antitrust laws. The price leadership arrangements of a number of industries — steel, tobacco, oil, and others — are typical of this class. But tacit unorganized collusion can occur in many other ways. Gentlemen's agreements of various sorts with regard to pricing, output, market sharing, and other activities of the firms within the industry can be worked out on the golf course and on "social" occasions of different kinds.

Independent Action

Cases of independent action are just what the name implies. The individual firms of an industry each go it alone. In some industries independent action often touches off price wars when the reactions of rivals to the actions of one firm are retaliatory in nature. In other industries independent action may be consistent with industry stability over time. Firms may have learned by experience what the reactions of rivals will be to actions on their part and may voluntarily avoid any activity that will rock the boat. Or it may be that the management of each firm is reasonably well-satisfied

---

[5]For an excellent discussion of cartel types *see* Karl Pribram, *Cartel Problems* (Washington, D.C.: The Brookings Institution, 1935), pp. 41–58.

with present prices, outputs, and profits, and is content to let things continue as they are rather than chance the start of a chain reaction.

Classification Limitations

Collusion is a matter of degree, with cases of perfect collusion and cases of independent action at the polar limits. We cannot with certainty say that all price leadership cases or all gentlemen's agreements fall under the heading of imperfect collusion. Ordinarily we would expect that to be the case, but in some instances terms of agreement and adherence to those terms may be strict enough to present us with a case of perfect collusion. Similarly, cartel arrangements may not always be enforced strictly enough to warrant calling them perfect collusion, but rather may fall in the category of imperfect collusion.

Reference to the number of firms in an industry is conspicuously absent from the classification we have made. Yet the degree of collusion achieved corresponds to some extent to the number of firms involved. The greater the number of firms in a given industry, the harder it will ordinarily be to achieve a high degree of collusion.[6] The smaller the number of firms involved, the easier it is for the activities of individual firms to come under the scrutiny of the others. Small numbers are more easily policed by the group as a whole; hence, collusive arrangements are less likely to be violated by individual firms.

The Short Run

We turn now to outputs and pricing in specific oligopoly cases in the short run. Typical examples under each of the three classifications of the preceding section will be examined so that a general grasp of the fundamental problems and principles involved in oligopolistic situations can be obtained. In the short-run analysis of the present section we should keep in mind that individual firms do not have time to change their plant sizes nor is it possible for new firms to enter the industry. The number of firms in the industry under consideration is fixed.

Perfect Collusion

The Centralized Cartel   The centralized cartel case illustrates collusion in its most complete form. Its purpose is the joint or monopolistic maximization of industry profits by the several firms of the industry. "Ideal" or

---

[6]State intervention has made collusion possible in some industries even though there are large numbers of producers involved. Certain agricultural crops—wheat, citrus fruits, and tobacco—are cases in point. *See* Arman A. Alchian and William R. Allen, *University Economics*, 2nd ed. (Belmont, Calif.: Wadsworth Publishing Company, Inc., 1967), pp. 319–349.

complete monopolistic price and output determination by a cartel will rarely be achieved in the real world, although it may be approached in some instances.

Suppose that individual firms of a certain industry have surrendered the power to make price and output decisions to a central association. Quotas to be produced are determined by the association, as is the distribution of industry profits. Policies adopted are to be those which will contribute most to total industry profits. To simplify the analysis we shall assume that the firms of the industry produce a homogeneous product.

Maximization of the cartel's profits is essentially a monopoly problem, since a single agency is making decisions for the industry as a whole. Profits are maximum where the industry output and price are such that industry marginal revenue equals industry marginal cost. These two concepts need explanation.

The association is faced with the industry demand curve for the product; the industry marginal revenue curve is derived from it in the usual manner. The industry marginal revenue curve shows how much each one-unit increase in the volume of sales per unit of time will increase industry total receipts. The industry demand curve and the industry marginal revenue curve are shown by *DD* and *MR*, respectively, in Figure 12-1.

The industry marginal cost curve is constructed from the short-run marginal cost curves of individual firms in the industry. The two-firm case in Figure 12-1 shows how this construction is done. For any given output level the central agency should minimize industry costs. This goal can be accomplished by allocating quotas to the member firms in such a way that the marginal cost of each firm when producing its quota is equal to the marginal cost of every other firm when each is producing its respective quota. If quotas are allocated to individual firms in any other way, industry costs for the given output will not be minimized. Suppose, for example, that the quota of Firm A with respect to the quota of Firm B is such that Firm A's marginal cost is greater than that of Firm B. Industry costs could be decreased by reducing Firm A's quota and by increasing Firm B's. Reducing Firm A's production rate by one unit will reduce industry total cost by an amount equal to Firm A's (higher) marginal cost. Increasing the production rate of Firm B by one unit will increase industry total cost by an amount equal to Firm B's (lower) marginal cost. Thus, the reduction of Firm A's quota will reduce total cost by more than the increase in Firm B's quota will increase it. When quotas are correctly allocated for each possible industry output, the industry marginal cost curve will be the horizontal summation of the individual firm short-run marginal cost curves. The industry marginal cost curve is ΣMC in Figure 12-1.

The profit-maximizing price for the cartel will be p and the industry output will be X. Each individual firm should produce the quota at which its

Figure 12-1   The Centralized Cartel

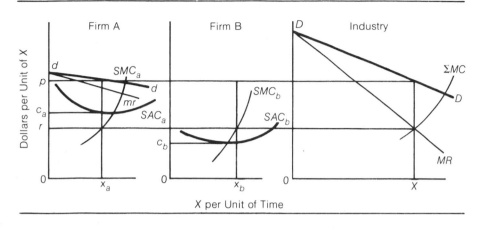

short-run marginal cost is equal to industry marginal revenue *r*. The quota of Firm A will be x_a and that of Firm B will be x_b. Ignore *dd* and *mr* in the Firm A diagram for the present. If industry output exceeds *X*, marginal costs of one or more firms will be greater than *r* and industry marginal revenue will be smaller. More will be added to industry total costs by these outputs than to industry total receipts; hence, profits will decrease. If industry output is less than *X* some or all firms' short-run marginal costs will be less than *r*, while industry marginal revenue will exceed *r*. Larger outputs up to *X* will add more to industry total receipts than to industry total costs, and profits will increase.[7]

Profits can be computed on a firm-by-firm basis and totaled for the industry. Profit per unit of output for a single firm will equal the industry price minus the firm's average cost at the output that the firm produces. Profit per unit multiplied by the firm's output equals the profit that the firm

---

[7]Let π = profits:

$R = f(x_a + x_b)$ = total revenue of the cartel
$C_a = g(x_a)$ = total cost for Firm A
$C_b = h(x_b)$ = total cost for Firm B.

Then:

$$\pi = R - (C_a + C_b) = f(x_a + x_b) - g(x_a) - h(x_b).$$

To maximize profits:

$$\frac{\delta\pi}{\delta x_a} = f'(x_a + x_b) - g'(x_a) = 0$$

$$\frac{\delta\pi}{\delta x_b} = f'(x_a + x_b) - h'(x_b) = 0$$

and:

$$f'(x_a + x_b) = g'(x_a) = h'(x_b)$$

or *MR* from cartel sales must equal the marginal cost of Film A's output and the marginal cost of Firm B's output.

contributes to total industry profits. Profit of Firm A is $c_a p \times x_a$, while that of Firm B is $c_b p \times x_b$. Total industry profits are the sum of the profits contributed by all individual firms. Industry profits may be distributed among firms on an "as earned" basis, or according to any other scheme deemed appropriate.

The "ideal" monopolistic determination of industry output and price just described is not likely to be achieved in practice. Decisions made by the association result from negotiation, give-and-take, and compromise among the points of view and interests of cartel members. Therefore it is not probable that the association would act precisely as would a monopolist who had the industry to himself. Profits, for example, may be distributed according to production quotas assigned to individual firms. Those firms able to exert the greatest pressure on the central association may receive the larger quotas, even though additional output per unit of time may run their marginal costs above those of other firms thus increasing industry costs and decreasing industry profits. In addition, pressure on the central association to increase the quotas of some firms may result in decisions to increase industry output beyond the profit-maximizing level. Prices and profits below the full monopolistic level would result. Additionally, inefficient high-cost firms may be assigned quotas that run their marginal costs substantially above industry marginal revenue, even though principles of economy may indicate that such firms should be shut down completely. These possibilities by no means exhaust the field, but they do serve to illustrate the point that political decisions on the part of the association, made to placate certain member firms, may sometimes take precedence over economic considerations.[8]

The larger the number of firms forming the cartel, the harder it will be to hold the cartel together, particularly if the individual firms' shares of the industry profits are small. There exists a strong incentive for individual firms to leave the cartel and operate independently. With the larger part of the industry adhering to the cartel price, an individual firm operating independently would be faced with a demand curve for its output that is much more elastic than the industry demand curve in price ranges around the cartel price.

Consider Firm A in Figure 12-1, for example. If Firm A could break away from the cartel, it would be faced with a demand curve such as *dd*, provided other firms in the cartel adhere to price *p*. The demand curve facing any one individual firm under these circumstances would be much more elastic than the industry demand curve at the cartel price, since a cut in price by the individual firm would attract buyers away from the rest of the cartel. Consequently, marginal revenue for Firm A, operating independently at output level x_a, would be higher than marginal revenue for the cartel

[8]*See* Machlup, *The Economics of Sellers' Competition*, pp. 476–480.

at output level X. Firm A's marginal revenue would exceed its marginal costs at output x_a, and the firm could increase its own profits by expanding its output beyond x_a. The firm that can break away from a cartel successfully can increase its profit possibilities if other firms do not try the same strategy. If all try it the cartel falls apart, industry output increases, the price falls, and all end up with smaller profits.

The Market-sharing Cartel   Market sharing of one type or another is characteristic of many cartel arrangements. Under certain conditions it can result in "ideal" monopoly price and output for the industry; that is, the industry profit-maximizing level of price and output. In practice it is likely to deviate from the monopoly position.

Suppose that the firms of the industry produce a homogeneous product and agree on the share of the market that each is to receive at each possible price. Homogeneity of the product will establish the rule of a single price in the product market. To simplify the analysis, assume further that there are only two firms in the industry. The two firms have equal costs and agree to share the market half and half.

Under the assumed conditions the two firms will have identical views regarding the price to charge and the output to produce. The industry demand curve for the product is *DD* in Figure 12-2. Each firm faces demand curve *dd* for its own output. Each has a short-run average cost curve and a short-run marginal cost curve of *SAC* and *SMC*, respectively. The marginal revenue curve faced by each firm is *mr*. The profit-maximizing output for each firm will be *x*, at which *SMC* is equal to *mr*. Each firm will want to charge price *p*. Profits for each firm will equal *cp* × *x*. Together the firms will produce an industry output of *X* that will fill the market at price *p*. Such will be the case since *dd* lies halfway between the market demand curve and the price axis.

Under the assumed conditions the market-sharing cartel, like the centralized cartel, will determine price and output at the levels that a monopolist would set were he in complete control of the producing facilities of the industry. Such a monopolist's marginal cost curve would be the horizontal summation of the two *SMC* curves of the two plants—it would lie twice as far to the right at each price level as the *SMC* curve of Figure 12-2 does. The monopolist would face the industry demand curve *DD*, and at output *X* industry marginal revenue would be at level *r*—the same level as individual firm marginal revenue at output *x*. Such would be the case because *DD* has the same elasticity at price *p* as does *dd*.[9]

---

[9]Two demand curves with equal elasticities at each of various price levels are said to be isoelastic. Demand curves are isoelastic when the quantities taken at each of various prices form a constant ratio to each other. [*See* Joan Robinson, *The Economics of Imperfect Competition* (London: Macmillan & Co., Ltd., 1933), p. 61.] Because *dd* lies halfway between *DD* and the price axis at different prices, the quantities taken as shown by *dd* are in constant ratio to the quantities taken as shown by *DD*. The ratio is one-half.

At output X industry marginal cost would be at level r. Output X would be the profit-maximizing output for the monopolist, since industry marginal revenue and industry marginal cost are equal at that output. The monopolist would sell output X at price p per unit.

But several factors may stand in the way of the achievement of an "ideal" monopolistic price and output. Costs of production for the individual firms are likely to differ rather than being identical as we assumed they were. Market sharing largely precludes the transferring of output quotas from firms with higher marginal costs to those with lower marginal costs at the outputs produced by each. Differing points of view and differing interests of the firms comprising the cartel may result in compromises that stand in the way of maximization of industry profits. Individual firms, assigned market shares and given a product price, may deliberately or in good faith overestimate the quantities of product that constitute their respective proportions of the total market, and thus may encroach on the markets of others.[10] Additionally, the degree of independent action left to individual firms may whet their desires to break away from the cartel and may increase the possibilities of their doing so.

Under a market-sharing cartel arrangement markets need not be shared equally. High-capacity firms may receive larger market shares than low-capacity firms. Market sharing may be accomplished on a regional basis, with each firm allocated a particular geographic area instead of sharing a common market. A whole host of difficulties may arise as a result of different demand elasticities at particular prices: different costs, inferior territories, encroachment upon each other's territories, and so on—all of which make pricing and output problems much more uncertain than they appear to be in the model.

Imperfect Collusion

Price Leadership by a Low-cost Firm   In the absence of a formal cartel arrangement price leadership by one firm in the industry is frequently the means of colluding. We shall suppose that there are two firms in the industry, that a tacit market-sharing arrangement has been established with each firm assigned half the market, that the product is undifferentiated, and that one firm has lower costs than the other.

A conflict of interest occurs with regard to the desirable price to charge. The market demand curve is DD in Figure 12-3. Each firm faces demand curve dd. The cost curves of the high-cost firm are SAC_1 and SMC_1. Those of the low cost firm are SAC_2 and SMC_2. The marginal revenue curve of each firm is mr. The high-cost firm will want to produce an

---

[10]To minimize sales in excess of market shares or quotas, most cartels exact penalties from the member who exceeds his quota.

Figure 12-2   The Market-sharing Cartel

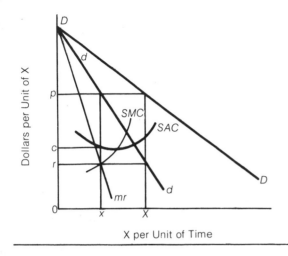

Figure 12-3   Price Leadership by a Low-cost Firm

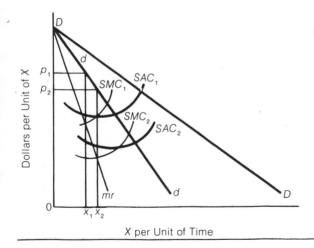

output of x_1 and charge a price of p_1, whereas the low-cost firm will want to produce an output of x_2 and charge a price of p_2.

Since the low-cost firm can afford to sell at a lower price than the high-cost firm can, the latter will have no recourse other than to sell at the price set by the low-cost firm. Thus, the low-cost firm becomes the price leader. This type of situation has several ramifications, depending on the comparative costs of the firms, the number of firms in the industry, the shape and position of the market demand curve, and the share of the market that each firm is to receive.[11]

Price Leadership by a Dominant Firm   Many oligopolistic industries are made up of one or more large firms, together with a number of small firms. To avoid large-scale price cutting tacit collusion may occur in the form of price leadership by one or more of the large firms.[12] We shall simplify the analysis by assuming that there is a single large dominant firm in the industry and a number of small firms. Suppose the dominant firm sets the price for the industry and allows the small firms to sell all they desire at that price. The dominant firm then fills out the market.

Each small firm will tend to behave as though it were in a competitive atmosphere. It can sell all it wants to sell at the price set by the dominant firm; it faces a perfectly elastic demand curve at the level of the established price. The marginal revenue curve of the small firm coincides with the demand curve faced by it; hence, to maximize profits the small firm should produce the output at which its marginal cost equals marginal revenue and the price set by the dominant firm.

A supply curve for all small firms combined is obtained by summing the marginal cost curves of all the small firms horizontally. It shows how much all small firms together will place on the market at each possible price. This curve is labeled ΣMC in Figure 12-4.

The demand curve faced by the dominant firm can be derived from this information. The market demand curve DD shows how much of the product consumers will take off the market at each possible price, whereas the ΣMC curve shows how much the small firms combined will sell at each possible price. The horizontal differences between the two curves at all possible prices show how much the dominant firm can sell at those prices. The demand curve faced by the dominant firm is dd and is obtained by subtracting the ΣMC curve from the DD curve horizontally. To show in detail how dd is obtained, suppose the dominant firm sets the price at p'. At this price, or any higher price, the small firms would fill the market, leaving no sales for the dominant firm. At a price of p'' the small firms would sell quantity $p''A''$, leaving $A''B''$ for the dominant firm to sell. In order to place the demand curve for the dominant firm's product in proper relationship to the quantity and dollar axes of the diagram, we can set point C'' so that $p''C''$ equals $A''B''$. This process can be repeated at various assumed prices. A line joining all points thus extablished will be dd, the demand curve faced by the dominant firm. At any price below their

[11]*See* Kenneth E. Boulding, *Economic Analysis*, vol. I, *Microeconomics*, 4th ed. (New York: Harper & Row, Publishers, 1966), pp. 475–482.

Figure 12-4 Price Leadership by a Dominant Firm

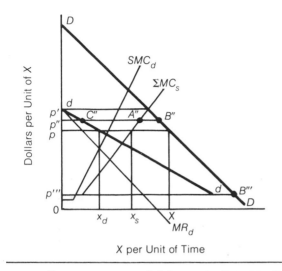

X per Unit of Time

respective average variable costs the smaller firms will drop out of the market, leaving the entire market to the dominant firm.

The profit-maximizing price and outputs are determined in the usual way. The marginal revenue curve of the dominant firm is MR_d, and its marginal cost curve is SMC_d. Profits are maximum for the dominant firm at an output level of x_d at which SMC_d equals MR_d. The price charged by the dominant firm is p. Each small firm maximizes profits by producing the output at which its marginal cost is equal to its marginal revenue, and marginal revenue for each small firm is equal to price p. Total output for the small firms combined is x_s, the output at which ΣMC equals p. Total industry output is x_d plus x_s which equals X. Profit for the dominant firm is x_d times the difference between price p and the dominant firm's average cost at output x_d. Profit for each small firm is equal to its output times the difference between price p and its average cost at that output. Average cost curves are omitted from Figure 12-4 to avoid cluttering the diagram.

Many variations of the dominant-firm model are possible. For example, if there are two or more large firms surrounded by a cluster of small firms, the small firms may look to one or all of the large firms for price leadership. The large firms collectively may estimate the amounts that the small firms will sell at various prices and proceed to share or divide the remaining market in any one of various possible ways. The present analysis assumes no product differentiation. Such product differentiation may occur in similar price leadership cases, causing price differentials for the prod-

---

[12]Price leadership has been common in the fabrication of nonferrous alloys, steel, agricultural implements, newsprint paper, and other industries. *See* Scherer *op. cit.*, pp. 164–173.

ucts of the various firms. The gasoline industry furnishes a case in point. Retail prices of the major companies—one or more of which often serve as the price leader—will be very close together in a given locality, while those of small independents will tend to be two or three cents per gallon below that of the majors.

Independent Action

Price Wars and Price Rigidity   A persistent danger of price wars exists in oligopolistic industries characterized by independent action on the part of individual firms. Little of a precise analytical nature can be said about these. One seller may lower his price to increase sales. But this move takes customers away from rivals, and the rivals may retaliate with a vengeance. The price war may spread throughout the industry, with each firm trying to undercut others. The end result may well be disastrous for some individual firms.

The specific causes of price wars are varied, but they originate from the interdependence of sellers. A new filling station opening up in a given locality or an existing one attempting to revive lagging sales may be the initiating factor. Surplus stocks at existing prices and limited storage facilities have touched off price wars in the sale of crude oil in the petroleum industry. In a young industry sellers may not have learned what to expect of rivals, or they may be scrambling to secure an established place in the industry and may inadvertently start a price war.

Maturity on the part of an industry may substantially lessen the dangers of price wars. Individual firms may at least have learned what not to do and may carefully avoid any activities that conceivably could touch off price wars. They may have established a price or a cluster of prices that is tolerable to all from the point of view of profits. Such prices are thought by many to be rather rigid over time, although there is no clearcut evidence that this is the case. Individual firms are thought to engage in nonprice competition rather than in price rivalry in order to increase their respective shares of the market and profits. Soft drinks and cigarettes are often cited as examples of mature rigid-price industries.

The "Kinked" Demand Curve   An analytical device frequently used to explain oligopolistic price rigidity is the kinked demand curve. This case is thought to occur when certain assumptions concerning the industry and the firms in the industry are fulfilled. First, the industry is a mature one, either with or without product differentiation. A price or a cluster of prices fairly satisfactory to all has been established. Second, if one firm lowers price, other firms will follow or undercut it in order to retain their shares of the market. For price decreases, the individual firm cannot hope to do

Figure 12–5 *The Kinked Demand Curve: Cost Changes*

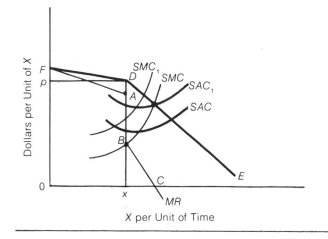

more than hold its former share of the market—and it may not succeed in doing that much. Third, if one firm increases price, other firms will not follow the price increase. The customers of the price-raising firm will shift to the other, now relatively lower-priced firms; and the price-raising firm will lose a part, if not all, of its share of the market.

The demand curve faced by a single firm in such a situation is pictured diagrammatically in Figure 12-5 as *FDE*. The firm has established price *p*. If it decreases the price below *p* other firms follow and it retains only its share of the market. For price decreases, then, the demand curve faced by the firm is *DE*, and it will have about the same elasticity at different prices as the market demand curve. Should the firm increase the price above *p*, other firms will not follow, and it loses a part or all of its share of the market to the other firms. The demand curve faced by the firm for price increases is *FD*, and at each possible price it will have a considerably greater elasticity than the market demand curve. The demand curve *FDE* is not a smooth one; it has a "kink" in it at the established price *p*.

The kinked demand curve has important implications for the marginal revenue curve of the firm. The marginal revenue curve is discontinuous at output *x*; that is, it has a gap in it at that point. We can visualize this gap by imagining first that only the *FD* portion of the demand curve exists and by drawing the appropriate marginal revenue curve for it. Second, we can imagine that the *DE* portion of the demand curve extends smoothly on up to the price axis, and we can then draw the appropriate marginal revenue curve for it. Since the imagined part of the *DE* curve does not exist, no marginal revenue curve exists for it at outputs less than *x*. Since the *FD* part of the demand curve does not go beyond *x*, neither does its marginal revenue curve. The two nonvertical sections of the marginal revenue curve can be thought of as the appropriate marginal revenue curves for two distinct continuous demand curves, and there would be no reason to expect them to be equal to each other at output x.

The discontinuous marginal revenue curve can be thought of also in terms of elasticity of demand. If the demand curve were continuous, its elasticity would be changing continuously as we move from higher to lower prices. Since $MR = p - p/\epsilon$, the marginal revenue curve would also be continuous as we move down the demand curve. However, the demand curve breaks at D . Elasticity at an output infinitesimally below x is substantially greater than elasticity at an output infinitesimally above x. Thus, marginal revenue must drop sharply at output x.

Cost curves SAC and SMC show a situation such that at price p some profit can be made. The marginal cost curve cuts the marginal revenue curve within its discontinuous part. Output x and price p are, in fact, the firm's profit-maximizing output and price. If the output level were less than x, marginal revenue would exceed marginal cost, and the firm's profits would be increased by expanding output to x. For output increases above x, marginal cost exceeds marginal revenue, and profits will decrease.

Discontinuous marginal revenue curves result in fairly rigid pricing policies on the part of individual firms in the industry. Suppose one firm's costs increase because of increases in the prices it must pay for resources. The cost curves will shift upward to positions such as SAC_1 and SMC_1. As long as the marginal cost curve continues to cut the discontinuous part of the marginal revenue curve, there is no incentive for the oligopolist to change either price or output. The reverse situation also holds. Resource price decreases will shift the cost curves downward, but as long as the marginal cost curve cuts the marginal revenue curve in its discontinuous part, no price-output changes will occur. If costs should go up enough for the marginal cost curve to cut the FA segment of the marginal revenue curve, the oligopolist will restrict output to the point at which marginal cost equals marginal revenue and will raise the price. Likewise, if costs decrease enough for the marginal cost curve to cut the BC segment of the marginal revenue curve, the oligopolist will lower the price and increase output up to the level at which marginal cost equals marginal revenue. Thus, there is room for the cost curves to shift up or down without changing the oligopolist's profit-maximizing price and output. Such will be the case as long as the marginal cost curve cuts the marginal revenue curve in its discontinuous part.

Price rigidity may also persist when demand changes. The initial position of the oligopolist is pictured by Figure 12-6 (a). Assume his costs do not change and market demand for the product increases. The demand curve faced by the oligopolist shifts to the right to $F_1D_1E_1$, as is shown in Figure 12-6 (b), but it remains kinked at price p. The marginal revenue

Figure 12-6 *The Kinked Demand Curve: Changes in Demand*

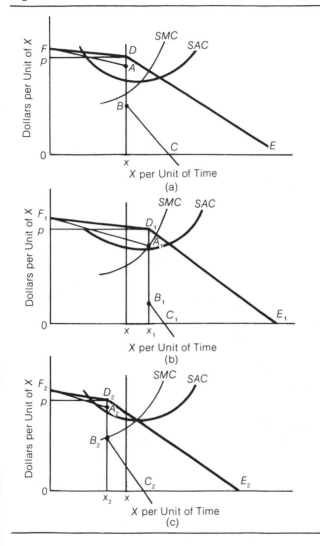

(a)

(b)

(c)

curve moves to the right also, with its discontinuous segment always occurring at the output at which the demand curve is kinked. If the increase in demand is limited enough so that the marginal cost curve still cuts the marginal revenue curve in the discontinuous segment B_1A_1, the firm will continue to maximize profits at price p but at a larger output x_1. If the increase in market demand should shift the firm's demand curve farther to the right than $F_1D_1E_1$, the marginal cost curve would cut the marginal revenue curve's F_1A_1 segment; and to maximize profits the firm should increase the price as well as the output. A decrease in market demand shifts the firm's demand curve to the left to $F_2D_2E_2$, as is shown in Figure 12-6 (c). Here there is no incentive to change the price, although output decreases, until the demand curve shifts far enough to the left for the marginal cost curve to intersect the B_2C_2 segment of the marginal revenue curve. This amount of shift would induce the firm to lower the price as well as to decrease output.

The case of the kinked demand curve is only one of many possible oligopolistic situations, and it rests on a special set of assumptions regarding the behavior of rivals when confronted with certain actions on the part of the firm under analysis. Often students (and some professors) become intrigued with the case and tend to think of it and the term "oligopoly" as being synonymous. We should avoid this inaccuracy in our thinking.

The Long Run

Two types of adjustment are possible in oligopolistic industries in the long run. In the first place individual firms are free to build any desired size of plant; thus, the relevant cost curves for the firm are the long-run average cost curve and the long-run marginal cost curve. Second, some industry adjustments may be possible in the form of entry of new firms into the industry or exit of old firms from the industry. These types of adjustment will be considered in turn.

Size of Plant Adjustments

The size of plant that the individual firm should build depends on its anticipated rate of output. For any given anticipated rate of output we can say as a first approximation that the firm attempts to produce that output at the least possible average cost; that is, it builds the plant size that makes its short-run average cost curve tangent to the long-run average cost curve at that output.

Under perfect collusion, and often under imperfect collusion, quotas, market shares, and outputs of individual firms may be predictable with some degree of accuracy. In such cases the firm would be expected to adjust its size of plant accordingly. Not much can be said with regard to whether the size of plant would be optimum size, less than optimum size, or greater than optimum size. It may be any one of the three, depending on the nature of the particular oligopolistic situation involved. Certainly, there is no reason for expecting that the firm would tend to construct an optimum size of plant.

For a firm in an industry characterized by independent action there will be no more certainty regarding the size of plant to build than there is regarding the output to produce and the price to charge. Growth possibilities of the industry may influence the decisions of the firm to a large extent. The existence of a large growth potential would make the individual firm optimistic with respect to anticipated sales and would result in plant enlargements. "Live and let live" policies or fear of "rocking the boat" on the part of individual firms may lead to fairly determinate outputs and consequently to some degree of certainty as to the sizes of plant to build. Again there is no reason for believing that optimum plant sizes would be built.

Entry into the Industry

When individual firms in an industry make profits, or when they incur losses, incentives exist for new firms to enter the industry or for old firms to leave. Exit from an oligopolistic industry will usually be much easier than entry and need not detain us here. Ease or difficulties of entry are much more important. The very existence of oligopolistic markets depends to some extent on whether or not entry into the industry can be partially or completely blocked. In addition, the degree of collusion that can be attained or maintained within the industry tends to be an inverse function of the ease of entry.

Entry and the Existence of Oligopoly   If entry into an oligopolistic industry is comparatively easy, it may not remain oligopolistic in the long run. Whether it does or not will depend on the extent of the market for the product, as compared with the optimum size of plant for an individual firm. Profits will attract new firms in, lowering the market price or the cluster of prices as industry output increases. When the price no longer exceeds long-run average costs for individual firms, entry will cease. If the market is limited, the number of firms may still be small enough to make it necessary for each firm to take account of the actions of the others. If so, the market situation remains one of oligopoly. If the market is extensive enough so that the number of firms can increase to the point at which each firm no longer considers that its activities affect the other firms, or that the activities of other firms affect it, the market situation will have become one of either pure or monopolistic competition.

Entry and Collusion   Easy entry tends to break down collusive arrangements. We have already seen that in a collusive arrangement a strong incentive exists for any one individual firm to break away from the group. The same sort of incentive operates to attract new firms into a cartelized industry and to induce those entering firms to remain outside the cartel. The entering firm, if it remains outside the group, will face a demand curve more elastic at various price levels than that of the group and, consequently, will be confronted with higher marginal revenue possibilities. At prices slightly below the cartel price it can pick up many of the cartel's customers. At prices slightly above the cartel price it can sell little or nothing. Entering firms that remain outside the collusive group will encroach more and more on the profits of that group or will cause the group to incur losses and force its eventual dissolution.

Even when the entering firms are taken into the cartel, a strong presumption exists that dissolution of the cartel will follow eventually. Refer to Figure 12-7. Suppose that ΣMC is the horizontal summation of individual firm short-run marginal cost curves. The price will be p and industry output will be X. The entry of new firms will move the ΣMC curve to the right,[13] increasing the industry profit-maximizing output and lowering the profit-maximizing price. When enough firms have entered to shift the industry marginal cost curve to ΣMC_1, forcing the price down to p_1 and increasing the level of output to X_1, profits for the industry may still exist. More firms will enter, shifting the industry marginal cost curve to some position ΣMC_2; however, industry profits will decrease if output is expanded beyond X_1. Industry marginal revenue for the additional output will be less than the industry's marginal cost. The more profitable course of action for the cartel is to keep the additional firms idle and simply cut them in on the industry's profits. Plant costs of additional firms augment industry total costs, and eventually enough firms will have entered the industry to cause all profit to be eliminated. A strong incentive now exists for individual firms to break away from the cartel. Any single firm, if it markets its own output, faces a more elastic demand curve in the neighborhood of the cartel price than does the cartel. Marginal revenue for the firm exceeds marginal revenue for the cartel. Also, average cost for the firm is lower than average cost for the cartel.[14] The firm which can break away can make profits, provided others remain in the cartel and the cartel price is maintained. The temptations facing each individual firm are likely to result in a breakup of the cartel.[15]

Barriers to Entry   Since ease of entry into an industry tends to be the nemesis of collusive oligopoly, collusion usually can be maintained only when entry is restricted; collusion has as one of its purposes the erection of barriers to potential entrants. Barriers to the entry of new firms may be inherent in the nature of the industry, or they may be established by the existing firms of the industry. These will be called "natural" barriers and "artificial" barriers, respectively. Natural barriers to entry may be inevitable in particular industries. Artificial barriers conceivably can be removed.

---

[13]Assume that M is the minimum price at which any firm will enter the industry.

[14]The individual firm's cost is lower since the cartel is holding the plant capacity of a number of firms idle, thus adding to cartel average costs.

[15]See Don Patinkin, "Multiple-Plant Firms, Cartels, and Imperfect Competition," *Quarterly Journal of Economics*, vol. LXI (February 1947), pp. 173–205.

Figure 12-7   Long-run Cartel Equilibrium and the Effects of Entry

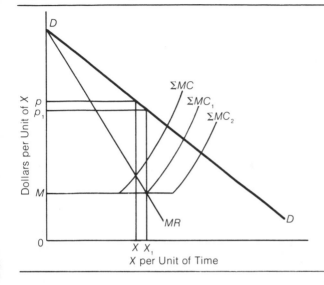

Probably the most important natural barrier to entry is the smallness of the product market in relation to the optimum size of plant for a firm in the industry. Suppose, for example, that there are two firms in the industry, and each is operating with a plant size somewhere near the optimum. Price exceeds average costs for each, and some profit exists. Heretofore we have considered the existence of profit as the signal for the entrance of new firms. Prospective entrants eye the profit and consider the possibility of entering. They discover that if a new firm enters with a plant size considerably smaller than optimum, average costs of the entrant will be so high that no profit could be made. Further, if a new firm enters with an optimum size of plant, industry output will be increased to the extent that price will be below average costs both for existing firms in the industry and for the entrant. Therefore, no new firms will enter.

Another natural barrier to entry consists of the difficulty of putting together a large and complex plant and of obtaining funds to build it. The automobile industry is a case in point. The initial investment outlay for a potential entrant is extremely high. Large amounts of space, several buildings, and specialized heavy equipment must be obtained. Highly skilled and well-paid personnel are necessary. A nationwide organization of dealership, maintenance, and repair facilities must be established. The difficulties of entry are so great that only a few firms have had the financial backing to try it since World War II, despite record profits in the industry. This barrier to entry is not the only one for the automobile industry, but it has been major.

Among the artificial barriers to entry those enforced or supported by the state loom large. Patent rights to key machines or technological processes may be obtained by certain firms of an industry. Those firms may then maintain control of the machines or processes by leasing them to a limited number of other firms.[16] Or the firms of an industry through cross-licensing arrangement may give each other access to the patents of each but refuse to allow any new firms to use them.[17]

Government-supported barriers to entry exist extensively in the field of transportation. On a local basis taxicab and bus companies operate under franchises guaranteeing limited "competition" in the industry. Entry into the interstate public transportation field, with the exception of air carriers, is regulated by the Interstate Commerce Commission. The Civil Aeronautics Board regulates entry into the air transportation field.

Local governments regulate entry into a host of local oligopolistic industries. Building codes in many cities prevent the entrance of firms producing prefabricated houses or parts of houses. Local licensing laws are frequently used to limit the number of barbers, taverns, plumbers, morticians, and others in service trades. Entry-restricting devices are usually rationalized as maintaining standards of competency, keeping undesirables out of the trades, and protecting the public in other ways.

A second artificial barrier to prospective entrants is the control by the firms already in the field of strategic sources of raw materials necessary for producing the product. This barrier will be of greatest importance where raw material sources are highly concentrated geographically, or, at least, where the better sources are highly concentrated. Concentration of raw material sources facilitates concentration of ownership. Magnesium, nickel, molybdenum, and aluminum provide examples.

Third, price policies of the established firms in an industry may barricade the door. The prospects of entry by new firms may set the established firms in motion, frightening away prospective entrants by threatening to lower the price enough to eliminate profit possibilities. Or, if new firms should be bold enough to enter, underselling by the established firms may promptly drive them out again. The classic example here was the Standard Oil case of the late 1800s. Additionally, recurrent price wars may create such an atmosphere of uncertainty about the profit possibilities of an industry that new firms will steer clear of it.

Fourth, product differentiation may form an artificial barrier to entry. The industry's product may have become so closely identified with particular

---

[16]Entry into the glass-container industry has been controlled in this manner. *See* Wilcox, *op. cit.*, pp. 73–78.

[17]Cross-licensing arrangements have been used extensively in the domestic branch of the electric lamp industry. *See* Stocking and Watkins, *op. cit.*, pp. 325–327, especially Footnote 75.

sellers' names that consumers will refuse to buy "off brands." Even though standard brands are differentiated from each other, the standard brands are well known to almost all consumers. What consumers fear and refuse to consume are the new, unknown, and consequently "inferior" brands. This reluctance is an important barrier to entry into the automobile industry.

Restricted entry into an oligopolistic industry makes it possible for profits to exist in the long run for the firms in the industry. We are not saying that pure profits will always exist in oligopolistic industries. Losses can and do occur. Or, the firms of an industry may be just covering average costs, showing neither profit nor loss. When no profits are being made, entry will not be desired regardless of whether it is restricted or open. The possibility of profits provides the motivation for entry, and when entry is restricted, profits may persist over time. Restricted entry prevents profits from playing their essential role in the organization of productive capacity in a free enterprise economy.

Nonprice Competition

Although oligopolists may be reluctant to encroach upon each other's market shares by lowering the product price, they appear to have little hesitancy in using other means to accomplish the same results. While open undercutting of the price(s) of rivals raises the specter of price wars that may be disastrous to some firms, product differentiation offers a more subtle and a much safer way of accomplishing approximately the same results. Product differentiation occurs in two major forms: (1) advertising and (2) variation in design and quality of product. Both forms may and do occur simultaneously, but for purposes of analysis we shall treat them separately.

Advertising

The primary purpose of advertising is to shift the demand curve faced by the single seller to the right and to make it less elastic. Thus the seller can sell a larger volume at the same or a higher price without the danger of touching off a price war. Each seller tries to encroach on the markets of others through advertising. When one firm launches an ingenious and successful advertising program, ordinarily there will be a time lag before rivals can embark on similar programs and profits can result during the time-lag interval.

Frequently the products of sellers in an industry can be differentiated effectively by advertising alone. Each seller attempts to attract customers to his particular brand name, although basically the product of each seller may be the same as that of other sellers in the industry. The success of sellers in this respect is especially evident in the aspirin industry. All five-grain aspirin tablets conform to certain United States pharmacopeia specifications, and one is as effective for the patient as another; nevertheless, some nationally known sellers are able to attract and hold customers at prices far greater than those of other sellers in the same industry.

In some instances rival advertising campaigns succeed only in increasing the costs of individual sellers. Attempts on the part of a single seller to encroach on the markets of others may be anticipated by the other sellers. They launch counteradvertising campaigns of their own, and all sellers succeed only in holding their original places in the market. The overall market for the product may not be expanded at all by advertising activity—the present-day cigarette industry is a case in point. But once rival advertising is started, no single seller can withdraw without losing his place in the market. The advertising outlays become "built-in" to the cost structures of individual firms and lead to higher product prices than would otherwise prevail.

How far should nonprice competition through advertising be carried by the individual seller seeking to maximize profits? The same principles that have guided us thus far in profit maximization apply in this case. Advertising outlays are expected to add to the seller's total receipts, but successively larger outlays per unit of time beyond some point will add successively less marginal revenue. That is, marginal revenue from advertising will decrease as outlays increase. Similarly, larger advertising outlays add to the seller's total costs; that is, marginal costs of advertising are positive. The profit-maximizing outlay on advertising will be that outlay at which the marginal cost of advertising is equal to the marginal revenue received from it.[18]

Differences in Quality and Design

Variations in quality and design of particular products are usually used, along with advertising, to differentiate the product of one seller from another. The objective of variations on the part of one seller is that of causing consumers to prefer his product over the products of others; that is, to shift his demand curve to the right (or to enlarge his share of the total market) and to make his demand curve less elastic. Additionally, quality

---

[18]In practice, probably less is known about the effects of advertising outlays than about the effects of any other cost outlays made by the firm. Nevertheless, any intelligent approach by management to the "correct" magnitude of the advertising budget must be made on the basis of estimated marginal revenue and estimated marginal cost resulting from its contraction or expansion.

variation may be used to extend the market vertically—different qualities to appeal to different classes or groups of buyers.

When quality and design variations are used to increase an individual firm's market shares, rival firms would not be expected to sit by idly while their markets shrink. Retaliation by rivals will occur. Successful innovations will be imitated and improved on. Individual firms may succeed in increasing their market shares temporarily, but if a permanent increase is to be obtained, such firms must be able to keep ahead of their rivals.

The automobile industry furnishes an excellent example of product variation to increase market shares of particular firms. One producer initiates power steering. Consumers take to the innovation, and other producers follow in order to regain their market positions. Another mounts the motor on rubber, and the process is repeated. Low-pressure tires, automatic transmissions, high horsepower, and many other improvements, both real and fancied, are introduced initially to enlarge the market share of one producer, and are in turn copied by other producers to regain or hold their shares of the market.

When quality differences are introduced to extend the market vertically for a product, we may find the same firm producing different product qualities to sell to different groups of buyers at different prices; or we may find different firms specializing in particular qualities of the product. Initially a product, say deluxe garbage disposals, may be produced for middle-income group markets. Sellers find that by producing "super deluxe" models the market can be expanded into upper-income levels. Likewise, by stripping the deluxe model of fancy gadgets, a standard model can be sold to lower-income groups at a lower price. When different firms specialize in a particular quality of the product, quality differences may become the basis for market sharing.

Product variation often operates in the best interests of consumers. When it passes along the fruits of industrial research in the form of an improved product to the consuming public, consumer desires may be more adequately met than before. The electric mixer in lieu of the old hand-driven egg beater, the more portable and more versatile tank-type of vacuum cleaner in lieu of the upright model, the no-frost refrigerator, the high-fidelity stereo sound system, the self-starter on the automobile, and many other variations in product probably represent increased fulfillment of consumer wants.

Some product variation falls in the same class as retaliatory advertising. It adds to costs but adds little to demand or to the fulfillment of consumer desires. Design changes adding nothing to the quality of the product may occur. The purpose of the design change may simply be to differentiate a 1974 model from a 1975 one. Each seller believes that other sellers will make some changes and decides he should do the same to hold his share of the market.

The principles of profit maximization with respect to design and quality changes are the familiar ones. Any changes that will add more to total receipts than to total costs will increase profits (or reduce losses); or any changes which will reduce total costs more than total receipts will increase profits (or reduce losses). To maximize profits with respect to changes in the product, the firm should carry out changes to the point at which the marginal revenue from the changes is equal to the marginal cost of making them.

The Welfare Effects of Oligopoly

Oligopolistic market structures, as compared with purely competitive market structures, would be expected to have adverse effects on consumer welfare. The problems are essentially the same as those brought about by pure monopoly. There is output restriction, internal inefficiency of the firm, and resource waste in sales promotion activities. There may, however, be some welfare gains from product differentiation.

Output Restriction

An oligopolistic firm ordinarily faces a demand curve for its output that is downward-sloping to the right, or that is less than perfectly elastic. As a consequence marginal revenue at each level of sales is less than the price; and since the profit-maximizing firm produces the output level at which marginal revenue equals marginal cost, marginal cost will be less than the product price. The important point here is that resources used in producing this product are more valuable to consumers in this use than in alternative uses. Welfare would be increased by transfers of resources into the product and expansion of its output to the point at which marginal cost is equal to the product price.

In addition, an oligopolistic firm may make profits in the long run because entry into the industry is restricted. The price of the product exceeds the average costs of production, indicating that an expansion of the productive capacity of the industry would increase welfare. However, restricted entry keeps this desirable reallocation of resources from taking place.

Efficiency of the Firm

The maximum potential economic efficiency for individual firms in the production of particular products is realized when those firms are induced to build optimum sizes of plant and operate them at optimum rates of output. As we have observed, there is no automatic tendency for this state of affairs to occur in the long run under oligopoly. The firm's output depends upon its quota, its market share, or its anticipations with regard to its marginal revenue and its long-run marginal costs. Once a long-run output is decided on, the firm will want to produce that output as cheaply as possible; that is, it will build the size of plant whose short-run average cost curve is tangent to the long-run average cost curve at that output. Coincidence of the desired output with the output of an optimum size of plant, operated at the optimum rate of output, would be sheer accident.

It should be emphasized that firms in an oligopolistic type of market, even though they do not use optimum plant sizes, operated at optimum rates of output, may provide more efficiency in producing a certain product than would firms of any other type of market organization. The optimum size of plant may be large enough in comparison with the market for the product so that there isn't room in the industry for enough firms to make the market one of pure competition. If the firms of the industry were broken up or atomized so that no one firm could appreciably influence market price, each might have a much smaller than optimum size of plant. Consequently, costs and price(s) of the product might be higher, and output levels smaller, with such an arrangement than they would be with the oligopolistic market structure.

Sales Promotion Wastes

Firms in oligopolistic markets engage in extensive sales-promotion activities designed to extend their own markets at the expense of the markets of rivals. As we have seen, the major forms of such activities are advertising and changes in product quality and design. To the extent that they add nothing to consumer satisfaction, resources used in these activities are obviously wasted. Often, however, they yield certain satisfactions to consumers in the forms of entertainment and improved product quality. In these instances the important question with regard to economic efficiency and welfare is whether or not the additional satisfactions obtained from resources used in sales-promotional activities are equal to their costs; that is, equal to the satisfactions that the resources could have produced in alternative employments. A strong case can be made that, since decisions regarding entertainment and product quality variations are made by business firms rather than by consumers in the market places of the economy, expenditures on resources so used will be too large and will be misdirected; and the value of consumer satisfaction obtained will consequently be less than the resource costs of providing it. To the extent that this phenomenon occurs, economic waste will be the result—welfare will be less than optimum.

Range of Products

Differentiated oligopoly provides consumers with a broader range of products among which to choose than does either pure competition or pure monopoly. Rather than being limited to a single kind and quality of automobile, each consumer can choose the kind and quality which best suits his needs and income. The same observations apply to television receivers, washing machines, refrigerators, or even entertainment. Gradations in product qualities, with each lower quality selling at a correspondingly lower price, increase the divisibility of the consumer's purchases of particular items. Consequently, his opportunities for allocating his income among different products may be so enhanced that he can achieve a higher level of want satisfaction than would otherwise be possible. Additionally, product differentiation enables consumers to give vent to their own individual tastes and preferences with regard to alternative designs for a particular product. The range of products available under differentiated oligopoly appears to work in the consumer's favor or to increase his welfare over what it would otherwise be.

Summary

In oligopolistic market structures there are few enough firms in the industry for the activities of a single firm to influence and evoke reactions from others. The demand curve faced by a single firm will be determinate when the firm can predict with accuracy what the reactions of rivals will be to market activities on his part. Otherwise it will be indeterminate.

We classified oligopolistic industries according to the degree of collusion that exists among firms of each of the industries. Under perfect collusion we included groups of firms such as cartels. Under imperfect collusion we included situations typified by price leadership and gentlemen's agreements. Under independent action we included noncollusive cases.

In the short run, perfectly collusive oligopolistic cases approximate the establishment of monopoly price and monopoly output for the industry as a whole. The less the degree of collusion, usually, the lower the price and the greater the output. In industries characterized by independent action on the part of individual firms, price wars are likely to be common occurrences. As the industry matures, the situation may become collusive, or it may develop into a "live and let live" attitude on the part of the firms in the industry. In the latter case price rigidity may occur. Firms may be afraid to change price for fear of touching off a price war.

In the long run the firm can adjust its plant size as desired and new firms can enter the industry, unless entry is blocked. The size of plant chosen by the firm will be the one that will produce its anticipated output at the least possible average cost for that output. Easy entry into the industry is largely incompatible with a high degree of collusion. Collusion exists partly to block entry. Barriers to entry may be classified as "natural" and "artificial." Restricted entry may enable firms in the industry to make long-run pure profits.

The firms of particular oligopolistic industries frequently engage in nonprice competition through product differentiation to avoid touching off price wars. Nonprice competition takes two major forms: advertising and quality and design variation. To the extent that firms using them succeed only in holding their respective market shares, costs of production and product prices will tend to be higher than they would otherwise be. The firm desiring to maximize profits will use each to the point at which the marginal revenue from it equals the marginal cost of extending its use.

Some of the welfare effects of oligopolistic markets on the economy are these:

(1) Outputs are restricted below and prices are increased above the levels that will yield Pareto optimality, since product price tends to be higher than marginal cost. With entry partially or completely blocked, pure profits and additional output restrictions occur.
(2) Individual firms are not induced to produce at their maximum efficiency plant sizes, although in many cases they produce more efficiently than they would if the industry were atomized.
(3) Some sales promotion wastes occur.
(4) The range of products available to consumers is broader under differentiated oligopoly than it would be under pure competition or pure monopoly.

Suggested Readings

Bain, Joe S., *Industrial Organization*, 2d ed. (New York: John Wiley & Sons, Inc., 1968).

Machlup, Fritz, *The Economics of Sellers' Competition* (Baltimore: The Johns Hopkins Press, 1952), Chaps. 4, 11–16.

Modigliani, Franco, "New Developments on the Oligopoly Front," *Journal of Political Economy*, vol. LXVI (June 1958), pp. 215–232.

Patinkin, Don, "Multiple-Plant Firms, Cartels, and Imperfect Competition," *Quarterly Journal of Economics*, vol LXI (February 1945), pp. 173–205.

Wilcox, Clair, *Competition and Monopoly in American Industry*, Temporary National Economic Committee Monograph No. 21 (Washington, D.C.: U.S. Government Printing Office, 1940).

Chapter 13:

Pricing and Output under Monopolistic Competition

There are many sellers of the product in an industry characterized by monopolistic competition; and the product of each seller is in some way differentiated from the product of every other seller. Questions may arise with regard to what "many sellers" means. How can we distinguish between differentiated oligopoly and monopolistic competition? How many sellers must there be in an industry to warrant calling the case one of monopolistic competition? These questions cannot be answered objectively in terms of numbers alone. When the number of sellers is large enough so that the actions of any one have no perceptible effect upon other sellers, and their actions have no perceptible effect upon him, the industry becomes one of monopolistic competition.

The theory of monopolistic competition provides few new analytical tools; it is very similar to that of pure competition. It furnishes a better description of those competitive industries in which product differentiation occurs—food processing, men's clothing, cotton textiles, the service trades in large cities, for instance—in that it recognizes small monopoly elements and the consequent different prices charged by different sellers of a particular type of product.

Some Special Characteristics

The conditions of demand faced by the firm set monopolistic competition apart from the three market situations discussed previously. Product differentiation leads some consumers to prefer the products of particular sellers over those of others. Consequently, the demand curve faced by an individual seller has some downward slope to it and enables the seller to exercise a small degree of control over his product price. Ordinarily the demand curve faced by the firm will be very elastic within its relevant range of prices because of the numerous good substitutes available for the product.

Product differentiation by the sellers in an industry increases the complexity of presenting the analysis in graphic terms. For example, in the analysis of pure competition, market demand and supply curves create no graphic problems. Under monopolistic competition the construction of market curves is rather unsatisfactory. Product differentiation makes the product units sold by one seller somewhat different from the product units sold by another. Tubes of toothpaste differ from cans of tooth powder. Bottles of liquid dentifrice are still different. Unless all of these can be converted into terms of a common denominator, difficulty in constructing the quantity axis for the industry curves will be encountered.

An additional difficulty arises. No single price prevails for the differentiated products of the industry. Different sellers will receive somewhat different prices, depending on consumers' judgments with regard to the comparative qualities of the differentiated products. These problems make it appear preferable to confine diagrammatic analysis to the individual firm. The market as a whole is there, but we shall discuss it in linguistic rather than in graphic terms.

The Short Run

Short-run output and pricing in an industry of monopolistic competition is very similar to that in other market situations. It is primarily an analysis of individual firm adjustment to the conditions each faces. The firm does not have time to change its plant size; therefore, there is insufficient time for new firms to enter the industry. Individual firms can make price and output adjustments. Additionally, they may be able to bring about small changes in demand for their individual outputs through advertising and slight variations of product quality and design.

Profit maximization with respect to output and price by the individual firm is governed by the principles set out in earlier chapters and is shown graphically in Figure 13-1. The firm's short-run average cost curve and short-run marginal cost curve are SAC and SMC respectively. The demand curve faced by the firm is dd. Since dd is less than perfectly elastic, marginal revenue for each possible level of sales is less than the product price, and the marginal revenue curve lies below the demand curve. The firm maximizes profits (or minimizes losses if the SAC curve

Figure 13–1   Short-run Profit Maximization

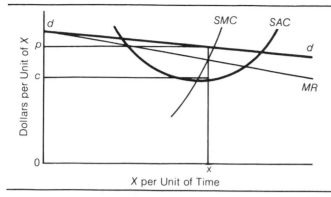

lies above *dd* for all possible outputs) by producing output *x* at which marginal cost equals marginal revenue. Profits per unit are *cp*. Total profits are *cp* × *x*.

The firm may also attempt to maximize profits with respect to advertising outlays and outlays on product variation; however, since there are many good substitutes for the product of the individual firm, neither strategy will be carried very far. To the extent that the firm does make advertising and product variation outlays, the principles involved are the familiar ones. Each should be carried to the point at which its marginal revenue is equated to its marginal cost, if profit maximization is the firm's objective.

Short-run equilibrium does not imply that all firms charge identical prices. Identity of prices would not be expected, since the firms of the industry do not produce homogeneous outputs. Each firm seeks its own profit-maximizing position. Each equates its own marginal cost to its own marginal revenue. Yet the prices charged by different producers will not be far apart. In short-run equilibrium we would expect prices to be clustered but not necessarily equal. Although each producer has some discretion in setting his own price, he is subjected to the restrictive effects of the many close substitutes for the product he produces.

The Long Run

All resources used by the firm are variable in the long run; consequently, two types of adjustment are possible: (1) the firm can build any desired size of plant; (2) unless entry into the industry is blocked, it will be possible for new firms to enter when profits are being made by existing firms. In the event losses are being incurred, existing firms can exit from the industry.

Adjustments with Entry Blocked

Blocked entry into an industry characterized by monopolistic competition clearly will not be the usual case; still it may, and sometimes does, occur. Where it occurs, it is usually the result of legislative activity of one kind or another. Owners or operators of the firms in a particular industry may belong to a trade association that has some political influence on a local, statewide, or perhaps even a nationwide basis. The industry may be fairly profitable; and the trade association may foresee the possibility of wholesale entry into the industry. Therefore, it may use its influence to secure the enactment of legislation that is rationalized as insuring an adequate supply of the commodity at prices allowing those in the trade to make fair and reasonable profits. Among the service trades in a particular city or state one can easily find licensing laws that tend to block entry.[1]

In such situations individual firms seek to adjust their respective plant sizes to those required for long-run profit maximization. The long-run average cost curve and the long-run marginal cost curve are the relevant ones for the firm. These are shown as LAC and LMC in Figure 13-2. The demand curve faced by the firm is dd, and the marginal revenue curve is MR. Profits will be maximum at output x, at which long-run marginal cost equals marginal revenue. Output x can be sold for price p per unit. To produce output x at the least possible cost per unit, the firm should build the plant size that has its short-run average cost curve tangent to the long-run average cost curve at that output. Since SAC is tangent to LAC at output x, short-run marginal cost is equal to long-run marginal cost and to marginal revenue at that output. Profits are equal to $cp \times x$.

If the firm should deviate from output x by increasing or decreasing its rate of output with the given size of plant, SMC would be greater than or less than MR, and profits would decline. If it should increase or decrease its rate of output by increasing or decreasing the size of plant, LMC would be greater than or less than MR, and profits would decline. Long-run equilibrium for the firm when entry into the industry is blocked means that the firm produces the output at which SMC equals LMC equals MR, and at which SAC equals LAC.

Adjustments with Entry Open

Ordinarily we would expect entry into or exit from a monopolistically competitive industry to be easy. Existing firms without the benefit of a trade association are likely to feel unconcerned about a few firms more or less in the industry; or, in the event they are concerned about the entry of new

---

[1]See Milton Friedman, *Capitalism and Freedom* (Chicago: The University of Chicago Press, 1962), Chap. IX.

Figure 13–2   Long-run Profit Maximization: Entry Blocked

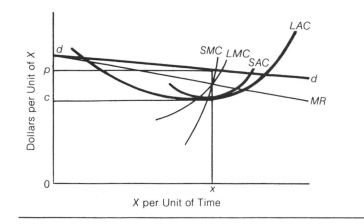

firms, they feel powerless to do anything about it. The mere fact that a large number of firms exists in the industry suggests that the size of each firm is something less than gigantic and that effective collusion without government support would be extremely difficult. Thus, most of the bars to entry that exist in oligopolistic markets are not effective in markets of monopolistic competition.

When pure profits exist for firms in the industry and potential entrants believe that they, too, can make pure profits, entry will be attempted. As new firms enter, they encroach on the markets of existing firms, causing the demand curve and the marginal revenue curve faced by each to shift downward. The downward shift of each firm's demand curve results from the increase in industry supply of the product as new firms enter. The increase in supply (and in the number of suppliers) pushes the whole cluster of price ranges for individual firms downward.[2]

The entry of new firms into the industry will affect costs of production for existing firms. As in pure competition (and in oligopoly to the extent that entry is possible), an increasing-cost, constant-cost, and decreasing-cost industry classification can be used. If the industry were one of increasing costs, the entry of new firms would cause resource prices to rise, which would shift the cost curves of existing firms upward and would raise the level of costs of entering firms. Under constant costs, the entry of new firms would have no effects on resource prices or on the cost curves of individual firms. In the unlikely case of decreasing costs the entry of new

---

[2]This analysis parallels that of pure competition. Larger market supply under pure competition shifts demand curves faced by individual firms downward.

firms would cause resource prices to decrease and the cost curves to shift downward. We shall examine only the case of increasing costs.

The entry of new firms will shift the demand curves faced by individual firms downward and cost curves of the firms upward. These shifts will cause profits to decrease, but new firms will continue to enter as long as profit possibilities remain. Eventually, enough firms will have entered to squeeze out pure profits.

This situation for the individual firm is pictured graphically in Figure 13-3. Compared with Figure 13-2 the demand curve faced by the firm has shifted downward as new firms enter, from dd in Figure 13-2 to d_1d_1 in Figure 13-3. The long-run cost curves have shifted upward to LAC_1 and LMC_1. The short-run cost curves have also shifted upward, and adjustments in the size of plant have occurred. When enough firms have entered to cause the demand curve faced by each firm to be just tangent to its long-run average cost curve, firms of the industry will no longer be making profits, and entry will stop.

Long-run equilibrium will be achieved by individual firms and by the industry as a whole when each firm in the industry is in the position shown in Figure 13-3. For each individual firm, long-run marginal cost and short-run marginal cost equals marginal revenue at some output such as x_1. Any deviation from that output with size of plant SAC_1 will cause losses to be incurred. Any change in the size of plant will cause losses to be incurred. Short-run average cost equals long-run average cost at that output, and both are equal to the price per unit received by the firm for its product. The industry as a whole will be in equilibrium, since no profits or losses occur to provide the incentive for entry into or exit from the industry.

Welfare Effects of Monopolistic Competition

Output Restriction

If one of the industries of a purely competitive economy in long-run equilibrium were to become monopolistically competitive, welfare would tend to be reduced by a slight restriction of output and a slight increase in the prices charged for the product. The demand curve faced by the monopolistic competitor, though very elastic, is less than perfectly elastic. Marginal revenue for the individual firm is less than price; and the rate of output is stopped short of that at which marginal cost equals the product price. The more elastic the demand curve faced by the firm, the less will be the deviation from purely competitive price and output.

In the long run price will equal average costs of production, unless entry into the industry is blocked. When entry is free and easy—as appears to be the usual case—new firms enter the profit-making industries and

Figure 13-3 *Long-run Profit Maximization: Entry Open*

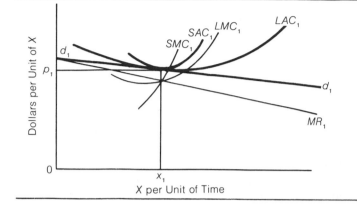

reduce profits to zero. Consumers pay just enough to enable firms to hold the desired quantities of resources in the production of the product. Organization of the economy's productive capacity can follow consumer tastes and preferences with a high degree of accuracy.

When entry into profit-making industries is blocked, the consequences with respect to prices and average costs are much the same as they are under pure monopoly and oligopoly. Productive capacity of the economy cannot be organized to conform accurately to consumer tastes and preferences. Additional quantities of resources are prohibited from moving into the profit-making industries where they would be more productive than they are in alternative employments.

Efficiency of Individual Firms

There will be some inefficiency of individual firms in the long run when entry into the industry is easy; that is, the firm will not be induced to build the optimum size of plant or to operate the one it does build at the optimum rate of output. This point can be seen best by reference to Figure 13-3. An optimum size of plant would involve the firm in losses, since average cost at such an output would be greater than price. If the long-run average cost curve lies below the demand curve for any range of outputs, pure profits can be made by any firm that builds the correct size of plant for any one of those outputs. New firms will enter until profits are eliminated. Profit possibilities are eliminated when individual firm long-run average cost curves are tangent to the demand curves faced by them. Losses are incurred when the long-run average cost curve lies above the demand curve for all outputs. Exit of firms from the industry will continue until the long-run average cost curve for each firm is again tangent to the demand curve faced by it.

In long-run equilibrium the output at which losses are avoided by the firm ($SMC = LMC = MR$) is the output at which the average cost curves are tangent to the demand curve. Since the demand curve faced by the firm is downward-sloping, the average cost curves must be downward-sloping also at their point of tangency with the demand curve. Thus, with easy entry into the industry, individual firms will build a less than optimum size of plant, such as SAC_1 in Figure 13-3, and they will operate at less than the optimum rate of output.

Some overcrowding with regard to the number of firms in the industry and some excess plant capacity may occur when entry is easy. Since each firm builds a less than optimum size of plant, there is room for more firms to exist than there would be if all were building plants of optimum size. Also, since each firm tends to operate the plant it does build at less than the optimum rate of output, it follows that excess plant capacity may exist. Empirical examples of both situations are not hard to find. The various textile industries illustrate both an excess of firms in an industry and excess capacity for individual firms.

The inefficiencies of the firm pointed out above should not be overemphasized, nor is the foregoing paragraph an argument for restriction of entry into monopolistically competitive industries. The demand curve faced by the firm is highly elastic; and the more elastic it is, the nearer the firm will come to building an optimum size of plant to operate near the optimum rate of output. Free entry into the industry will cause the total industry output to be greater than it would be if entry were restricted, and it will cause prices to be correspondingly lower.

When entry is restricted, the firm will build the appropriate size of plant to produce the output at which long-run marginal cost equals marginal revenue. There is no inducement for the firm to build an optimum size of plant. The plant built will be optimum only in the event that the firm's marginal revenue curve passes through the minimum point on its long-run average cost curve. Such an occurrence would be purely accidental.

Sales Promotion Wastes

Some waste advertising or design changes may occur under monopolistic competition. Efforts on the part of individual firms to expand their markets in this way may be counteracted by similar efforts on the part of the others, and the resources so used merely add to costs of production. Any such waste of resources will be much smaller under monopolistic competition than under oligopoly, where efforts on the part of one to expand his share of the market induces others to put forth similar efforts to prevent such expansion. Such rivalries do not exist under monopolistic competition. Advertising done by one firm induces no retaliatory action by others.

When the advertising done by one is counteracted by that of others, this is simply the result of all firms trying to do the same thing—expand their own markets. None are reacting to encroachments of other firms on their particular markets.

Range of Products Available

Consumers will have a broad range of types, styles, and brands of particular products from which to choose in market situations of monopolistic competition. The consumer can choose the type, style, or color of package that most nearly suits his fancy and pocketbook.

The different kinds of a specific product may be so numerous that they prove confusing to the consumer, and problems of choice may become very complicated. Ignorance with regard to actual differences of quality results in a willingness by the consumer to pay higher prices for particular brands, which in reality are not superior to lower-priced brands of the same product. What housewife can possibly be familiar with the comparative qualities of all the many different brands of soaps and detergents, floor waxes, electric irons, and so on?[3]

Summary

In a market situation of monopolistic competition there are enough sellers of differentiated products so that the activities of each have no effect on others and their activities in turn have no effect on him. The demand curve faced by the firm has some downward slope because of product differentiation and the attachment of consumers to particular brand names. However, it is highly elastic within the relevant price-output range.

Short-run profit maximization by the firms in the industry will occur at the prices and outputs at which each is equating his marginal cost to his marginal revenue. There is no single industry price. There will be a cluster of market prices reflecting consumer opinions of comparative qualities of the product.

In the long run the nature of the adjustment of firms and the industry to a position of equilibrium will depend on whether entry into the industry is blocked or easy. With entry blocked, individual firms will produce the output and sell at the price at which long-run marginal cost equals marginal revenue. The firm will build the appropriate size of plant for that output,

---

[3]For a partial solution to the problem *see* Eugene R. Beem and John S. Ewing, "Business Appraises Consumer Testing Agencies," *Harvard Business Review*, vol. XXXII (March-April 1954), pp. 113–126.

and with the appropriate size of plant short-run marginal cost will also equal marginal revenue.

With entry easy the existence of profits will induce new firms to enter, decreasing the demand curve faced by the firm and shifting the cost curves upward, if the industry is one of increasing costs. Entry will continue until profits are squeezed out. The long-run average cost curve and the short-run average cost curve for each firm will be tangent to the demand curve faced by it at the appropriate output. Long-run marginal costs and short-run marginal costs will equal marginal revenue.

Monopolistic competition existing along with pure competition tends to reduce welfare through: (1) output restriction and price increases, (2) inefficient plant size, and (3) some advertising wastes. There will also be a broader range of products among which consumers may choose than will occur in the other three market situations, a condition that may or may not affect welfare.

Suggested Readings

Chamberlin, Edward H., *The Theory of Monopolistic Competition*, 8th ed. (Cambridge, Mass.: Harvard University Press, 1962), Chaps. IV and V.
Machlup, Fritz, *The Economics of Sellers' Competition* (Baltimore: The Johns Hopkins Press, 1952), Chaps. 5–7, 10.
Stigler, George J., "Monopolistic Competition in Retrospect," *Five Lectures on Economic Problems* (New York: The Macmillan Company, 1949), pp. 12–24; reprinted in Stigler, George J., *The Organization of Industry* (Homewood, Ill.: Richard D. Irwin, Inc., 1968).

Chapter 14:

Pricing and Employment of Resources: Pure Competition[1]

In this chapter we turn from the markets for consumer goods to the markets for the resources used in producing them. Resource prices play a key role in guiding and directing a private enterprise economy. They are important in determining the employment levels of resources; and, as we shall see in Chapter 16, they allocate resources among different uses, drawing them away from less important uses toward more important ones. They induce individual firms to move toward more efficient resource combinations. Also, since all of us are resource owners, resource prices and employment levels affect us personally. They determine our incomes and the share of the economy's output that each of us receives. We shall con- sider distribution of the economy's output in Chapter 17.

The principles of resource pricing and employment under conditions of pure competition in both product markets and resource markets are de- veloped here.[2] Pure competition in resource markets implies several things. No one firm takes enough of any given resource to be able to influ- ence its price. No one resource supplier can place enough of a given re- source on the market to be able to influence its price. Variable resources

---

[1]The material of this chapter is based on the principles of production already covered in Chapter 8. A re- reading of that chapter should prove worthwhile unless the reader is thoroughly familiar with this subject matter.

[2]A simple definition of the market for a resource will suffice for most purposes. The market for a resource is the area within which the resource is free to move (or is mobile) among alternative employments. The extent of the market for a given resource will vary, depending on the time span under consideration. The longer the period of time, the broader the market will be.

are mobile as among different employments, and their market prices are flexible. Using these assumptions, we shall analyze first the simultaneous employment of several variable resources by the firm; next we shall turn to the pricing and employment of any given variable resource.

Simultaneous Employment of Several Variable Resources

Up to this point profit maximization by the firm has been considered in terms of product outputs and sales, with little specific attention given to resource inputs. In this section profit maximization will be viewed in terms of resource inputs and least-cost resource combinations.

Profit Maximization and Least-cost Combinations

The least-cost combination of variable resources for a given output was discussed in Chapter 8.[3] Resources must be so combined that the marginal physical product per dollar's worth of one is equal to the marginal physical product per dollar's worth of each of the other resources used, if such a combination is to be achieved. The given output is not necessarily the profit-maximizing output of the firm. Suppose, in Figure 14-1, that the firm produces an output of x_0 and uses two variable resources, A and B. To produce output x_0, resources A and B must be combined so that MPP_a/p_a equals MPP_b/p_b, if average variable costs are to be kept down to v_0. If the product price is p_x, the firm's output is too small for profit maximization. Although A and B are used in proper proportions, not enough of either is being used.

To maximize profits the firm's output must be increased to x. Additional output can be obtained by using more of both resource A and resource B. To keep average variable costs as low as possible as output is increased, increases in the quantities of resources A and B must be in such relationship to each other that the marginal physical product per dollar's worth of A continues to equal the marginal physical product per dollar's worth of B. When output x is reached, the firm will be using the resources not only in the least-cost combination but also in correct absolute quantities.

Marginal Physical Products and Marginal Cost

The least-cost combination conditions for resources A and $B-MPP_a/p_a$ equals MPP_b/p_b—are the reciprocal of the marginal cost of product X. Consider resource A first. Any one unit of resource A contributes an amount to the firm's total costs equal to p_a. It adds an amount to the firm's

---

Figure 14–1   Least-cost Combinations and Profit Maximization

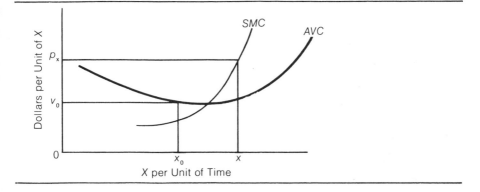

total product equal to MPP_a. Thus, the fraction p_a/MPP_a should be read as "the change in the firm's total costs per unit change in the product." This is the same thing as the marginal cost of product X; hence, we can state that MC_x equals p_a/MPP_a. Likewise, MC_x equals p_b/MPP_b. Since MPP_a/p_a equals MPP_b/p_b, when the firm is using a least-cost combination of A and B, we can state that:

$$\frac{MPP_a}{p_a} = \frac{MPP_b}{p_b} = \frac{1}{MC_x}.$$ [14.1]

Or we can consider the reciprocals of the foregoing terms and state that:

$$\frac{p_a}{MPP_a} = \frac{p_b}{MPP_b} = MC_x.$$ [14.2]

The last statement means that at whatever output the firm is producing, if it uses the least-cost combination of resources the amount of A or the amount of B or the combined amounts of both necessary to add a single unit to the firm's output brings about the same addition to the firm's total costs. Suppose the product is men's suits and the variable resources used are labor, machines, and materials. The last one-unit increment in quantity produced per unit of time should increase total costs of the firm by the same amount, regardless of whether the increment in product was obtained by increasing the ratio of labor to materials and machines, materials to labor and machines, or machines to labor and materials. Total costs should be increased by the same amount if the increment in product was obtained by simultaneous increases in the quantities of all three resources. When resources are used in the correct combination they are equally efficient at the margin. The last dollar outlay on one resource adds the same amount to total product as the last dollar outlay on any other resource. The increment in cost necessary to bring about the last unit increase in product output per unit of time is the marginal cost of the product.

Suppose we again consider profit maximization by the firm in terms of the quantities of resources that should be used. With reference to Figure 14-1 at output x_0, MC_x is less than p_x, or:

$$\frac{MPP_a}{p_a} = \frac{MPP_b}{p_b} = \frac{1}{MC_x} > \frac{1}{p_x}. \qquad [14.3]$$

Here the firm is using the resources in correct proportions to produce output x_0; however, output x_0 is too small for profit maximization, since MC_x is less than p_x. In the pursuit of maximum profits the firm will increase output by increasing the inputs of A and B. Additional quantities of A and B used with the constant quantities of fixed resources cause the marginal physical product of each to decrease. The prices of A and B remain constant since the firm purchases them under conditions of pure competition; consequently, MPP_a/p_a and MPP_b/p_b decrease as does $1/MC_x$.

Decreases in $1/MC_x$ mean increases in MC_x. Thus, decreases in the marginal physical products of A and B are the same as increases in the marginal cost of product X. Larger quantities of A and B will be employed to expand the firm's output up to the point at which:

$$\frac{MPP_a}{p_a} = \frac{MPP_b}{p_b} = \frac{1}{MC_x} = \frac{1}{p_x}, \qquad [14.4]$$

or up to the point at which the firm's marginal cost equals its marginal revenue or product price. At the profit-maximizing output the firm will be using its variable resources both in the correct combination and in the correct absolute amounts.

Pricing and Employment of a Given Variable Resource

Demand and supply analysis is used to show how the market price and employment level of a given resource are determined. First, the individual firm demand curve, the market demand curve, and the ·market supply curve for the resource must be constructed. Once we have accomplished these objectives, we can then determine the market price, the firm's employment level, and the market level of employment of the resource.

The Demand Curve of the Firm: One Resource Variable

The demand curve of a firm for a given variable resource should show the different quantities of it that the firm will take at various possible prices. But the factors influencing the quantities that a firm will take when confronted by various alternative prices of the resource differ when the given resource is the only variable resource used by the firm from the factors that prevail when the given resource is one of several variable resources used by the firm. Assume for the present that the given resource is the only variable one used by the firm; that is, the quantities of all other resources employed remain constant.[4] Assume also that the firm's objective is to maximize its profits.

The firm considers different quantities of the resource — suppose we call it resource A — with regard to their effects on its total receipts and total costs. If larger quantities of A per unit of time will add more to the firm's total receipts than to its total costs, those quantities will increase profits (or decrease losses). On the other hand, if larger quantities of A will add more to the firm's total costs than to its total receipts, they will cause profits to decrease (or losses to increase). The firm should employ that quantity of, the resource at which a one-unit increase in its employment level increases both total receipts and total costs by the same amount.[5]

Value of Marginal Product   The market value of the increment in product when a firm increases the employment level of resource A (or any other resource) by one unit per unit of time is called the *value of marginal product* of the resource, or VMP_a. In computing the value of marginal product of resource A, we note first that a one-unit increase in the employment level adds a certain amount (MPP_a) to the firm's total output. The output increment can be sold at its market price (p_x). Thus, the extra product produced multiplied by the price per unit at which it can be sold is the value of the marginal product of a unit of resource A; that is, VMP_a is the same as $MPP_a \times p_x$ when the quantity of resource A used is increased by one unit.

In Table 14-1, which represents Stage II for resource A, column (2) lists the marginal physical product of A when various quantities of it are used with constant quantities of other resources. The price per unit of the final product of the firm is shown in column (3). The value of marginal product of resource A is shown in column (4). For the purely competitive seller of

---

[4]The assumption is the same as that made in defining the law of diminishing returns.

[5]Consider the case of a major integrated oil company employing pipeline riders. Intelligent decisions regarding how many riders to employ will turn on the stated conditions. The company must estimate the value of the waste avoided against the additional expense incurred by hiring the rider. If the value of waste avoided exceeds the wages of the additional rider, it pays to hire him. Pipeline riders should be added up to the point at which the marginal contribution of any one rider to the firm's total receipts is just equal to the extra expense incurred in hiring him.

product one-unit increases in the level of employment of a resource will add amounts to the firm's total receipts equal to the value of marginal product of the resource.

Table 14-1   Value of Marginal Product, Resource Price, and Profit
            Maximization

(1)	(2)	(3)	(4)	(5)
	Marginal		Value of	
	Physical	Product	Marginal	Resource
Quantity	Product	Price	Product	Price
of A	(MPP_a)	(p_x)	(VMP_a)	(p_a)
4	7	$2	$14	$4
5	6	2	12	4
6	5	2	10	4
7	4	2	8	4
8	3	2	6	4
9	2	2	4	4
10	0	2	0	4

In Stage II for resource A the value of marginal product decreases as larger amounts of A per unit of time are employed. This decrease is caused by the operation of the law of diminishing returns — in Stage II for resource A the marginal physical product of A declines as larger quantities of it are employed. Thus, A's value of marginal product declines even though the price at which the final product is sold remains constant.

Level of Employment   A one-unit increase in the employment level of a resource adds an amount equal to its price to the firm's total costs when resources are purchased under conditions of pure competition. One firm takes such a small proportion of the total supply of the resource that by itself it cannot affect the resource price. If the price of the resource (p_a) is $4 per unit each one-unit increase in the amount of A employed adds $4 to the firm's total cost. These amounts are shown in column (5) of Table 14-1.

The profit-maximizing level of employment of A by the firm is that level at which the value of the marginal product of A is equal to the price per unit of the resource. Refer to Table 14-1. A fourth unit of A per unit of time adds $14 to the firm's total receipts but adds only $4 to the firm's total costs; therefore, it adds $10 to the firm's profits. A fifth, six, seventh, and eighth unit of A each add more to total receipts than to total costs and, consequently, make a net addition to profits. A ninth unit of A adds the same amount to both total receipts and total costs. A tenth unit of A, if employed, will decrease profits by $4. Hence, when p_a is $4, profits are maximized with respect to resource A at an employment level of 9 units.

Figure 14-2   A Value of Marginal Product Curve

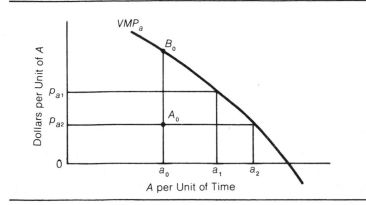

We can write the profit-maximizing condition in either of the following forms:

$$VMP_a = p_a$$

or   [14.5]

$$MPP_a \times p_x = p_a$$

The second form is simply an elaboration of the first.

The Demand Curve   The value of marginal product schedule for resource A, as listed in columns (1) and (4) of Table 14-1, is the firm's demand schedule for A if A is the only variable resource employed. It shows the different quantities that the firm will take at different possible prices. If p_a were \$10 per unit, 6 units would be employed. If p_a were \$14 per unit, 4 units would be employed.

The demand curve of the firm for the resource is the value of marginal product schedule plotted. Figure 14-2 shows such a curve. With reference to the quantity axis, it occupies Stage II for resource A. With reference to the dollars per unit axis, the value of marginal product at each quantity of A is found by multiplying the marginal physical product by the price per unit at which the final product is sold.

It may be instructive to consider profit maximization by the firm with respect to resource A again—this time in terms of the demand curve or the value of marginal product curve. If the price of A in Figure 14-2 were p_{a2}, the firm would maximize profits by using quantity a_2. If the firm were to use quantity a_0, the a_0 unit would add a_0A_0 to the firm's total costs but would add $a_0 B_0$ to the firm's total receipts. It would add $A_0 B_0$ to the firm's profits. Increasing the employment level of A up to a_2 adds more to total receipts than to total costs, and therefore increases profits. Beyond a_2 larger quantities add more to the firm's total costs than to its total receipts and cause profits to decrease. If the price of A were p_{a1}, the firm would maximize profits by using that quantity at which the value of marginal product of A equals its price per unit.

The Demand Curve of the Firm: Several Resources Variable

When a firm uses several variable resources its demand curve for any one of them is no longer the value of marginal product curve of the resource. When several variable resources are used by the firm a change in the price of one, assuming the prices of the others remain constant, will bring about changes in the quantities used of the other resources; and these changes will in turn affect the utilization of the one as the firm attempts to maximize profits and to re-establish a least-cost combination of resources. Suppose we call such changes the firm or *internal effects* of a change in the price of a resource.

To illustrate the internal effects, suppose that we want to derive the firm's demand curve for resource A, which is one of several variable resources. Suppose that initially the firm is producing the profit-maximizing output of product X and is using the appropriate least-cost combination of variable resources. As shown in Figure 14-3, the price of A is p_{a1} and the quantity employed is a_1. The VMP_{a1} curve shows the value of marginal product of A when the quantity of A, only, is varied.

Now suppose that for some reason the price of A falls to p_{a2}. Since $VMP_a > p_a$, the firm will tend to expand employment of A toward a_1'. This increased utilization of A will shift the marginal physical product and the value of marginal product curves of variable resources complementary to A to the right. The corresponding curves of substitute resources will be shifted to the left. Since the prices of other resources remain constant, the utilization of complementary resources will increase while that of substitute resources will decrease. Such changes in the utilization of other resources will shift the marginal physical product and the value of marginal product curves of A to the right. Each different level of utilization of each other variable resource will result in a different marginal physical product curve and value of marginal product curve for A.

When these and higher order complementary and substitute effects have worked themselves out, the firm will be on some such value of marginal product curve as VMP_{a2} and will be employing that quantity of A at

Figure 14–3   The Firm's Demand for One of Several Variable Resources

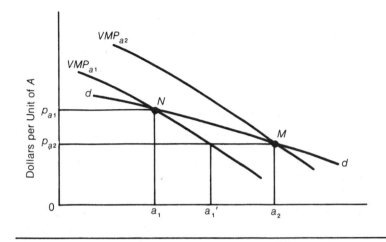

which its value of marginal product equals its price — that is, quantity a_2.[6] The employment levels of other variable resources will also be such that for each one its value of marginal product equals its price when the firm is again maximizing profits and using the appropriate least-cost combination.

Points N and M are on the firm's demand curve for resource A. They show the quantities of A that the firm would take at alternative prices of A when the prices of other resources are held constant and the quantities of all other resources are adjusted appropriately for each price of A. Other points on the firm's demand curve for A can be established in a similar fashion and would trace out a curve such as *dd*. Ordinarily the firm's demand curve for a resource will be more elastic than will any single value of product curve of the resource. The better the substitutes available for a resource, the more elastic its demand curve will be.

The Market Demand Curve

A first approximation to the market demand curve for a resource is the horizontal summation of individual firm demand curves for it. However, a straightforward horizontal summation leaves out what we shall call the *market* or *external effects* of changes in the price of a resource.

[6]The increasing ratios of resource A to fixed resources of the firm will insure that the marginal physical product and the value of marginal product of A decline, even though the changing utilization of other variable resources tends to shift the curves for A to the right.

In a purely competitive world an individual firm is small enough relative to the markets in which it operates to anticipate that its actions will have no effect on the price of anything it buys or sells. Consequently, the firm's demand curve for a resource should show the different quantities that the firm would take at various alternative resource prices when the firm anticipates that its actions will have no effect on the price of whatever product the firm sells. The firm only considers the firm or internal effects of resource price changes.

The market or external effects come about as a result of simultaneous expansion or contraction of industry outputs of products by all firms using a given resource as the price of the resource changes. If industry X is one of the industries using resource A, a decrease in the price of resource A will cause all firms using A to increase their employment of it. Although no one firm's increase in output is sufficient to cause a decrease in the price of X, the simultaneous increases in output of all firms may cause such a price decrease to come about. Each such decrease in the price of X will cause shifts to the left or decreases in the whole family of individual firm value of marginal product curves, and consequent shifts to the left or decreases in individual firm demand curves for resource A.

The external effects of changes in the price of a resource and the construction of the market demand curve for the resource are illustrated in Figure 14-4. Suppose that the firm of the diagram, and every other firm that uses resource A, is in equilibrium; and that the price of A is p_{a1}. The firm's demand curve for A is d_1d_1; the firm is employing a_1 of A. By summing the amounts that all firms employ at price p_{a1}, we determine the total amount taken off the market at that price, A_1. Thus, Q is a point on the market demand curve for A.

Now suppose the price of A falls to p_{a2}. Each firm will expand its employment of A, but as the firms in each industry that use A expand employment of it and, consequently, the industry outputs of product, market prices of products decrease. Individual firm demand curves for resource A shift to the left toward positions such as d_2d_2. Thus, the individual firm employment levels of A will increase toward such quantities as a_2 rather than toward a_1'.

Restricted expansion in the employment of A results from the market or external effect of the decrease in the resource price. When each individual firm has made the necessary adjustments to achieve a least-cost combination of resources and a profit-maximizing product output, and each firm's level of employment is some such level as a_2, the amounts that all firms together employ at price p_{a2} can be totaled to obtain quantity A_2; and R is a second point on the market demand curve for A. Other points on the market demand curve can be found in a similar way; they trace out the market demand curve D_aD_a.

Figure 14-4   The Market Demand Curve for a Resource

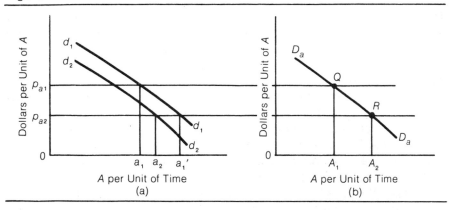

The Market Supply Curve

The market supply curve for resource *A*, or for any other resource, shows the different quantities per unit of time that its owners will place on the market at different possible prices. Generally it will be upward-sloping to the right, indicating that at higher prices more of it will be placed on the market than at lower prices. If resource *A* is a certain kind of labor, there are several forces that may cause the quantity supplied to be greater at higher than at lower wage rates. First, as we noted in Chapter 5, individual workers will be induced to provide more hours of work if substitution effects are not outweighed by income effects.[7] Second, higher wage rates tend to induce more workers to enter the occupation. Third, higher wage rates in a given occupation tend to induce workers qualified for that occupation who have been working in other jobs to re-enter it.

Nonhuman resources used in any one industry are in general the outputs of other industries. Their supply curves, then, will be the appropriate industry or market supply curves. Except in constant-cost and decreasing-cost cases they will slope upward to the right. In the petroleum industry, for example, increases in crude oil prices lead to a more rapid rate of recovery and vice-versa. The precise shapes of resource supply curves are not of paramount importance for our purposes, although for certain types of economic problems they will be. Here, they may be upward-sloping to the right, they may be absolutely vertical, or they may bend back on themselves at high prices. The basic analysis will be the same in each case.

---

[7]*See* pages 94-96.

Resource Pricing and the Level of Employment

The conditions of market demand and market supply, as summed up in the market demand curve and the market supply curve, determine the market price of the resource. Its equilibrium price will be that at which resource buyers are willing to take the same quantity per unit of time that sellers want to sell.

In Figure 14-5 the market demand curve and the market supply curve are D_aD_a and S_aS_a, respectively. Resource A will be priced at p_a. At a higher price sellers will want to sell more than buyers will want to employ at that price. Some unemployment will occur, and the owners of unemployed units will undercut each other to secure full employment of their particular supplies. Thus, the price will be driven down to the equilibrium level of p_a. At prices lower than p_a there will be a shortage of the resource. Resource buyers will bid against each other for the available supply, driving the price up to the equilibrium level.

In the economy with which we are working determination of the equilibrium market price for a given resource will tend to occur as we have described, but it may be good to reiterate the assumptions underlying that economy. We have assumed that the economy is a stable one—free of major fluctuations up and down—and that high levels of resource employment exist. To put the matter in a slightly different way, we assume that the fiscal-monetary policies of the federal government are such that national income is stabilized at high levels of resource employment.

In a private enterprise economy in which stability is not assured, the determination of resource prices and employment levels is more complex. Resource supplies and resource demands are not independent. In the Great Depression of the 1930s in the United States, for example, decreasing demand for products and resources created unemployment and lowered resource prices. But resource employment levels and prices determine individual incomes. Hence, individual incomes dropped, decreasing demand for products and for resources still more. Demand curves for resources in the unstable economy thus depend in some degree upon the levels of unemployment and prices of resources. Additionally, in a contracting economy a fear of unemployment and declining incomes may induce resource owners to offer larger quantities at given prices; that is, supply curves may shift to the right, augmenting the problem of unemployment. We need not pursue this line of reasoning, since it lies outside the scope of our analysis. It does, however, point up the intricate relationships between macroeconomics and microeconomics, as well as show that the theory of price developed in terms of a stable economy has certain limitations.

Returning to the stable economy, an individual firm, purchasing resource A competitively, can get as much as it wants at a price of p_a per

Figure 14-5   Determination of Market Price, Market Level of Employment, and Firm Level of Employment of a Resource

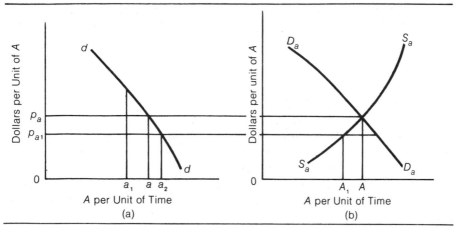

(a)　　　　　　　　　　　(b)

unit. A single construction firm in Chicago will not be able to influence the market price of steel. The supply curve of the resource from a single firm's point of view is shown in Figure 14-5 as a horizontal line at the equilibrium market price. The dollars per unit axes on the firm and market diagrams are identical. The scale of the quantity axis of the market diagram is greatly compressed, as compared with that of the single firm. The level of employment of the resource by the single firm is quantity a, assuming that dd is the demand curve of the firm associated with price p_a; and at that quantity value of marginal product is equal to its price per unit. The market level of employment of the resource is the summation of the quantities employed by the individual firms and is shown as quantity A in the market diagram.

The belief that resources are often paid lower than equilibrium prices is widespread enough to warrant consideration of such a situation in some detail. Suppose in Figure 14-5 that resource A is priced at p_{a1}. At that price individual firms want quantity a_2 in order to maximize their profits with respect to the resource. All firms cannot get as much as they desire, since the entire quantity placed on the market at that price is A_1. In fact, many or perhaps all firms will each get some quantity even less than a, say, a_1. For such firms the value of marginal product of A is greater than the resource price. These firms desire to expand employment of the resource in order to increase profits. Each firm believes that by offering a slightly higher price than p_{a1} it will be able to get as much of the resource as it desires. In the absence of collusion among the firms employing the resource—and in pure competition there is no collusion—each attempts the same strategy. No firm succeeds in getting as much as it wants until the price has been driven up to p_a. Under pure competition in resource buying, independent action on the part of each firm and the desire to maximize profits preclude the permanent location of price below the equilibrium level.

It is worth noting that under pure competition a particular resource receives a price per unit equal to the value of its marginal product. Thus, a unit of resource A is paid just what it contributes to the value of the economy's product. The market demand curve for A shows the value of marginal product for A in all its uses combined. The market demand curve and the market supply curve determine the price; hence, the resource price is equal to its value of marginal product in any one or in all of the firms that use the resource. Any one firm takes the market price as given and adjusts the quantity of the resource employed in such a way that the value of its marginal product in that firm is equal to the market price of the resource.[8]

The conditions set out in the first part of the chapter for employing the correct amounts and correct proportions of several resources simultaneously to maximize the firm's profits can also be established considering resources one by one. Suppose the firm uses two resources, A and B. To maximize profits with respect to A, it should employ A up to the point at which:

$$MPP_a \times p_x = p_a, \text{ or } \frac{MPP_a}{p_a} = \frac{1}{p_x}. \qquad [14.6]$$

Likewise, B should be employed up to the point at which:

$$MPP_b \times p_x = p_b, \text{ or } \frac{MPP_b}{p_b} = \frac{1}{p_x}. \qquad [14.7]$$

Equations [14.6] and [14.7] can then be combined as follows:

$$\frac{MPP_a}{p_a} = \frac{MPP_b}{p_b} = \frac{1}{p_x}. \qquad [14.8]$$

---

[8]This point is frequently misconstrued. A firm is said to pay a resource a price equal to the value of its marginal product—implying that the firm determines the value of the marginal product of the resource, then pays it accordingly. This implication misrepresents the nature of marginal productivity theory under pure competition. The firm has nothing to say about the price. It must pay the market price, but it adjusts the quantity taken to the point at which the value of marginal product equals that price.

Since MPP_a/p_a and MPP_b/p_b are the same as $1/MC_x$, then:

$$\frac{MPP_a}{p_a} = \frac{MPP_b}{p_b} = \frac{1}{MC_x} = \frac{1}{p_x}. \qquad [14.9]$$

When the firm employs each of its variable resources in the correct absolute amount for profit maximization, it necessarily will be using them in the correct combination.

Alternative Costs Reconsidered

The alternative cost doctrine, which we discussed in Chapter 9, can be restated in terms of the value of marginal product of any given resource. Under pure competition each firm using a given resource employs that quantity of it at which its value of marginal product equals its price. Any discrepancy in resource prices offered by different firms induces units of the resource to move from the lower-paying to the higher-paying uses until a single price prevails throughout the market. The resource price, or its cost to any firm, will be equal to the value of its marginal product in its alternative employments.

Economic Rent

Perfect mobility of all resources does not occur in the short run even under conditions of pure competition. Those resources constituting the firm's size of plant are not mobile—they are fixed in quantity for particular uses or users. The longer the time period under consideration, the fewer will be the fixed resources.

The returns received by fixed resources are not determined according to the principles set out above. Since those resources are not free to move into alternative employments, their short-run remuneration will be whatever is left over after the mobile resources have been paid whatever it takes to hold them to the particular firm. The mobile resources must be paid amounts equal to what they can earn in alternative employments; that is, amounts equal to the values of their marginal product in alternative employments. The residual left for the fixed resources is called economic rent.[9]

A short-run cost-price diagram for an individual firm should help make the concept of economic rent clear. The short-run average cost curve, average variable cost curve, and marginal cost curve are drawn in Figure

---

[9]These returns are sometimes called *quasi rents*. This term introduced by Alfred Marshall, is used so ambiguously in economic literature that we shall avoid it here altogether.

14-6. Suppose the market price of the product is p. The firm's output will be x. Total cost of the variable (mobile) resources is $0vAx$. This is the outlay necessary if the firm is to hold its variable resources.

Should the firm attempt to reduce the payments made to variable resources, some or all of them would move into alternative uses where their values of marginal product and remunerations are greater. Thus, the average variable cost curve shows the necessary outlays per unit of product output that the firm must make for variable resources. The fixed resources get whatever is left from the firm's total receipts; that is, they receive economic rent. Total rent for the fixed resources is $vpBA$. The lower the market price of the product, the less the rent will be. The higher the market price of the product, the higher the economic rent will be.

A problem now arises with regard to the nature of the SAC curve. What does it show? To get at the problem, suppose we lump the fixed resources together and call them investment in the firm. The rent represents the return on investment in the firm. Only that part of rent that represents a return on investment equal to what that amount of investment could earn elsewhere in the economy (or in alternative uses) constitutes fixed costs for the firm. Thus, the part of rent represented by $vcDA$ is fixed costs for the firm. The rest of the rent we have defined previously as pure profits. Average cost at any output is equal to average fixed cost plus average variable cost at that output.

Economic rent may be equal to, greater than, or less than enough to cover the firm's fixed costs. When investment in the firm yields a higher rate of return than investment on the average elsewhere in the economy, rents are greater than total fixed costs; and we say that the firm is making pure profits. The firm's profits are zero when rents equal total fixed cost; that is, when investment in the firm yields the same rate of return as investment elsewhere. When product price is not sufficient for rents to equal total fixed costs, or when investment elsewhere in the economy yields a higher rate of return than it does with the firm, we say that the firm is incurring losses.

Summary

This chapter applies the principles of production to the pricing and employment of resources under conditions of pure competition both in product selling and resource buying. First, the principles underlying the employment of several variable resources by a firm were established. Second, the principles underlying pricing and employment of any given variable resource were determined.

Figure 14-6   Economic Rent

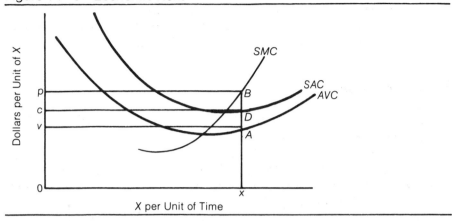

• When several variable resources are used by the firm, two problems are solved simultaneously by the firm in the process of maximizing its profits. It must use resources in the correct (least-cost) combination; and it must use the absolute amounts necessary to produce the quantity of the product that maximizes profits. Use of resources in the correct absolute amounts means that they are used in the correct combination also. The firm should employ those amounts of resources and produce that amount of product at which:

$$\frac{MPP_a}{p_a} = \frac{MPP_b}{p_b} = \cdots = \frac{MPP_n}{p_n} = \frac{1}{MC_x} = \frac{1}{p_x}.$$

The individual firm demand curve, the market demand curve, and the market supply curve for a resource are necessary for determining the market price, the individual firm level of employment, and the market level of employment of the resource. When the firm employs one variable resource only, the value of marginal product curve for the resource is the firm's demand curve for it. If the firm employs several variable resources, the firm's demand curve for a given resource shows the different quantities that the firm would take at various alternative prices when prices of other resources are held constant; and at each price of the given resource the firm makes all the adjustment necessary in the quantities of all resources used in order to maximize its profits. The market demand curve is obtained by summing the quantities that all firms in all industries using the resource will take at each possible resource price. The market supply curve shows the quantities of the resource that its owners will place on the market at various possible prices. Once the market price is established, the firm will employ a quantity of the resource at which its value of marginal product is equal to its market price. The market level of employment is the summation of individual firm levels of employment.

Suggested Readings

Hicks, John R., *Value and Capital*, 2nd ed. (Oxford, England: The Clarendon Press, 1946), Chaps. VI, VII, and VIII.

Robertson, Dennis H., "Wage Grumbles," *Economic Fragments* (London: R.S. King & Son, Ltd., 1931), pp. 42–57. Reprinted in *Readings in the Theory of Income Distribution* (Philadelphia: P. Blakiston's Sons & Company, 1946), pp. 221–236.

Scitovsky, Tibor, *Welfare and Competition,* Rev. ed. (Homewood, Ill.: Richard D. Irwin, Inc., 1971), Chap. 7.

Stigler, George J., *The Theory of Price*, 3rd ed. (New York: Crowell-Collier and Macmillan, Inc., 1966), Chap. 14, pp. 239–244.

Chapter 15:

Pricing and Employment of Resources: Monopoly and Monopsony

In markets other than pure competition the principles of resource pricing and employment operate in a modified fashion. We shall examine how they work where: (1) firms sell products as monopolists while buying resources under conditions of pure competition and (2) firms buy resources as monopsonists while selling products either as pure competitors or as monopolists. In order to take product monopoly into account the firm's demand curve for a resource must be redefined. The analysis as modified covers product markets of monopolistic competition and oligopoly, as well as those of pure monopoly. To take monopsony into account a modified view of the resource supply curve facing the firm is necessary. The modification also includes cases of oligopsony and monopsonistic competition. Monopoly and monopsony will be considered in turn.

Monopoly in the Selling of Products

Simultaneous Employment of Several Variable Resources

A monopolist who uses several variable resources must determine the combinations of resources necessary to produce alternative outputs at the least possible costs. If he purchases resources under purely competitive conditions, his least-cost conditions are the same as those faced by a pure competitor. The least-cost combination for a given output is that at which the marginal physical product per dollar's worth of one variable resource is equal to the marginal physical product per dollar's worth of every other variable resource used. If A and B are two such resources, they should be combined so that:

$$\frac{MPP_a}{P_a} = \frac{MPP_b}{P_b}. \qquad [15.1]$$

But to maximize profits the monopolist must do more than determine least-cost combinations of variable resources. He must use enough of each to produce the product output at which marginal revenue from his product sales and marginal cost of his product output are equal. With reference to Figure 15-1, suppose he uses the least cost combination for the production of x_0 units of product. The marginal cost of the product is less than the marginal revenue from it. The output of X and quantities used of resources A and B are all too small. These conditions can be summarized as follows:

$$\frac{MPP_a}{P_a} = \frac{MPP_b}{P_b} = \frac{1}{MC_x} > \frac{1}{MR_x}. \qquad [15.2]$$

The monopolist can increase output by increasing the quantities of A and B used in combination with his fixed resources. The marginal physical product of both A and B will decrease, causing the marginal cost of the product to rise. The larger output and sales of the monopolist cause marginal revenue from the product to fall. The quantities of A and B, together with the firm's output, will be increased until the marginal cost and the marginal revenue are equal. At output x and price p profits will be maximized. Variable resources will be used in the least-cost combination, as well as in the correct absolute quantities. The profit-maximizing conditions with respect to resource purchases, resource combinations, and product output can be summarized as follows:

$$\frac{MPP_a}{P_a} = \frac{MPP_b}{P_b} = \frac{1}{MC_x} = \frac{1}{MR_x}. \qquad [15.3]$$

These principles of profit maximization apply to all types of sellers' markets—pure competition, pure monopoly, oligopoly, and monopolistic competition—as long as pure competition prevails in the buying of resources.[1]

---

[1]The only difference between this and the similar purely competitive situation of the preceding chapter is that p_x in the competitive case is replaced by MR_x in the monopolistic case. Since p_x and MR_x are the same for the competitive firm, the conditions states here hold for a competitive firm as well as for the monopolistic firm.

Figure 15–1   Least-cost Combinations and Profit Maximization

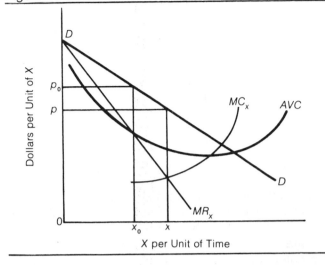

Pricing and Employment of a Given Variable Resource

The price and employment level of a given variable resource are determined in much the same way when resource purchasers are monopolistic sellers of product as when they are purely competitive product sellers. The monopolist's demand curve for a resource, while defined in the same way as that of the pure competitor, is computed in a slightly different manner. As in the purely competitive market, we differentiate between the case in which the given resource is the only variable one employed by the firm and the case in which it is one of several variable resources employed.

The Demand Curve of the Firm: One Resource Variable   To maximize profits with respect to a single variable resource the monopolist must employ that quantity at which a one-unit change in the quantity employed per unit of time changes total revenue and total cost in the same direction by the same amount. The effects on total receipts and on total costs of one-unit changes in the quantities employed are determined in the same way as they were for the pure competitor.

Changes in the firm's total receipts and the causes of those changes are shown in Table 15-1. Columns (1) and (2) show a portion of the marginal physical product schedule for resource A lying in Stage II for that resource. Resource A is the only variable resource used by the firm; the quantities of all other resources are fixed. Columns (3) and (4) show the portion of the product demand schedule of the monopolist corresponding to the quantities of A shown in column (1).

Table 15-1   The Computation of the Marginal Revenue Product of a
              Resource

(1)	(2) Marginal Physical Product (MPP_a)	(3) Total Product	(4) Product Price (p_x)	(5) Total Revenue	(6) Marginal Revenue Product (MRP_a)
Quantity of A					
4	8	28	$10.00	$280.00	—
5	7	35	9.80	343.00	$63.00
6	6	41	9.60	393.60	50.60
7	5	46	9.50	437.00	43.40
8	4	50	9.40	470.00	33.00

Column (6) is the important one for the present. It shows the additions to the firm's total receipts made by one-unit increments in the quantity of A employed per unit of time and is called the *marginal revenue product* of resource A. The marginal revenue product of a given quantity of A can be computed directly from column (5), but in a fundamental sense it is the marginal physical product of A at that quantity multiplied by the marginal revenue obtained from sale of the final product. Marginal revenue product of A or MRP_a when, say, 5 units are employed, equals marginal physical product of A at that point multiplied by the marginal revenue from each of the additional units of sales.[2]

Increases in the level of employment of A by the monopolist cause the marginal revenue product of A to decrease for two reasons. First, they cause the marginal physical product of A to decline, because of the operation of the law of diminishing returns. Second, marginal revenue for the monopolist ordinarily will decrease as he markets larger quantities of product.

The marginal revenue product curve is the monopolist's demand curve for A when he buys the resource competitively and when resource A is the only variable resource used by the firm. The monopolist will buy that quantity of A at which the additions made to total receipts by a one-unit increment are equal to the additions made to total cost by the increment. Since the resource is purchased competitively, the additions to total cost made by each additional unit of A purchased per unit of time are the same as the price per unit of A. Thus, in Figure 15-2, if MRP_a is the monopolist's marginal revenue product curve for A, and p_a is the price per unit of A, the monopolist will use quantity a. The profit-maximizing conditions can be

[2]A fifth unit of A per unit of time increases output and sales of X from 28 units to 35 units, and total receipts of the firm from $280 to $343. The increment in revenue per unit increment in sales, or MR_x, equals $63 ÷ 7 or $9 per unit for each of the 7 units. Marginal revenue product of A, then, when five units are employed, must equal $MPP_a \times MR_x$; that is, 7 × $9 = $63.

Figure 15–2   The Marginal Revenue Product Curve for a Resource

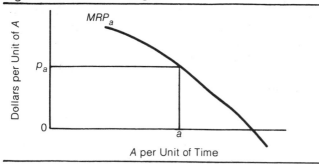

written as:

$$MRP_a = p_a$$

or: [15.4]

$$MPP_a \times MR_x = p_a.$$

At different possible prices of A the marginal revenue product curve shows the different quantities that the monopolist will purchase per unit of time.

The Demand Curve of the Firm: Several Resources Variable   The procedure for establishing the monopolist's demand curve for a given resource when several variable resources are employed is very little different from that used in the purely competitive case. Assuming that the prices of all other resources remain constant, changes in the price of the given resource will give rise to the same sort of firm or internal effects.

These effects are shown in Figure 15-3, in which A is the given variable resource. Suppose that the initial price of A is p_{a1}; the firm is using a least-cost combination of variable resources and is producing the profit-maximizing quantity of product X. The quantity of A employed is a_1. The curve MRP_{a1} is valid for changes in the quantity of A only.

A decrease in the price of A to p_{a2} will provide an incentive for the monopolist to increase employment of the resource toward $a_1{}'$. But, as the employment of A is expanded, the marginal physical product curves and marginal revenue product curves of complementary resources will be shifted to the right, causing larger quantities of these resources to be used at their given prices. The corresponding curves of substitute resources will be shifted to the left by the greater utilization of A, and smaller quantities of substitute resources will be employed at their given prices by the monopolist. Both effects will shift the marginal physical product curve and the marginal revenue product curve of resource A to the right. When the monopolist has again established a least-cost profit-maximizing combination of variable resources, the marginal revenue product curve for A will be in some position such as MRP_{a2}, and the quantity of A employed will be a_2. Thus, the firm's demand curve for resource A will consist of points tracing out a curve such as dd.

The Market Demand Curve and Resource Pricing   If all purchasers of resource A were purely monopolistic sellers of product, the market demand curve for A would be the horizontal summation of all individual firm demand curves for it. There would be no external or industry effects resulting from a decrease in the price of A, since each monopolist is the sole supplier of product for his industry. The effect of a decrease in the price of A on the quantity of product produced in any given industry and, consequently, on the price of that product has already been taken into account in the marginal revenue product curves and in that monopolist's demand curve for the resource.

If the purchasers of resource A are oligopolists or monopolistic competitors, the market demand curve for the resource is no longer the horizontal summation of individual firm demand curves for it. A change in the price of A changes not only the output that any single firm in a given industry will produce but the outputs of all the firms in the industry as well. These changes will occur in every such industry that uses the resource. As in the purely competitive case of the last chapter, changes in product outputs of other firms in the industry will shift the product demand curve facing any given firm and, consequently, the firm's demand curve for resource A. Thus, at any given price of A the quantities employed by all firms in all industries using A, when each firm is maximizing its profits, must be totaled to locate a point on the market demand curve for A. Other points on the market demand curve can be obtained in the same fashion.

The procedure just outlined is applicable for establishing the market demand curve for a resource regardless of the type of product market in which the firms using the resource sell. The usual case will be that some of the firms using resource A will sell in one type of product market and some will sell in other types. The only market structure requirement to be met is that all firms purchase the resource competitively.

With regard to market supply, resource pricing, and resource employment, monopoly in the product market adds nothing new to the analysis presented in the preceding chapter. The market supply curve for resource A again shows the different quantities of it which its owners will place on the market at various alternative prices. The market price of the resource moves toward the level at which firms are willing to employ the quantity per unit of time that its owners are willing to place on the market.

Figure 15–3   The Firm's Demand Curve for a Resource

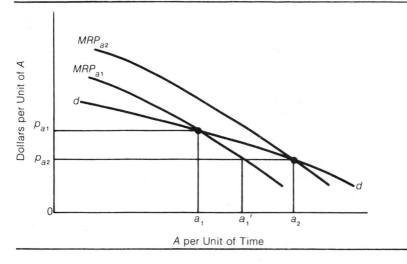

The market price of *A* determines its level of employment. The mono-polist, like a firm selling under conditions of pure competition, is faced with a horizontal supply curve for resource *A* at a level equal to its market price. The monopolist will employ the resource up to the point at which it is maximizing his profits with respect to it. At this point marginal revenue product of the resource is equal to its price. The market level of employ-ment of the resource is the summation of all individual firm employment levels, whether those firms be monopolists, pure competitors, oligopolists, or monopolistic competitors.

When the monopolist is maximizing profits with respect to each vari-able resource used, those resources will necessarily be used in a least-cost combination. Suppose that *A* and *B* are the only two variable re-sources used by a monopolist producing product *X*. When profits are max-imized with respect to *A*, then:

$$MPP_a \times MR_x = p_a. \tag{15.5}$$

Similarly, maximization of profits with respect to *B* means:

$$MPP_b \times MR_x = p_b. \tag{15.6}$$

Consequently:

$$\frac{MPP_a}{p_a} = \frac{MPP_b}{p_b} = \frac{1}{MC_x} = \frac{1}{MR_x}. \tag{15.7}$$

Monopolistic Exploitation of a Resource

Monopoly in a product market is said to result in exploitation of resources used by the monopolist. In this respect exploitation means that units of a resource are paid less than the value of the product that any one of them adds to the economy's output. A monopolist employs that quantity of a resource at which its price equals its marginal revenue product—marginal physical product multiplied by marginal revenue from the sale of the product. But the value of product added to the economy's output by a unit of the resource is its value of marginal product—marginal physical product multiplied by price per unit at which the product is sold. The marginal revenue product of the resource to a particular firm facing a downward-sloping product demand curve is less than the value of marginal product of the resource, since marginal revenue is less than product price in such cases. Hence, the prices paid resources used by monopolistic firms are less than the values of the products that they add to the economy's output.

Nevertheless, the price paid a resource must be equal to what it can earn in alternative employments. Exploitation does not mean that the monopolist pays units of the resource less than do competitive firms hiring units of the same resource. Exploitation under monopoly occurs because the monopolist, faced by the market price of the resource, stops short of the employment level at which value of marginal product of the resource equals resource price. Units of the resource contribute more to the value of the economy's output when employed by the monopolist than they do when employed by the purely competitive firm, but they are paid the same price in each market situation. Thus, market forces will not induce resources to move into their more valuable uses.

Monopsony in the Buying of Resources

A resource market situation in which there is a single buyer of a particular resource is called one of *monopsony*.[3] A monopsonistic situation is the polar extreme of the situation of pure competition among resource buyers—the situation that we have heretofore assumed exists. Two additional resource market situations can be distinguished. The first is oligopsony, in which there are a few buyers of a particular resource that may or may not be differentiated. One buyer takes a large enough proportion of the total supply of the resource to influence the market price of the resource. The other situation is one of monopsonistic competition. Here there are many buyers of a particular kind of resource, but there is differentiation within

---

[3]The term *monopsony* is applied also to cases in which there is a single buyer of a particular product; however, our discussion will be confined to monopsony in resource markets.

the resource category that causes specific buyers to prefer the resource of one seller to that of another. Our analysis will center around monopsony — one buyer of the resource — but it may also be applied to oligopsony and to monopsonistic competition.

Resource Supply Curves and Marginal Resource Costs

As the only buyer of a resource, the monopsonist faces the market supply curve for it. Ordinarily that supply curve is upward-sloping to the right. A producer who furnishes virtually the entire source of employment in an isolated area would be in this position, in the short run at least. Contrast the supply curve faced by a monopsonist with that faced by the firm that buys a resource under conditions of pure competition. Under pure competition the firm can get as many units of the resource per unit of time as it desires at the going market price; hence, it is faced with a horizontal or perfectly elastic resource supply curve even though the market supply curve may be upward-sloping to the right or less than perfectly elastic.

The upward slope of the resource supply curve faced by the monopsonist gives monopsony the characteristics that distinguish it from pure competition. To obtain larger quantities of the resource per unit of time the monopsonist must pay higher prices per unit. Columns (1) and (2) of Table 15-2 present a portion of a typical resource supply schedule illustrating this situation. Column (3) shows the total cost of resource A to the firm for different quantities purchased. Column (4) shows marginal resource cost of A to the firm.

Table 15-2   The Computation of Marginal Resource Cost

(1) Quantity of A	(2) Resource Price (P_a)	(3) Total Resource Cost (TC_a)	(4) Marginal Resource Cost (MRC_a)
10	$0.60	$6.00	—
11	0.65	7.15	$1.15
12	0.70	8.40	1.25
13	0.75	9.75	1.35

Marginal resource cost is defined as the change in the firm's total costs resulting from a one-unit change in the purchase of the resource per unit of time. When the resource supply curve faced by the firm is upward-sloping to the right, marginal resource cost will be greater than the resource price for any quantity purchased by the firm. This relationship can be explained with reference to Table 15-2.

Suppose the firm increases the quantity of A that it purchases from 10 units to 11 units. The eleventh unit costs the firm $0.65. However, in order to obtain 11 units per unit of time, the firm must pay $0.65 per unit for *all 11 units*. Therefore, the cost of obtaining the other 10 units has increased from $0.60 to $0.65 per unit. An additional cost of $0.50 is incurred on the 10. Add this to the $0.65 that the eleventh unit costs, and the increase in the firm's total cost is $1.15. The marginal resource cost of the twelfth and thirteenth units can be computed in a similar way.[4]

A graphic illustration of the resource supply curve and the marginal resource cost curve faced by a monopsonist is shown in Figure 15-4. The market supply curve for resource A is S_aS_a. The marginal resource cost curve is MRC_a and lies above the supply curve. The marginal resource cost curve bears the same relationship to the supply curve that a marginal cost curve bears to an average cost curve. In fact, the market supply curve of resource A is the average cost curve of resource A alone; and the marginal resource cost curve is the marginal cost curve of resource A alone. Obviously then, if the supply (average cost) curve of A is increasing, the marginal resource cost (marginal cost) curve must lie above it.[5]

Pricing and Employment of a Single Resource

Profit maximization with respect to resource A is governed by the same general principles for the monopsonist as for firms buying resources competitively. Larger quantities of A per unit of time will be purchased if they add more to the firm's total receipts than to its total costs. Additions to the monopsonist's total receipts as more A is employed are shown by the curve MRP_a in Figure 15-4. Additions to total costs are shown by the marginal resource cost curve. Profits are maximized when quantity a of the resource is employed. Larger quantities would add more to total costs than to total receipts and would cause profits to decline. We can state the profit-maximizing conditions in equation form. When the monopsonist's profits are maximized, he employs that quantity of A at which:

$$MRP_a = MRC_a$$

or: [15.8]

$$MPP_a \times MR_x = MRC_a.$$

---

[4]Marginal resource cost to the firm buying under conditions of pure competition is equal to the price of the resource. Since the firm can purchase as much as it desires at a constant price per unit, each additional unit adds an amount to the firm's total costs that is equal to the resource price.

[5]See pages 177–179.

Figure 15-4 Marginal Revenue Product, Marginal Resource Cost, and Profit Maximization for a Monopsonist

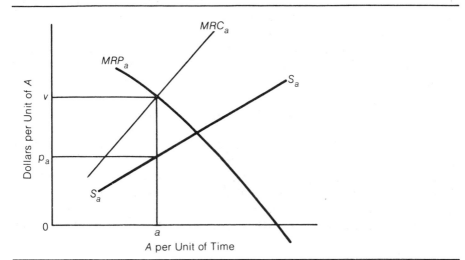

The monopsonist differs from the competitive buyer of resources with respect to the price paid for the resource at the profit-maximizing level of employment. For quantity *a* of the resource it is necessary for the monopsonist to pay a price of only p_a, although the marginal revenue product of the resource at that level of employment is *v*. Should the monopsonist employ that quantity of *A* at which its marginal revenue product is equal to its price—as does the competitive resource buyer—he would make less profit. To maximize his profits he restricts the quantity of the resource used and pays it a price per unit that is less than its marginal revenue product. The important consideration for profit maximization is the employment of that quantity at which the marginal resource cost equals the marginal revenue product—and for the monopsonist, the resource price is less than the marginal resource cost. Monopsony profits, resulting from the excess of the marginal revenue product of the resource over its price per unit, are equal to $p_a v \times a.$[6]

---

[6]In terms of the calculus the general solution to the problem of profit maximization by a firm with respect to one variable resource *A* runs as follows:

Let:

$x = f(a)$ = the firm's production function

$p_x = h(x)$ = the product demand curve facing the firm

$p_a = g(a)$ = the resource supply curve facing the firm.

On the revenue side:

$R = x \cdot p_x$ = total revenue of the firm

Simultaneous Employment of Several Variable Resources

The conditions that must be met by the monopsonist if he is to employ least-cost combinations of variable resources for given outputs differ slightly from those that apply to purely competitive resource buyers. As before, the least-cost combination for the monopsonist is that combination at which the marginal physical product per dollar's worth of one resource is equal to the marginal physical product per dollar's worth of every other resource. The difference between the monopsonistic and the competitive buyer rests on what constitutes the marginal physical product per dollar's worth of a resource.

An illustration will help make this difference clear. Suppose a coal-mining firm buys miners' labor monopsonistically. At the current level of employment a single miner's labor adds a ton of coal per day to the firm's output. This is the marginal physical product of the miner's labor. It adds $20 to the firm's total costs. This is the marginal resource cost of the miner's labor, and it exceeds the daily wage rate. The addition made to the

$$\frac{dR}{dx} = p_x - x \cdot h'(x) = \text{marginal revenue of the firm}$$

and:
$$\frac{dR}{da} = \left(\frac{dR}{dx}\right)\left(\frac{dx}{da}\right) = [p_x - x \cdot h'(x)]\, f'(a) = \text{marginal revenue product of } A \text{ to the firm.}$$

On the cost side:
$$C = k + a \cdot p_a = \text{total costs of the firm}$$

$$\frac{dC}{da} = p_a + a \cdot g'(a) = \text{marginal resource cost.}$$

To maximize profits:
$$\pi = R - C = x \cdot p_x - (k + a \cdot p_a)$$

$$\frac{d\pi}{da} = [p_x - x \cdot h'(x)]\, f'(a) - [p_a + a \cdot g'(a)] = 0$$

or:
$$[p_x - x \cdot h'(x)]\, f'(a) = p_a + a \cdot g'(a)$$

or:
$$MRP_a = MRC_a.$$

If the firm is a purely competitive seller of product then:
$$p_x = h(x) = k$$

and:
$$h'(x) = 0.$$
If it is a purely competitive purchaser of A then:
$$p_a = g(a) = k$$

and:
$$g'(a) = 0.$$
The profit-maximizing conditions thus become:
$$p_x \cdot f'(a) = p_a$$
or:
$$VMP_a = p_a$$

as well as: $MRP_a = MRC_a.$

firm's total product per additional dollar's expenditure on labor is 1/20 of a ton of coal, or is equal to MPP_ℓ/MRC_ℓ. The same calculation applies to any other resource purchased monopsonistically. The marginal physical product per dollar's worth of any resource is found by dividing its marginal physical product by its marginal resource cost.

If a firm purchases variable resources A and B monopsonistically, to achieve the least-cost combination for a given output it must use them in such proportions that:

$$\frac{MPP_a}{MRC_a} = \frac{MPP_b}{MRC_b}. \qquad [15.9]$$

The reciprocal of either or both of the fractions in the equation represents the marginal cost of the product at whatever output the firm is producing. A unit of A used adds an amount MRC_a to total costs and an amount MPP_a to total product. Therefore, the addition to total costs per unit increase in output is MRC_a/MPP_a. Similarly, the marginal cost of the product in terms of resource B is MRC_b/MPP_b.

Suppose that initially the monopsonist is using too little of A and B for profit maximization, but is using the least-cost combination for the product output he is producing. Marginal cost of the product is less than marginal revenue from its sale. These conditions can be summed up as follows:

$$\frac{MPP_a}{MRC_a} = \frac{MPP_b}{MRC_b} = \frac{1}{MC_x} > \frac{1}{MR_x}. \qquad [15.10]$$

Profit maximization requires the employment of greater quantities of the variable resources per unit of time. The additional resource units will increase the output and decrease the marginal revenue received from the product. Additional quantities of A and B cause the marginal physical products of both resources to decline. At the same time, the marginal resource costs of A and B increase. Thus, the marginal cost of the product to the firm rises as a result of two forces working simultaneously—declining marginal physical products and rising marginal resource costs. Additional quantities of A and B will be employed per unit of time until the marginal cost equals the marginal revenue. At this point the resources are used in the correct absolute quantities, as well as in the least-cost proportions. The conditions necessary for profit maximization can be stated as follows:

$$\frac{MPP_a}{MRC_a} = \frac{MPP_b}{MRC_b} = \frac{1}{MC_x} = \frac{1}{MR_x}. \qquad [15.11]$$

The conditions necessary for profit maximization by the monopsonist also can be established by considering resources A and B individually. Resource A should be used up to the point at which:

$$MPP_a \times MR_x = MRC_a, \text{ or } \frac{MPP_a}{MRC_a} = \frac{1}{MR_x}. \qquad [15.12]$$

Likewise, resource B should be used up to the point at which:

$$MPP_b \times MR_x = MRC_b, \text{ or } \frac{MPP_b}{MRC_b} = \frac{1}{MR_x}. \qquad [15.13]$$

From (15.12) and (15.13) we can write:

$$\frac{MPP_a}{MRC_a} = \frac{MPP_b}{MRC_b} = \frac{1}{MC_x} = \frac{1}{MR_x}. \qquad [15.14]$$

The profit-maximizing conditions set forth above for the monopsonist are general enough to apply to all classifications of both product sellers' markets and resource buyers' markets. Under conditions of pure competition in resource buying MRC_a and MRC_b become p_a and p_b, respectively. Under conditions of pure competition in product selling MR_x becomes p_x.

Conditions Giving Rise to Monopsony

Monopsony results from either or both of two basic conditions. First, monopsonistic purchases of a resource may occur when units of the resource are specialized to a particular user. This statement means that the marginal revenue product of the resource in the specialized use is enough higher than it is in any alternative employments in which it conceivably can be used to eliminate the alternative employments from the consideration of resource suppliers. Thus, the resource supply curve facing the monopsonist will be the market supply curve of the resource and usually will be upward-sloping to the right. The more he is willing to pay for the resource, the greater will be the quantity placed on the market.

A situation of the kind described may occur when a special type of skilled labor is developed to meet certain needs of a specific firm. The higher the wage rate offered for the special category of labor, the more individuals there will be who are willing to undergo the necessary training to develop it. No other firm utilizes labor with this or similar skills; consequently, once trained, the workers' only options are to work for this firm or to work elsewhere at jobs where their marginal revenue products and their wage rates are significantly lower.

Specialization of resources to a particular user is not confined to the labor field. A large aircraft or automobile manufacturer may depend on a number of suppliers to furnish certain parts used by no other manufacturer. In the tightest possible case such suppliers sell their entire outputs to the manufacturer, and complete monopsony by the manufacturer exists. Given time, the suppliers may be able to convert production facilities to supply other types of parts to other manufacturers, and the degree of monopsony enjoyed by the one may be decreased correspondingly.

Special monopsonistic cases occur in the field of entertainment. Performers are placed under contract by specific employers and are then no longer free to work for alternative employers. Major league baseball players fall in this category also. Under the well-known reserve clause, once he is signed to play for a given team, a player either accepts the best salary terms he can get from that employer or else is forbidden to play in the major leagues at all. He cannot transfer from one major league team to another of his own volition, although his contract can be sold to another team by his employer.

The second condition from which monopsony may stem is the immobility of certain resources. It is not necessary that resources in general be immobile. It is only necessary that mobility out of certain areas or away from certain firms be lacking, thus creating unique monopsonistic situations. Various forces may hold workers in a given community or to a given firm. Among these are emotional ties to the community together with a fear of the unknown. Ignorance regarding alternative employment opportunitites may exist. Funds may not be sufficient to permit job seeking in and movement to alternative job areas. Seniority and pension rights accumulated with a firm may make workers reluctant to leave. Specific cases of immobility among firms within a given geographic area may result from agreements among employers not to "pirate" each other's work forces.

Monopsonistic Exploitation of a Resource

Monopsony in the purchase of a resource also is said to result in exploitation of that resource. Monopsonistic exploitation can be understood best by comparing monopsony with pure competition in resource buying. In a purely competitive situation each firm will add to its profits by taking larger quantities of the resource up to the point at which the marginal revenue product of the resource is equal to the resource price. The resource receives a price per unit equal to what any one unit of it contributes to the firm's total receipts.[7]

---

[7]Monopolistic exploitation will occur if the resource-buying firms face downward-sloping product demand curves, but there is no monopsonistic exploitation.

In contrast, the monopsonist maximizes profits by stopping short of the resource employment level at which marginal revenue product of the resource is equal to its price per unit. This situation is shown in Figure 15-4. The profit-maximizing level of employment is that at which the marginal revenue product equals the marginal resource cost. Since the marginal resource cost exceeds the resource price, the marginal revenue product of the resource does also. Hence, units of the resource are paid less than what any one of them contributes to the total receipts of the firm. This situation is called monopsonistic exploitation of the resource. The monopsonist restricts the quantity of the resource used and holds down its price.

Measures to Counteract Monopsony

What can be done to counteract monopsonistic exploitation of resources? Two alternatives will be considered. First, administered or fixed minimum resource prices can be used. Second, measures successful in increasing resource mobility will reduce the monopsonistic power of particular resource users.

Minimum Resource Prices   Minimum resource prices can be established by the government or by organized groups of resource suppliers. The typical monopsonistic situation is pictured in Figure 15-5. The level of employment of resource A is quantity a. Its price per unit is p_a; however, marginal revenue product is v, and the resource is being exploited. Suppose a minimum price is set at p_{a1} and that the firm must pay a price of at least p_{a1} per unit for all units purchased. Should the firm want more than a_1 units, it faces the mn sector of the resource supply curve. The entire supply curve now faced by the firm will be $p_{a1}mn$.

The alteration in the resource supply curve facing the firm also alters the marginal resource cost curve. For quantities between zero and a_1, each additional unit of A employed per unit of time adds an amount equal to p_{a1} to the firm's total costs. The new marginal resource cost curve coincides with $p_{a1}m$, the new supply curve, out to quantity a_1. For quantities greater than a_1 the regular supply curve mn is the relevant one, and the corresponding sector of the marginal resource cost curve becomes ℓk. The altered marginal resource cost curve is $p_{a1}m\ell k$. At quantity a_1 it is discontinuous between m and ℓ.

The quantity of A that the firm should now use to maximize profits will differ from the quantity used before the minimum price was set. The firm should use quantity a_1, at which the new marginal resource cost is equal to the marginal revenue product of A. The minimum price not only eliminates monopsonistic exploitation of the resource; it increases the level of employment in the process.

Figure 15-5 *Control of Monopsony by Minimum Resource Prices*

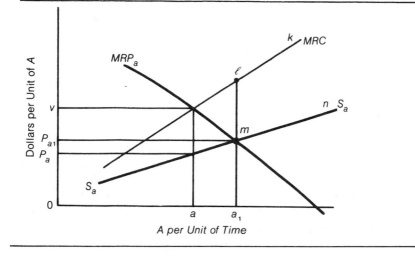

This analysis assumes that the minimum price of resource A is set at just the correct level to counteract monopsony completely. Such precision may or may not be achieved in fact. However, any minimum price between p_a and p_{a1} will counteract monopsony to some extent. The nearer to p_{a1} the price is set, the more nearly will exploitation be eliminated. Prices set between p_{a1} and v will counteract exploitation also, but at the expense of employment. Unemployment will occur, since at any price level about p_{a1}, resource sellers will want to put more on the market than buyers are willing to buy.

Countering of monopsony by price regulation is at best a difficult job. The precise price level at which monopsony is offset completely is hard to determine. In the labor field—where monopsony is most publicized—minimum-wage laws may be the counteracting device used. Different degrees of monopsony for different kinds of labor and for different situations make blanket price fixing of this type impractical as an overall monopsonistic offset. Collective bargaining on a firm-by-firm basis could more nearly meet and offset individual monopsonistic cases. Even here the problem of determining—leaving aside the difficulty of obtaining—the "correct" minimum price for the resource remains.

Measures to Increase Mobility   Measures to increase resource mobility among alternative employments get directly at the causes of monopsony. Immobility of resources is thought by many economists to be most serious in labor markets; hence, our discussion will be centered on the labor resource. We shall present a few general lines of approach rather than specific and detailed programs. With regard to the labor resource, mobility among geographic areas and firms, horizontal mobility among occupations at the same skill level, and vertical occupational mobility to higher skill classifications will be of value in counteracting monopsony.

An efficient system of federal employment exchanges should provide one avenue of attack on labor immobility. An important function of such a system is the collection and dissemination of information regarding alternative employment opportunities. It should make data available to the entire labor force — including those in now isolated communities — with regard to high-wage, scarce-labor-supply areas, and give descriptions of the requisite skills for obtaining employment in such areas. In addition, the system should perform the more common function of bringing together job opportunities and workers seeking alternative jobs.

The educational system offers a second avenue of attack. It can increase both the vertical and horizontal mobility of labor resources. With regard to vertical mobility, the availability and use of educational opportunitites can channel larger numbers of the younger generation toward higher-paying, higher-level occupations. By means of vocational and trade schools the educational system can provide older workers with training for upward movement through skill classifications. With regard to horizontal mobility, vocational guidance can assist in steering the potential labor force away from lower-paying occupations toward those providing higher remuneration. Additionally, adult education programs can furnish the retraining necessary to escape from particularly low-paying occupations.

Still a third line of attack is that of a limited amount of subsidization of worker migration out of areas characterized by monopsony, since one of the causes of immobility is lack of funds needed by workers to move into alternative employment areas. Subsidization of migration may occur in the form of government loans or outright grants of funds to assist in worker relocation.

The Concept of Mobility

A few observations regarding the meaning of mobility are in order, so that no wrong impression be given. To some people a mobile labor force may imply a drifting one with a high job turnover rate — an undesirable social situation. Mobility, as the term is used in economics, does not mean a complete lack of ties to particular communities and social institutions; nor does it mean that all workers must be ready to pack up and move at the slightest provocation. The amount of actual movement necessary to prevent monopsony from occurring usually will be quite small. The possibility or likelihood of migration is the important factor. Also, there is at all times considerable change and turnover of the labor force—workers changing jobs, new workers entering the labor force, and old workers retiring. This constant change constitutes mobility. The primary problem is that of directing the mobility that already exists into economically desirable channels.

Summary

The principles of resource pricing and employment in situations other than pure competition are a modification of the principles established in the preceding chapter. Monopoly in product markets alters the nature of individual firm demand curves for resources. Monopsony in the purchase of resources alters the nature of the resource supply curve faced by the firm.

The monopolistic firm employing several variable resources must determine the least-cost resource combinations for various possible outputs and also the profit-maximizing quantities of variable resources to use. The least-cost combination for a given product output is the one at which the marginal physical product per dollar's worth of one resource is equal to the marginal physical product per dollar's worth of every other resource used. To maximize profits the firm must use both a least-cost combination and the correct absolute amounts of each resource. Resources must be used so that:

$$\frac{MPP_a}{P_a} = \frac{MPP_b}{P_b} = \cdot \ \cdot \ \cdot = \frac{MPP_n}{P_n} = \frac{1}{MC_x} = \frac{1}{MR_x}$$

Monopoly in product markets is said to result in monopolistic exploitation of resources, since the resource price equals its marginal revenue product for the firm and is less than the value of its marginal product for the economy as a whole.

The market price and the employment level of a resource are determined simultaneously. Where monopoly occurs in product markets, marginal revenue product of each variable resource used must be equal to its price if profits are to be maximized. If the monopolist uses only one variable resource, the marginal revenue product curve of the resource is the firm's demand curve for it. If several variable resources are used, internal or firm effects of price changes in any given resource must be taken into account in determining the firm's demand curve for it.

The market demand curve for a resource is obtained by summing up the quantities of it that all firms will employ at each possible price, whether those firms operate as monopolists or as pure competitors in selling products. Resource price is determined by the conditions of market demand and market supply. As the market price is established, the firm adjusts its employment of the resource to the level at which the marginal revenue product equals the resource price. The market employment level is the summation of individual firm employment levels.

Monopsony means a single buyer of a particular resource; hence, the monopsonist faces a resource supply curve that slopes upward to the right. He also faces a marginal resource cost curve that lies above the supply curve. He maximizes profits by employing the quantity of the resource that equates its marginal revenue product to its marginal resource cost. The marginal resource cost and the marginal revenue product of the resource exceed the resource price at the profit-maximizing level of employment, thus resulting in monopsonistic exploitation of the resource.

Suggested Readings

Cartter, A. M., and F. R. Marshall, *Labor Economics* (Homewood: Richard D. Irwin, Inc., 1967), Chap. 10.

Fellner, William, *Modern Economic Analysis* (New York: McGraw-Hill, Inc., 1960), Chap. 19.

Nicholls, William H., *Imperfect Competition within Agricultural Industries* (Ames: The Iowa State College Press, 1941), Introduction and Chaps. 1–3.

Robinson, Joan, *The Economics of Imperfect Competition* (London: Macmillan & Co., Ltd., 1933), Chaps. 25 and 26.

Chapter 16:

Resource Allocation

One of the most important functions performed by resource prices in a private enterprise economy is that of allocating resources among different uses and different geographic areas. If a high level of efficiency is to be attained in the economy, constant reallocation of resources must occur in response to changes in human wants, in the kinds and quantities of resources available, and in available techniques of production. In developing the principles of resource allocation we shall first discuss the concept of resource markets; then consider the conditions of resource allocation leading to maximum efficiency in resource use; and finally examine certain factors that prevent resources from being correctly allocated.

The Conditions of Maximum Welfare

What are the allocation conditions that must be met if any given resource is to make its maximum contribution to welfare? In general terms the requirement is that the value of marginal product of the resource in any one of its uses must be the same as its value of marginal product in all of its other uses. Suppose some other allocation prevails—for example, that a tractor used on a farm contributes at the margin $2000 worth of farm products annually to the economy's output, and that an identical tractor used in construction can contribute $3000 worth of products annually to the economy's output. If a tractor were switched from farming to construction, there would be a net gain to consumers of $1000 worth of product. Obviously, some consumers can be made better off without making anyone worse off. Transfers of resources from lower value of marginal product uses to higher value of marginal product uses always yield a welfare increase; and maximum welfare results when these transfers have been carried to the point that for each resource its value of marginal product is the same in all its alternative uses.

Resource Markets

When the price system is used to allocate resources the concept of a resource market becomes important. The extent of a resource market depends on the nature of the resource under consideration and on the time span relevant to the problem at hand. Within a given time span some resources are more mobile than others, and, consequently, their markets tend to be larger. Mobility depends on a number of things—shipping costs, perishability, social forces, and the like—and resources differ with respect to these characteristics.

Ordinarily, the mobility of any given resource varies with the time span under consideration. Over a short period of time its mobility is more limited than it is over a longer period. Consider labor of a certain kind, say, machinists. Over a short time period of a few months, or perhaps a year, machinists in the United States will not move freely from one geographic area to another, although they may be fairly free to move from one employer to another within a single locality. The longer the period of time under consideration, the larger the geographic area within which they are free to move. Over a period of twenty-five years they will be fairly mobile over the entire economy.[1]

Over short periods of time all the machinists, or all the units of any other resource in the economy, do not necessarily operate in the same market. The economy can be divided into a number of submarkets, each submarket being the area within which units of a resource are mobile in the given time span. The longer the time span considered, the greater the interconnections among the submarkets. Over a sufficiently long period the submarkets tend to fuse into a single market.

The submarkets for a resource tend to be conceptual rather than real in the sense that boundaries between submarkets are blurred. Each submarket overlaps others. But if we think of them as being separate and apart

---

[1]Mobility does not require the physical transference of a machinist from one area to another or even from one employer to another. As old machinists retire from the work force and new machinists enter, mobility can exist; for in certain areas the retiring machinists may not be replaced, while in others the number of entries into the trade may exceed retirements.

from each other, we can make better progress with the analysis of re-source allocation. Also, in place of the whole continuum of time periods, only two need be considered: (1) a short period during which the submar-kets for a given resource are separate and (2) the long period in which resources have sufficient time to move freely among the submarkets and create a fusion of these into a single market.

Resource Allocation under Pure Competition

Will the price system allocate resources among their various uses so that optimal welfare tends to be approached? If pure competition exists in both product markets and resource markets, such an allocation will occur; therefore, the competitive model provides a convenient starting point for our analysis. First we shall discuss the short-period allocation of a re-source within a given submarket. Then this will be expanded to include long-period allocation among submarkets or over the entire economy.

Allocation within a Given Submarket

When units of a resource are so allocated that the value of marginal prod-uct in one use is greater than it is in other uses, the allocation is incorrect from the point of view of economic efficiency and welfare. The resource units would be more valuable to society in the higher value of marginal product use; and if they were transferred from the lower to the higher val-ue of marginal product uses, the total value of the economy's output would be increased.

Resource prices furnish the mechanism for reallocation when resources are incorrectly allocated under a purely competitive system. Suppose that units of a given resource are allocated between two industries in such quantitites that the value of marginal product of the resource is higher in one than in the other. Given this allocation, firms in the industry in which the value of marginal product is higher will also be willing to pay more per unit for the resource, since in each industry the resource will be paid an amount equal to its value of marginal product. Consequently, resource owners, seeking maximum income, transfer resource units from the lower-paying to the higher-paying uses.[2] As units of the resource are transferred, its value of marginal product decreases in the employments to which it is transferred, and increases in the employments from which it is transferred. The transfer continues until its value of marginal product is equalized in

---

[2]New resource units just entering the market, say, college graduates, may be attracted to the jobs offering higher pay. This attraction, together with the failure to replace resource units retired from the market in lower-paying employments, provides an important method of transfer.

all its uses, and all firms in the submarket are paying a price per unit equal to that value of marginal product. At this point the resource is correctly allocated and, within the submarket, is making its maximum contribution to net national product.

To illustrate the role of resource prices in allocating resources among different uses in more detail, suppose the firms of two different industries produce X and Y and operate in the same submarket for resource A. Suppose also that initially units of A are correctly allocated among the firms of the two industries. The value of marginal product of A in firms of the industry producing X (VMP_{ax}) is equal to the value of marginal product of A in firms of the industry producing Y (VMP_{ay}). Suppose further that there is neither a surplus nor a shortage of A on the market, so that:

or:
$$VMP_{ax} = VMP_{ay} = p_a$$

$$MPP_{ax} \times p_x = MPP_{ay} \times p_y = p_a,$$

where p_a is the price per unit of resource A and p_x and p_y are the respective prices of product X and product Y.

Suppose an increase occurs in the market demand for commodity X, while demand for commodity Y remains unchanged. The level of aggregate demand remains constant, and the increase in demand for X is offset by decreases in demand for commodities other than X and Y. The price of X rises, thereby increasing VMP_{ax}. Resource A has become more valuable to society in the production of X than it is in the production of Y. The original allocation of A no longer maximizes welfare; that is, this allocation is no longer the correct one. At price p_a for the resource employers in the industry producing X find that a shortage of A exists. Consequently, they will bid up the price of A enough to cause owners of A to transfer units of it from the industry producing Y to the industry producing X. As the quantity of A employed by firms in the industry producing X increases relative to the quantities of other resources used, MPP_{ax} declines. As the output of X increases, p_x declines. Thus, VMP_{ax} declines.

Changes within the industry producing Y will accompany changes in the industry producing X. As units of A are transferred from the production of Y to X, the proportions of A to other resources used by firms in the industry producing Y decrease, and MPP_{ay} increases. Smaller amounts of Y are produced and sold; consequently, p_y rises. Increases in MPP_{ay} and p_y increase VMP_{ay}.

Reallocation of A from the production of Y to X continues until units of the resource are again correctly distributed between the two industries. Units of A move from the industry producing Y to the industry producing X until the VMP_{ax} has gone down enough and the VMP_{ay} has gone up enough for the two to be equal. The new price per unit of A will be somewhat higher than the old price, since its value of marginal product is now higher in both industries than it was previously. In bidding against each other for the available supply of A firms in both industries have raised the price of A to the level of its value of marginal product in both uses.

Resource A will again be making its maximum contribution to net national product. When VMP_{ax} was greater than VMP_{ay}, every movement of a unit of A from the industry producing Y to the industry producing X increased A's contribution to net national product. Withdrawal of a unit of A from the industry producing Y decreased A's contribution to net national product by an amount equal to VMP_{ay}. Putting the unit of A to work in the industry producing X increased A's contribution to net national product by VMP_{ax}. Hence, a net gain in A's contribution to net national product resulted from such transfers until A's value of marginal product was once more equalized among firms in the two industries.

Allocation among Submarkets

We extend the analysis by increasing the time span under consideration, joining short-period with long-period analysis. Consider two resources: (1) a certain kind of labor and (2) capital. The total supply of the kind of labor involved is a small proportion of the economy's total supply of all kinds of labor, and all units of it are homogeneous. Capital is fixed in specific forms and is immobile for the short period; but over the long period it is mobile, can change its form, and can be reallocated from one use to others.[3]

Allocation of Labor Suppose that Area I and Area II initially constitute separate and almost identical short-period submarkets. The products produced in the two submarkets are the same; capital facilities are the same; and their labor demand curves, D_1D_1 and D_2D_2, as in Figure 16-1, are the same. However, labor supplies for the two areas differ. Area I has a larger labor supply than Area II; thus, the labor supply curve S_1S_1 of Area I lies farther to the right than S_2S_2 of Area II.

---

[3]Capital is usually considered in two contexts: (1) as concrete agents of production and (2) as a fluid stock of productive capacity. The first context is a short-run concept, with capital taking such specific forms as buildings, machinery, wheatland, and so on. The second is a long-run concept. Concrete pieces of equipment have time to wear out and be replaced. But replacement of the same kind and in the same place does not necessarily occur. Replacement can be in the form of new and different kinds of concrete agents: In agriculture, horse-drawn machinery was allowed to depreciate as the use of tractors became widespread and special machinery adapted to the tractor gradually came into use. Or capital may flow from one industry to another and from one location to another through depreciation in the one and the building of new equipment in the other. Thus, while capital may be almost completely immobile in the short run, in the long run it becomes quite mobile. *See* Frank H. Knight, *On the History and Method of Economics* (Chicago: University of Chicago Press, 1956), pp. 56–57.

Figure 16–1   Allocation of Labor between Submarkets

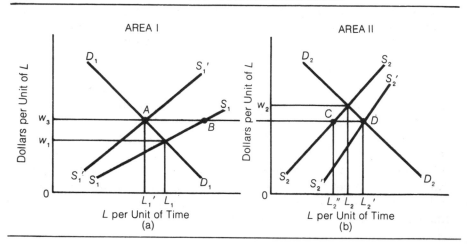

Labor is malallocated, and its maldistribution causes its value of marginal product and its price to differ between the two areas. The price of labor, or the wage rate, in Area I will be w_1, and in Area II it will be w_2. The level of employment in Area II is L_2, while that in Area I is higher at L_1. The higher ratio of labor to capital in Area I causes the marginal physical product and value of marginal product of labor to be lower in that area. The reverse holds in Area II. The ratio of labor to capital is smaller; consequently, the marginal physical product and value of marginal product of labor are higher.

The disparate submarket prices for labor furnish the incentive for long-period movement or reallocation of labor from Area I to Area II; and reallocation tends to eliminate the wage differential. As workers leave Area I the short-period supply curve for that submarket shifts to the left. As they enter Area II its short-period supply curve shifts to the right. As the ratio of labor to capital declines in Area I labor's value of marginal product and the wage rate increase. In Area II the increasing ratio of labor to capital decreases labor's value of marginal product and the wage rate. Reallocation continues until wage rates of the two submarkets are equal at w_3. The labor supply curve of Area I is now $S_1' S_1'$, and that of Area II is $S_2' S_2'$.

The reallocation of labor between Areas I and II increases real net national product and welfare. Before the movement began, the value of marginal product of labor in Area I was w_1. In Area II it was substantially higher at w_2. The movement of a unit of labor from Area I to Area II causes a loss of w_1 dollars' worth of product in Area I and a gain of almost w_2 dollars' worth of product in Area II. This gain more than offsets the loss in Area I, and creates a net increase in total value of product produced in the economy. Each transfer of a unit of labor from Area I to II brings about such a net increase until the values of marginal product and the wage rates of labor are the same in the two submarkets. Labor is then correctly allocated between the two areas—it is making its maximum contribution to welfare. No further transfer of labor in either direction can increase net national product, but will decrease it instead. Also, equalization of the wage rates will have removed the incentive for labor migration to occur.

Allocation of Capital   The entire burden of adjustment will not be thrown on labor in the long period as this analysis suggests, but will be partly absorbed by reallocation of capital. The high ratio of labor to capital in Area I amounts to the same thing as a low ratio of capital to labor. Likewise, the low ratio of labor to capital in Area II means a high ratio of capital to labor. Therefore, we would expect the value of marginal product of capital in Area I to exceed that in Area II. Differing productivities of capital and returns on investment between the two areas furnish the incentive for capital to migrate from Area II to I.

Long-period capital migration affects the short-period labor demand curves and the wage rates of the two areas. As units of capital leave Area II the demand curve (value of marginal product curve) for labor in that area shifts to the left, augmenting the decline in wage rates caused by the increasing labor supply. As units of capital enter Area I the demand curve for labor in Area I increases. The increases in demand join the decreases in supply in raising the wage rates of Area I.

When the reverse migrations of labor and capital have been sufficient to equalize wage rates and the returns on investment between the two areas, both labor and capital will be correctly allocated. Further transfers of either resource in either direction will reduce the real net national produce yielded by the two submarkets combined.

Factors Preventing Correct Allocation

A number of forces in the real world prevent the price system from allocating resources correctly. Even with the price system free to operate and with resource prices free to guide resource allocation, three important causes of incorrect allocation can be cited. These are monopoly in product markets, monopsony in resource markets, and certain nonprice impediments to resource movements. Additionally, direct interference with the price mechanism by the government or by private groups of resource owners and resource purchasers constitutes a cause of incorrect allocation. We shall consider these causes in turn.

The term *monopoly* is used in a broad context to include pure monopoly, oligopoly, and monopolistic competition—all cases in which individual firms face downward-sloping product demand curves. Similarly, the term *monopsony* is used broadly. Complete monopsony in resource purchases precludes any reallocation whatsoever. With less than complete monopsony units of a given resource may be free to move among a limited number of buyers, any one of which can influence market price of the resource.

Monopoly

Monopoly in product markets may not affect all resource movements directly. Some resources may be free to move among alternative employers even though some of the firms employing them enjoy a degree of product monopoly. Steel, common labor, certain raw materials, and other resources are employed by many firms and may be free to flow from one to another without regard to the types of product market in which individual firms sell. Where price discrepancies for any such resource exist within or among submarkets, long-period reallocation of the resource tends to occur to whatever extent necessary to eliminate the discrepancies. Every firm in every submarket tends to employ that quantity of the resource at which its marginal revenue product equals the resource price. Reallocation tends to occur until the marginal revenue product and the price of the resource are the same in all its alternative employments.

When some degree of product monopoly exists, real net national product and welfare would not be maximized even though all resources were so allocated that the marginal revenue product of each is the same in all its alternative employments. Individual firms face downward-sloping product demand curves. For each firm marginal revenue is less than product price. Thus, for any given resource, value of marginal product in each of its uses would exceed marginal revenue product. But discrepancies would occur among the values of marginal products of the resource in its various uses even though its marginal revenue product were the same in all of them. Such will be the case because of the differing demand elasticities of the various products that the resource aids in producing. Differing demand elasticities mean that product prices and corresponding marginal revenues are not proportional to each other among the different products. Hence, values of marginal products of the resource in its various uses are not proportional to its marginal revenue products. When the latter are equal, the former will be unequal. Inequalities among values of marginal product of a resource in its various uses show that net national product could be increased by transferring units of the resource from lower value of marginal product uses to higher value of marginal product uses.

It is the *value of marginal product* of a resource that measures the contribution of a unit of it to the value of the economy's output — its marginal physical product multiplied by the price of the final product. *Marginal revenue product* shows the contribution that a unit of the resource makes to the total receipts of a single firm; but where monopoly exists, this is less than the value of the product added to the economy's output by the resource unit. Thus, when a resource is so allocated that its marginal revenue product is equalized in all alternative uses, and when its price equals its marginal revenue product, the price system has done its job. Even though further reallocation from lower value of marginal product uses to higher value of marginal product uses will increase net national product, there is no automatic motivation to make it occur.

Suppose that machinists in Detroit work both for firms selling as oligopolists and those selling as pure competitors. An automobile manufacturer furnishes an example of the former type of firm, whereas any one of many small independent machine shops is an example of the latter. Suppose an equilibrium allocation of machinists exists—they are paid $8 per hour in all alternative employments. The small machine shop hires that quantity at which the value of marginal product of machinists if $8 per hour. The automobile manufacturer hires that quantity at which marginal revenue product equals $8 per hour. But since the automobile manufacturer faces a downward-sloping product demand curve, value of marginal product of machinists employed by him exceeds their marginal revenue product. Value of marginal product may thus be $12 per hour. Society would gain in terms of net national product if some machinists would transfer from the small independent machine shops to automobile manufacturers. However, since both pay $8 per hour, the price system will not motivate the transfers.

In addition, partially or completely blocked entry into monopolistic industries may prevent other resources from being so allocated that their respective marginal revenue products and prices are equalized within and among submarkets. We can think of such resources as being inseparable from the existence of individual firms—they are certain ones of the short-run "fixed" resources. They can enter industries only in the form of plant for new firms. The existence of long-run profits for the firms in an industry indicate that the marginal revenue products of such resources are greater in that industry than they are elsewhere in the economy.

Monopsony

The existence of monopsony in resource purchases may also prevent the price system from allocating resources correctly. Where some degree of monopsony is present, an individual firm purchases that quantity of the resource involved at which its marginal revenue product equals its marginal resource cost. When the resource supply curve to the firm slopes upward to the right, marginal resource cost exceeds the price that the firm pays the resource. When equilibrium in the purchase of the resource is reached on the part of any single firm, the price paid the resource is below its marginal revenue product.

Differential prices of the resource guide its allocation among the few firms using it, just as they did in the previous analysis. Voluntary reallocation of the resource will cease when its price is the same in its alternative uses. Resource owners will have no incentive to transfer units of it from one employment to another, and an equilibrium allocation will have been achieved.

Even though an equilibrium allocation may be achieved and all firms may be paying the same price for the resource, it will not be making its maximum contribution to net national product. To the extent that the supply curves of the resource facing different firms have differing elasticities, marginal resource costs and marginal revenue products of the resource among different firms will not be equal. Some degree of monopoly in product markets will create further distortions in the pattern of values of marginal products. Hence, there is no reason for believing that the values of marginal products of the resource will be the same among its alternative employments even though it is everywhere paid the same price. About the most we can say on this point is that resource transfers from lower value of marginal product uses to higher value of marginal product uses would increase real net national product; but since the resource price is the same in its alternative employments, resource owners will not make such transfers voluntarily.

Nonprice Impediments

Ignorance   Lack of knowledge on the part of resource owners may prevent resources from moving from lower-paying to higher-paying uses. In the most obvious case resource owners may lack information concerning the price patterns of the resources over the economy as a whole. Bricklayers may not be aware of the areas and firms paying the highest wages for bricklayers. Farmers may sell products at unnecessarily low prices when they are not aware of the higher prices which can be obtained elsewhere. Investors make mistakes when they lack knowledge of alternative investment opportunities throughout the economy.[4]

Lack of knowledge may also prevent potential resources from being channeled into the resource supply categories in which they will contribute most to net national product. Various kinds of labor resources will illustrate the point. For what trade or profession should potential entrants to the labor force be trained? Do those responsible for influencing or selecting the vocation possess full knowledge of the future returns to be derived

---

[4]The classic examples here are the many single proprietorships that fail in such fields as neighborhood grocery stores, eating and drinking establishments, and filling stations.

from alternative vocations? Usually they do not. Sons may follow fathers as sharecroppers or coal miners, when alternative occupations would be more lucrative. Or, where sons do not follow fathers' occupations, the information on which decisions are made is often sketchy. Frequently the potential entrant and his advisers do not discover until the training program is well advanced or completed that the choice of occupation has been an unfortunate one economically—and at this point it may be too late to change.

Sociological and Psychological Impediments   Sociological and psychological factors may throw blocks in the way of allocation of resources that will maximize net national product.[5] They include those ties to particular communities, friends, and to the family that restrict mobility regardless of the monetary incentives to move. Or, the virtues of a particular occupation, community, or way of living may be so extolled by various social groups that mobility is restricted. Glorification of the family farm, or of southern California, or of the teaching profession may be cases in point.

Institutional Factors   Various institutional barriers to reallocation of resources are evident in the economy. In the industrial world workers accumulate rights of various kinds with particular firms. These include pension and seniority rights. In some cases labor unions may restrict entry directly into particular occupations. Patent rights held by one firm or a group of firms in an industry may block the entry of new firms into the industry and thus condemn quantities of certain resources to other occupations in which their values of marginal products and rates of pay are lower. The list can be extended considerably, but these cases serve to illustrate the point.

Interferences with the Price Mechanism

Sometimes the price mechanism is not allowed to perform its function of signaling the spots where quantities of certain resources should be transferred in or out. Some resource prices are fixed or controlled by the government. Control may be exercised through such devices as minimum-wage legislation, agricultural price supports, or the general price and wage controls so common during times of war. Some resource prices may be partially or completely controlled by organized private groups of resource owners and resource purchasers. Some labor unions fall within this category, as do certain farm-marketing cooperatives and some employer associations. These hypothetical examples illustrate some of the effects of controlled resource prices on the equilibrium allocation of resources and

---

[5]We are not saying that such blocks constitute mistakes on the part of society. The "good life" is not necessarily achieved through maximization of net national product. It may be desirable to sacrifice some product, in some instances, for the achievement of other objectives or values.

on net national product. We shall assume that in the absence of control pure competition would exist; however, even if some degree of monopoly in product markets were to exist, the results would be approximately the same.

Two submarkets for a given resource are shown in Figure 16-2. As a matter of convenience we shall call the resource labor. The two submarkets are essentially alike except for the initial distribution of labor. They produce the same products and have identical supplies of capital. The demand curves for labor are the same for each submarket. Since Area I has a greater labor supply than Area II, the short-period price of labor will be lower in Area I and the employment level will be higher. We shall consider three possible cases.

Case I   Assume first of all that the workers of Area II are organized and that those of Area I are not. The initial labor demand and labor supply situations are shown in Figure 16-2. The equilibrium wage rate and employment level in Area I are w_1 and L_1, respectively. In Area II they are w_2 and L_2, respectively. Assume further that organized workers, through collective bargaining, succeed in placing a floor of rate w_2 under Area II wage rates.

The immediate or short-period effects of the minimum-wage rate of w_2 in Area II will be nil. Since w_2 is initially the equilibrium wage rate in Area II, the union should have little difficulty in obtaining it. At that wage rate employers of Area II are willing to employ as much labor as is willing to go to work. The wage differential between the two areas continues to reflect the existence of the initial maldistribution of labor.

The effects of the minimum-wage rate set in Area II are felt in the long period. The wage differential creates an incentive for workers to migrate from Area I to Area II. However, if additional workers were hired in Area II, the ratio of labor to capital would increase, the marginal physical product of labor would decrease, and the value of marginal product of labor would decrease. Since the wage rate of such additional workers would be w_2, and since this rate would exceed their values of marginal product, they would not be hired. Any workers migrating from Area I to Area II would find themselves unemployed; and this prospect would keep migration from occurring. Employment in Area I at the lower wage rate of w_1 would be preferable to no employment at all in Area II, regardless of how high wage rates are. Labor would remain poorly allocated between the two areas, and welfare would be permanently below its optimum level.

This situation sets the stage for interesting repercussions with regard to capital. An incentive for capital to migrate in the long period will be present in this case also. In fact, capital migration is the only adjustment in resource allocation that can occur. As capital migrates from Area II to Area I, demand for labor will decrease in Area II and will increase in Area I. This demand change will increase wage rates and employment in Area I.

Figure 16-2 The Impact of Minimum Resource Prices on Labor Allocation

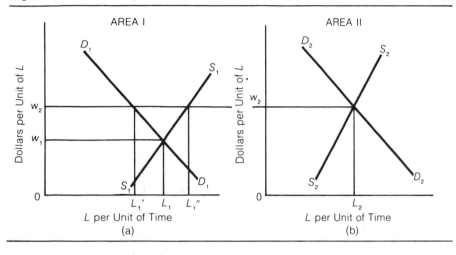

AREA I

AREA II

(a)

(b)

However, unemployment will develop among the organized workers of Area II, and welfare will still be below its maximum potential level.[6]

Case II   Assume that the organized workers of Area II succeed in extending their organization to Area I. Once Area I is organized, assume that workers in both places can bring wage rates in Area I up to w_2 (Figure 16-2). Immediate short-period effects occur. There will be no initial effect on the employment level in Area II. In Area I, unemployment amounting to $L_1'L_1''$ will occur. In Area I, at the old wage level of w_1, employment level L_1 equates value of marginal product of labor to the wage rate. The minimum-wage rate of w_2 makes the wage rate greater than the value of marginal product of labor at the old employment level of L_1. Employers find that a reduction in employment will decrease their total receipts by less than it reduces their total costs; hence, workers are laid off. The decreasing ratio of labor to capital increases the value of marginal product of labor until, when only L_1' workers are employed, their value of marginal product is again equal to the wage rate. Here the layoffs will stop.

The long-period effects of the minimum-wage rate of w_2 will be approximately the same as the immediate effects. Since the wage differential is eliminated, there is no incentive for employed workers of Area I to migrate to Area II. Employers of Area II will not find it profitable to employ more workers than L_2 at a wage rate of w_2; hence, unemployed workers of Area I will not find migration to Area II of any benefit.

---

[6]The women's full-fashioned hosiery industry furnishes an excellent example of the migration of capital from high-cost union areas to low-cost nonunion areas. *See* Sumner H. Slichter, *Union Policies and Industrial Management* (Washington, D. C: The Brookings Institution, 1941), pp. 353–360.

With regard to capital, the minimum-wage rate of w_2 in Area I and the reduced ratio of labor to capital (increased ratio of capital to labor) eliminate the incentive for capital to migrate to Area I in the long period. The ratio of capital to labor in Area I is increased sufficiently by the worker layoffs to make the value of marginal product of capital in Area I equal to that in Area II.[7] Thus, the minimum-wage rate of w_2 extended to both areas prevents the effects of the initial malallocation of resources from being alleviated by either labor or capital migration; and, in addition, it creates unemployment.

Case III   A third possibility, in which controlled resource prices may not affect resource allocation adversely, deserves some consideration. Assume that both areas are organized or, alternatively, that the government sets a minimum-wage rate applicable to both. The wage rate is set through collective bargaining or by the government at level w_3, as is shown in Figure 16-3; that is, at precisely the level that would prevail in free markets in the long period after workers had had sufficient time to migrate. The initial demand and supply relationships are D_1D_1 and S_1S_1, respectively, in Area I. In Area II they are D_2D_2 and S_2S_2, respectively. In Area I the minimum wage rate of w_3 will cause unemployment equal to *AB*. In Area II a labor shortage equal to *CD* will occur at wage rate w_3, and the wage rate in that submarket will rise to w_2.

Unemployment will assist the price system in reallocating labor from Area I to Area II in the long period. The unemployed and the lower-paid workers of Area I will seek the higher-paying jobs of Area II. The supply curve for labor in Area I will shift leftward to $S_1'S_1'$, and that of Area II will shift rightward to $S_2'S_2'$. Labor will be reallocated so that its value of marginal product is equalized between the two submarkets and so that labor is making its maximum contribution to net national product.

Again, some migration of capital from Area II to Area I may occur in the long period. At wage rate w_3 the initial employment level is L_1' in Area I and is greater than the initial employment level of L_2 in Area II. Therefore, the ratio of capital to labor is smaller, and the marginal revenue product of capital is greater, in Area I than in Area II. Capital migration will reduce the demand for labor in Area II and will increase the demand for labor in Area I, thus reducing the amount of labor migration necessary to secure full employment and maximum net national product.

---

[7]Since the initial capital facilities and products produced in the two areas were assumed to be the same, the labor demand curves are also the same. At wage rate w_2 each market employs the same quantity of labor; that is, L_1' units of labor equals L_2 units of labor in Figure 16-2. Consequently, ratios of labor to capital in the two areas, when the wage rate for both is w_2, will be the same; and the value of marginal product of capital will also be the same.

Figure 16-3   Job Opportunities as Incentives for Labor Migration

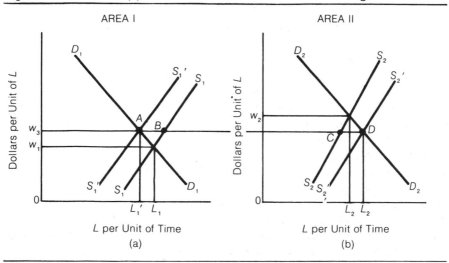

AREA I   AREA II

L per Unit of Time   L per Unit of Time
(a)   (b)

Summary

Any given resource is "correctly" allocated—makes its maximum contribution to economic welfare—when its value of marginal product is the same in all of its alternative uses. In a private enterprise economic system resource prices serve the function of directing the allocation of resources.

Only under pure competition in product markets and resource markets will resources automatically be allocated so as to maximize real net national product or welfare. Under pure competition a malallocation of any given resource causes its values of marginal products in different employments to differ from each other. Consequently, employers for whom its value of marginal product is higher bid resources away from those for whom its value of marginal product is lower. Transfers of resource units from lower to higher value of marginal product uses increase the contributions of the resource to welfare. Its maximum contribution occurs when value of marginal product of the resource is the same in all its possible uses. Price of the resource will also be the same in all its alternative uses; therefore, no incentive will exist for further transfers to be made.

With some degree of monopoly in product markets a resource will be reallocated among its alternative uses until its price is the same in all of them. However, where employers are monopolists in some degree, they employ those quantities of the resource at which its marginal revenue product equals its price. The marginal revenue products of the resource will be the same in alternative employments. Differing product demand elasticities cause values of marginal products of the resource to differ in alternative employments. Thus, the resource does not makes its maximum contribution to net national product.

Where employers have some degree of monopsony, but there is no resource differentiation, a resource will again be reallocated until its price is the same in alternative employments. But a monopsonist employs the resource up to the point at which marginal revenue product equals marginal resource cost. Different monopsonists may face resource supply curves of differing elasticities and, if so, marginal resource cost will be different for each even though all pay the same price per unit for the resource. With equilibrium allocation of the resource achieved, marginal revenue products differ. The usual case will be that differences in values of marginal product also occur, and the resource will not be making its maximum contribution to net national product.

Nonprice impediments to correct allocation of resources include ignorance, sociological and psychological factors, and institutional restrictions. In some instances the achievement of noneconomic values may be of more importance to society than correct resource allocation.

Direct interferences with the price mechanism by the government and by private groups may prevent resources from being correctly allocated in some cases. In other cases they may not lead to adverse effects.

Suggested Readings

Clark, John Bates, *The Distribution of Wealth* (New York: The Macmillan Company, 1923), Chap. XIX.

Pigou, A. C., *The Economics of Welfare*, 4th ed. (London: Macmillan & Co., Ltd., 1932), Pt. III, Chap. IX.

Rees, Albert, "The Effects of Unions on Resource Allocation," *Journal of Law and Economics* (October, 1963) pp. 69–78. Reprinted in Breit, William and Harold M. Hochman. *Readings in Microeconomics* (New York: Holt, Rinehart, and Winston, Inc., 1968), pp. 375–382.

Chapter 17:

Product Distribution

Of the four functions of an economic system with which we are concerned, we have yet to consider the distribution of the economy's product, or income. Income distribution among the families and individuals of economic systems has been an age-old source of unrest and concern. In fact, a promise always extended by socialist economic systems is that they will improve the distribution of income. In this chapter we shall examine the way in which a private-enterprise system distributes income, the possibilities of redistribution, and the welfare implications of both.

Individual Income Determination

The principles of individual income determination and of income distribution in a private-enterprise economic system are called *the marginal productivity theory*. These principles were set out in previous chapters, but we shall draw together and summarize them here.

The principles of income determination where pure competition prevails, both in product markets and resource markets, were developed in Chapter 14. The owner of a given resource is paid a price per unit for the units employed equal to the value of marginal product of the resource. The price of the resource is not determined by any single employer or by any single resource owner. It is determined by the interactions of all buyers and all sellers in the market for the resource.

If for some reason the price of a resource should be less than the value of its marginal product, a shortage will occur. Employers want more of it at that price than resource owners are willing to place on the market. Employers, bidding against each other for the available supply, will drive the price up until the shortage disappears and each is hiring (or buying) that quantity of the resource at which its value of marginal product equals its price.

A price high enough to create a surplus of the resource will set forces in motion to eliminate the surplus. Employers take only those quantities sufficient to equate its value of marginal product to its price. Resource owners undercut each other's prices to secure employment for their unemployed units. As price drops, employment expands. The undercutting continues until employers are willing to take the quantities that resource owners want to place on the market.

Where some degree of monopoly[1] exists in product markets, these principles are altered to some extent. Monopolistic firms employ those quantities of the resource at which its marginal revenue product is equal to its price. Thus, the price per unit received by owners of the resource is less than its value of marginal product, and the resource is exploited monopolistically.

Some degree of monopsony in the purchase of a given resource will cause it to be paid still less than its marginal revenue product. The monopsonist, faced with a resource supply curve sloping upward to the right, employs that quantity of the resource at which its marginal revenue product is equal to its marginal resource cost. Marginal resource cost is greater than the price paid for the resource. Monopsonistic exploitation of the resource occurs to the extent that its marginal revenue product exceeds its price. If the resource purchaser is also a monopolist, marginal revenue product of the resource will in turn be less than its value of marginal product, and the resource will be exploited monopolistically as well as monopsonistically.

As we noted in Chapter 2 an individual's income per unit of time is the sum of the amounts earned per unit of time from the employment of the various resources which he owns. If he owns a single kind of resource, his income will be equal to the number of units placed in employment multiplied by the price per unit which he receives. If he owns several kinds of resources, the income from each one can be computed in the same manner; and then all can be totaled to determine his entire income.

---

[1]Again, we use the term to refer to all cases in which the firm faces a downward-sloping product demand curve. They include cases of pure monopoly, oligopoly, and monopolistic competition.

Table 17-1   Distribution of Total Money Income in the United States Before Taxes, 1970

Total money income	Families		Unrelated Individuals	
	Number (Thousands)	Percent	Number (Thousands)	Percent
Under $1,500	4,601	8.9	3,562	23.2
$1,500 to 3,000			3,891	25.4
$3,000 to $4,999	5,341	10.4	2,720	17.7
$5,000 to $6,999	6,148	11.1	1,873	12.2
$7,000 to $9,999	10,348	19.9	1,895	12.3
$10,000 to $14,999	13,925	26.8	969	9.1
$15,000 and over	11,585	22.3	447	
Total	51,948	100.0	15,357	100.0
Median Income	$9,867 (Families)		$3,137 (Individuals)	

Source: U.S. Department of Commerce, Bureau of the Census, *Consumer Income*, Series P-60, No. 80 (October 4, 1971), pp. 1, 22.

Personal Distribution of Income

Personal distribution of income refers to income distribution among spending units of the economy. We shall survey first the distribution of income by size, and then point up certain problems involved in discussing income differences and equality.

Distribution among Spending Units

Some idea of the distribution of income in the United States is provided by Table 17-1. It is worth noting that almost half of the families had incomes of $10,000 or over per year. Note also that 8.9 percent of families fell below the $3000 per year level. Among unrelated individuals—persons fourteen years of age or over who are not living with any relatives—almost half had incomes under $3000 per year. In fact, 23.2 percent of these had annual incomes under $1500.

Income Equality and Income Differences

Any discussion of income distribution inevitably raises questions of whether the distribution is just or fair. These questions are often confused with those of income equality or differences. We shall not discuss issues of justice and fairness since these are concepts not subject to objective measurement. They mean different things to different individuals, depending on individual value judgments. Equality or differences in incomes *are* subject to objective measurement.

As Table 17-1 indicates, we usually look at the distribution of income among spending units. But these differ in size and composition; hence, equality among spending units does not really mean equality among individuals.

With regard to size spending units are composed either of unrelated single individuals or families. Family units vary in size from two persons up. Usually they include relatives living as members of the same household.

Differences in the composition of spending units of the same size lead to further complications in assessing the extent of income differences. Variations in the ages of members occur among different spending units. Cultural differences exist. Differences in regional locations occur. These and other differences of a similar nature lead to differences in tastes and preferences among spending units, and to differences in capacities of enjoying product consumption.

The difficulties encountered in trying to define and measure income equality or income differences will not be of major importance for our purposes. We are interested in the causes of differences rather than in their ethical implications. We shall have occasion to refer to "movements toward greater equality," but this statement should be accepted for what it is—a loose statement meaning some mitigation of income differences among heterogeneous spending units. It means some lopping off of incomes at the top and some augmenting of incomes at the bottom. It does not mean that we can state with any precision the point at which income distribution is "equalized."

Causes of Income Differences

With reference to the determinants of individual[2] incomes, it becomes clear that differences in incomes arise from two basic sources: (1) differences in the kinds and quantities of resources owned by different individuals and (2) differences in prices paid in different employments for units of any given resource. The former are the more fundamental. The latter arise from various types of interference with the price system in the performance of its functions and from any resource immobility which may occur.

It will be convenient to discuss labor and capital resources separately. To enable us to see the importance of each in perspective it is worthwhile to note the *functional distribution* of income in the United States; that is, distribution according to the resource classes into which resources are divided. In Table 17-2 compensation of employees represents income

---

[2]The term *individual* will be used throughout the rest of the chapter to refer to a spending unit, regardless of its size or composition.

Table 17-2 National Income by Type of Income: 1939-1971

Type of Income	1939		1949		1959		1969		1971	
	Income (Billions of Dollars)	Percent of Income	Income (Billions of Dollars)	Percent of Income	Income (Billions of Dollars)	Percent of Income	Income (Billions of Dollars)	Percent of Income	Income (Billions of Dollars)	Percent of Income
Compensation of employees	48.1	66.3	140.8	64.7	278.5	69.6	565.5	72.8	641.9	75.4
Business and professional proprietors' income	7.3	10.0	22.7	10.4	35.1	8.8	50.3	6.5	52.1	6.1
Farm proprietors' income	4.3	5.9	12.9	5.9	11.4	2.8	16.8	2.0	16.3	1.9
Rental income	2.7	3.7	8.3	3.8	11.9	3.0	22.6	2.9	24.3	2.9
Net interest	4.6	6.3	4.8	2.2	16.4	4.1	29.9	3.8	35.6	4.2
Corporate profits (before taxes)	5.7	7.9	28.2	13.0	47.2	11.8	78.6	12.0	81.0	9.5
Total	72.8	100.0	217.7	100.0	400.5	100.0	763.7	100.0	851.1	100.0

Sources: Economic Report of the President (Washington, D.C.: Government Printing Office, 1965), p. 203.
U.S. Department of Commerce, Survey of Current Business (Washington, D.C.: Government Printing Office, April 1972), S-2.

received by the owners of labor resources for the listed years; while corporate profits, interest, and rental income represent income received by capital owners. All are understated substantially, because proprietors' income includes both income from labor and from capital. Since accounting records for such enterprises often do not differentiate between returns to labor and returns to capital, we cannot split this item into categories labeled capital and labor. We can guess roughly that labor resources account for 80 to 85 percent of national income and that capital resources account for some 15 to 20 percent.

In this section we shall first consider differences in the kinds and quantities of labor resources owned by different individuals. Next, differences in capital resources owned will be discussed. Finally, we shall examine the effects on income distribution of certain interferences with the price mechanism.

Differences in Labor Resources Owned

The labor classification of resources is composed of many different kinds and qualities of labor. These have one common characteristic — they are human. Any single kind of labor is a combination or complex of both inherited and acquired characteristics. The acquired part of a man's labor power is sometimes referred to as human capital. We shall make no attempt to separate inherited and acquired characteristics.

Labor can be subclassified horizontally and vertically into many largely separate resource groups. Vertical subclassification involves grading workers according to skill levels from the lowest kind of undifferentiated manual labor to the highest professional levels. Horizontal subclassification divides workers of a certain skill level into the various occupations requiring that particular degree of skill. An example would be the division of skilled construction workers into groups — carpenters, bricklayers, plumbers, and the like. Vertical mobility of labor refers to the possibility of moving upward through vertical skill levels. Horizontal mobility means the ability to move sideways among groups at a particular skill level.

Horizontal Differences in Labor Resources   At any specific horizontal level individuals may receive different incomes because of differences in the demand and supply conditions for the kinds of labor they own. A large demand for a certain kind of labor relative to the supply of it available will make its marginal revenue product and its price high. On the same skill level a small demand for another kind of labor relative to the supply available will make its marginal revenue product and its price low. The difference in prices tends to cause differences in income for owners of the kinds of labor concerned.

Suppose, for example, that bricklayers and carpenters initially earn approximately equal incomes. A shift in consumer tastes occurs from wood to brick construction in residential units. The incomes of bricklayers will increase, while those of carpenters will decrease, because of the altered conditions of demand. Over a long period of time horizontal mobility between the two groups tends to decrease the income differences thus arising, and welfare will be increased in the process.

Quantitiative differences in the amount of work performed by individuals owning the same kind of labor resource may lead to income differences. Some occupations afford considerable leeway for individual choice of the number of hours to be worked per week or month. Examples include independent professional men such as physicians, lawyers, and certified public accountants, along with independent proprietors such as farmers, plumbing contractors, and garage owners. In other occupations hours of work are beyond the control of the individual. Yet in different employments of the same resource differences in age, physical endurance, institutional restriction, custom, and so on can lead to differences in hours worked and to income differences among owners of the resource.

Within a particular labor resource group qualitative differences or differences in the abilities of the owners of the resource often create income differences. Wide variations occur in public evaluation of different dentists, or physicians, or lawyers, or automobile mechanics. Consequently, within any one group variations in prices paid for services and variations in the quantities of services sold to the public will lead to income differences. Usually a correlation exists between the ages of the members of a resource group and their incomes. Quality tends to improve with accumulated experience up to a point. Data reported by Friedman and Kuznets suggest, for example, that the incomes of physicians tend to be highest between the tenth and twenty-fifth years of practice, and the incomes of lawyers tend to be highest between the twentieth and thirty-fifth years of practice.[3]

Vertical Differences in Labor Resources   The different vertical strata themselves represent differences in labor resources owned and give rise to major labor income differences. Entry into high-level occupations, such as the professions or the ranks of business executives, is much more difficult than is entry into manual occupations. The relative scarcity of labor at top levels results from two basic factors: (1) individuals with the physical and mental characteristics necessary for the performance of high-level work are limited in number; and (2) given the necessary physical and

[3] Milton Friedman and Simon Kuznets, *Income from Independent Professional Practice* (New York: National Bureau of Economic Research, 1945), pp. 237–260.

mental characteristics, many lack opportunities for training and the necessary social and cultural environment for movement into high-level positions. Thus, limited vertical mobility keeps resource supplies low relative to demands for them at the top levels; and it keeps resource supplies abundant relative to demands for them at the low levels.

Differences in labor resources owned because of differences in innate physical and mental characteristics of individuals are accidents of birth. The individual has nothing to do with choosing them. Nevertheless, they account partly for restricted vertical mobility and for income differences. The opportunities of moving toward top positions and relatively large incomes are considerably enhanced by the inheritance of a strong physical constitution and a superior intellect; however, these by no means insure that individuals so endowed will make the most of their opportunities.

Opportunities for training are more widely available to individuals born into wealthy families than to those born into families in lower-income groups. Some of the higher-paying professions require long and expensive university training programs—often beyond the reach of the latter groups. The medical profession is a case in point. However, we often see individuals who have had the initial ability, drive, and determination necessary to overcome economic obstacles thrown in the way of vertical mobility.

Differences in social inheritance constitute another cause of difference in labor resources owned. These are closely correlated with differences in material inheritance. Frequently, individuals born "on the wrong side of the tracks" face family and community attitudes that sharply curtail their opportunities and their desires for vertical mobility. Others, more fortunately situated, acquire the training necessary to be highly productive and to obtain large incomes because it is expected of them by the social group in which they move. The social position alone, apart from the training induced by it, may be quite effective in facilitating vertical mobility.

When vertical mobility can occur but is blocked, income differences persist and welfare is below its potential maximum. If those who are denied access to higher value of marginal product jobs and occupations were able to attain these, the result would be higher real net national product, as well as greater equality in income distribution.

Differences in Capital Resources Owned

In addition to inequalities in labor incomes large differences occur in individual incomes from differences in capital ownership. Different individuals own varying quantities of capital—corporation or other business assets, farmland, oil wells, and property of various other types. We shall examine the fundamental causes of inequalities in capital holdings.

Material Inheritance Differences in the amounts of capital inherited or received as gifts by different individuals create large differences in incomes. The institution of private property on which private enterprise rests usually is coupled with inheritance laws allowing large holdings of accumulated property rights to be passed from generation to generation. The individual fortunate enough to have a wealthy father inherits large capital holdings; his resources contribute much to the productive process; and he is rewarded accordingly. The son of a Southern sharecropper—who may be of equal innate intelligence with the son of a wealthy father, but inherits no capital—contributes less to the productive process and receives a correspondingly lower income.

Fortuitous Circumstances Chance, luck, or other fortuitous circumstances beyond the control of individuals constitute a further cause of differences in capital holdings. The discovery of oil, uranium, or gold on an otherwise undistinguished piece of land brings about a large appreciation in its value or its ability to yield income to its owner. Unforeseen shifts in consumer demand increase the values of certain capital holdings, while decreasing the values of others. National emergencies, such as war, lead to changes in valuations of particular kinds of property, and hence to differential incomes from capital. Fortuitous circumstances can work in reverse also, but even so, their effects operate to create differences in the ownership of capital.

Propensities to Accumulate Differing psychological propensities to accumulate and differing abilities to accumulate lead to differences in capital ownership among individuals. On the psychological side a number of factors influence the will to accumulate. Stories circulate of individuals determined to make a fortune before they reach a certain age. Accumulation sometimes occurs for purposes of security and luxury in later life. It sometimes occurs from the desire to make one's children secure. The power and the prestige accompanying wealth provide the motivating force in some cases. To others, accumulation and manipulation of capital holdings is a gigantic game—the activity involved is fascinating of itself. Whatever the motives, some individuals have such propensities and others do not. In some instances the will to accumulate may be negative, and the opposite of accumulation occurs.

The ability of an individual to accumulate depends largely on his original holdings of both labor and capital resources. The higher the original income, the easier saving and accumulation tend to be. The individual possessing much in the way of labor resources initially is likely to accumulate capital with his income from labor—he invests in stocks and bonds, real estate, a cattle ranch, or other property. Or the individual possessing substantial quantities of capital initially—and the ability to manage it—receives an income sufficient to allow saving and investment in additional capital. In the process of accumulation labor and capital resources of an individual augment each other in providing the income from which further accumulation can be accomplished.

Manipulation of the Price Mechanism

Various groups of resource owners throughout the economy, dissatisfied with their current shares of national income, seek to modify income distribution through manipulation or fixing of the prices of resources that they own or the prices of products they produce and sell. Certain groups of farmers—wheat, cotton, dairy farmers, and others—have been able to obtain government-enforced minimum prices for the products they sell. Certain groups of retailers have been able to secure state laws forbidding product-selling prices below a fixed percentage of markup over cost. Labor organizations seek to increase, or in some cases to maintain, their shares of national income by fixing wages through the collective-bargaining process. People all over the economy, concerned with small distributive shares of low-paid workers, support minimum-wage legislation. We shall examine typical cases of administered prices[4] in an attempt to assess their effects on income distribution. In each case we shall assume that the particular resource concerned constitutes a small proportion of the economy's total resources.

Administered Prices: Pure Competition   Suppose that owners of a given resource, dissatisfied with their shares of national income, seek and obtain an administered price above the equilibrium level for their resource. Will the incomes of the resource owners involved increase relative to the incomes of the owners of other resources? In other words, will the owners of the given resource receive a larger share of the economy's product? Equally important, what will happen to the share of total earnings of the resource received by each of its owners? What will the effects on the efficiency of the economy's operation or on welfare be?

Assuming that demand for the given resource remains constant,[5] the effect of the administered price on total income earned by the resource

---

[4]Administered prices are prices fixed by law, by groups of sellers, by groups of buyers, or by collective action of buyers and sellers. They are the antithesis of free-market prices established by free interactions of buyers and sellers in the marketplaces.

[5]There seems to be no valid reason for assuming that a change in the price of the resource will change the demand for it, especially if the resource concerned constitutes a small proportion of the economy's total supplies of resources—and such is usually the case for any given resource. Even if the administered price raises the total income of the resource owners involved, it seems unlikely that demand for the products which the resource assists in producing will be increased to any significant degree. In a stationary economy, particularly, it seems logical to assume independence between resource price changes and consequent changes in demand for the resource.

Figure 17–1   Effects of Administered Prices on Income Distribution

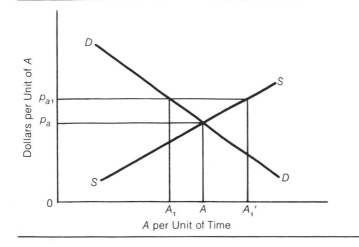

will depend on the elasticity of demand. If elasticity is less than one, total income will increase and owners of the resource as a group will have increased their distributive share. If elasticity equals one, no change in total income will occur. If elasticity is greater than one, total income and the distributive share of owners of the resource as a group will decline.

Reference to Figure 17-1 will help to answer the second problem—the effects of the administered price on the distribution among the owners of the total income earned by the resource. The demand curve and supply curve in the figure for resource A are DD and SS, respectively. The equilibrium price is p_a and the level of employment is quantity A.

Suppose now that an administered price of p_{a1} is set for the resource— none can be sold for less. Whether the administered price is set by the government, through bargaining between organized groups of buyers and sellers, or through unilateral action on the part of either resource buyers or resource sellers is of no consequence. The effects will be the same. Confronted by the higher price, each firm using resource A finds that if it employs the same quantity as before, marginal revenue product for the resource will be less than its price. Consequently, each firm finds that reductions in the quantity of the resource used will reduce total receipts less than they decrease total costs, and will increase the firm's profits. When all firms have reduced employment sufficiently for the marginal revenue product of the resource in each to equal p_{a1}, they will again be maximizing profits. The market level of employment will have dropped to A_1.

The administered price p_{a1} will create unemployment, thus causing income differences between those whose resources are employed and those whose resources are unemployed.[6] At price p_{a1} employers will take quantity A_1, but quantity A_1' of the resource seeks employment. Unemployment amounts to A_1A_1'. Those whose units of the resource remain employed gain greater distributive shares of the economy's product; however, those owning unemployed units now receive nothing for them. Units of the resource still are paid according to their marginal contributions to the total receipts of the firm. For the employed units marginal revenue product is greater than formerly because of the reduction in the ratio of resource A to the other resources used by individual firms. The marginal revenue product of the unemployed units is zero.

The unemployed units of resource A may seek employment in another resource classification. Suppose, for example, that units of resource A are carpenters. Carpenters denied employment in that skill category, at a wage rate of p_{a1}, may seek employment as common laborers rather than remain as unemployed carpenters. Their marginal revenue product and their wage rate will be lower in the lower skill classification. The administered wage rate increases income differences in two ways: (1) employed carpenters receive higher wage rates and incomes than they would otherwise receive; and (2) the wage rates and incomes of common labor are lower than they would otherwise be, as unemployed carpenters join the ranks and increase the supply of common labor.

The effects of the administered price on welfare are clear. The unemployed units of A contribute nothing to the value of the economy's output, or to the extent that they shift into lower productivity classifications they contribute less than they would otherwise have. If the resource price were allowed to drop to its equilibrium level, greater employment in the higher value of marginal product uses would raise the real value of the economy's output—and at the same time would contribute toward greater income equality among owners of the resource.

Supply Restrictions: Pure Competition   Resource prices in particular employments may be increased indirectly through restriction of the resource supplies that can be used in those employments. Examples are furnished by governmental acreage restrictions placed on cotton and wheat farmers. Or the same result may be obtained by labor union activity. The milk wagon drivers' union in a large city may succeed in making union membership a condition of employment, while at the same time it restricts entry into the union.The effects on income distribution and total output of the economy are about the same as those resulting from directly administered prices. The employment level of the resource in its restricted

---

[6]Unless the unemployment is shared equally by all owners of the resource.

use is decreased, leaving some of the resource units either unemployed or seeking employment in alternative uses. Land excluded from cotton and wheat farming may be switched to the production of other products. Light-truck drivers excluded from driving milk wagons may secure such alternative employments as delivery-truck or taxi driving. Value of marginal product and price of resource units in the restricted use increase,[7] while value of marginal product and price of those placed in other employments decrease. These changes lead to differential prices for the resource and to greater income differences. At the same time they lead to net national product smaller than the economy is capable of producing.

Administered Prices: Product Monopoly Do administered resource prices set above the equilibrium level offset the restrictive effects of monopoly when resource buyers sell a product as monopolists? The argument is frequently made that they do, and that the advance in resource prices comes from the monopolists' profits. Suppose that initially the equilibrium price for a given resource prevails. Firms with some degree of monopoly in product markets are among those who buy the resource, and the resource is so allocated that its price is the same in its alternative uses. The resource price equals its marginal revenue product in its various employments, and those units of the resource employed by monopolistic sellers are exploited monopolistically—they receive less than they contribute to the value of the economy's output.

Will an administered resource price above the equilibrium price regain what is lost by resource owners from monopolistic exploitation? Suppose such an administered price is obtained. Marginal revenue product of the resource for individual firms will be less than the administered price if firms continue hiring the same quantities as before. Consequently, each firm reduces its employment of the resource to the level at which its marginal revenue product equals the administered price. But note that it is still marginal revenue product and not value of marginal product of the resource that is equal to its price. Despite the administered price, monopolistic exploitation of the resource continues to occur.[8]

---

[7]In the case of wheatland or cottonland the ratio of land to other resources is decreased both through decreased acreage allowances and through more intensive application of labor and fertilizer. Greater marginal physical product of the land and possibly higher prices for smaller crops increase the value of marginal product of land.

About the same thing happens with regard to milk-wagon drivers. Firms faced with restricted supplies attempt to make each driver as productive as possible. Slightly larger trucks may be used to minimize the number of trips back to the plant for reloading. Trucks may be made more convenient to get into, to get out of, and to operate. Idle truck time is avoided through better maintenance and repair facilities for trucks. Such measures increase the marginal physical product of the drivers. Additionally, the employment of fewer drivers may lead to smaller milk sales and higher milk prices. Thus, the value of marginal product of milk-wagon drivers will be higher than before.

[8]Thus, measures to offset monopolistic exploitation of resources must attack the monopolistic product demand situation. They must eliminate the difference between marginal revenue and price for the monopolist and, hence, between marginal revenue product and value of marginal product of resources.

In addition, the level of employment of the resource by monopolistic firms, already too low for maximum welfare, is reduced still further. At the higher price the firms employ fewer units of the resource. More units seek employment. Unemployment and even greater differences in income among owners of the resource occur. If the unemployed units then find employment in lower marginal revenue product resource classifications or uses, income differences are mitigated to some extent; but they still occur.

Administered Prices: Monopsony　In monopsonistic cases administered resource prices can offset monopsonistic exploitation of a resource. The employment level of the resource can be increased at the same time that its price is raised above the market level. The income and the distributive shares of the owners of the resource are increased relative to those of other resource owners in the economy. At the same time the level of real net national product and welfare will be increased.

The detailed explanation of how an administered resource price offsets monopsonistic exploitation was presented in Chapter 15. To recapitulate the analysis, an administered price set above the market price makes the resource supply curve faced by the firm horizontal at that price. For prices higher than the administered price, the original supply curve is the relevant one. For the horizontal section of the resource supply curve, marginal resource cost and resource price will be equal. By judicious setting of the administered price the firm can be induced to employ that quantity of the resource at which marginal revenue product equals resource price. Without the administered price the firm restricts employment and pays units of the resource less than their marginal revenue product.

Price Increases Accompanying Demand Increases　The effects of administered resource price increases, when demand for the resource remains constant, are often confused with the effects of resource price increases that accompany increases in demand for the resource. Suppose demand for a given resource is increasing while, simultaneously, resource owners organized as a group succeed in *bargaining out* a series of price increases with the buyers of the resource. Suppose further that the contract prices at no time exceed the rising equilibrium price. No adverse distributive effects for the owners of the resource arise. Their positions are continuously improving as individual resource owners and as a group. However, it is erroneous to conclude from situations of this kind that administered resource price increases will in general have no adverse effects on total income of the owners of the resource in question, or on the distribution of income within the group. We must distinguish carefully between those administered price increases which are accompanied by increases in demand for the resource and those which are not. Although the former may have no adverse effects on total income of the owners of the resource, or on the distribution of income among owners of the resource, adverse effects—except in the case of monopsony—are likely to arise from the latter.

A Greater Measure of Equality

For various reasons—economic, ethical, and social—many people favor some mitigation of income differences. The causes of differences should furnish the clues for measures leading toward their mitigation—if movement toward greater equality is thought by society to be desirable. Thus, equalizing measures may be (and are) attempted via the price system, or they may be (and are) attempted through redistribution of resources among resource owners. We shall consider each of these in turn.

Via Administered Prices   Equalizing measures attempted via administered prices are likely to miss their mark except in monopsonistic cases. Where competitive and monopolistic conditions prevail in product markets, and where competitive conditions prevail in the purchase of a given resource, the equilibrium price of the resource tends to be equal to its value of marginal product or its marginal revenue product, as the case may be. Additionally, the resource tends to be so allocated that its price is the same in its alternative employments. Successful administered price increases are likely to result in unemployment and malallocation of the resource, and these in turn contribute toward greater rather than smaller income differences. As we have observed before, administered resource prices in monopsony cases can offset monopsonistic exploitation of a resource by increasing both its price and its level of employment.

Via Redistribution of Resources

The major part of any movement toward greater income equality must consist of redistribution of resources among resource owners, since this is the major cause of income differences. Redistributive measures can take two forms: (1) redistribution of labor resources and (2) redistribution of capital resources.

Labor Resources   Labor-resource ownership can be redistributed through measures designed to increase vertical mobility. Greater vertical mobility will increase labor supplies in the higher vocational levels and decrease labor supplies in the lower levels. Greater supplies at the higher levels will decrease values of marginal product or marginal revenue products, and will reduce the top incomes. Smaller supplies at the lower levels will increase values of marginal product or marginal revenue products, thereby increasing incomes at the lower occupational levels. The transfers from lower to higher occupations will mitigate income differences and will increase net national product in the process.

At least three methods of increasing vertical mobility can be suggested. First, greater equality in educational and training opportunities can be provided. Second, to the extent that differences in capital ownership are reduced, greater equality in economic opportunities for development of high-grade labor resources will tend to occur. Third, measures may be taken to reduce the barriers to entry established by groups and associations of resource owners in many skilled and semiskilled occupations.[9]

Measures to increase horizontal mobility also can serve to decrease income differences. These include the operation of employment exchanges, perhaps some subsidization of movement, vocational guidance, adult education and retraining programs, and other measures of a similar nature. The argument is really for a better allocation of labor resources, both among alternative jobs within a given labor resource category and among the labor resouce categories themselves. Greater horizontal mobility, as well as greater vertical mobility, will increase net national product at the same time that it decreases income differences.

Capital Resources   Policy measures to redistribute capital resources meet considerable opposition in a private enterprise economy. Many advocates of greater income equality will protest measures designed to redistribute capital ownership—and these measures are the ones that will contribute most toward such an objective. The opposition centers around the rights of private property ownership and stems from a strong belief that the right to own property includes the right to accumulate it and to pass it on to one's heirs.

Nevertheless, if income differences are to be mitigated, some means of providing greater equality in capital holdings among individuals must be employed. The economy's system of taxation may move in this direction. In the United States, for example, the personal income tax, the capital gains tax, and estate and gift taxes, both federal and state, already operate in an equalizing manner.

The personal income tax by its progressive nature serves to reduce income differences directly, and in so doing, it reduces differences in abilities to accumulate capital. But the personal income tax alone cannot be expected to eliminate income differences without seriously impairing incentives for efficient employment of resources and for reallocation of resources from less-productive to more-productive employments.

The capital gains tax constitutes either a loophole for escaping a part of the personal income tax or a plug for a loophole in the personal income

---

[9]An example of such a barrier is provided by the professional association that controls the licensing standards which prospective entrants must meet in order to practice the profession.

tax, depending on one's definition of income. The capital gains tax is applied to realized appreciation and depreciation in the value of capital assets. Those who can convert a part of their income from capital resources into the form of capital gains have that part of their remuneration taxed as capital gains at a rate ordinarily below the personal income tax rate. For them the capital gains tax provides a loophole through which personal income taxes can be escaped. Yet if certain capital gains would escape taxation altogether under the personal income tax, but are covered by the capital gains tax, the latter can be considered as a supplement to the personal income tax. In either case the capital gains tax allows some remuneration from capital resources to be taxed at rates below the personal income tax rates, and, if differences in opportunities to accumulate capital are to be mitigated, this tax must be revised to prevent individuals from taking advantage of its lower rates.

Estate and gift taxes will play the major roles in any tax system designed to reduce differences in capital ownership. The estate taxes in such a system would border on the confiscatory side, above some maximum amount, in order to prevent the transmission of accumulated capital resources from generation to generation. Gift taxes would operate largely to plug estate tax loopholes. They would be designed to prevent transmission of estates by means of gifts from the original owner to heirs prior to the death of the original owner.

Redistribution and the Price System   Redistribution of labor resource and capital resource holdings can be accomplished within the framework of the price system and the private enterprise economic system if movement toward greater income equality is thought by society to be desirable. Redistribution measures, such as those sketched above, need not seriously affect the operation of the price mechanism. In fact the price mechanism can act as a positive force assisting the measures to reach desired objectives. Some of the fundamental measures — educational opportunities, progressive income taxes, gift and estate taxes — are already in existence, although their effectiveness could be greatly increased. Redistribution measures can be thought of as rules of the free enterprise game — along with a stable monetary system, monopoly control measures, and other rules of economic conduct.

SUMMARY

Individual claims to net national product depend on individual incomes; thus, the theory of product distribution is really the theory of income distribution. Marginal productivity theory provides the generally accepted principles of income determination and income distribution. Resource owners tend to be remunerated according to the marginal revenue products of the resources they own, except in cases where resources are purchased monopsonistically.

Incomes are unequally distributed among spending units in the United States. Income differences stem from three basic sources: (1) differences in labor resources owned, (2) differences in capital resources owned, and (3) restrictions placed on the operation of the price mechanism. With regard at the same general skill level. We call these horizontal differences in labor resources. Different individuals also own different kinds of labor graded vertically from undifferentiated manual labor to top-level professions. Differences in capital resources owned result from differences in material inheritance, fortuitous circumstances, and differences in propensities to accumulate.

Administered prices for a given resource often lead to unemployment or malallocation of some units of the resource and, hence, to differences in incomes among owners of the resource. The case of monopsony provides an exception. Under monopsony administered resource prices can offset monopsonistic exploitation of the resources involved.

Attacks on income differences, if society desires to mitigate those differences, should be made by way of redistribution of resources among resource owners. Attacks made by way of administered prices are not likely to accomplish this task. Redistribution of labor resources can be accomplished through measures designed to increase both horizontal and vertical mobility. These will in turn increase net national product.

The tax system offers a means of effecting redistribution of capital resources. Estate and gift taxes will bear the major burden of effective redistribution and may be supplemented by personal income and capital gains taxes.

Redistribution of resources can be accomplished within the framework of the price system and the private enterprise economy.

Suggested Readings

Friedman, Milton, *Capitalism and Freedom* (Chicago: University of Chicago Press, 1960), Chaps. X, XI, and XII.

Pigou, A.C., *The Economics of Welfare*, 4th ed. (London: Macmillan & Co., Ltd., 1932), Pt. IV, Chap. V.

Chapter 18:

Equilibrium and Welfare

In this chapter we summarize and tie together the subject matter of this book. First we will review what is involved in the concepts of welfare and equilibrium. Then we will examine the conditions that must be met in order to maximize welfare, in the sense of a Pareto optimum. Finally, we consider the conditions required for equilibrium to exist in a private enterprise economic system, and the implications of these general equilibrium conditions for welfare.

The Concepts of Equilibrium and Welfare

Welfare and equilibrium are different concepts, although they are frequently confused with one another. We have defined *welfare* as the state of well-being of the persons comprising an economic system. We have defined *equilibrium* as a state of rest, a position from which there is either no incentive or no opportunity to move. We shall look at some of the principal aspects of each of these concepts.

Welfare

Most economic analysis is concerned with the welfare aspects of economic activity—how to achieve maximum or optimum welfare for the population in the economic system. An objective definition of optimum welfare constitutes a major problem. As we noted in the introductory chapter, where only one person is being considered, the concept is straightforward and is synonomous with the well-being of that person. But when more than one person is being considered, an objective definition of a unique optimum welfare position for the group as a whole becomes impossible, since such a definition would require interpersonal comparisons of satisfaction. The Pareto optimum situation, in which no one can be made better off without making someone else worse off, is the best solution we can attain.

Equilibrium

Equilibrium concepts are important, not because equilibrium positions are ever in fact attained but because these concepts show us the direction in which economic processes move. When equilibrium positions are *stable* —as they have been assumed to be throughout this book—economic units in disequilibrium move toward equilibrium positions. But even as they are doing so, changes in consumer preference patterns, resource supplies, and technology change the equilibrium positions themselves, thus redirecting the movements that are occurring. If equilibrium positions are *unstable*, economic units will move farther away from the equilibrium positions rather than toward them.

Partial Equilibrium   A large part of the analytical structure that we have built up is called *partial equilibrium analysis*. It has been concerned with the movements of individual economic units toward equilibrium positions in response to the given economic conditions confronted. Thus, the consumer, with his given tastes and preferences, is confronted with a given income and with given prices of goods and services. He adjusts his purchases accordingly to move toward equilibrium. The business firm—faced with given product demand situations, a given state of technology, and given resource supply situations—moves toward an equilibrium adjustment. The resource owner possesses given quantities of resources to place in employment. He faces given alternative employment possibilities and resource price offers. His equilibrium adjustment is made on the basis of the given data. The conditions of demand and of cost in a particular industry cause profits or losses to be made, and these motivate entry of new firms (if entry is possible) or exit of existing firms, thus leading toward equilibrium for the industry. Changes in the given data facing economic units and industries change the positions of equilibrium that each is attempting to reach and motivate movements toward the new positions.

Partial equilibrium is especially suitable for the analysis of two types of problems, both of which we met time and again throughout the book. Problems of the first type are those arising from economic disturbances that are not of sufficient magnitude to reach far beyond the confines of a certain industry or sector of the economy. Problems of the second type are concerned with the first-order effects of an economic disturbance of any kind.

As an illustration of the first type of problem, suppose the production workers of a small manufacturer of plastic products go on strike. Suppose further that the plant is located in a large city, and that the workers are fairly well dispersed among the residential areas of the city. The effects of the strike will be limited largely to the company and the employees concerned. Partial equilibrium analysis will provide the relevant answers to most of the economic problems arising from the strike.

As an example of the second type of problem, suppose a rearmament program increases the demand for steel suddenly and substantially. Partial equilibrium analysis will provide answers to the first-order effects on the steel industry—what happens to its prices, output, profits, demand for resources, the resource prices, and its resource employment levels. However, the first-order effects by no means end the repercussions from the initial disturbance.

General Equilibrium   As individual economic units and industries seek equilibrium adjustments to what appear to be given facts, their total group actions change the facts that they face. If some units were in equilibrium and others were not, those in disequilibrium would move toward equilibrium. Their activities would change the facts faced by units in equilibrium and would throw the latter into disequilibrium. General equilibrium for the entire economy could exist only if all economic units were to achieve simultaneous partial, or particular, equilibrium adjustments. The concept of general equilibrium stresses the interdependence of all economic units and of all segments of the economy on each other.

A hard-and-fast line between partial equilibrium analysis and general equilibrium analysis is difficult to draw. Instead of establishing a dichotomy, it will be preferable to think in terms of moving along a continuum from partial to general equilibrium, or from first-order effects of a disturbance into second-, third-, and higher-order effects. For example, in discussing pricing and output under market conditions of pure competition, we were concerned first with partial equilibrium, or equilibrium of the individual firm. Next we extended the analysis to an entire industry and observed the impact of individual firm actions on each other. Finally, we observed how productive capacity is organized in a purely competitive free enterprise economy according to consumer tastes and preferences. This series of topics represents progressive movement from the application of partial equilibrium analysis to the application of general equilibrium analysis.

General equilibrium theory provides the analytical tools for accomplishing two objectives: (1) from the standpoint of pure theory it provides the means of viewing the economic system in its entirety—the means of seeing what holds it together, what makes it work, and how it operates; (2)—and this objective is really an application of the first one—is the determination of the second-, third-, and higher-order effects of an economic disturbance. When the impact of an economic disturbance is of sufficient magnitude to have repercussions throughout most of the economy, general equilibrium analysis provides the more relevant answers regarding its ultimate effects. First comes the big splash from the disturbance. Partial equilibrium analysis handles this. But waves, and then ripples are set up from it, affecting one another and affecting the area of the splash. The ripples run farther and farther out, becoming smaller and smaller, until eventually they dwindle away. The tools of general equilibrium are required for analysis of the entire series of readjustments.

Suppose the higher-order repercussions from the increase in demand for steel are to be examined. The first-order, or partial, equilibrium effects are higher prices, larger outputs with given facilities, larger profits, and larger payments to the owners of resources used in making steel. These effects generate additional disturbances. Higher incomes for the resource owners increase demand for other products, setting off disturbances and adjustments in other industries. Demands also increase for steel substitutes, generating another series of disturbances and adjustments. Productive capacity will be diverted from other activities toward the making of steel. Eventually, effects will be felt over the entire economy. If the full impact of such a disturbance is to be determined, general equilibrium analysis must provide the tools to do so.

Since general equilibrium analysis covers the interrelationships of all parts of the economy, it necessarily becomes exceedingly complex. There are two principal variants of it. In the first one, following Walras, most economists find it convenient to discuss general equilibrium in mathematical terms. The interdependence of economic units is shown through a system of simultaneous equations relating the many economic variables to each other. It can be demonstrated that there are as many variables to be determined as there are equations relating them. Solving the system of equations establishes those values of the variables that are consistent with general equilibrium for the economic system.[1] The Walrasian version of general equilibrium provides essentially the theoretical apparatus for understanding the interrelationships of the various sectors of the economy.

---

[1] *See* C.E. Ferguson, *Microeconomic Theory*, 3rd. ed. (Homewood, Ill.: Richard D. Irwin, Inc., 1972), Chap. 15.

The second variant of general equilibrium analysis is Wassily W. Leontief's input-output analysis.[2] The input-output approach is an empirical descendant of the abstract Walrasian approach. It divides the economy into a number of sectors or industries, including households and the government, as "industries" of final demand. Each industry is viewed as selling its output to other industries; these outputs become inputs for the purchasing industries. Likewise, each industry is viewed as a purchaser of the outputs of other industries. Thus, the interdependence of each industry on the others is established. Statistical data gathered around the basic framework of the system provide an informative and useful picture of the interindustry flows of goods, services, and resources. The input-output approach shows promise for analyzing and measuring the effects of major economic disturbances statistically, as well as for mobilizing an economy in periods of national emergency.

The attainment of general equilibrium in an economic system does not imply that Pareto optimality is also attained. A price system tends to move the economy toward general equilibrium. But unless pure competition exists in both product and resource markets, Pareto optimality will not follow.

The Conditions of Optimum Welfare

Maximum welfare conditions in an economy are usually grouped into three sets. The first consists of the set of conditions leading to maximum consumer welfare when supplies of goods and services are fixed. The second consists of the conditions of maximum efficiency in production, assuming that resource supplies are fixed. In the third the conditions of consumer welfare and maximum productive efficiency are brought together to determine conditions under which the outputs of different goods and services are optimal.

Maximum Consumer Welfare: Fixed Supplies

The conditions of maximum consumer welfare with fixed supplies of goods and services per time unit are illustrated in the two-good, two-person model of Figure 18-1. If the distribution of goods X and Y between the two consumers H and J is initially off the contract curve at some such point as D, exchanges can be made that will increase the welfare of either without decreasing the welfare of the other. A movement from distribution

---

[2]For an excellent survey and analysis of this approach *see* Robert Dorfman, "The Nature and Significance of Input-Output," *Review of Economics and Statistics*, XXXVI (May 1954), pp. 121–133.

Figure 18–1   Optimum Consumer Welfare: Fixed Supplies

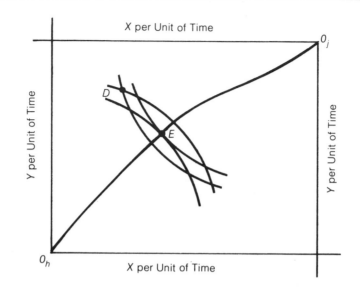

D to distribution E increases the welfare of both. Once a contract curve distribution is achieved, any further exchanges will benefit only one consumer at the expense of the other. Any point on the contract curve represents a Pareto optimal distribution of X and Y between the two consumers. Each such point is defined by the condition that:

$$MRS_{xy}{}^h = MRS_{xy}{}^j \qquad\qquad [18.1]$$

The condition can be extended to as many goods and services and as many consumers as there are in the economy.

Sometimes there are *externalities* involved in the consumption of a good or service. An externality occurs if the consumption of a good by someone else affects the level of satisfaction attained by any given consumer. Suppose, for example, that H and J are neighbors; that H increases his stereo capacity; and that J, whose musical tastes parallel those of H, can now hear and enjoy the music played by H. J receives an external benefit from H's consumption—his set of indifference curves between music and other goods and services is shifted inward toward the origin of his indifference map. On the other hand, the externality could have operated in the opposite direction. The music played by H could have annoyed J, shifting his set of

Figure 18-2   *Externalities in Consumption*

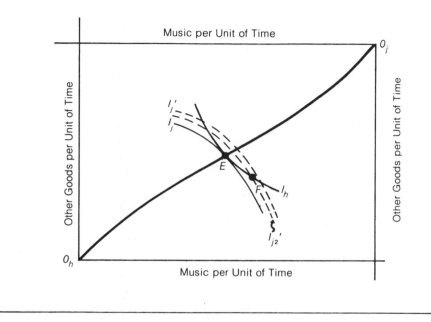

indifference curves between music and other goods and services outward from the origin of his indifference map.[3]

When an externality in consumption occurs, we can no longer be sure that a point on the contract curve such as *E* in Figure 18-2 is Pareto optimal. Suppose that *J*'s satisfaction is enhanced by *H*'s increased purchase of music via an expansion of stereo capacity. An exchange of other goods and services for music that moves the consumers from distribution *E* to distribution *F* would not change *H*'s level of satisfaction. Suppose the external benefits that *J* receives from *H*'s increased consumption of music, shift *J*'s indifference curves toward origin 0_j so that the satisfaction level formerly represented by I_j is now represented by I_j'. At point *F*, *J* will be at a higher level of satisfaction, represented by I_{j2}', than before; and, since *H*'s satisfaction has not been lessened, the welfare of the two consumers combined is greater than it was at point *E*.

---

[3]The preference function of *J* takes the form of:

$$U_j = f(x_j, y_j, x_h)$$

in which x_j and y_j represent *J*'s consumption of two goods, *X* and *Y*, and x_h represents *H*'s consumption of *X*.

Figure 18–3   Optimum Productive Efficiency

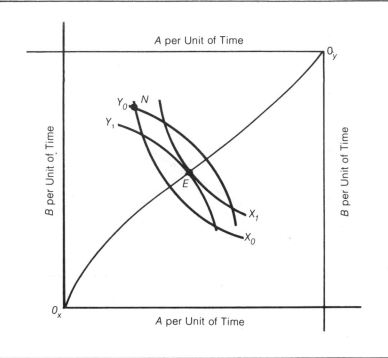

Maximum Efficiency in Production: Given Resource Supplies

The Conditions of Efficiency: No Externalities   Maximum efficiency in production refers to Pareto optimality in production processes. Given the supplies of resources available, these must be allocated among the production of goods and services in such a way that the production of any one good cannot be increased unless the production of another is decreased.

The conditions of efficiency are illustrated in the two-resource, two-product model of Figure 18-3. Fixed supplies of resources A and B are used in the production of products X and Y. Any distribution of resources between the two products that lies on the contract curve, such as that at E, is more efficient than is any distribution not on the contract curve, such as that at N. Given any initial distribution such as N, the output of either product can be increased with no sacrifice of the other. It is also possible to increase the outputs of both products by allocating more A and less B to the output of X, and less A and more B to the output of Y, and thus moving from N to E. Given any distribution such as E, the output of neither product

Figure 18–4   A Transformation Curve

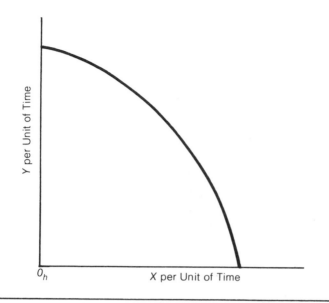

can be increased unless some of the other is sacrificed. Any point on the contract curve represents a maximum efficiency allocation of resources. The condition that determines any such point is that:

$$MRTS_{ab}^{\ x} = MRTS_{ab}^{\ y}. \tag{18.2}$$

These conditions can be expanded to include as many resources and as many goods and services as exist in the economy.

The infinite number of efficiently produced combinations of X and Y shown by the contract curve of Figure 18-3 are also shown by the transformation curve of Figure 18-4. For every combination of X and Y on the transformation curve, resources are allocated to each product in the optimal combinations. The transformation curve is often appropriately called the production possibilities curve. Its slope at any point measures the rate at which one product must be given up to obtain an additional unit of the other; that is, the MRT_{xy}.

The Effects of Externalities   If externalities occur in the production of a product the contract curve may no longer show the conditions of maximum efficiency. Congested facilities represent a very common type of externality. Suppose, for example, that highway facilities, along with other

Figure 18–5   Externalities in Production

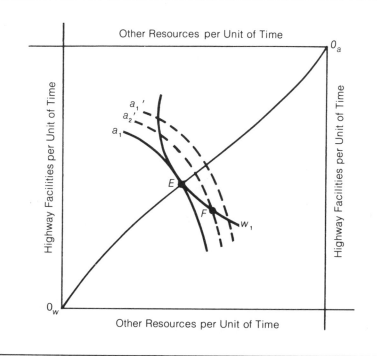

resources, are used by the producers of wheat and also by the producers of automobiles for getting their products to consumers. Initially, these two groups of users cause the highways to be congested to the extent that transportation delays result. In Figure 18-5 the marginal rate of technical substitution between highway facilities and other resources is the same for producers of wheat and producers of automobiles at point E. But this allocation of resources is not necessarily optimal. If highway congestion exists at E, a reduction in the use of the highways by firms in one industry will increase the productivity of highway facilities for those in the other.

Suppose wheat producers reduce their use of the highways but maintain their output level at w_1 by increasing their use of alternative forms of noncongested transport, thus moving from point E to point F. This move shifts the set of isoquants of automobile producers toward the 0_a origin and a_1 units of automobiles is now shown by the dashed line a_1'. At point F automobile production will be at a_2', a higher level than before. At the same time there will have been no change in total wheat production. The efficiency of production has been increased by the resource exchange.

Figure 18-6   *The Full Conditions of Maximum Welfare*

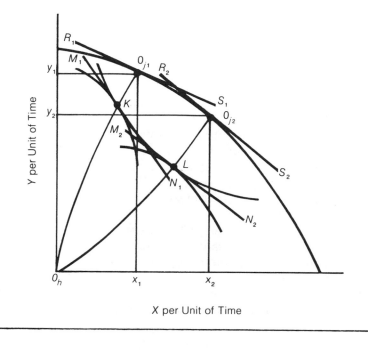

X per Unit of Time

Optimal Outputs of Goods and Services

We have not yet determined which of the combinations of products represented by a transformation curve yield optimal welfare to consumers. Assuming that there are no externalities of production, the transformation
curve of Figure 18-6 shows the combinations of X and Y that resources A
and B can produce when those resources are used efficiently; that is,
when $MRTS_{ab}{}^{x} = MRTS_{ab}{}^{y}$ for each combination. The slope of the transformation curve at any point, the MRT_{xy}, shows the rate at which it is possible
technically to transform Y into X at that combination of goods.

For any combination of X and Y on the transformation curve an Edgeworth box for consumers can be constructed to show the optimal distributions of supplies making up the combination. For the combination at O_{j1} in
Figure 18-6 the Edgeworth box $O_h y_1 O_{j1} x_1$ is the appropriate one for a two-
consumer, two-good model. For the combination at O_{j2} the appropriate
box is $O_h y_2 O_{j2} x_2$. Note that since the origin O_h for consumer H remains in a
fixed position, his indifference curves, drawn with respect to the X and Y

axes of the transformation diagram, are the same for all possible boxes. The origin of the indifference map for consumer J, however, is different for each different combination of X and Y shown on the transformation curve and for each different box. Consequently, his set of indifference curves must be redrawn for each different box.

If the combination of X and Y being produced were 0_{j1}, would this be the optimal output of each product? Since it lies on the transformation curve the outputs are being produced with maximum efficiency. Moreover any distribution (such as K) of the output combination between consumers H and J that lies on the contract curve $0_h 0_{j1}$ is a welfare-maximizing distribution of the specific combination. Still, combination 0_{j1} of product outputs, together with distribution K of the products between consumers, does not result in maximum welfare. The slope of line $M_1 N_1$ through point K and tangent to the indifference curves of H and J measures the MRS_{xy} for both consumers at point K. It indicates the rate at which *both* consumers would be willing to give up Y for X. The slope of $R_1 S_1$ through point 0_{j1}, tangent to the transformation curve, measures the MRT_{xy} — the rate at which it is technically necessary to give up Y to produce more X. Since $MRS_{xy} > MRT_{xy}$ (that is, consumers are willing to give up more Y to obtain an additional unit of X than is necessary in the production processes), the welfare of both consumers can be increased by increasing the output of X and decreasing the output of Y.

The conditions for optimum welfare in terms of the output levels of X and Y and the distribution of that output between consumers H and J are that:

$$MRS_{xy} = MRT_{xy}.$$ [18.3]

Consider combination 0_{j2} and distribution L. The lines $M_2 N_2$ and $R_2 S_2$ are parallel, indicating that $MRS_{xy} = MRT_{xy}$; therefore, this is an optimum welfare output combination and distribution. A small movement away from L or away from 0_{j2} will decrease the welfare of at least one of the consumers.

The optimum welfare combination of outputs and distribution of product among consumers is not a unique one, however. There may be an infinite number of output combination-product distribution possibilities at which the $MRS_{xy} = MRT_{xy}$. For output combination 0_{j1}, even though at distribution K the $MRS_{xy} \neq MRT_{xy}$, there may be other distributions on contract curve $0_h 0_{j1}$ at which the $MRS_{xy} = MRT_{xy}$, although it is not certain that there are. The same thing can be said for other output combinations represented by the transformation curve.

Summary of Optimum Welfare Conditions   In summary, then, for Pareto optimality to exist in an economic system three conditions must be met:

(1) the distribution of product outputs must be such that the marginal rate of substitution of any one product for any other product is the same for all consumers; (2) the allocation of resources must be such that the marginal rate of technical substitution of any one resource for any other resource is the same in the production of all products for which those resources can be used; and (3) the outputs of product and their distribution among consumers must be such that the marginal rate of substitution of any one product for any other product is equal to the marginal rate of transformation of the products.

The conditions of Pareto optimality leave us uninformed about which of the optimal distributions of product among consumers is the "optimum" optimum and about which of the optimal combinations of product output is the "optimum" optimum. We can eliminate those distributions of any output combination at which marginal rates of substitution are not equal to the corresponding marginal rates of transformation. But after these deletions we may still have a great many alternative possibilities.

Private Enterprise and General Equilibrium

Will a private enterprise economic system guided and directed by the price mechanism move toward optimum welfare positions as it moves toward general equilibrium positions? The optimum welfare conditions of the preceding subsection apply to any kind of economic system—socialist, private enterprise, or other. To evaluate the performance of a private enterprise system, then, it is necessary to examine the conditions of the equilibrium toward which it moves, in order to determine whether these coincide with the conditions of optimum welfare or at least approach those conditions. Toward this end we draw on, summarize, and extend the principles developed throughout the book.

Consumer Equilibrium: Fixed Supplies

Consider first the problem of consumers' choice. Assume that the supplies of goods and services are fixed—they automatically come into being on the first of each month. The distribution among consumers may be any distribution, but it will not vary from month to month. Consumer preference patterns are fixed. A monetary system exists. The price pattern is initially random. Each good or service is in the hands of many individuals, with the result that pure competition will exist in the event that exchange occurs. What happens at this point if individuals are free to buy and sell, that is, to exchange? Each consumer will seek to maximize satisfaction.

If for two goods, X and Y, priced initially at p_x and p_y, the consumer finds that $MRS_{xy} \neq p_x/p_y$, he will want to engage in exchange. Any consumer for whom $MRS_{xy} > p_x/p_y$ will want to sell Y and buy X, in order to move to higher indifference curves. Any consumer for whom $MRS_{xy} < p_x/p_y$ will want to sell X and purchase Y in order to move to higher indifference curves.

At the initial price pattern the supplies of some items are likely to be exhausted before all consumers get as much as they desire. The prices of these items will rise, reducing the quantities that consumers want relative to the quantities of other goods. Prices will move to those levels at which consumers are just willing to ration themselves to the entire quantities available per month.

The supplies of other goods may be overabundant at their initial price levels. In order to reduce the quantities they have on hand those who hold surpluses will reduce the asking prices. Prices will fall to the levels at which consumers are just willing to take the entire quantities available per month.

General equilibrium exists when goods and services are so priced that each consumer gets the quantity of each of them that he desires relative to the quantities of others, and when there is neither a shortage nor a surplus of any item. For each consumer the MRS_{xy} of any one good, X, for any other good, Y, is equal to p_x/p_y. It follows that the MRS_{xy} for any one consumer is equal to the MRS_{xy} for any other consumer, since the price ratios faced by all consumers are the same. Since the MRS_{xy} is the same for all consumers, all consumers are on the contract curve. Thus, under conditions of pure competition and in the absence of externalities, the conditions of general equilibrium with fixed supplies coincide with the conditions of optimum welfare with fixed supplies.

Producer Equilibrium: Given Resource Supplies

We turn now to the operation of the price mechanism in organizing production. To facilitate the discussion several assumptions are useful. We shall assume that resource supplies are fixed quantities per month and that their initial prices are random. The range of production techniques is given. First we shall view the organization of production in terms of the purely competitive model. Then we shall modify the analysis to take monopoly and monopsony into account.

Pure Competition   Suppose that the fixed supplies that consumers receive are being produced by firms operating in purely competitive industries, and that these firms seek to maximize their profits. Confronted with the initial resource prices, each firm attempts to acquire those quantities of different resources at which the marginal revenue product of each resource is equal to its marginal resource cost.

At the initial set of resource prices firms will find that they are not able to obtain enough of some resources to bring their marginal revenue products into line with their respective marginal resource costs; that is, short-ages occur. The prices of these resources will rise, inducing firms to at-tempt to substitute other resources for them. Prices will reach equilibrium levels when each firm is just able to obtain the quantities that it desires.

Some other resources will not be fully employed when, at the initial prices, every firm takes the quantities at which their marginal revenue products equal their marginal resource costs. Surpluses of these re-sources will cause those who own them to cut the prices at which they are offered in order to induce firms to substitute them for now relatively more expensive resources. The prices will be in equilibrium when firms are just willing to absorb the entire quantities placed on the market.

General equilibrium exists when each resource is priced so that neither a surplus nor a shortage exists, and when each firm is taking that quantity of each resource at which its marginal revenue product is equal to its marginal resource cost. These conditions, together with pure competition in both resource and product markets, lead to important additional conse-quences, as described below.

Since pure competition exists, the value of marginal product of each resource will be equal to the resource price. For any given resource, A, $MRP_a = MRC_a$ means also that $VMP_a = p_a$, because for any product, X, that A assists in producing $MR_x = p_x$; and for any firm purchasing A, $MRC_a = p_a$.

When firms using several common resources to produce several products employ resources in profit-maximizing quantities, they will also be employing them efficiently from a Pareto optimal point of view. Suppose two resources, A and B, are employed by firms producing X and Y. Any firm in industry X employs those quantities of the resources at which:

$$MPP_{ax} \times p_x = p_a$$

and:

$$MPP_{bx} \times p_x = p_b.$$

Thus:

$$\frac{MPP_{ax}}{p_a} = \frac{1}{p_x} \text{ and } \frac{MPP_{bx}}{p_b} = \frac{1}{p_x}.$$

Therefore:

[18.4]

$$\frac{MPP_{ax}}{p_a} = \frac{MPP_{bx}}{p_b} \text{ and } \frac{MPP_{ax}}{MPP_{bx}} = \frac{p_a}{p_b}$$

or:

$$MRTS_{ab}^{x} = \frac{p_a}{p_b}.$$

Similarly, we can show that:

$$MRTS_{ab}{}^y = \frac{p_a}{p_b}.$$

Therefore:

$$MRTS_{ab}{}^x = MRTS_{ab}{}^y,$$

which is the condition for a Pareto efficient allocation of any two resources between any two products.

Monopoly and Monopsony   Monopoly in the sale of products will not deter the price system from allocating resources among different products so that they are used efficiently in the production of each product, but some degree of monopsony will act as a deterrent. If monopoly exists in the sale of products X and Y, but the firms in both industries purchase resources A and B competitively, we can show that when A and B are purchased in each industry in a manner such that the marginal revenue products of the resources equal their respective resource prices, then:

$$MRTS_{ab}{}^x = MRTS_{ab}{}^y \qquad\qquad [18.5]$$

However, if some degree of monopsony exists in the purchase of A and B then:

$$MPP_{ax} \times MR_x = MRC_{ax}$$

and: $\qquad\qquad\qquad\qquad\qquad\qquad\qquad\qquad\qquad\qquad\qquad [18.6]$

$$MPP_{bx} \times MR_x = MRC_{bx}.$$

Therefore:

$$\frac{MPP_{ax}}{MRC_{ax}} = \frac{MPP_{bx}}{MRC_{bx}} \text{ and } \frac{MPP_{ax}}{MPP_{bx}} = \frac{MRC_{ax}}{MRC_{bx}}$$

or:

$$MRTS_{ab}{}^x = \frac{MRC_{ax}}{MRC_{bx}}.$$

We can show similarly that:

$$MRTS_{ab}{}^y = \frac{MRC_{ay}}{MRC_{by}}. \qquad [18.7]$$

The firm producing X must pay the same price for resource A as the firm producing Y.[4] But if the elasticity of the supply of A to the firm producing X differs from the elasticity of supply of A to the firm producing Y, at whatever the supply price of A to both firms may be, then:

$$MRC_{ax} \neq MRC_{ay}. \qquad [18.8]$$

Similarly, under the same set of circumstances:

$$MRC_{bx} \neq MRC_{by}.$$

Consequently:

$$MRTS_{ab}{}^x \neq MRTS_{ab}{}^y,$$

and the price system will not bring about optimum efficiency in the use of the resources in the two industries.

Product Output Levels: Given Resource Supplies

In this subsection we shall continue to trace the implications of the general equilibrium results brought about by the price mechanism. Equilibrium exists when: (1) price levels of goods and services are such that there are no shortages and no surpluses; (2) price levels of resources are such that there are no shortages and no surpluses; (3) firms purchase those quantities of different resources at which their marginal revenue products equal their respective marginal resource costs. Again we shall consider purely competitive markets first, and then turn to the effects of monopoly and monopsony.

Pure Competition   Under conditions of pure competition in both product and resource markets, and in the absence of externalities, the allocation of resources and the output levels of product determined by the price system

---

[4]Rather than assume pure monopsony, in which resource A would be specialized to one firm only, we assume a degree of monopsony in which units of the resource are mobile among a few firms, any one of which buys a sufficient proportion of the total available supply to have an effect on the resource price.

will maximize welfare. We will show that the price system brings about an output combination for any two products X and Y at which:

$$MRT_{xy} = MRS_{xy}. \qquad [18.9]$$

Consider first the allocation of resources between any two products, X and Y. When firms of industry X are using two resources, A and B, and are maximizing profits, then for each firm:

$$\frac{MPP_{ax}}{P_a} = \frac{MPP_{bx}}{P_b} = \frac{1}{MC_x} = \frac{1}{P_x}, \qquad [18.10]$$

or:

$$MC_x = P_x.$$

Similarly, for firms in industry Y:

$$\frac{MPP_{ay}}{P_a} = \frac{MPP_{by}}{P_b} = \frac{1}{MC_y} = \frac{1}{P_y}, \qquad [18.11]$$

or:

$$MC_y = P_y.$$

The MRT_{xy}, at whatever combination of X and Y is being produced, is the measure of the amount of Y that must be given up by the economic system to produce an additional unit of X; MRT_{xy} can be expressed as $\Delta y / \Delta x$.

Since resources are used efficiently in the production of both X and Y, the cost of giving up Δy of Y must equal the cost of adding Δx of X to the economy's output;[5] that is:

$$\Delta y \times MC_y = \Delta x \times MC_x$$

and: [18.12]

$$\frac{\Delta y}{\Delta x} = \frac{MC_x}{MC_y}.$$

---

[5]This relationship must obtain since the identical quantities of resources released in giving up Δy of Y are used to produce Δx of X.

Since the price system leads to a product output combination at which:

$$MC_x = p_x \text{ and } MC_y = p_y,$$

then: [18.13)

$$MRT_{xy} = \frac{\Delta y}{\Delta x} = \frac{MC_x}{MC_y} = \frac{p_x}{p_y}.$$

We can now put the pieces together. The price system induces consumers to establish a price ratio for the supplies of any two goods, X and Y, such that for each consumer;

$$MRS_{xy} = \frac{p_x}{p_y}.$$ [18.14]

These prices in turn bring about an allocation of resources between the two goods such that:

$$MC_x = p_x$$ (18.15)

and:

$$MC_y = p_y$$

or:

$$\frac{MC_x}{MC_y} = \frac{p_x}{p_y}.$$

The ratio MC_x/MC_y in turn is the measure of the MRT_{xy}; thus, the price system leads to general equilibrium outputs of X and Y such that:

$$MRS_{xy} = MRT_{xy}.$$ [18.16]

This condition for general equilibrium is also the condition for a set of optimum outputs of X and Y.

An output combination on the transformation curve such that $MRS_{xy} \neq MRT_{xy}$ simply means that $MC_x \neq p_x$ and $MC_y \neq p_y$. For example, if $MRS_{xy} > MRT_{xy}$, as is the case at point K in Figure 18-6, it follows that $MC_x < p_x$ and $MC_y > p_y$. The price system will bring about an expansion in the output of X and a reduction in the output of Y. These changes will decrease MRS_{xy}, causing p_x to decrease and p_y to increase. At the same time they cause MRT_{xy} to increase, increasing MC_x and decreasing MC_y until $MC_x = p_x$, $MC_y = p_y$, and $MRS_{xy} = p_x/p_y = MC_x/MC_y = MRT_{xy}$.

Monopoly   Monopoly in the sale of a product will prevent the attainment of optimal outputs by way of the price mechanism. Suppose that product X is sold monopolistically and product Y is sold competitively. The price system will lead to a set of outputs such that for each consumer:

$$MRS_{xy} = \frac{p_x}{p_y}. \qquad [18.17]$$

But profit maximization will induce the monopolist to produce the output at which $MC_x = MR_x < p_x$. Purely competitive producers of Y produce outputs at which $MC_y = p_y$. Thus:

$$MRT_{xy} = \frac{MC_x}{MC_y} = \frac{MR_x}{p_y} < \frac{p_x}{p_y} = MRS_{xy}. \qquad [18.18]$$

The output level of X is too small and the output level of Y is too large for optimum welfare.

Summary

In this chapter we summarized the conditions that must be met in an economic system in order to achieve maximum welfare in the sense of a Pareto optimum. Then we summarized the operation of the price mechanism in a private enterprise type of economic system, examining it to see if its results are Pareto optimal. The price system will lead to Pareto optimality if all markets are purely competitive and if no externalities occur in consumption or production. Where selling markets are monopolized, outputs will be short of the optimal quantities. Monopsony in resource purchases has a further adverse effect, in that it leads to inefficiency in the use of resources by the purchasers.

Suggested Readings

Bator, Francis M., "The Simple Analytics of Welfare Maximization," *American Economic Review* (March 1957), pp. 22–59. Reprinted in Breit, William, and Harold M. Hochman *Readings in Microeconomics*, 2nd ed. (New York: Holt, Rinehart and Winston, Inc., 1971), Chapter 32.
Baumol, William J., *Economic Theory and Operations Analysis*, 3rd ed. (Englewood Cliffs, N. J.: Prentice-Hall, Inc., 1972), Chap. 16.

Chapter 19:

Linear Programming

Linear programming is the simplest and most widely used of the mathematical programming techniques that have come into vogue since World War II. It is a technique for solving maximization and minimization problems confronting decision-making agencies subject to certain side conditions or constraints that limit what the agencies are able to do. Its development has been concurrent with and tremendously enhanced by the advent of electronic computers.

Linear programming techniques provide little information regarding the operation of the economy beyond that provided by the conventional theory of the firm. Their prime virtue is that they provide computational possibilities that are not present in conventional theory owing to the smooth, continuous and frequently nonlinear nature of conventional theory's production, cost, and revenue functions. The observable data confronting decision-making agencies are ordinarily not continuous and may not be amenable to marginal analysis or calculus techniques. From an assumption that relations among observable data are linear, straightforward solutions to complex maximization and minimization problems can be obtained through linear programming. Moreover, problems programmed for this sort of solution can make extensive use of electronic computers that are not yet able to perform the operations of the infinitesimal calculus. Sometimes the distortions resulting from the exclusive use of linear relationships may render worthless the solutions arrived at by means of the technique, but in many cases distortions of this kind may be more or less negligible. Like any other technique, if its results are to be useful it must be applied with good judgment and common sense.

This chapter presents the nature and method of linear programming. First, we will establish the assumptions on which linear programming problems rest. Next we will formulate and solve graphically a general maximization problem involving one and two inputs. Third, we will formulate and solve a maximization problem involving multiple outputs and inputs. Finally we will consider the dual solution to a maximization problem.

The Assumptions

The linear programming technique rests on several basic assumptions. In the first place the decision making to which it is applied always involves constraints on the decision-making agency. In the second place input and output prices are assumed to be constant. In the third place the firm's[1] input-output, output-output, and input-input relations are presumed to be linear. These will be discussed in turn.

The Constraints

In linear programming problems the firm is viewed as facing various limitations on its activities. There may be quantity limitations on particular kinds of inputs or facilities used by the firm. An automobile final assembly line, for example, can turn out some maximum number of automobiles per twenty-four-hour period. A firm's warehouse space contains a fixed number of square feet. A candy factory can wrap only so many bars per day. The firm's access to credit may be restricted. And so on.

The firm is viewed also as facing a limited number of alternative production processes. Any one process is defined in terms of a constant ratio of inputs. Suppose process A involves the use of one man of a given skill and one machine of a given kind and size. Production carried on with process A can be increased or decreased until input quantity limitations are reached, but always will involve one man per machine regardless of the total number of machines used.

Constant Prices

Linear programming techniques make use of the purely competitive approach to prices. Output prices and input prices are assumed to be unaf-

---

[1] As a matter of convenience the decision-making agency will be designated as a firm throughout the chapter. Linear programming techniques can be and are used by agencies other than firms, for example, military procurement units.

fected by the actions of any one individual firm. Output prices are the same whether the firm's output is large or small. Input prices are the same regardless of how much or how little of the inputs the firm uses. As sellers and buyers firms are thought of as being price takers rather than price makers.

Linear Relations

Linear programming techniques take advantage of the simplicity of linear relations. In many instances linear relations are found in fact. A firm purchasing an input at a constant price per unit faces a linear total resource cost curve for that input. The total revenue curve from the sale of a product will be linear when the product sells at a constant price per unit. An iso-cost curve for two inputs will be linear, given the prices of the inputs. An isorevenue curve for two outputs will be linear, given the prices of those outputs.

In other cases relations among variables that may not actually be linear can be represented usefully by a series of (different) discrete linear relationships or by a single linear relationship. An isoquant, for example, is ordinarily a nonlinear constant product curve for two resources. The linear programming counterpart is a series of connected linear relations. Similarly, actual production functions may very well show nonlinear relations between inputs and output. In linear programming problems they are taken as being homogeneous of degree one.

Maximization Problems

Two maximization problems will be considered in this section. In the first we shall be concerned with the optimum use of inputs in the production of a single output. In the second we shall be concerned with the optimum output mix to be produced with particular inputs.

One Output, Two Inputs

Cost Outlay Constraints   Suppose that a firm producing one output X and using inputs A and B seeks to maximize output subject to a given cost outlay. This problem is familiar from our previous study of the theory of production and serves as a good introduction to linear programming. However, suppose that the possibilities of continuous substitution between A and B that characterize the usual theoretical presentation of the problem are absent. Instead, suppose that there are only four processes—

possible ratios of B to A—by which the firm can produce the product. The firm faces constant input prices and a constant output price.[2]

The nature of a process is illustrated in Figure 19-1. Units of input A per unit of time are measured along the horizontal axis and units of input B per unit of time are shown on the vertical axis. If process C—one of the four processes available to the firm—requires three units of input B to every one unit of input A, the process can be represented by the linear ray 0C. Ignore for the moment the scale numbers along 0C. The various points making up the ray 0C show the fixed ratio of B to A, but at different levels of utilization. Similarly process rays 0D, 0E, and 0F can be drawn for the other three processes available to the firm. Each process ray shows a given ratio of B to A throughout its length. The ratio of B to A is different for each of the process rays.

The assumption that the production function is homogeneous of degree one enables us to measure product output along each of the process rays. A production function is of this type if, when *all* inputs are increased in a given proportion, output is increased in the same proportion. Focusing for the moment on process ray 0C, suppose that 3 units of B used with 1 unit of A will produce 10 units of output X. The point on 0C representing this combination of A and B can be marked off as 10 units of X. Now if the inputs are doubled to 6 units of B and to 2 units of A, output is doubled to 20 units of X. The point on 0C representing the new combination of A and B can be scaled as 20 units of X and will lie twice as far from the origin as the point representing 10 units of X does. The output scale along 0C is thus easily established.

Output scales can be established in a similar way along each of the other three process rays. However, the distance measuring 20 units of output (or any other given quantity of output) will not ordinarily be the same along one process ray as it will be along another. The technological efficiency of the other three processes are assumed to be such that the 20-unit output marks on their respective process rays are those indicated in Figure 19-1.

The points on the various process rays representing any given quantity of output can be joined by a series of straight lines, as they are at the 20-unit level in Figure 19-1. The resulting kinked curve can be called an isoquant, just as was its counterpart in traditional theory. A different isoquant can be drawn for each possible output level. The higher the output level, the farther from the origin the isoquant lies. The linear segment of an isoquant between any two process rays will always be parallel to the corre-

---

[2]The problem would not be changed if total revenue were stated as the quantity maximized. Since price per unit of output is given, maximization of output also maximizes total revenue.

Figure 19–1   Process Rays and Isoquants

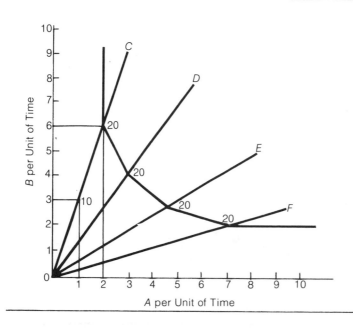

A per Unit of Time

sponding linear segment of any other isoquant. For example, in Figure 19-2 the G_1H_1 segment of isoquant x_1 is parallel to the G_0H_0 segment of isoquant x_0.[3]

Any point such as K on isoquant x_1 represents the simultaneous use by the firm of two processes to produce a given amount of output. In this case the firm would be using process C and D. The processes are assumed to be technologically independent of one another. The productivity of process C is unaffected by the level at which process D is used and vice-versa. Quantity $0G_0$ of X is produced by means of process C. Quantity G_0K ($= H_0H_1$) of X is produced using process D. The output scale measuring G_0K (or H_0H_1) of X is different from that measuring $0G_0$ of X. The scale of process ray $0D$ is used for the former while the scale of process ray $0C$ is used for the latter.

In general we would expect isoquants to exhibit the shapes illustrated in Figures 19-1 and 19-2. In Figure 19-2 supppose that B is capital and A is labor. Continuous substitution of one for the other is assumed to be impossible. Nevertheless, the same general type of reasoning as that

---

[3]This must be so because the sides $0G_1$ and $0H_1$ of triangle G_1H_10 are cut into proportional segments by line G_0H_0; that is, $0G_0/G_0G_1 = 0H_0/H_0H_1$.

Figure 19–2   Simultaneous Use of Two Processes

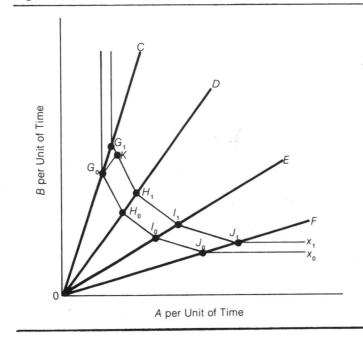

used in discussing conventional isoquant shapes still applies. If the firm were using process *F* to produce a given amount of product, the ratio of labor to capital would be relatively high. Therefore, if the firm were to consider a process using smaller ratios of labor to capital, say, process *E*, it is likely that it could give up a rather large amount of labor to obtain the additional capital—the amount of output remaining constant. But as the firm moves to processes using relatively smaller ratios of labor to capital, say, processes *D* and *C*, the amounts of labor that could be given up to obtain additional units of capital, output remaining constant, would be expected to become smaller and smaller.

The cost constraint on the firm is represented by a conventional isocost curve. Its position and shape are determined by the fixed cost outlay and the fixed prices per unit of the firm's inputs. In Figure 19-3 suppose the cost outlay is T_1 while the prices of A and B are p_{a1} and p_{b1}, respectively. The cost outlay divided by the price of A, or T_1/p_{a1} establishes point S_1, which is the number of units of A that can be obtained if no B is purchased. Similarly, T_1/p_{b1} is the number of units of B that can be purchased if no A is taken; it is represented by point R_1. A straight line joining R_1 and S_1 is the isocost curve showing the combinations of A and B available with the cost

figure 19–3   Output Maximization, Total Cost Constraint

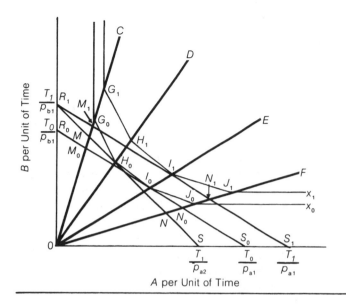

outlay T_1. The isocost curve has a negative slope equal to $0R_1/0S_1 = T_1/P_{b1} \div T_1/P_{a1} = T_1/P_{b1} \times P_{ai}/T_1 = P_{a1}/P_{b1}$[4]

The isocost curve and process rays $0C$ and $0F$ place limits on what the firm is able to do. Any point on or within the triangle $0M_1N_1$ is a possible combination of inputs A and B and will lie on some isoquant of the firm; that is, it will produce some specific level of output. The area bounded by $0M_1N_1$ is called the area of *feasible solutions* to the firm's problem. No production possibilities outside this area are open to the firm.

From the feasible solutions to the firm's problem the *optimal solution* must be found. This has already been postulated as the one that maximizes the firm's output subject to the cost outlay constraint. The optimal solution will occur at point I_1, at which the isocost curve touches the highest possible isoquant. Output x_1 is the highest output possible with the given cost outlay. The firm will use process E. Cost level T_1 expended on any of the other processes will not produce outputs as high as x_1.

---

[4]The equation of the isocost curve will be:
$$ap_{a1} + bp_{b1} = T_1$$
or:
$$b = \frac{T_1}{P_{b1}} - a\frac{P_{a1}}{P_{b1}}$$
for which T_1/P_{b1} is the B axis intercept and P_{a1}/P_{b1} is the slope.

A change in the cost constraint, with the prices of A and B remaining constant, will not affect the process used, but will affect only the level at which it is used. Changes in T will shift the position of the isocost curve but will not affect its slope. A reduction in the cost outlay to T_0 shifts the isocost curve to the left parallel to itself to $R_0 S_0$. The area of feasible solutions is now bounded by $0 M_0 N_0$. The firm maximizes output by using process E at level I_0. The maximum output is x_0. Isocosts parallel to $R_1 S_1$ will always touch those isoquant corners falling along process ray $0E$. This will be so because, due to the assumption that the production function is homogeneous of degree one, the corresponding segments of the various isoquants are parallel to each other.

If the price of A relative to the price of B were to increase enough, the firm would shift to a different process. Suppose the total cost outlay were to remain the same and the price of A were to rise to p_{a_2}. The restricting isocost curve now becomes $R_1 S$ and the area $0MN$ encloses the feasible solutions. To maximize output subject to the constraint, the firm would use process D at level H_0. It is possible, too, that the price of A relative to that of B could change just enough to make the isocost curve coincide with a linear segment of an isoquant, say, a segment corresponding to $G_1 H_1$. If this were the case process C and process D would be equally efficient. It would make no difference which the firm uses. Or any combination of the two processes shown by the linear isoquant segment $G_1 H_1$ could be used.

Where the firm is faced by a single constraint, not more than one process is required to maximize whatever the firm is maximizing. In the case at hand the process to be used will be determined by the ratio of input prices. Once the output-maximizing process has been identified, it becomes apparent that a considerable change in input price ratios may occur without inducing the firm to switch from one process to another. The extent to which input price ratios must change to induce a change in the process used will depend on the number of processes available and the measures of the angles formed by linear segments of the isoquants.

Input Quantity Constraints   The optimal solution to the problem of output maximization is different if, instead of being faced with a total cost outlay constraint, the firm is faced with quantity limitations per time period on one or more of its inputs. Common examples of this sort of thing are warehouse space, number of machines available, size of a drying kiln, and so on. We shall look first at a situation in which only one of two inputs is limited in quantity. Then we shall extend the constraint to include both of the inputs that the firm uses.

In Figure 19-4 we assume first that not more than b_0 of B is available to the firm and that A is available in unlimited quantities. The area of feasible solutions would be on or within triangle $0PJ_2$—the area on or between

Figure 19-4   Output Maximization, Input Quantity Constraints

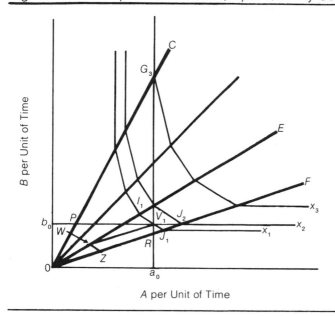

A per Unit of Time

process rays 0C and 0F and on or below the horizontal line extending to the right from b_0. There will be some isoquant the horizontal segment of which coincides with the horizontal line. This isoquant is designated x_2 in the diagram and represents the highest output level available with quantity b_0 of B. Process F used at level $0J_2$ will maximize the firm's output.

If A were limited to a_0 while B were unlimited in quantity, the area of feasible solutions would lie between process rays 0C and 0F and on or to the left of a vertical line extending upward from a_0. Output would be maximized by using process C at level $0G_3$ and would be x_3. In each of the two cases output maximization requires but a single process. In neither case is the ratio of input prices a determinant of the process to be used.

Turning now to the case in which both inputs are limited in quantity, assume in Figure 19-4 that the availability of input A is limited to a_0 while that of B is limited to b_0. Subject to these limitations, the area of feasible solutions is on or within the polygon $0PV_1R$. The solution lies at point V_1 and the maximum output of the firm is x_1. In the case illustrated, process E and process F will both be used. Quantity $0W$ will be produced using process E, and quantity $WV_1(= ZJ_1)$ will be produced using process F. Conceivably, if the available quantity of A were smaller and that of B were larger the solution to the problem would fall at an isoquant corner such as

I_1. If this were the case, process E only would be required. Again the ratio of the price of A to the price of B plays no part in determining the process or processes to be used.

The problems discussed illustrate a fundamental principle in linear programming techniques. No larger number of processes than the number of constraints placed on the firm will be required in whatever the firm is maximizing or minimizing. In the example in which total cost outlay was the only constraint, one process was required. In the example in which the constraint was the quantity of one input, no more than one process was required. When two inputs were limited in quantity, no more than two processes were required. Where there are more inputs limited in quantity, more processes may be required, but these will not exceed the number of inputs for which there are effective limitations.

Multiple Outputs, Multiple Inputs

Moving now to a more complex problem, suppose that the objective of a firm is to maximize the excess of its total receipts over its total variable costs; that is, its total economic rent as defined in Chapter 14[5], subject to limitations in the capacities of certain fixed facilities. Suppose the firm produces two kinds of output, X and Y. It has four kinds of facilities each of which is fixed in capacity. We shall designate these as facilities $M, N, R,$ and S. These could be such things as paint shop capacity, final assembly capacity, packaging capacity, and the like.

Rent yielded per unit of X and per unit of Y will depend on the prices received for each of the products and the average variable costs of each. We shall assume that given quantities of variable inputs are required per unit of X regardless of the amount of X produced; therefore the average variable cost of X will be constant. The same assumption will be made for product Y. Rent yielded per unit of product X produced is equal to its price minus its average variable cost and thus will be a constant amount. Rent yielded per unit of product Y is computed in the same way. These can be designated as r_x and r_y, respectively.

If r_x and r_y were $8 and $6, respectively, the following *objective equation* could be extablished showing what it is that the firm wants to maximize:

$$8x + 6y = W. \qquad\qquad [19.1]$$

---

[5]Maximization of rent also means that profit will be maximized, since profit is equal to rent minus total fixed costs. In the problem being formulated the firm's fixed costs will not be known. Thus, rent can be computed but profit cannot.

Figure 19–5   Multiple Outputs, Facility Constraints

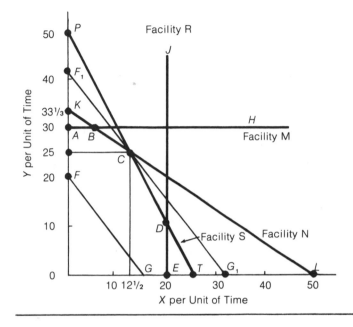

Rent yielded per unit of X multiplied by the total amount of X produced will be total rent received from the production of X. Rent yielded per unit of Y multiplied by the quantity of Y produced will show total rent obtained from the production of Y. The sum of the two will be W, or total rent received by the firm.

The objective equation is the equation for a family of *isorent curves* — one for every possible value of W. In Figure 19-5 the line FG is the isorent curve for W equals $120. It shows all combinations of X and Y which will yield that amount of rent. Its slope is r_x/r_y, or in this case, 8/6. Isorent curves for higher values of W lie farther to the right but have the same slope. Those for lower values of W also have the same slope, but lie farther to the left.

The constraints on the firm's activities are the fixed facilities M, N, R, and S. Suppose we designate the entire amount of each as unity. In Table 19-1 that part of each facility required in the production of one unit of X and that part of each required in the production of one unit of Y are shown.

Essentially, Table 19-1 defines the processes involved in the problem. There will be two processes used if both outputs are produced. The production of X requires one process — fixed proportions of facilities M, N, S,

Table 19-1   Multiple Outputs, Facility Constraints

Facility	Facility Input per Unit of Output	
	X	Y
M	0.0	0.033
N	0.02	0.03
S	0.04	0.02
R	0.05	0.0

and R. Similarly, the production of Y requires one process—fixed proportions of the four facilities, but proportions that are different from those required to produce X.

From Table 19-1 we can construct a set of algebraic representations of the constraints placed on the production of X and Y by the fixed facilities. These are:

$$0.033y \leq 1 \tag{19.2}$$

$$0.05x \leq 1 \tag{19.3}$$

$$0.02x + 0.03y \leq 1 \tag{19.4}$$

and:

$$0.04x + 0.02y \leq 1 \tag{19.5}$$

in which:

$$x \geq 0 \text{ and } y \geq 0$$

Inequality (19.2) sums up the constraint exercised by facility M. This facility is useful in the production of Y only. It is not useful in the production of X. The amount required in the production of one unit of Y is 0.033 of the entire facility. If we consider (19.2) as an equation, solving for y we find that the entire facility will permit the production of 30 units of Y per unit of time. It will also permit the production of smaller quantities. Graphically, the horizontal straight line AH in Figure 19-5 at 30 units of Y represents the limitations on production inherent in facility M.

Similarly, inequality (19.3) sums up the constraint exercised by facility R, which is used only in the production of X. An amount 0.05 of the entire facility is required for each unit. The maximum quantity of X that facility R will permit is 20 units per time period. This is shown graphically by the vertical line EJ at that output level in Figure 19-5.

The production possibilities of facility N are shown by inequality (19.4) and includes both outputs. Because 0.03 of facility N are required for a unit of *Y* and 0.02 of it are required for a unit of *X*, (19.4) treated as an equation marks off possible combinations of outputs that the facility will allow from those it will not allow. If *x* were zero, 33 1/3 units of *Y* could be handled by the facility. If *y* were zero, 50 units of *X* could be handled by it per time period. Locating these two points at *K* and *L*, respectively, the straight line joining them in Figure 19-5 is the graphic representation of the equation.

Similarly, (19.5) treated as an equation separates the combinations of *X* and *Y* that facility *S* will permit from those it will not permit. If no *X* were produced, *y* could be 50 units per time period. If no *Y* were produced, *x* could be 25 units. The graphic representation of the equation is the line *PT* in Figure 19-5.

The area of feasible solutions, showing all combinations of *X* and *Y* that can be turned out per unit of time by the firm, is *0ABCDE*. Facility *M* limits the firm to combinations equal to or smaller than those represented by *AH;* facilities *M* and *N* limit it to combinations equal to or smaller than those represented by *ABL;* facilities *M, N,* and *S,* further limit it to combinations equal to or smaller than those represented by *ABCT;* facilities *N, S,* and *R* limit it to combinations equal to or smaller than those represented by *BCD;* facilities *S* and *R* limit it to combinations equal to or smaller than those represented by *DE;* and facility *R* limits it to combinations equal to or smaller than those represented by *EJ.*

The optimal solution to the firm's problem can be found graphically by moving to higher and higher isorent curves until the one just touched by the area of feasible solutions is reached. This will be isorent curve F_1G_1, which is just touched by point *C* in Figure 19-5. No other point either within or on the boundary of the area of feasible solutions touches an isorent curve as high as F_1G_1. Every point other than *C* on the isorent curve F_1G_1 lies outside the area of feasible solutions. The firm would produce and sell 25 units of *Y* receiving rent of $6 per unit. It would produce and sell 12 1/2 units of *X* receiving rent of $8 per unit. Thus, the maximum total rent obtainable would be $250 per time period.

The facilities limitations are not all effective as constraints on the firm. At point *C* facility *M* is not used to capacity and therefore does not restrict the firm's output. Similarly, facility *R* is not used to capacity. To produce combination *C*, only facilities *N* and *S* are used to their full capacities. If more of these two facilities were available the firm could move to a higher isorent curve.

Algebraically the solution to the problem can be found by examining the "corners" of the area of feasible solutions. We need only to examine the corners since the number of processes involved in the problem will not exceed the number of effective constraints on the firm. Thus, the points at which both X and Y are positive (that is, where two processes are used) and that would be possible optimal solutions must lie at corners formed by two constraints (that is, where two constraints would be effective). A possible optimal solution in which only X is produced would require but one effective constraint and would be the corner at the intersection of the X axis and the constraint that exercises the greatest restriction when used exclusively in the production of X. Similarly, the corner on the Y axis represents the only possible optimal solution if Y alone were produced. If the optimal solution were a zero output for both X and Y, the necessity of a corner solution at the origin is obvious.

Suppose now that we start with the corner at the origin and proceed clockwise around the area of feasible solutions, attempting to find the one at which total rent to the fixed facilities is maximum; that is, at which the objective equation (19.1) yields the maximum W. At 0 we find that W equals zero. To find the coordinates of corner A we solve the facility M equation (19.2). At this corner x equals zero and y equals 30. Plugging these values for X and Y into equation (19.1) we find that W equals $180. The simultaneous solution of equations (19.2) and (19.4) for facilities M and N gives us corner B, at which y equals 30 and x equals 5. Thus, from equation (19.1), total rent is found to be $220. The simultaneous solution to equations (19.4) and (19.5) for facilities N and S is represented by corner C where y equals 25 and x equals 12½. Substituting these values in equation (19.1), total rent is $250. When equations (19.5) and (19.3) for facilities S and R are solved simultaneously for the coordinates of corner D, x equals 20 and y equals 10. Substituting these values in equation (19.1), total rent is $220. The solution to (19.3) provides the coordinates of corner E with x equal to 20 and y equal to zero. Substituting in (19.1) we find that total rent would be $160.

Comparing the results obtained at the various corners shows that corner C provides maximum total rent. In problems where the number of outputs and constraints are too great for graphic analysis this sort of algebraic examination of the "corners" of the area of feasible solutions can be used to find the one that provides the optimal solution.[6]

Different ratios of r_x to r_y may result in different optimal solutions to rent maximization. The slope of an isorent curve $(-r_x/r_y)$ could conceivably be small enough so that the area of feasible solutions touches the highest isorent curve at point B. Or it could be great enough for the highest possible isorent curve to be touched at point D. If $-r_x/r_y$ were equal to the slope of the line segment CD in Figure 19-5—that is, if the highest attaina-

---

[6]The method used here is called the complete description method. An alternative is provided by the simplex method. See Robert Dorfman, Paul A. Samuelson, and Robert M. Solow, *Linear Programming and Economic Analysis* (New York: McGraw-Hill, Inc., 1958), Chap. 4.

ble isorent curve were to coincide with the graphic representation of equation (19.5) — any combination of X and Y on line segment CD would be an optimal solution to maximization of total rent. In this case the limitations imposed by facility S would be the only effective constraint on the firm.

The Dual Problem

Every linear programming problem has a counterpart problem called its *dual*. The original problem is referred to as the *primal* problem. If the primal problem requires maximization, the dual problem is one of minimization; or if the primal is a minimization problem, the dual is a maximization problem. An illustration of the relationship between a primal problem and its dual is provided in the theory of production and costs. Suppose that the primal problem were that of maximizing output with a given cost outlay. The dual would be that of minimizing costs for the given product output. Whether or not a particular problem to be programmed should be set up for solution in its primal or its dual form depends on: (1) which formulation yields the desired information more directly and (2) which formulation can be more easily solved.

In this section the dual of the primal problem of the preceding section will be formulated and solved. In the primal problem we sought the outputs of X and Y that would maximize total rent received by the firm, subject to capacity limitations of its fixed facilities M, N, R, and S. In the dual problem we seek to impute minimum values — sometimes called shadow prices — to the firm's fixed facilities just sufficient to absorb the firm's total rent.

The data available to us are those of the primal problem. Table 19-1 shows the amount of each fixed facility available (one unit of each) and the portion of each fixed facility required in the production of a unit of X and a unit of Y. The contribution per unit of product X to total rent is given as \$8 while that unit of product Y is given as \$6. The objective equation of the dual problem can be stated as

$$v_m + v_n + v_r + v_s = V. \qquad [19.6]$$

The term v_m denotes the value to be imputed to facility M, while v_n, v_r, and v_s denote, respectively, the values to be imputed to facilities N, R, and S.[7]

---

[7]In the present problem the coefficient of each of the variables on the left side of the equation will be one, since the entire capacity of each fixed facility is taken as being unity. If each fixed facility were to consist of some certain number of units, then the value per unit of each facility would have as its coefficient the number of units of the facility which are available.

On the right side of the equation V denotes the total valuation of the fixed facilities.

The constraints placed on the assigning of minimum values to the fixed facilities are summed up in the following inequalitites:

$$0.0v_m + 0.02v_n + 0.04v_s + 0.05v_r \geq 8 \qquad [19.7]$$

and:

$$0.33v_m + 0.03v_n + 0.02v_s + 0.0v_r \geq 6 \qquad [19.8]$$

in which:

$$v_m \geq 0, v_n \geq 0, v_s \geq 0, \text{ and } v_r \geq 0.$$

Inequality (19.7) states that the values assigned to the various fixed facilities must be such that the values of productive capacity necessary for the production of one unit of X (see Table 19-1) when added together must not be less than the value of a unit of X. Inequality (19.8) states the same thing with respect to the production of Y. Together and treated as equations they state that the values assigned to each kind of productive capacity must be such a dollar's worth of that productive capacity used in producing either X or Y must yield a dollar in rent.

We face the dilemma of having more unknowns than there are equations [treating (19.7) and (19.8) as equations] to solve for the unknowns. However, the linear programming principle cited earlier, together with conventional economic analysis, can rescue us. The linear programming principle tells us that the number of fixed facilities operating as effective constraints on the firm's output should not exceed the number of processes used. There are two processes used — one for producing X and one for producing Y. Consequently, only two of the fixed facilities can be effective constraints on the firm's output and the other two must be underutilized.

Consider now an underutilized facility from the point of view of conventional economic analysis. A small increase — say, 1 percent — in such a facility would add nothing to the firm's output or total receipts. The marginal revenue product of such an increment would thus be zero, and so would its imputed value. Every other 1 percent of the facility would also have an imputed value of zero and so would the whole underutilized facility. Since we must have two underutilized facilities, two of the variables of (19.7) and (19.8) should have values of zero and the other two will take on positive values.

The problem now is to find which two of the variables—v_m, v_n, v_s, and v_r—have imputed values of zero and which two have positive values when the firm is minimizing total valuation of the fixed facilities. We can proceed by first assigning values of zero to any two of these, solving for the other two. Then we assign values of zero to another pair (one of the pair may be from the previous pair) and solve for the remaining pair. We proceed in this manner until every possible pair of the variables has been assigned zero values and the corresponding solutions in terms of the remaining variables have been obtained. Six solutions of this sort are possible. We shall examine them in turn.

Suppose first of all that we let v_m and v_n take on values of zero. Equations (19.7) and (19.8) become:

$$0.04v_s + 0.05v_r = 8 \qquad\qquad [19.7a]$$

and:

$$0.02v_s + 0.0v_r = 6. \qquad\qquad [19.8a]$$

Solving equation (19.8a) for v_s we find that v_s equals $300. Substituting this value of v_s in equation (19.7a) we find that v_r equals −$80. This is recorded as solution (1) in Table 19-2.

Second, suppose we let v_m and v_s take on values of zero. Equations (19.7) and (19.8) become:

$$0.02v_n + 0.05v_r = 8 \qquad\qquad [19.7b]$$

and

$$0.03v_n + 0.0v_r = 6. \qquad\qquad [19.8b]$$

Solving equation (19.8b) for v_n, we find that v_n is $200. Substituting in equation (19.7b), v_r is found to be $80. These values are recorded as solution (2) in Table 19-2.

Table 19-2   Imputation of Input Values

Solution	Imputed Value in Dollars				Total Valuation in Dollars
	v_m	v_n	v_s	v_r	
(1)	0	0	300	−80	. . .
(2)	0	200	0	80	280
(3)	0	100	150	0	250
(4)	181.82	0	0	160	341.82
(5)	66.66	0	200	0	266.66
(6)	−181.82	400	0	0	. . .

Third, let v_m and v_r assume zero values. Equations (19.7) and (19.8) become:

$$0.02v_n + 0.04v_s = 8 \qquad \text{[19.7c]}$$

and:

$$0.03v_n + 0.02v_s = 6. \qquad \text{[19.8c]}$$

Solving these simultaneously we obtain v_n equal to $100 and v_s equal to $150. These are recorded as solution (3) in Table 19-2.

Fourth, let v_n and v_s be zero. Equations (19.7) and (19.8) become:

$$0.05v_r = 8 \qquad \text{[19.7d]}$$

and:

$$0.033v_m = 6. \qquad \text{[19.8d]}$$

The solutions will be: v_r equals $160 and v_m equals $181.82. These are shown as solution (4) in Table 19-2.

Fifth, if v_n and v_r were zero, equations (19.7) and (19.8) would become:

$$0.0v_m + 0.04v_s = 8 \qquad \text{[19.7e]}$$

and:

$$0.033v_m + 0.02v_s = 6. \qquad \text{[19.8e]}$$

Solving equation (19.7e) for v_s yields a value of $200. Plugging this value for v_s into equation (19.83), v_m becomes $66.66. These are listed as solution (5) in Table 19-2.

Finally, when we let v_s and v_r take on values of zero, we will have exhausted the possibilities. In this case equations (19.7) and (19.8) become:

$$0.0v_m + 0.02v_n = 8 \qquad \text{[19.7f]}$$

and:

$$0.033v_m + 0.03v_n = 6. \qquad \text{[19.8f]}$$

In equation (19.7f), v_n is equal to $400. Substituting this value for v_n in equation (19.8f), we find that v_m is $-$181.82. These are shown as solution (6) in Table 19-2.

All six possible combinations of minimum values that may be assigned to the four facilities are shown in Table 19-2. Of the six possible solutions two can be ruled out immediately. Solutions (1) and (6) yield negative values for one variable, thus violating the requirement that imputed values must be zero or larger. To find which of the remaining four solutions will

Figure 19-6   Imputation of Input Values

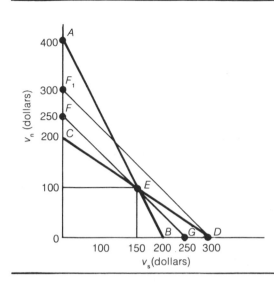

minimize *V* of the objective equation (19.6) we can evaluate (19.6) using each of the four in turn. The results are listed in Table 19-2 in the last column. Thus, of the four solutions it appears that solution (3) is the one we seek. Facilities *M* and *R* are assigned imputed values of zero. They are the ones that are not fully utilized. Facility *N* is assigned an imputed value of $100. Facility *S* is assigned an imputed value of $150. Thus the minimum possible valuation of the fully utilized fixed facilities is $250 when the productive capacity of each of these is equally valuable in the production of either *X* or *Y*.

Alternatively, suppose we look at the problem geometrically. Since facilities *M* and *R* have imputed values of zero, the objective equation (19.6) becomes:

$$v_n + v_s = V \tag{19.6a}$$

This equation yields a family of isovalue curves, each having a slope of -1. If *V* were $300 then F_1D in Figure 19-6 would be the graphic representation of the objective equation. If *V* were $250 then *FG* would be its graphic representation. For every different value assigned to *V* a different isovalue curve is established. All such curves are parallel to each other.

Equations (19.7c) and (19.8c) are plotted in Figure 19-6 as *AB* and *CD*, respectively. Curve *AB* shows the minimum possible combinations of values that could be assigned to facilities *N* and *S* such that a dollar's worth of productive capacity would yield a dollar in rent in the production of X. Curve CD shows the minimum possible combinations of values that could be assigned to facilities N and S such that a dollar's worth of productive capacity would yield a dollar in rent in the production of Y. Pairs of values represented by CE would undervalue the facilities in the production of X. Those represented by EB would undervalue the facilities in the production of Y. Thus the lines joining A, E, and D represent the minimum possible combinations of values of facilities N and S at which a dollar's worth of productive capacity would produce a dollar's worth of either X or Y. The area above and to the right of AED is the area of feasible solutions to the imputation problem.

The optimal solution is approached geometrically by locating first the lowest isovalue curve touched by the area of feasible solutions. This is curve FG. The pair of values of facilities N and S represented by point E is the optimal solution with v_n equal to $100 and v_s equal to $250. At no other point on, above, or to the right of AED will the total imputed value as shown by an isovalue line through that point, be as low. At point E a dollar's worth of productive capacity will produce a dollar's worth of either X or Y or both. It is worth noting that the optimal solution to the dual problem, like that of the primal problem is a "corner" solution — the "corner" representing the simultaneous solution of two of the linear constraints on the firm.

A comparison of the dual solution with that of the primal problem shows that they provide the same information. In both we found that facilities M and R were underutilized and that only facilities N and S were utilized to capacity. We found that the minimum values that could be imputed to these two facilities total to an amount equal to the maximum rent that they can produce. Further, in the primal problem we found that maximum rent is obtained when 25 units of Y and $12\frac{1}{2}$ units of X are produced. Twenty-five units of Y, yielding $6 in rent per unit, yield a total rent of $150. Twelve and one-half units of X, yielding $8 in rent per unit, provide total rent of $100. From Table 19-1 we can determine that the production of 25 units of Y requires 75 percent of the capacity of facility N and 50 percent of the capacity of facility S. The production of $12\frac{1}{2}$ units of X requires 25 percent of the capacity of facility N and 50 percent of the capacity of facility S. From the dual problem, in which v_n and v_s were found to be $100 and $150, respectively, we find that the 75 percent of the facility N used in producing Y is valued at $75, while the 50 percent of facility S used in producing Y is valued at $75. Thus, the total value imputed to that part of facilities N and S used in the production of Y is $150 — equal to the total rent that Y yields. Similarly, the 25 percent of facility N used in producing X is valued at $25, while the 50 percent of facility S used in its production is valued at $75. The total value of that part of the facilities used in the production of X is $100 — equal to the total rent yielded by product X.

Summary

Linear programming is a technique for solving maximization and minimization problems subject to certain side conditions or constraints. The technique is based on certain assumptions. Decision making is accomplished subject to certain constraints on the decision-making agency; input and output prices are assumed to be constant; and the firm's input-output, output-output, and input-input relationships are assumed to be linear.

The first problem considered was that of maximization of a firm's output (total revenue) subject to the constraint of a given cost outlay to be made by the firm. The production function of the firm was assumed to be linearly homogeneous, and the firm was limited to a choice among four different processes in producing its product output. Isoquants and isocosts were established for the firm. The area of feasible solutions to the problem was established, and then the optimal solution was found at the point where the isocost curve touched a corner of one of the firm's isoquants. Changes in cost outlay, given the prices of inputs, will not change which of the processes available is the optimal one, but will affect only its level of use. Changes in the relative prices of inputs may result in changes in which of the processes available is the optimal one. If the constraints under which the firm maximizes output are quantity limitations on inputs, these rather than input prices determine the process or processes chosen. In general the number of processes required to carry on its activities will be equal to the number of constraints under which the firm operates.

The second problem was that of maximizing the firm's total rents where multiple outputs are produced and several limited facilities are used to produce them. The processes for producing each output are specified. These, together with constraints, determine the area of feasible output solutions to the problem. Given the amount of rent yielded by each output, isorent lines for the outputs can be established, and the optimal solution of the problem is that at which the area of feasible solutions just touches the highest possible isorent line. This will ordinarily be at a corner of the area of feasible solutions. Not all input or facility quantity limitations need be effective constraints on the firm. The number of effective constraints will generally be equal to the number of processes used. Changes in relative rents yielded by each output may change the optimal solution and, consequently, the input limitations which act as effective constraints.

Attention was then turned to the dual solution to a linear programming primal problem. For the primal linear programming problem summarized in the preceding paragraph the dual problem consists of imputing values to the inputs that serve as effective constraints on the firm. The imputed values of the total amounts available of such inputs must be such that their sum will not exceed the firm's total rent. This involves finding the combination of minimum valuations at which a dollar's worth of any one input yields a dollar in rent in any one of the products it is used to produce.

Suggested Readings

Baumol, William J., "Activity Analysis in One Lesson," *American Economic Review*, vol. XLVIII (December 1958), pp. 837–873.

Dorfman, Robert, "Mathematical or 'Linear' Programming: A Nonmathematical Exposition," *American Economic Review*, vol. XLIII (December 1953), pp. 797–825.

Liebhafsky, H.H. *The Nature of Price Theory*, rev. ed. (Homewood, Ill.: The Dorsey Press, Inc., 1968), Chap. 17.

Wu, Yuan-Li and Ching-Wen Kwang, "An Analytical Comparison of Marginal Analysis and Mathematical Programming in the Theory of the Firm," reprinted in Kenneth E. Boulding and W. Allen Spivey, eds., *Linear Programming and the Theory of the Firm*. (New York: McGraw-Hill, Inc., 1960), pp. 94–157.

Index:

Administered prices and income distribution, 370–375
Advertising (*see* Nonprice competition)
Agricultural Adjustment Acts, 56n, 58
Alchian, Arman A., 263n
Allen, R. G. D., 69n
Allen, William R., 263n
Allocation of resources (*see* Resource allocation)
Alternative cost principle, 163–164, 315
American Medical Association, 58–59

Bain, Joe S., 287
Bator, Francis, 400
Baumol, William J., 97, 400, 424
Beem, Eugene R., 297n
Blocked entry
  effects on resource allocation, 350–351
  under oligopoly, 277–281
  under pure monopoly, 236
Boulding, Kenneth E., 53, 97, 113n, 121, 191, 226, 270n, 424
Breit, William, 358
Brozen, Yale, 66
Budget line, 76–78

Capital
  accumulation of, 24
  differences in ownership of, 368–370
  nature of, 4–5, 347n
  reallocation of, 349
  redistribution in ownership of, 376–377

Cartels
  centralized, 262, 263–267
  limitations to profit maximization by, 266–267
  marginal cost curve of, 264
  market sharing, 267–268
  nature of, 128–129, 261
  pricing and output by, 263–268
Cartter, A. M., 340
Cassels, John M., 161
Chamberlain, Edward H., 298
"Circular flow" model, 15–18
Civil Aeronautics Board, 280
Clark, John Bates, 358
Collusion, incentives for, 261
Compensating variation in income, 88
Competitive goods (*see* Substitute goods)
Competition in the United States, 30
Complementary goods, 34, 74–76, 104
Constant cost industries, 218–219, 293
Constant returns to scale, 144–145
Consumer behavior
  constraints on, 76–78, 108
  objectives of, 78–81, 108
Contract curve, 90–91, 158
Cost curves
  assumptions underlying, 165–166
  long-run
    average, 180–186
    marginal, 186–188
      relation to short-run marginal, 188–190
    total, 186–188
  short-run
    average, 174–175, 194–195
      relation to long-run average, 179–186

average fixed, 172–173, 192–193
average variable, 173–174, 193–194
marginal, 175–176
  derivation from total, 175–176
  relation to average and average variable,
    177–179, 195–196
total, 168, 171
total fixed, 168–169
total variable, 168–171
Costs of production
alternative cost principle, 163–164
explicit, 164
fixed, 168
implicit, 164–165
variable, 168
See also Cost curves
Cross elasticity of demand
for complementary goods, 51
industry definition in terms of, 51
for substitute goods, 51

Decreasing cost industries, 219–221, 293
Deductive reasoning, 7
Demand curve faced by the firm
definition of, 123
under monopolistic competition, 130–132,
  289–290
under oligopoly, 126–130, 260
under pure competition, 124–125
under pure monopoly, 125–126
See also Kinked demand curve
Demand for goods and services
changes in, 33–34, 38
definition of, 31–33
determination of market demand, 116
See also Individual consumer demand curves
Demand for a resource
assumptions underlying, 305
market, 309–311
under monopoly, 323–328
under pure competition, 304–311
Dewey, Donald, 251
Differentiated products (*see* Product
    differentiation)
Diminishing marginal utility, 100–102.
Diminishing returns
definition of, 144
and marginal cost, 302–303
Diseconomies of size, 184
Distribution of output, 21–22
Dorfman, Robert, 385n, 416n, 424

Economic activity, 1–6
Economic efficiency
in allocation of resources, 156–158, 388–390
in distribution of final goods, 90–91, 385–387
under monopolistic competition, 295–296
nature of, 20
under oligopoly, 284–285
under pure competition, long-run, 225
under pure monopoly, 245

in relation to resource combinations, 144–154
Economic growth, requirements for, 23–24
Economic rent, 315–317
Economic system
functions of, 18–24
model of, 15–18
Economic theory
construction of, 6–8
functions of, 8
macroeconomics, 8–10
microeconomics, 8–10
Economics, definition of, 1–2
Economies of size, 182–183
division, and specialization of labor, 182
technological factors, 182–183
Edgeworth box, 89–91, 156–158
Edgeworth, Francis Y., 69n
Efficiency (*see* Economic efficiency)
Einhorn, Henry A., 30
Elasticity
of demand
  arc elasticity, 42–43
  definition of, 40–42
  factors influencing, 48–50
  measurement of, 40–46
  point elasticity, 43–46
  in relation to total money outlays, 46–48
  and tax incidence, 65
of supply 65, 200–202
Employment of resources
competitive firm level of, 306–307
market level of, 312–315
monopolistic level of, 323–327
monopsonistic level of, 320–324, 336–337
Engel, Ernst, 81n
Engel curves, 84–86
Entry into an industry
barriers to, 278–281
effects upon collusion, 277–281
under monopolistic competition, 292–294
under oligopoly, 277–281
under pure competition, 213–215
under pure monopoly, 236
Envelope curve, 181
Equilibrium
general
  importance of, in economic theory, 382–385
  nature of, 383–385
  See also General equilibrium theory
partial, 382–383
Equilibrium price, 37–38
Equilibrium resource prices, 312–315
Ewing, John S., 297n
Exchange, 89–91, 116–120
Expansion path of the firm, 155–156
Explicit costs of production, 164
Exploitation of resources
under monopoly, 328
under monopsony, 335–336
External diseconomies, 216–218
External economies, 219–221
Externalities
in consumption, 386–387
in production, 389–390

Fair Labor Standards Act of 1938, 58
Fellner, William, 133, 340
Ferguson, C. E., 385n
Firm
    nature of, 15–16
    role in free enterprise system, 15–18
Fixed resources, 166–167
Friedman, Milton, 12, 63, 292n, 367n, 378
Fringe benefits, 92–94
Functional distribution of income, 364–366
Functions of an economic system, 18–24

General equilibrium
    nature of, 383–385
    with constant product supplies, 393–394
    with constant resource supplies, 394–396
    monopoly impact on, 396
    monopsony impact on, 396–397
    and welfare, 393–400
General equilibrium theory
    objectives of, 383–385
    variants of, 384–385
Gentlemen's agreements, 262, 263
Gideonse, Harry D., 15n, 25
Gilbert, Milton, 17n
Goods and services, valuation of, 18–19

Hague, Douglas C., 53
Harrod, R. F., 251
Heady, Earl O., 161
Hicks, John R., 69n, 97, 318
Hochman, Harold M., 358
Households
    nature of, 15–16
    role in free enterprise system, 15–18
Hypotheses, 7–8

Implicit costs of production, 164–165
Income-consumption curve, 84–86
Income determination, 21, 361–362
Income differences
    causes of, 364–375
    nature of, 363–364
    and resource allocation, 21–22, 345–349
Income distribution
    determinants of, 21–22
    effect on
        of administered prices, 370–375
        of supply restrictions 372–373
    functional, 364–366
    personal, 363–364
Income effects on a price change, 87–89
Income elasticity, 86–87
Income redistribution
    effects on free enterprise system, 375–377
    via administered prices, 375
    via resource redistribution, 375–377
Increasing cost industries, 215–218, 293
Increasing returns, 144
Indifference curves
    characteristics of, 72–74

definition of, 70–72, 104–108
Individual consumer demand curves
    definition of, 81
    establishment of
        by indifference curve analysis, 81–83
        by utility analysis, 112–115
Inductive reasoning, 7
Inferior good, 85, 88
Inflation control, 62–64
Input-output analysis, 385
Interstate Commerce Commission, 280
Isocosts, 154–156, 408–409
Isoquants
    characteristics of, 138–139
    nature of, 137–138
    in linear programming, 406–408
Isorent curves, 413
Isovalue curves, 421

Jazi, George, 17n
Jevons, William S., 99

Kinked demand curve, 272–277
Knight, Frank H., 15n, 25, 53, 161, 357n, 370
Knight, Wyllis R., 66
Koopmans, Tjalling C., 12
Kuznets, Simon, 367n
Kwang, Ching-Wen, 424

Labor resources
    allocation of, 345–357
    definition of, 4
    differences in ownership of, 366–368
    redistribution of, 375–376
Labor supply, 94–96
Lange, Oscar, 12
Least-cost resource combinations
    and average variable cost, 174
    determination of, 154–156
    for a given product output, 302–303
    and long-run average cost, 181
    under monopsonistic buying, 332–334
    for profit-maximizing output, 302–304,
        321–322
Liebhafsky, H. H., 424
Leontief, Wassily W., 385
Levels of living, 3–4
Licensing laws, 280
Linear programming
    assumptions underlying, 404–405
    complete description method, 412–417
    constraints, 404
    dual problem, nature of, 417
    feasible solution defined, 409
    objective equation, 412, 417
    optimal solution defined, 409
    output maximization problems, 405–417
    primal problem, nature of, 417
    processes
        definition, 405–406
        relation to constraints, 410–412

profit or rent maximization problems
    shadow prices, 417-423
Long run, definition of, 167
Loss minimization
    under pure competition, 206-208
    under pure monopoly, 234-235

Machlup, Fritz, 53, 133, 261n, 266n, 287, 298
Macroeconomic theory, 8-10
Marginal costs
    as determined by resource inputs, 302-304
    nature of, 175-179
    See also Cost curves
Marginal productivity theory, 361-362
Marginal rate of substitution, 73-74, 107
Marginal rate of technical substitution, 138-139,
        152-154
Marginal rate of transformation, 160
Marginal resource costs
    discontinuous curves, 336-337
    nature of, 329-330
    relationship to resource supply curve,
        329-330
Marginal revenue
    derivation from demand curve, 252-256
    discontinuous curves, 273-276
    under monopoly, 230-232
    under pure competition, 204-205
    relationship to price and to demand elasticity,
        231-232, 257
Marginal revenue product
    definition of, 324
    as demand for a resource, 324-325
    relationship to value of marginal product, 328
Market price determination, 36-38
Markets
    consumer goods and services, 16-18
    resources, 16-18, 301, 344-345
Marshall, Alfred, 12, 41, 42n, 53, 121, 226, 251,
        315n,
Marshall, F. R., 340
Maximization of satisfaction
    in terms of indifference curves, 78-81
    in terms of utility, 108-112
Menger, Karl, 99
Methodology, 6-8
Microeconomic theory, 8-10
Minimum wage rates, 57-59, 336-337,
        353-357
Mobility of resources
    meaning of, 28, 338-339, 344-345
    in relation to time, 344-345
Modigliani, Franco, 287
Monopolistic competition
    characteristics of, 130, 289
    equilibrium under
        long-run
            entry blocked, 292
            entry open, 292-294
        short-run, 290-291
    long-run profits under, 291-294
    output restriction, 294-295
    pricing and output

long-run, 291-294
short-run, 290-291
sales promotion under, 132, 296-297
and welfare, 294-297
Monopoly
    effects on resource allocation, 349-351
    See also Pure monopoly
Monopsony
    conditions causing, 334-335
    counteraction
        through aids to resource mobility, 337-339
        by price fixing, 336-337
    nature of, 328-329
    profits, 330-331
Multiple products, 156-160

National income analysis, 8-10
Nicholls, William H., 340
Nonprice competition
    advertising
        effects of, 281-282
        purposes of, 281-282
        under monopolistic competition, 291,
            296-297
    variations in quality and design
        effects of, 282-284
        purposes of, 282-284
Normal good, 85
Nutter, G. Warren, 30

Oligopoly
    characteristics of, 126-127, 259
    classification of types, 261-263
    collusion under, 261-263, 263-272
    differentiated, 127, 260
    independent action under, 262-263, 272-276
    long-run profits under, 276-281
    output restriction under, 284
    pricing and output under
        long-run, 276-281
        short-run, 263-276
    pure, 127, 260
    sales promotion under, 129-130, 285
    and welfare, 284-286
Opportunity cost principle, 163-164
Optimal outputs of goods and services,
        391-393
Optimum rate of output (see Size of plant)
Optimum size of plant, 184-186
Organization of production, 19-21, 221-224
Output restriction
    under monopolistic competition, 294-295
    under oligopoly, 284
    under pure monopoly, 242-245

Pareto optimum, 10-11, 90-91, 118, 158, 382,
        392-393
Pareto, Vilfredo, 69n
Partial equilibrium, 382-383
Patents, 280
Patinkin, Don, 278n, 287

Perfect competition, 28–29
Personal income
   determinants of, 361–362
   differences in, 363–364
   distribution of, 363–364
Pigou, A. C., 358, 378
Postulates, 6–7
Premises, 6–7
Pribram, Karl 262n
Price-consumption curve
   and elasticity of demand, 82–83
   nature of, 82
Price discrimination
   conditions necessary for, 240
   distribution of sales under, 240–241
   examples of, 242
   profit maximization under, 241–242
Price leadership
   by dominant firm, 270–272
   by low-cost firm 268–270
Price rigidity, 272–276
Price ceilings, 59–64
Price supports, 55–57
Price wars, 272, 280
Principles, nature of, 7
Product schedules and curves of a resource
   average product, 140–154
   and efficiency, 144–154
   marginal physical product, 140–154
   total product, 139–140, 144–154
Product differentiation, 127–130, 280–281,
        281–284, 289–291
Product distribution, 21–22, 361–378
   See also Income distribution
Product homogeneity, 27–28
Production, organization of, 19–21, 221–224
Production functions
   nature of, 135–143
   linearly homogeneous, 144–145, 406
Production surface, 136–139
Production techniques, 62, 136, 165–166
Profit
   as incentive for efficiency, 20
   measurement of, 203–206, 210–211
   nature of, 212–213
Profit maximization
   under monopolistic competition, 290–294
   under oligopoly, 263–281
   under pure competition, 203–207, 211–221
   under pure monopoly, 232–242
   for resource inputs
      under monopoly, 321–322
      under monopsony, 330–334
      under pure competition, 302–309
Propensity to accumulate, 369–370
Pure competition
   adjustments
      to disturbances under, 215–221
   firm and industry
      long-run, 211–221
      short-run, 203–211
   characteristics of, 27–28, 199
   equilibrium under
      long-run, 211–221

      short-run, 203–211
   marginal revenue under, 204–205
   as a "norm," 29
   price and average cost relationships
      under, long-run, 213–215
   pricing and output under
      long-run, 211–221, 223–224
      short-run, 203–211, 222–223
   total revenue under, 204–205
   use of, in economic analysis, 29–30
   very short-run pricing under, 199–203,
        221–222
   and welfare, 221–225
Pure monopoly
   characteristics of, 125–126, 229
   elasticity of demand under, 234–235
   equilibrium under
      long-run, 236–239
      short-run, 232–235
   examples of, 229
   long-run profits under, 236–239
   output restriction under, 242–245
   price discrimination under, 239–242
   pricing and output under
      long-run, 236–239
      short-run, 232–235
   regulation of, 246–249
   sales promotion under, 126, 245
   and welfare, 242–245

Quasi rent (*see* Economic rent)

Radford, R. A., 66
Rationing in the very short run, 22–23, 200–203
Rees, Albert, 358
Regulation of monopoly
   through maximum prices, 246–247
   by taxation, 247–249
Rent (*see* Economic rent)
Resource allocation
   administered price distortions of, 353–357
   among different uses, 20, 21–22, 345–347
   and economic efficiency, 346–349
   among industries, 345–347
   long-run, 347–349
   for maximum welfare, 343–344, 345–349
   monopoly distortions of, 349–351
   monopsony distortions of, 351–352
   and net national product, 345–349
   nonprice distortions of, 352–353
   under pure competition, 345–349
   short-run, 345–347
Resource employment (*see* Employment of
        resources)
Resource exploitation (*see* Exploitation of
        resources)
Resource immobility, 344–335
Resource prices
   determination of
      under monopoly, 326–327
      under monopsony, 330–334, 336–337
      under pure competition, 304–315

functions of, 345–349, 352
and resource allocation, 345–349
Resource supply curve, 311, 313, 326–327,
     329–330
Resources
  characteristics of, 5–6
  classification of, 4–5
  economic, 5, 151
  efficient combinations of, 20, 144–154
  fixed, 166–167
  free, 5
  nature of, 4–6
  scarcity of, 5
  variable, 166–167
  variations in proportions of, 6
  versatility of, 6
Revenue curves
  marginal
    under monopoly, 230–232, 252–256
    under pure competition, 204–205
  total
    under monopoly, 230–232
    under pure competition, 204–205
Ridge lines, 153–154
Robertson, Dennis H., 318
Robinson, Joan, 251, 267n, 340

Sales promotion
  under monopolistic competition, 132,
     296–297
  under oligopoly, 129–130, 285
  under pure competition, 225
  under pure monopoly, 126, 245
Samuelson, Paul A., 416n
Size of plant
  definition of, 167
  and long-run output, 180–186
  optimum rate of output of, 179
  variability of, in long-run, 180–186
Size of plant adjustments
  under monopolistic competition
    with entry blocked, 292
    with entry open, 292–294
  under oligopoly, 276–277
  under pure competition, 211–221
  under pure monopoly, 237–239
Scitovsky, Tibor, 318
Sherer, F. M., 20, 271n
Sherman Antitrust Act, 30
Shortage, 37
Short run, nature of, 166–167
Slichter, Sumner, H., 355n
Smith, Adam, 182n
Solow, Robert M., 416n
Specialized resources, 61, 334–335
Speculation, 23, 202
Spivey, W. Allen, 424
Standard Oil case, 280
Standards of living (see Levels of living)
Stigler, George J., 25, 43n, 81n, 121, 191, 298,
     318
Stocking, George W., 261n
Stonier, Alfred W., 53

Substitute goods, 34, 74–76, 104
Substitution effects of a price change, 87–89
Supply
  changes in, 36, 39–40
  long-run industry
    under constant costs, 219
    under decreasing costs, 219–220
    under increasing costs, 218
  nature of, 34–36
  restriction of, 58–59
  short-run
    firm, 209
    market, 209–211
Surplus, 37, 56

Tangri, Om P., 161
Taxes
  capital gains, 376–377
  estate and gift, 377
  excise tax incidence, 64–65
  payroll, 65
  personal income, 376
Techniques of production, 6, 136, 165–166
Transformation curves, 159–160, 388–389,
     391–392

Unemployment, 58, 354–357
Utility
  marginal utility
    and consumer tastes and preferences,
       102–103
    definition of, 100–103
    diminishing, 100–102
    for nonrelated goods, 100–103
    for related goods, 103–108
  maximization of, 108–112
  measurement of, 100n
  total utility, 100–103

Value
  in exchange, 119–120
  in use, 119–120
Value of marginal product
  nature of, 305–307
  relationship to marginal revenue product, 328
Variable resources, 166–167
Very short run
  nature of, 22, 199–200
  pricing under, 199–203, 221–222
  rationing among consumers, 200–201
  rationing over time, 200–202
Viner, Jacob, 191, 226

Walras, Léon, 99, 112n
Wants
  as ends of economic activity, 2
  origins of, 2–3
Watkins, Myron W., 261n
Weintraub, Sidney, 138, 161
Welfare

effects of monopolist competition on,
294–297
effects of pure competition on, 221–225
effects of pure oligopoly on, 284–286
effects of pure monopoly on, 242–245

exchange and, 89–91, 116–120
nature of, 2, 10–11, 381–382
optimum, 385–393
Wilcox, Clair, 280n, 287
Wu, Yuan-Li, 424